THE FIRST YEAR OF
WORLD WAR II
1919

THE FIRST YEAR OF
WORLD WAR II
1919

by
Richard E. Osborne

Richard E. Osborne

Riebel-Roque Publishing Company, Inc.

Indianapolis, Indiana

Other books by this author:

World War II Sites in the United States
Casablanca Companion
World War II in Colonial Africa
If Hitler Had Won
Tour Book for Antique Car Buffs

ISBN 0-9628324-8-0
Published and printed in the U.S.A.
Book design and production by *k2design*, Zionsville, IN

Editorial advice and assistance provided by
Jane Miller

RIEBEL-ROQUE PUBLISHING COMPANY, INC.
6027 Castlebar Circle
Indianapolis, Indiana 46220

TABLE OF CONTENTS

INTRODUCTION
"DER DIKTAT" und "DER TAG"

‖‖

On June 28, 1919, the German government was forced to sign the Versailles Peace Treaty after having lost the Great War. This document reduced Germany to a third-rate economic and military power. Land was taken from her in Europe; all of her colonies were taken, her military was reduced to a level where it could only maintain internal order, a huge, and as yet, unspecified reparations bill was presented, and Germany was blamed for starting the War. Within days, this universally hated document became known in Germany as *"Der Diktat"* (The Dictate).

By the end of 1919, another phrase was being used throughout Germany, *"Der Tag"* (The Day). It referred to the day when Germany would get even and regain all that she had lost.

Der Tag came on September 1, 1939, when a new and powerful German Army, under a powerful and dictatorial leader, invaded Poland and Danzig to reclaim the majority of the land that had been lost in Europe as a result of Der Diktat.

This event started World War II. Accordingly, the Great War was then renamed World War I.

CHAPTER 1
SETTING THE STAGE

||||||||||||||||||||||||||||||||||||||||||||||||||||||||||||||||||||||||||||||||||||||||||||||||||||||||||||||||||||||||||||||||||||||||||||||

The Great War had ended, and the peacemakers were gathering. It would be a whole new world and it would never happen again. So went the hopes and aspiration of most of the people of the world at the beginning of 1919. Unfortunately, history would take them down another course.

CONDITIONS IN EUROPE

One by one, the Central Powers had surrendered to the Allies, accepted armistices, and were awaiting peace treaties to follow.

But, there were still battles and wars in progress in other parts of Europe — and in other parts of the world.

In Russia, a terrible revolution was underway; in Berlin, there was a communist uprising; in Mexico, there was an ongoing revolution; and in eastern Europe, Italy, the Balkans, the Baltic, the Middle-East, and China, there was political instability and great tensions.

In eastern Europe, the Germans had, before and during the Great War, structured that region to their liking, but now Germany was defeated and nationalism surged to great heights throughout those lands. Nine new nations emerged in the latter months of 1918 — all of them politically and militarily weak, with inexperienced leaders and long-standing feuds and grudges against their neighbors. The new nations (some of them resurrections of formerly independent states) were Finland, Estonia, Latvia, Lithuania, Belorussia, Ukraine, Poland, Czechoslovakia, and The Kingdom of Serbs, Croats, and Slovenes (also known as Jugoslavia — later Yugoslavia). Here was a hotbed of problems that would dominate much of Europe for decades to come.

As for the various peace treaties that were being planned between the victorious Allies and the defeated Central Powers, the most important would be that with Germany, the major power in that wartime alliance. Work on this treaty began in Paris in January

1919 and the others would follow. The formal meetings between the Germans and Allies were to take place in the former royal palace at Versailles, a suburb of Paris. The immense and sumptuous palace was a fitting place for such a gathering because it was large enough to hold all the many delegates who were expected to attend the conference, and it would be a fitting place to punish Imperial Germany for starting the Great War. That punishment was a unique and fitting form of retribution. In early 1871, it was the Germans and *their* allies who had gathered in the Versailles Palace to punish the French after the latter had lost the Franco-Prussian War of 1870-71. On January 18, 1871, Kaiser Wilhelm I, the predecessor of Germany's leader during the Great War, Wilhelm II, came to Versailles personally to proclaim the new German Empire — the Second Reich — and the defeat of France. He made this historic proclamation in the palace's famous Hall of Mirrors. Now, the pendulum had swung in the other direction and the delegates who would punish Germany would meet in, and issue their decision from, that same Hall of Mirrors.

THE THIRD REICH

The German Second Reich collapsed in 1918 with the ending of the Great War. In 1933, Hitler and the Nazis would proclaim the creation of the Third Reich. It would last until 1945.

REALIGNMENT OF THE GERMAN STATES

Inside defeated Germany, a curious and spontaneous political re-alignment of the German states was underway. The various German states that comprised the Second Reich had all retained some measure of autonomy under the central government in Berlin. Now, with the central government in Berlin in disarray, the leaders of the various states exerted these powers and concluded agreements with one another for a variety of reasons that resulted the states dividing, combining, or spinning off portions of their territories. For example, during November and December 1918, the Duchy of Saxe-Coburg-Gotha had split into two halves and the half containing Coburg joined the Kingdom of Bavaria. There were other realignments taking place and by the end of 1918, the 26 states of the Kaiser's German federation had been reduced to 18. None of the states involved had strong inclinations of leaving the German federation, although there were forces at work in every state that would, if they could, detach that state from Germany and proclaim adherence to the rapidly growing utopian society that was emerging in the east — Soviet Russia.

Many of the German states changed their names to "Free State of..." or "People's State of..." such as the "Free State of Brunswick" and the "People's State of Wurttemberg." Some of the states gave up their traditional state flag and adapted the solid red flag of leftist revolution (the flag the Bolsheviks were using in Russia), and some changed the names of their state councils to the "Workers' and Soldiers' Council" or something similar. As for political parties, the Social Democratic Party (SPD), Germany's largest, held most of the power in most of the states and in Berlin. Some of the states, however, where the Social Democrats were not strong, acquired far leftist regimes while a few others acquired a far right regime.

This would not be the end of it. During the next few years, the process of German states combining and recombining would continue, as would the trend toward left wing politics.

This was a very unhealthy process for Germany, implying that secession and/or revolution were just under the surface.

THE MAJOR PLAYERS

The host of the Paris peace conference was the French Premier, Georges Clemenceau, age 76, a politician with great experience and the man who had led France during the last two years of the war. He was a man of firm convictions and determination, and a man who drove a hard bargain. These attributes had earned him the nickname "The Tiger." Clemenceau had a strong American connection, though. He had lived for a while in the United States; his first wife had been an American and he spoke fluent American English.

On the darker side of his personality, however, Clemenceau hated the Germans and made no secret of it. He once said that he wanted to be buried standing up, facing Germany, so that even in death, he could confront the hated enemy on the other side of the border.

And, like the experienced politician that he was, he had prepared his case well for the coming peace conference. In December 1918, he had called a special national election that would test the mood of the French people in their moment of victory. It was his hope that the election would give him a powerful mandate from the people to pursue his goals for France and the punishment of the hated enemy, Germany. This was an old and accepted political maneuver in European politics. Clemenceau campaigned almost exclusively on the issue of punishing Germany to the maximum and he was well-rewarded. He won the election by a four-to-one landslide. Now, with a mandate from the French people, he would use it to the fullest degree at Versailles. In the process,

Clemenceau would prove to be the group's curmudgeon.

Representing Great Britain would be the Prime Minister, David Lloyd George, age 56, who, like Clemenceau, had led the British government during the last years of the war. He had a reputation for being a charismatic orator, a social reformed, a powerful Cabinet member in previous governments and an economic wizard who had reformed Britain's tattered economy in the time of war and substantially increasing Britain's ability to produce arms and munitions. Lloyd George had no love for the Germans but his hatred was less intense than that of Clemenceau. Also like Clemenceau, he had called a special election in the wake of the Allied victory, campaigned on punishing Germany, and won handily. He too, would have a popular mandate when he arrived at Paris.

Lloyd George, however, had a domestic problem. He headed a coalition government whose structure was somewhat tenuous and was under pressure to conclude a peace agreement quickly. As a result, time would not be on his side.

Representing the United States would be President Woodrow Wilson, age 63, serving his second term in the White House, a late-comer to the war, a former university professor, liberal, intellectual, and a person with strong Christian beliefs. Unlike his compatriots, Wilson did not have a recent mandate from the American people; rather, he had something of a chastisement. Whereas Clemenceau and Lloyd George had been given popular mandates, the American people had rejected Wilson's political party in the Congressional election of November 1918 and given control of Congress to his opposition — the Republicans. If the Americans had had a political system like the Europeans, it would have been a

Republican who would arrive in Europe rather than a Democrat.

Nevertheless, Wilson had gained a great measure of self-confidence from the way he had successfully conducted the war, the support the American people gave him in that effort, and the praise and admiration he was currently enjoying at home and abroad.

When the US entered the war, Wilson insisted that the US was not a member of the Allies, but an "Associated Power" which implied a looser bond than that of a fully committed Ally. This phrase would appear repeatedly in the Versailles Peace Treaty.

Also unlike Clemenceau and Lloyd George, Wilson did not have any great animosity toward the defeated enemy and sought a just and equitable peace. He had put this message into writing a year earlier, in January 1918, when he produced a document known as "The Fourteen Points." Unfortunately, The Fourteen Points were not necessarily compatible with the attitudes of Clemenceau and Lloyd George and would cause considerable discord at the peace conference. During the making of the peace treaty, the atmosphere would be that of the vindictive French against the forgiving Americans with the British somewhere in between.

The American delegation to Versailles was officially known as "The American Commission to Negotiate Peace," and was composed almost entirely of Democrats and close Wilson aides such as Robert Lansing, Secretary of State; Colonel (honorary title from Texas) Edward House, Wilson's foreign affairs advisor and closest confidant; General Tasker Bliss, representing the American armed forces; Bernard Baruch, Chairman of the War Industries Board; Herbert Hoover, Director-General of the International Food Relief Program; and others.

And there were complications between Lansing and Wilson. They had seldom seen eye-to-eye and Wilson, more often than not, ignored Lansing's advice. Lansing's presence in Paris was a form of window dressing because the other Allied leaders had brought along their advisors of Lansing's rank.

WILSON AND LANSING – ROOSEVELT AND HULL

During Would War II, President Franklin Roosevelt often ignored the advice of his Secretary of State, Cordell Hull. Roosevelt was a northern liberal and Hull a southern conservative. Roosevelt did not have a Col. House, but he often relied on others than Hull for advice on foreign affairs.

The American delegation stayed at the elegant Hotel Crillon overlooking the Seine River and the Champs Elysees. Wilson remained apart from the delegation and stayed at the Palais Murat, also an elegant hotel. It was in the second floor library of this hotel that Wilson often met with Clemenceau, and Lloyd George and others.

The makeup of Wilson's delegation, as might be expected, did not sit well with the Republicans back home because they would be left out of the all-important negotiations in Paris. There was also criticism from the Republicans, and in the American press, that it was a mistake for Wilson to go personally to Versailles and that he should remain in the White House during these critical times. They pointed to the fact that at the end of America's last major conflict, The Spanish-American War, President McKinley remained in Washington and sent others to make the peace. Furthermore, by going to Paris, Wilson would be putting himself on the world stage whereby his every action would be closely scrutinized and subjected to international appraisals.

Then, there was the matter of the proposed "League of Nations," a hot-button issue for many Americans. Various political leaders throughout America, including the powerful Senator Henry Cabot Lodge (R-MA), Chairman of the Senate's Foreign Affairs Committee, had announced that they had grave apprehensions about such an organization and even greater apprehensions about the United States becoming one of its members. This attitude reflected the sentiment of a large segment of the American public whose view of foreign entanglements had, traditionally, been one of mind-your-own-business. Wilson further complicated the issue by insisting that the League of Nations be an integral part of the peace treaty. Since the Senate was required by the Constitution to ratify the peace treaty, this meant that the Senators would be faced with an all or-nothing-at-all situation — no League of Nations — no peace treaty.

Also sitting at the peace table would be Italian Premier, Vittorio Orlando, age 59, who, again like Clemenceau and Lloyd George, had led Italy during the last years of the war. Italy's war had been primarily against Austria-Hungary so Orlando had no great score to settle with Germany. At home, his political position had been insecure from its beginning. He came to power after Italy had suffered a major defeat at the Battle of Caporetto and was forced to restructure Italy's High Command. He also had to radically extend government economic war powers to avoid a financial crisis and to arrest large numbers of anti-war pacifists and Socialists to keep peace in the streets. Orlando's position at Versailles would not be strong.

Representing Japan was Prince Kimmochi Saionji, the senior member, and Baron Nobuaki Makino, his second in command. Saionji had lived in France for ten years and had taken a law degree from the Sorbonne. Clemenceau was at the Sorbonne at the same time and they remembered each other. The Prince participated in very few meetings and was seldom seen; therefore the Baron spoke most of the time for Japan.

In Japan, much favorable publicity was given to the fact that Japan had been included as one of the "Big 5." Their war effort had been small compared to their European Allies, but it had been totally successful in that the Japanese had successfully occupied all the German colonial territories in the Far East and Pacific north of the equator. Those south of the equator had been conquered by the Australians and New Zealanders. Japan was, by far, the most powerful nation in the Far East and had a military and economy equal to that of Italy.

Also at the peace table would be presidents, prime ministers, and representatives from the several dozen nations that had been at war with Germany. There would be no representatives from one of the original Allied nations, Imperial Russia, because that state no longer existed and no one wanted to see a Bolshevik in Paris.

WHO WAS AT WAR WITH GERMANY DURING THE GREAT WAR AND IN WW II?

Those countries at war with Germany or one of the other Central Powers during the Great War were the following: Australia, Belgium, Bolivia, Brazil, Britain, Canada, China, Cuba, Czechoslovakia, Ecuador, France, Greece, Guatemala, Haiti, Hijaz, Honduras, India, Italy, Japan, Liberia, Montenegro, New Zealand, Nicaragua, Panama, Peru, Portugal, Poland, Romania, San Marino, Serbia, Siam, Union of South Africa, United States of America, and Uruguay.

Those countries at war with Germany or one of the other Axis Powers during World War II were: Argentina, Australia, Belgium, Bolivia, Brazil, Canada, Chile, China, Columbia, Coast Rica, Cuba, Czechoslovakia, Dominican Republic, Ecuador, Egypt, El Salvador, Ethiopia, France, Great Britain, Greece, Haiti, Honduras, Iran, Iraq, Lebanon, Liberia, Mexico, Mongolia, The Netherlands, New Zealand, Nicaragua, Norway, Panama, Paraguay, Peru, Poland, San Marino, Saudi Arabia, The Soviet Union, Syria, Turkey, Union of South Africa, United States of America, Uruguay, Venezuela, and Yugoslavia. In addition, some of the defeated Axis powers, such as Italy, Romania, Hungary, and Bulgaria switched sides and joined the Allies.

In addition to those who were entitled to a seat at Versailles, there were those who came to Paris of their own accord hoping to be heard, or to forward some specific program. These were the "lobbyists," as it were, who vied for the time and attention of the gathered world leaders. Their presence in Paris made for good press and good political positioning back home.

THE FOURTEEN POINTS: A NOBLE COMMITMENT OR A DIPLOMATIC BOONDOGGLE

In January 1918, President Wilson had taken it upon himself to lay out a set of conditions for ending the Great War and providing for world peace thereafter. This unilateral declaration became known as The Fourteen Points. Wilson formally presented the program to Congress on January 8, 1918, and soon afterwards, his Administration began a large-scale propaganda campaign in support of it.

At the time, an end to the war seemed close at hand because the German war effort was clearly faltering and there had been attempts by the last two German Chancellors to start a dialogue for peace with the Western Allies. It was Wilson's thinking, and that of Col. House and others, that a fair and equitable peace proposal to Germany would hasten the end of the war. There were those in Germany who saw the advantage of such a proposal but, unfortunately, they were not the individuals in power. The Kaiser and his generals saw The Fourteen Points as an affront and insult and quickly rejected it.

Furthermore, Wilson's Fourteen Points were not received well in many Allied quarters. Those most disturbed by the program were the leaders of America's major Allies, the French, British, and Italians. They had neither been informed nor consulted beforehand and, upon reading the Fourteen Points, were aghast at its wide-sweeping and, in their opinions, overly-generous commitments. Immediately, these leaders recognized conditions in the Fourteen Points to which they could never agree. But, for the most part, the Allied leaders held their respective tongues because Allied harmony was most important at this time, and would continue to be, until the Central Powers were clearly defeated. The Allied leaders went one step further, however. By using their wartime censorship powers, they forbade their respective media organizations from engaging in public discussions of the program.

In the United States, however, there were no such restraints. Opponents of the program, and of Wilson and his administration in general, became vocal and highly critical. Former President Teddy Roosevelt soon emerged as one of the program's most notable and ardent critics. Roosevelt disagreed with Wilson on many issues and was especially bitter toward Wilson personally because the President had consistently refused his (Roosevelt's) offers to help in some manner toward America's war effort. Roosevelt's view of The Fourteen Points was that Wilson had created another diplomatic blunder of the first order. In attacking the program, Roosevelt called it "sheer nonsense" and stated on many occasions that the American people wanted to see Germany smashed and not coddled.

Others speaking out against the program used such words as "naive," "ill-timed," "repugnant," and "socialist."

Given Wilson's strong religious beliefs, it might be said that The Fourteen Points constituted an epistle issued by a self-proclaimed messiah of democracy without the consent or advice of those who would be expected to become true believers.

As a measure of Wilson's beliefs of directions from above, the word "should" appeared 14 times in the document.

THE FOURTEEN POINTS

Wilson' Fourteen Points program, and the controversies they created were as follows:

1. *Open covenants of peace, openly arrived at, after which there should be no private international understandings of any kind, but diplomacy shall proceed always frankly and in the public view.*

This was a concept also proposed by the Bolsheviks in Russia from the inception of their revolution in November 1917, and for this reason, the program was seen by some as being "socialistic." To most people at this time, the terms "Bolshevik" and "Socialist" were synonymous.

As it turned out, this first of The Fourteen Points was adapted by the delegates at Versailles and put into Article XXVIII of the covenant of the League of Nations. This was not necessarily because the delegates approved of Wilson's proposal, but that it was politically untenable for those who had been parties to the agreements to argue otherwise.

As time would show, Article XXVIII would be widely ignored.

2. *Absolute freedom of navigation upon the seas, outside territorial waters, alike in peace and in war, except as the seas may be closed in whole or in part by international action for the enforcement of international covenants.*

To the leaders in London, this appeared to be American meddling into the affairs of the British Navy which was the largest in the world and whose freedom of action was absolutely necessary to the maintenance and security of the British Empire — also the largest in the world. Similarly, other nations dependent on naval strength such as France, Italy, and Japan could take exception to this proposal.

3. *The removal, so far as possible, of all economic barriers and the establishment of an equality of trade conditions among all the nations consenting to the peace and associating themselves for its maintenance.*

Here was one of the long-standing battle cries of the political left — free trade. To the political and economic conservatives of the world, such a broad statement affecting international economic conditions was unacceptable. This point could do nothing else but set the stage for conflicts on economic matters at the future peace conferences.

4. *Adequate guaranties given and taken that national armaments will be reduced to the lowest points consistent with domestic safety.*

"Domestic safety" — what did that mean? The ability to quell a rebellion or to repulse an invader? Fortunately, disarmament was a goal of almost everyone and this point was vague enough so that virtually everyone could agree to it. As a result, it was incorporated into the League of Nations Covenant as Article VIII.

5. *A free, open-minded, and absolute impartial adjustment of all colonial claims, based upon a strict observance of the principle that in determining all such questions of sovereignty the interests of the populations concerned must have equal weight with the equitable claims of the government whose title is to be determined.*

"Whose title is to be determined" — referred directly to the German colonies and the lands that would be taken from the Ottoman Empire (Turkey). Here, Wilson is expressing America's long-standing anti-colonialism foreign policy. On this issue, Wilson had many allies who, like himself, did not want to see the huge colonial empires of the world grow even larger. This, in turn, led to the concept of creating mandated territories whereby the supervisory power would guide and direct the territory in question to political maturity and eventual self-rule. The concept of mandates was eventually included in the League's Covenant and was, perhaps, Wilson's greatest victories at Versailles.

6. *The evacuation of all Russian territory and such a settlement of all questions affecting Russia as will secure the best and freest co-operation of the other nations of the world in obtaining for her an unhampered and unembarrassed opportunity for the independent determination of her own political development and national policy and assure her of a sincere welcome into the society of free nations under institutions of her own choosing, and more than a welcome, assistance also of every kind that she may need and may herself desire.*

The treatment accorded Russia by her sister nations in the months to come will be the acid test of their good will, of the comprehension of her needs as distinguished from their own interests, and of their intelligent and unselfish sympathy.

Here, in lofty and wordy diplomatic rhetoric, Wilson was offering an olive branch to the Bolsheviks to join peacefully and willingly into the community of nations.

The Bolsheviks ignored Wilson's plea and the civil war continued unabated; consequently, and the world remained frightened by the Bolsheviks' international aspirations. After all, Lenin had said, "As an ultimate objective, peace simply means communist world control." This phenomena had another name, the "Red Scare."

7. *Belgium, the whole world will agree, must be evacuated and restored, without any attempt to limit the sovereignty which she enjoys in common with all other free nations. No other single act will serve to restore confidence among the nations in the laws which they have themselves set and determined for the government of their relations with one another. Without this healing act the whole structure and validity of international law is forever impaired.*

None of the Allies could object to this point. The reason Belgium was singled out in The Fourteen Points was that the Germans planned to dismantle the nation and acquire for themselves Flanders and its Germanic-speaking population as well as small bits of territory along the Belgian-German border. This statement obviously decreed that Belgium was to be restored to her pre-war status and favored in territorial disputes.

THE NAZIS ALSO PLANNED TO DISMANTLE BELGIUM

During WW II the Nazis planned to dismantle Belgium and, as during the

Great War, take control of Flanders and several border areas. The remainder of Belgium, French-speaking Wallonia, was to be incorporated into a new state named "Burgundy" to serve as a buffer state between Germany and France. A state by that name had existed in the same general area centuries earlier and had served as a buffer state.

||||||||||||||||||||||||||||||||||||||||||||||||||||||||||||||||||||||||||

8. All French territory should be freed and the invaded portions restored, and the wrong done to France by Prussia in 1871 in the matter of Alsace-Lorraine, which had unsettled the peace of the world for nearly fifty years, should be righted, in order that peace may once more be made secure in the interest of all.

Here, Wilson was courting the French and acknowledging one of their primary war aims, that being the recovery of the provinces of Alsace and Lorraine which had been lost to the "Prussians" after the Franco-Prussian War of 1870-71. The delegates at Versailles agreed wholeheartedly with this proposal and the two provinces were, in fact, returned to France by the Versailles Peace Treaty.

9. A readjustment of the frontiers of Italy should be effected along clearly recognizable line of nationality.

In this statement Wilson was giving notice that he would not necessarily agree to the territorial concessions made to Italy by the British and French in the secret Treaty of London of 1915. These concessions were made to Italy in return for her entering the war on the side of the Allies. At the peace table, this would become one of the most delicate issues between the United States and Italy.

10. The peoples of Austria-Hungary, whose place among the nations we wish to see safeguarded and assured, should

be accorded the freeset opportunity of autonomous development.

Here, Wilson was advocating the dismantling of the huge Austro-Hungarian Empire that sprawled across central and eastern Europe and encompassed many different nationalities. More specifically, Wilson was advocating the right of the Poles, Czechs, Slovaks, Croats, and others to determine their own future. The splitting apart of Austria and Hungary as a united nation was not specifically stated but was very much implied. Virtually all of the Allied leaders agreed with this point and the Austro-Hungarian Empire was, in fact, dismantled.

11. Romania, Serbia and Montenegro should be evacuated; occupied territories restored; Serbia accorded free and secure access to the sea; and the relations of the several Balkan States to one another determined by friendly counsel among historically established line of allegiance and nationality; and international guaranties of the political and economic independence and territorial integrity of the several Balkan States should be entered into.

The Balkan area had been a hotbed of unrest since the departure of the Turks at the turn of the Twentieth Century. The nations there had fought each other over the spoils and became involved in two local wars, the First and Second Balkan Wars. Then, on June 24, 1914, a Serbian nationalist, Gavrilo Princip, hoping to liberate Bosnia, a region claimed by Serbia, from the Austro-Hungarians, assassinated Arch Duke Ferdinand and his wife in the Bosnian city of Sarajevo. At first, it appeared that the third Balkan war was about to erupt, but due to complicated political entanglements, the situation escalated out of control and resulted in the Great War. Here, Wilson was calling for peace and order in this very troubled part of Europe. Since Romania, Serbia, and Montenegro had been Allied nations, Wilson approved of them taking the lead in settling matters there.

Few at the peace conference could disagree with Wilson's assessment of the situation and agreed that something had to be done in the Balkans. This resulted in the creation of the state of Jugoslavia with its capital being Belgrade, the capital of Serbia, and its head of state being the King of Serbia. Ironically, this was the goal sought by Gavrilo Princip when he assassinated the Arch Duke because Bosnia was incorporated into the new state.

12. The Turkish portions of the present Ottoman Empire should be assured a secure sovereignty, but the other nationalities which are now under Turkish rule should be assured an un-doubted security of life and an absolute unmolested opportunity of autonomous development, and the Dardanelles should be permanently opened as a free passage to the ships and commerce of all nations, under international guaranties.

Few at the peace conference disagreed with Wilson's assessment as to what should be done with regard to the Ottoman Empire. But there were those who resented Wilson's meddling into this affair because the United States had not been at war with the Turks and had suffered no casualties or economic losses in defeating that enemy.

Unfortunately for Wilson, this pronouncement would backfire on him at the peace conference. When the discussion as to what to do about the liberated areas of the former Ottoman Empire got underway, the concept of creating mandated territories was widely accepted. With this, Wilson was then asked to make good this commitment by accepting one or more mandates in the Middle East — or in other words — help pay part of the costs of the peace with Turkey. Back home, the idea of the US government committing resources and personnel to that far away region of the globe in an effort to quell the activities of those wild Mohammedans (the popular word at the time for Muslims) would not sit well with the U.S. Congress nor with the American public. As a result, Wilson was forced to go on the defensive and back down with regard to issues regarding Turkey.

13. An independent Polish state should be erected which should include the territories inhabited by indisputably Polish populations, which should be assured a free and secure access to the sea, and whose political and economic independence and territorial integrity should be guaranteed by international covenants.

Here, Wilson was supporting the concept, widely held by the other Allied nations, that Poland should become a free and independent nation. By calling for Polish access to the sea, Wilson was giving his approval to the concept that an area of land should be cut through the German state of Prussia and given to Poland to provide that access. This, in effect, would split Germany into two parts, Germany proper and East Prussia. This action was taken by the peacemakers and the infamous Polish Corridor was created. This action would become a most bitter issue for the German people and provide political ammunition for almost every current and future German politician until the end of WW II. The Nazis would work this concept to the maximum, and recovery of the Polish Corridor would become one of their primary political goals.

14. A general association of nations must be formed under specific covenants for the purpose of affording mutual guar-

anties of political independence and territorial integrity to great and small states alike.

Here, Wilson was promoting one of the programs he considered most important to world peace — the League of Nations. Wilson would have his way; the League of Nations would come into being, but the United States would not become a member. Wilson would not give up, however. He fought doggedly for American entrance into the League and that effort would cost him his health.

FDR DID IT TOO

At the Casablanca Conference in January 1943, President Franklin Roosevelt made a similar unilateral declaration which could be compared to The Fourteen Points. It, too, concerned the conduct of the war and came as a surprise to the other Allied leaders and gave them considerable concern. In a press conference, he made what appeared to be an off hand remark stating that the Allies would accept nothing less than "unconditional surrender" from the Axis Powers. Such an understanding had not been agreed to among Roosevelt's equals. Furthermore, calling for unconditional surrender ruled out any hope for a negotiated settlement to end the war. After much consideration, the other Allied leaders, unlike those of Wilson, accepted the concept and it became a formal part of the Allies' war aims.

SELF-DETERMINATION

The phrase "self-determination" did not appear in Wilson's Fourteen Points but, nevertheless, became associated with that document because of the overall tone of that document which offered the subject peoples of the world the right to choose their own political future. The

phrase, "self-determination," would be widely used in the post 1918 era.

THE FOUR PRINCIPLES

On February 11, 1918, Wilson went before Congress again and presented an addendum to his Fourteen Points. This became known as the "Four Principles." This document was a refinement of The Fourteen Points and another call upon Germany to end the war. The Four Principles were:

First: Each part of the final settlement must be based upon the essential justice of the particular case and upon such adjustments as are most likely to bring a peace that will be permanent.

Second: Peoples and provinces are not to be bartered about from sovereignty to sovereignty as if they were mere chattels and pawns in a game, even the great game, now forever discredited, of the balance of power but that

Third: every territorial settlement involved in this war must be made in the interest and for the benefit of the populations concerned, and not as a part of any mere adjustment or compromise of claims amongst rival states; and

Fourth: all well-defined national aspirations shall be accorded the utmost satisfaction that can be accorded them without introducing new or perpetuating old elements of discord and antagonism that would be likely in time to break the peace of Europe and consequently of the world.

UPSURGE OF ANTI-SEMITISM

At the time Wilson was composing his Fourteen Points and Four Principles, there was another phenomenon occurring in the world. In November 1917, the Bolsheviks burst onto the world stage when they overthrew the democratic Kerenski government in Petrograd (St. Petersburg), Russia. At once, the anti-semites of Europe and much of the world pointed out that the Bolshevik organization was heavily riddled with Jews. It was common knowledge that Karl Marx, the creator of communism, was a German Jew and now, in Russia, home to half of the world's Jews, Jews were in prominent positions of authority. While Lenin, the leader of the Bolshevik Party and the real leader of the revolution, was not a Jew, it was widely rumored that his wife, Krupskaya, was part Jewish. It was definitely known that Lenin's second in command, Leon Trotsky (Lev Davidovich Bornstein), Commissar for War and Commander of the Red Army, was Jewish, as were Lev Kamenev (Rosenfeld), "President" of the Soviet government; Yakov Sverdlov (Solomon), the Communist Party's executive secretary; Grigori Zinoviev (Radomyslsky), head of the Communist Internationale

Some people believed that it was actually Trotsky who was in control of the Bolsheviks. This cartoon, published by the Russian Whites, suggests this. Trotsky (right) is seen as the dominant figure and Lenin (left) as his subordinate. The Soviet government was often called the Lenin-Trotsky government in both Russia and Europe.

(Comintern); and Moses Uritsky, head of CHEKA, the State Secret Police.

In January 1918, just two months after the beginning of the Bolshevik Revolution, David R. Francis, the still-functioning US Ambassador to Russia, reported to the State Department "The Bolshevik leaders here, most of whom are Jews and 90 percent of whom are returned exiles, care little for Russia or any other country but are internationalists and they are trying to start a worldwide social revolution."

On May 2, 1918, the US Consul General in Moscow sent a report to the State Department saying in part "Jews prominent in local Soviet government, anti-Jewish feeling growing among population."

On July 5, 1918, the US Consul General in Vladivostok sent the message "Fifty percent of the Soviet government in each town consists of Jews of the worst type."

THE "PROTOCOLS" BOOK

As a result of the suspected Jewish/communist connection, the opponents of communism and the anti-semites of Europe united to resurrect a notorious book from the literary scrap heap — a book entitled *Protocols of the Elders of Zion* (or *Protocols of the Wise Men of Zion*). This book, apparently published by the Czar's secret police in the 1880s, claimed to have uncovered a secret conspiracy by the leaders of international Jewry to take over the world by economic means. Many people then, as now, believe the book to be a fake and a crude justification by the Czar's secret police to justify the many pogroms that were carried out against the Jews in Russia. Nevertheless, the message the book conveyed was a message that many people found easy to believe, especially in light of the international nature of the Jews and their propensity for things economic.

So, when communism — an economic system designed by a Jewish Elder, Karl Marx — suddenly appeared on the scene calling for a classless society in which everyone was considered equal and prescribing an economic system that everyone in the world should adhere to, it was easy to associate communism with the predictions in Protocols.

During the latter months of the war, the book popped up in various countries and in several languages and it was read by many influential people. Adolf Hitler, an avid reader, read the book as a young man and said of it later that the found it "enormously instructive" and "useful and valid."

A NEW KIND OF ARMY

During the Great War a new kind of army, commonly called the "Red Army," emerged in Bolshevik-controlled Russia. It was a heavy mix of communist political theory and military science. In the new Red Army, political authorities, called "commissars," worked side-by-side with officers and outranked them. Every decision had to politically approved and on some issues, the soldiers were allowed to vote. The old ranks of private, corporal, lieutenant, captain, and others were replaced by new ranks with different names. There were "revolutionary tribunals" in every units that passed judgment on individuals whose loyalties and abilities came into question. Within the Red Army, there was also a large bureaucracy to manage and administer virtually every aspect of military life.

GROSSE POLITISCHE SCHAU IM BIBLIOTHEKSBAU DES DEUTSCHEN MUSEUMS ZU MÜNCHEN · AB 8. NOVEMBER 1937 · TÄGLICH GEÖFFNET VON 10-21 UHR

The Nazis used the Jewish-communist connection extensively in their anti-Jewish propaganda. Above is a Nazi poster advertising "The Eternal Jew" exhibition in Germany in 1937. Under his arm, the Jew holds a map of Soviet Russia marked with the communist symbol, the hammer and sickle.

A NEW VOCABULARY OF WAR

Many terms used during the Great War carried over to WW II. Some of them included: air raids, air fields, airmen, D-Day, depth charge, dogfights, doughboys (used in the early years of WW II until it was replaced by "GI"), poison gas, TNT, flamethrowers, tanks, home front, land mines, Q-ships, RAF, shell shock, strategic bombing, U-boats, and war crimes.

CHAPTER 2
JANUARY 1919, A VERY DYNAMIC MONTH...
VERY

||||||||||||||||||||||||||||||||||||||||||||||||||||||||||||||||||||||||||||||||||||||||||||||||||||||||||||||||||

JANUARY 1, 1919

On this date, peace in Europe was 51 days old.

Corporal Adolf Hitler, age 29, was in the Pasewalk Military Hospital near Berlin, recovering from his second war wound, an attack of poison gas that had left him temporarily blinded.

Hitler was a highly decorated enlisted man having won the Iron Cross 1st Class (a very high honor), Iron Cross 2nd Class, Military Cross 3rd Class with Swords, Service medal 3rd Class, Regimental Diploma for Outstanding Bravery, and the Wound Badge.

During his stay in the hospital, he was examined by a military physician who specialized in psychiatry. In his notes, the doctor stated that the corporal was "incompetent to command people" and "dangerously psychotic." In later years, Hitler himself contributed to this psychotic diagnoses by telling people that, while he was in the hospital, he had had a "vision" which told him that he had a mission to save Germany.

Adolf Hitler, age 29.

HITLER'S EYESIGHT

Hitler often complained about his eyes and when he reached his early 50s, the troubles worsened. Soon, he was wearing glasses and using a magnifying glass to read documents and maps. He had large-type typewriters installed in his various headquarters so he could more easily read typed documents.

Benito Mussolini, age 34, was a relatively well-known socialist journalist in Italy having been editor of a prominent socialist newspaper before the war. He fought with the Italian Army on the Austrian front, then was wounded and discharged. He now published his own newspaper in Milan, *"Il Popolo d'Italia"* and had changed his political philosophy from the one-size-fits-all concept of international socialism to one favoring a form of national socialism tailored for the needs of Italy. By making this move, he had deserted the political far left and now advocated a program that covered almost the entire political spectrum.

Winston Churchill, age 34, was a well-known British politician on the rise. In December 1918, he had been appointed War Minister in Lloyd George's Cabinet and was now preparing to play his role in the forthcoming peace negotiations at Versailles.

Franklin D. Roosevelt, age 31, was in Washington, DC, serving in the Wilson Administration as Assistant Secretary of the Navy. This was a very important government position because the US now had the world's largest navy. He would be sent to Paris for a few weeks in 1919, not as an American delegate to the peace conference, but to oversee the sale of surplus naval property.

GIANTS AND PYGMIES

On the night of the German armistice, November 11, 1918, Churchill commented to Lloyd George, "The War of the giants has ended...The quarrels of the pygmies have begun."

At the end of WW II, in his last letter to Franklin Roosevelt, dated March 17, 1945, Churchill wrote " ... when the war of the giants is over, the war of the pygmies will begin." Roosevelt did not reply. He died on April 12, 1945.

Joseph Stalin, age 39, was in Russia, deeply involved in the Bolshevik Revolution; and he had become a close associate of Lenin.

Harry S Truman, age 34, had served in the US Army in France as a captain of artillery. He was awaiting discharge and intended to return to his home in Independence, MO, where he would go into the haberdashery business. Upon returning home, Truman would resume his career in the National Guard.

Neville Chamberlain, age 49, had served as a Conservative member of Parliament from the constituency of Ladywood and was now Mayor of Birmingham.

Lt. Colonel Dwight D. Eisenhower, age 28, had not gone overseas but served as commander of Camp Colt, PA, a tank training center where he had the temporary rank of Lt. Col.

Chiang Kai-shek, aged 22, had obtained military training in both China and Japan and was now a close associate of Dr. Sun Yat-sen, founder of the Republic of China.

Mao Tse-tung, age 25, was fairly well-educated and working in a university library in China as a library assistant.

Hirohito, age 17, was the Crown Prince of Japan and was attending a special school created exclusively for Japanese royalty.

Hideki Tojo, age 34, was a professional officer in the Japanese Army during the war, but he saw little action. He was from a well-respected military family and was considered to be an officer with a bright future. In 1919, he would be sent to Germany to serve as a military attache in the Japanese embassy in Berlin.

Captain Charles de Gaulle, age 28, had served as a subaltern in General Henri Petain's regiment, and was wounded and captured by the Germans in 1916 at Verdun. He spent 32 months in captivity during which time he wrote the first draft of a book on military theory entitled "Discord Among the Enemy," which he published in 1924. De Gaulle would remain in the French Army, rise rapidly, and ultimately become an authority on military theory.

Joseph Goebbels, age 21, was a student at Heidelberg University. He had not been called up for military service because he had a club foot. He would go on to obtain a doctorate degree in 1921 in Romantic Drama.

Hermann Goering, age 25, was a well-known, and highly decorated German aviator and war hero. He would soon leave the military and take a position in commercial aviation.

Heinrich Himmler, age 18, was a student studying agriculture at Munich Technical High School.

Martin Bormann, age 18, had served in the German Army during the last months of the war, but the war ended before he reached the front. In 1919 he joined a Free Corps.

Brigadier General Douglas MacArthur, age 38, was one of America's best-known war heros. He served with distinction in France, was wounded several times, and highly decorated. He had acquired the nickname "the Dude" because

of his unorthodox attire. MacArthur was awaiting reassignment.

Lt. Erwin Rommel, age 26, was a highly decorated hero of the German Army because of his exploits on the Italian front. He left the Army after the war, but returned and made it his career.

Albert Speer, age 13, was a school boy in Mannheim which had been bombed several times by the Allies. His father was an architect and he would also become an architect.

Rudolf Hess, age 23, had served as a shock troop leader in the German Army since 1914. He spent time serving in the same regiment as Corporal Adolf Hitler. During the latter part of the war, he became an aircraft pilot. In 1919 he joined General Ritter von Epp's Free Corps.

Col. George C. Marshall, age 38, had served in France on the General Staff of the US First Army. He had gained the reputation of being a very knowledgeable officer and a good organizer.

Wilhelm Keitel, age 29, was an accomplished professional soldier who had served on the German General Staff as an artillery officer; he was wounded several times. In 1919 he joined a Free Corps.

George S. Patton, Jr. age 33, was seen early in his military career as an officer of great promise and was an expert on tanks. He was assigned to Pershing's staff and later led American tank units in combat. He was badly wounded and was in the hospital when the war ended.

Brigade Major Bernard L. Montgomery, age 31, had served with distinction in the British Army during the war and saw lots of action. He was awarded the DSO.

Heinz Guderian, age 30, had served as an officer in the German Army and would later become a member of a Free Corps.

Harold "Hap" Arnold, age 32, had risen rapidly from private to Lt. Colonel in the US Army Air Service. By the end of the war, he commanded the Service's 1st Pursuit Group. He returned to the US and was assigned to pilot training.

Robert J. Oppenheimer, age 14, was a high school student in New York City.

Joachim von Ribbentrop, age 25, was a well-educated (having studied in France, Britain, and Switzerland) and socially well-connected army officer. He had fought in the war and won the Iron Cross. He would be appointed a member of the German negotiating team that went to Versailles to sign the peace treaty.

Isoruku Yamamoto, age 33, was a professional naval officer who had served in the Japanese Navy throughout the war. In 1919 he went to the United States to study at Harvard University.

Georgi K. Zhukov, age 22, had been a sergeant in the Czar's Army but in 1918 joined the Bolsheviks and was now serving as a cavalry officer in the Red Army. The Red Army was very short of officers so experienced and dedicated men, such as Zhukov, were rapidly promoted.

Omar N. Bradley, age 25, graduated from West Point in 1915 and spent the war in the US training infantry units.

Mark W. Clark, age 22, graduated from West Point in 1917, saw action in France, and was wounded. He returned to the US determined to make the Army his career.

Karl Doenitz, age 27, had commanded a German submarine in the Mediterranean. His vessel malfunctioned and he was captured by the British.

Chester Nimitz, age 33, had become an expert on submarine warfare before the war and had studied diesel engines in Germany. By 1919, he had risen to the rank of Lt. Commander and was on the staff of Captain Samuel Robison.

William F. "Bull" Halsey, age 36, had graduated from the US Naval Academy in 1904 and commanded a destroyer which served as a convoy escort during the war. Halsey was awarded the Navy Cross.

Eva Braun, age 6, was a school girl living with her family in Munich. Her father was a school teacher.

Wernher von Braun, age 5, was a school boy living with his family in Wirsitz, Prussia. His father had founded a successful bank and had served in the government as Minister of Agriculture.

Albert Einstein, age 38, was a well-known German physicist having published papers on the theory of relativity.

John Foster Dulles, age 30, and Allen Dulles, age 25, These two brothers had long-standing and high level political connections and were up-and-coming stars at the US State Department. They were the grandsons of John Watson Foster, who served as President Benjamin Harrison's Secretary of State and were nephews of Robert Lansing, Wilson's Secretary of State. They had also caught the eye of Wilson because their father, Allen Macy Dulles was, like Wilson's father, a Presbyterian minister. John Foster, who had studied at the Sorbonne, served as a legal counsel to the American delegation and Allen, who had had experiences in the US diplomatic service and served in Berlin, Paris, Constantinople, Vienna, and Berne, was an advisor within the State Department. John Foster went on after the signing of the Versailles Peace Treaty to serve on the war reparations commission and Allen was appointed in 1922 as the State Department's Chief of Division for Near Eastern Affairs.

Colonel Erich von Manstein, age 30, was a professional soldier who had fought on both the eastern and western fronts. He remained in the German Army after the war.

Joseph Stilwell, age 35, held the temporary rank of Lt. Col. in the US Army and saw combat at Meuse-Argonne. In 1919 he served with the US Army of occupation in the Rhineland and in 1920 was sent to China.

David Ben-Gurion, age 32, was an American citizen who had fought as an enlisted man in the American Battalion of the Jewish Legion of the British Army in Palestine. He would remain in Palestine and become a leader of Jewish right-wing political factions.

On this first day of the new year, Wilson, his wife Edith, and members of his entourage were on the King of Italy's private train which had been sent to pick them up for their planned visit to Italy. They would meet and talk with King Victor Emmanuel III, Premier Orlando, and Pope Benedict XV.

KING VICTOR

King Victor Emmanuel III would still be on the throne in December 1941 and would sign Italy's declaration of war against the United States. He was Italy's King throughout WW II and reigned for 46 years.

All along the way, crowds gathered at trackside, hoping to get a glimpse of the great man from across the sea. Such public adulation had become commonplace ever since Wilson arrived at Brest, France, on December 13, 1918 (Friday the 13th). In both France and Britain, as he journeyed to meet Clemenceau, Lloyd George, and others, he was hailed and cheered on every occasion. Now that he was coming to Italy, the Italian media covered his every move and reported glowingly on his activities. Even Mussolini's newspaper, *Il Popolo d'Italia*, welcomed the great American President. For Wilson, personally, these first weeks in Europe had to have been a very stimulating experience and a highlight of his career.

On January 3, Wilson and his entourage arrived in Rome to another tumultuous public greeting. The diplomatic reception he received from the Italian leaders was, however, a different matter. They had, all along, been counting on their European Allies, Britain and France, to honor their commitments in the secret Treaty of London of 1915 which gave Italy major territorial concessions in Europe and the Middle East in return for Italy entering the war on the Allied side. They knew, full well, of Wilson's disapproval of such secret treaties and fully expected him to oppose the promises made, especially since the US had not been a signatory to the London Treaty nor had even been informed of it until later.

JANUARY 3, 1919:
FOOD FOR THE EUROPEAN MASSES

Long before the guns fell silent on the Western Front, the need was foreseen by the Allies to feed the peoples of Europe immediately after the end of the conflict. Extensive plans were made in this regard and on January 3, an American, Herbert Clark Hoover, who was already in Europe, was appointed Director General of a newly-created food relief organization called the "International Food Relief Program." Its goal was to feed 125 million people — including Germans, Austrians, and others in need. His efforts would be seen as a vital weapon against the spread of Bolshevism and anarchy. Several nations would contribute to the program, but most of the food and money would come from America.

Herbert Hoover was well suited for the job. In 1900 he directed food relief in China during the Boxer Revolution; in late 1914 he headed the "American Relief Committee" to get food to submarine-blockaded Britain, and from 1915 to 1919, he headed an American relief program to aid the people of Belgium. Hoover had also been involved in rationing at home. One of his most prominent proposals was "wheatless Mondays" and "meatless Tuesdays." This was soon known as "Hooverizing."

Hoover's job was not easy. He had his opponents who felt that the program, and the Americans in particular, were coddling the enemy who had caused so much misery throughout all of Europe. Furthermore, Hoover's appointment came on the heels of Lloyd George's and Clemenceau's recent elections, in which they both promised their people that they would come down hard on the "Huns." One of Hoover's strongest opponents was Winston Churchill in the British Admiralty. Churchill and Hoover became involved in an exchange of verbal abuses. Churchill called Hoover an "S.O.B." and Hoover labeled the British Admiralty "a sanctuary of British militarism." One of the problems Hoover had, which was created in part by Churchill, was that the British Admiralty refused to lift blockade restrictions on Germany's fishing fleet and kept it bottled up in the German ports. The British government was continuing the wartime blockade to put economic pressure on Germany to comply with the armistice agreement and the coming Versailles Peace Treaty.

Hoover argued that this action was counterproductive and contributing to the food problems inside Germany. But it was the Admiralty which would have its way with regard to the German fishing fleet. Hoover's food program would have to make up for the food that the fishing fleet could not provide.

To add to Hoover's burden, the British press frequently made unfavorable comments about his relief program because some saw it a competitor to the legitimate interests of the Empire's food producers. This attitude was also prevalent in France and Italy. Hoover had planned to set up

his operation in London, but because of the British opposition, moved it to Paris. Even there, Hoover had problems. Clemenceau said once, referring to the relief program, "There are 20 million Germans too many."

To mollify some of the criticism, Hoover allowed the name of his organization to be changed to "The Supreme Council of Supply and Relief" to give it a more international image, and he allowed representatives from the various Allied nations to serve on its board.

One of the staples badly needed in Europe was cereals. Central and Eastern Europe had relied heavily over the years on supplies from Russia, but that source was no longer available and, by now, all available inventories were depleted. Fortunately, in America, there was a bumper crop in the fall of 1918. It was grain grown in Kansas and Indiana that would now feed people in Czechoslovakia and Germany. Some of Hoover's critics even pounced on this, arguing that the U.S was dumping its farm surpluses in Europe. This argument was countered, to some degree, by the fact that the British Commonwealth nations would also supply significant quantities of food.

In Washington, DC, Wilson asked Congress for $100 million to fund Hoover's program. There was some opposition in the Senate about feeding the Germans, but the appropriation passed, 53 to 18.

This action came none too soon. Soon after being appointed, Hoover reported back to Washington that one of his inspection teams had estimated that, in northern Germany, some 800 people were dying per day of starvation.

HERBERT HOOVER'S RELIEF PROGRAM AND THE MARSHALL PLAN

There are a number of interesting parallels between Hoover's activities

Rosa Luxemburg

in Europe after the Great War and the "Marshall Plan" following World War II.

John Maynard Keynes, a guru economist of his day and an advisor to the British delegation in Paris in 1919, wrote of American economic assistance to Europe in his forthcoming and best-selling book, The Economic Consequences of the Peace (1920) that "Europe...should never forget the extraordinary assistance afforded her during the first six months of 1919 through the agency of Mr. Hoover and the American Commission on Relief."

In May 1945, President Harry S Truman, faced with the problems of supplying food to a war-torn Europe, called Hoover to the White House and sought his advice with regard to the problem of feeding the people of Europe.

JANUARY 5, 1919:
GERMAN COMMUNISTS
TAKE CONTROL OF BERLIN

As the Great War was coming to an end, the Allies declared that they would not negotiate an armistice with the Kaiser's government. Therefore, the Kaiser had to go. Soon after he abdicated in early November 1918 and fled to The Netherlands, a broad-based coalition government was formed in Berlin under a prominent Social Democrat, Friedrich Ebert, who was given the thankless job of running the country in its most desperate hour of need. A sizeable communist-oriented organization, known as the Sparticus League (named after the Roman slave and gladiator, Sparticus, who had led a revolt against Rome in 73 BC), was a part of the coalition and the dominant organization on the extreme political left. The leaders of the League, Karl Liebknecht and Rosa Luxemburg, a Jew, soon realized that they could not work with the Ebert government and left the coalition.

QUEEN WILHELMINA AND THE KAISER

When the Kaiser fled to The Netherlands, he accepted asylum from the country's Head of State, Queen Wilhelmina, who was married to German Grand Duke Henry of Mechlenburg-Schwerin. The Queen gave the Kaiser and his family a grand estate at Doorn in which to live and protected him from extradition by the Allied Powers.

When WW II began in 1939, Wilhelmina was still on the throne and the Kaiser was still in The Netherlands. When the Germans invaded The Netherlands in May 1940, Wilhelmina fled the country and headed a Government-in-Exile in Britain. The Kaiser remained in The Netherlands and thereby came under Hitler's control. Hitler was vehemently opposed to the Kaiser, or any member of his family, returning to the throne of Germany but let the Kaiser live out the rest of his life in peace. Kaiser Wilhelm died in The Netherlands on June 4, 1941.

Rebellious German soldiers and sailors, sympathetic with the communist cause, patrolled the streets of Berlin, displaying the red flag.

Leftist strikes and demonstrations soon followed and law and order in the German capital began to deteriorate. It had been rumored that Lenin saw in this action the potential of Germany becoming a communist satellite, and had sent Liebknecht and Luxemburg sizeable support in the form of gold and the services of one of Lenin's closest associates, Karl Radek, a Ukrainian Jew.

By late December, the situation in Berlin had turned to open revolt, and the possibility of a full-scale civil war loomed. The Berlin police were losing control of the situation and the German Army, demoralized by defeat and riddled with leftist sympathizers and rebellious soldiers and sailors, was incapable of providing meaningful support. But the military leaders, virtually all of whom were on the political right, had a solution — the "Free Corps."

THE EMERGENCE OF THE "FREE CORPS"

On December 14, 1918, General Ludwig von Maercker, commander of the 214th Infantry Division, with Hindenburg's and Ludendorff's approval, issued an order establishing the *"Freiwillige Landesjager-korps"* (Volunteer Rifle Corps). These units would become known as the "Free Corps."

Maercker's order read in part:

1. *Aim:* The Volunteer Rifle Corps is created for the maintenance of order within the Reich and for the defense of its frontiers.

2. *Constitution:* The Rifle Corps is composed entirely of volunteers.

3. *Discipline:* The fighting strength of troops can only be manifested in its full strength if it gives implicit obedience to its leaders...To achieve [this], an iron discipline is necessary...(and) should be founded upon ready and consenting obedience.

4. *Trusted Men:* These should be a bond between non-commissioned officers and subordinates...[and] They should have no authority as regards the (German Army) command."

An intensive recruiting campaign followed. Experienced officers, NCOs and men, untainted by leftist political leanings, were sought as volunteers. These efforts were fruitful. By Christmas, eleven days after Maercker's order, the Freiwillige Landesjagercorps had 4000 men. Money and some weapons were supplied by the army and by secret organizations and militant groups that had hidden weapons and other military assets from both the Allied authorities and the German government.

By the end of December, the first Free Corps, Reinhardt's Free Corps, named after its commander, was ready for action and others were rapidly being formed. Within weeks, tens of thousands of men would become Free Corpsmen in units popping up all over Germany. As they grew, the Free Corps took over army posts, headquarters, training facilities, and other army assets while Hindenburg, Ludendorff, and others looked on in silence.

Out of desperation, Ebert called upon the Free Corps for help in Berlin. But, it took time and planning to get these hoped-for saviors gathered together and transported.

In the meantime, the Sparticans gained more control over the city, and, on the last day of the year, dropped the name, Sparticus League, and renamed their organization the "Communist Party of Germany" (KDP).

Then, Liebknecht and Luxemburg made their move. They called upon their followers to converge on Berlin on January 5 and take full control of the city — by force of arms if necessary — and establish a communist government for Germany. They counted on their followers to be well-armed, because, at the time, army rifles were plentiful in the marketplace because many of the returning soldiers had brought them home and sold them. The going price for a used army rifle was about two marks.

Seeing what was coming, Ebert called upon the Allies for help. They responded and both the French and American promised to send small military contingents to Berlin. But again, the time factor favored the communists, and they struck first.

On the nights of January 5/6, an estimated force of some 200,000 workers, leftist soldiers, sailors, and others, most of them armed, streamed into Berlin and took control of large sections of the city. Ebert consolidated his meager forces in a redoubt around the Chancellory building and waited for the Free Corps.

COMMUNISTS IN THE RUHR AND IN SAXONY

Berlin was not the first area in Germany to go communist. In the Ruhr, Germany's industrial heartland, communist-oriented Workers' Councils had taken over some areas and proclaimed them the "Autonomous Republic of the Ruhr."

In the state of Saxony, in southeastern Germany on the border of the new nation of Czechoslovakia, the local leaders in Dresden, the state capital, proclaimed Saxony to be a communist state. Unlike the communists in Berlin and the Ruhr, Saxony would remain within the German federation and would continue to submit to Berlin's authority on national issues. The Saxons, though, changed their state flag to that of an all-red field (the symbol of revolution) with a large black hammer and cycle in the center.

From the standpoint of the Ebert government and the German Army, the state of Saxony could wait, but the rebellion in Berlin and the Autonomous Republic of the Ruhr had to be eliminated as soon as possible.

DRESDEN

During Ww II, the Allied bombing of Dresden in October 1944 and again in January 1945 has remained a controversy over the years. Why Dresden? Clearly, it was not a city that the western Allies would conquer, but would, almost certainly, fall to the Red Army which was advancing from the east. Many believe that Dresden was bombed as a warning to the Soviets to live up to their agreement to halt their advance in Europe at the agreed-upon line of demarcation. If that was, in fact the intent of the Western Allies, what better target could have been selected that the former capital of communist Saxony?

TWO OTHER EVENTS

Two other events of significance occurred on the same day the communists took over Berlin — January 5, 1919.

In the Baltic Sea, the British Navy was maintaining a naval blockade of the southern coastline of that body of water from Denmark to Finland. This was not only against the Germans, but also against the Bolsheviks. On this day, British war ships shelled Bolshevik headquarters in the city of Riga, Latvia, which had recently come under the control of the Bolshevik VII Army. This was only a small episode of a much larger conflict that had begun during the summer of 1918 when Allied forces (British, French, American, Canadian, Japanese and others), invaded areas of the former Russian Empire in an effort to contain, or possibly defeat, the Bolshevik revolutionaries. As such, the Allies were working in conjunction with the Russian "Whites," the name given to the accumulation of armed and loosely-connected organizations actively fighting the Bolsheviks inside Russia.

In the Baltic area, there was a very unique situation. The Germans had "liberated" the area from the Russians during the Great War and had intended, over the years, to Germanize the people and eventually annex the area to Germany. This area that was to become part of Germany was called "Kurland." The territories in question were the three Baltic regions traditionally known (from north to south) as Estonia, Latvia, and Lithuania. After the German defeat, German forces withdrew from Kurland and the Bolsheviks started to move in. The local people resisted but with only limited success and two of the three states, Latvia and Lithuania, fell to the invader. But Estonia was saved due the effective resistance of the newly-created, but small, Estonian army and two allies who came to their aide. These were the Finns, who were fighting for their own freedom, and a White force, known as the "Northwestern White Army" which had been operating in the area since early 1918.

THE NAZIS ALSO PLANNED TO ANNEX THE BALTIC AREA

During WW II, the Nazis also planned to annex this Baltic region and Germanize the people. The Nazis called the region "Ostland" (Eastland) and it was much larger than Kurland would have been. Ostland would have included the three Baltic states, the Leningrad (St. Petersburg) area up to the Finnish border, and territories to the east to within about 150 miles of Moscow.

Anton Drexler, co-founder of the Munich discussion group that would eventually become the German Workers' Party, and later, the Nazi Party.

In contrast to what was actually happening in the Baltic areas, the Allies could not accept the German plans for the area and, in 1918, declared that the three Baltic states should have their freedom and independence. As a result, during the interim between the time when the Germans withdrew and the Bolsheviks invaded, provisional governments were formed in all three states, each proclaimimg the independence of their respective state based on the Allied declaration. Consequently, by making their declaration, the Allies had committed themselves to go to the support of the Baltic states but they had no coherent plan to do so. Furthermore, the situation was complicated because the new state of Poland had claims on Lithuanian territory and some Russian White leaders, notably Admiral Alexander V. Kolchak who commanded White forces east of Moscow, wanted to see no part

of the former Russian Empire became independent. It was his hope to reconstitute the entire Russian Empire under his leadership.

By January 1919, however, the Allies were hard-pressed to launch military operations anywhere and especially in the Baltic area. They could, though, take limited actions such as the shelling of Bolshevik-occupied Riga by the British warships.

Ironically, the Allies and the Ebert government in Berlin concurred in the belief that the Baltic states should be free and independent. It would be the Germans, not the Allies, who would try to make this happen.

The second event that occurred on this day, January 5, 1919, happened in a beer hall in Munich, Germany. It was insignificant at the time, but would eventually have earth-shaking consequences.

A group of about two dozen politically-minded men gathered in the back room of the Furstenfelder Hof Beer Hall in Munich to form a discussion group which focused on the subject of German politics. At this time, with the war having been over for only two months, Germany's politics was in a very volatile state of flux. The group was headed by two individuals, Karl Harrer, a sports writer for the right wing newspaper "Munchener-Augsburger Abenzeitung," and Anton Drexler, a toolmaker in a local locomotive works. Many of the participants were Drexler's fellow workers.

Harrer was a member of the Thule Society, a sizeable right-wing political group, and wanted to form a smaller tight-knit organization of his own that would study and discuss Germany's new post-Kaiser political structure and her many economic problems.

Drexler called himself a socialist and a worker and had been recruited by Harrer to help form the group. Their union was very compatible and the group would soon advance beyond a mere discussion group and enter into the political arena. Within a short time, it would give itself a name, the "German Workers Party" (DAP), and Harrer would become the National Chairman with Drexler the Deputy Chairman.

This was the symbol of the Thule Society, one of the first right wing, anti-republican, anti-Semitic groups that formed in Germany at the end of the Great War.

In the heady days of December 1918 and January 1919, many small groups were coming together in Germany and giving themselves political names. The DAP was just one of many.

Drexler and some of the other participants were, like Harrer, active members of the Thule Society which was a right-wing, anti-republican, anti-Semitic political action organization that had been formed in August 1918 and had grown rapidly in the Munich area. The Thule Society was named after a mythical island in northern Europe which was reported to have been the initial home of the White race.

There was one overriding factor that bonded the two groups, the Thule Society and the DAP, in a common cause. Both highly respected the efforts and memory of Bismarck, the "Iron Chancellor," who had wielded dictatorial power and uniting Germany in the 1860s and 1870s. This feeling was still strong in Germany and many believed that another Iron Chancellor might be needed to keep Germany united and bring her back to the powerful state they believed she should be. But the chances of another Iron Chancellor emerging under the new liberal republic, with its constant intra-party political squabbling, were weak at best.

The Thule Society had a symbol which included a swastika and a dagger. At this time in European cultures, the swastika did not have the extreme right-wing, anti-Semitic meaning it would soon acquire. Rather, it had been looked upon for generations as a symbol of good fortune and, at times, a Christian symbol. In this respect,

it was sometimes called the "twisted cross." The dagger, since early times, represented strong centralized government. Therefore, the Thule logo stood for good fortune for the German people under a strong and powerful leadership.

Others in Europe were also using this symbol of good fortune at this time. The Finns, who were fighting to obtain their independence and had fought the Bolsheviks and, more recently, their own Finnish communists, used a light blue swastika as their symbol. Then too, some of the Free Corps units that were forming in Germany at this time adopted the swastika. And, a right wing political organization in Austria used a flag showing a swastika on a red background. There was also another political group in Munich, the "Germanen Orden" (Teutonic Order), that used the swastika.

TEDDY ROOSEVELT DIED

On January 6, former President Teddy Roosevelt died at his home on Long Island. With his passing, the leadership of the progressive wing of the Republican Party became leaderless. This opened the door for the conservative Republicans to take more control of their party. For Wilson, it meant that his opponents at home were moving further to the political right and away from his more liberal positions espoused by "TR."

A captured British tank was used by the Free Corps to help subdue the communists in Berlin. The Allies had impounded all German tanks but neglected to impound tanks captured by the Germans.

On this day, Wilson was in Milan, Italy, making speeches and still enjoying the adulation of the Italian crowds. This was Mussolini's hometown and his newspaper, *Il Popolo d'Italia*, covered Wilson's every move and joined in the praise. It was a honeymoon that would not last long.

And in Rome, things were turning from bad to worse for Premier Orlando. It was becoming clear that Wilson, despite his words of conciliation and respect for the Italian people, would not support Italy's territorial claims on Italy's eastern border. Of primary interest was the strategically located deep-water port of Fiume at the northern end of the Adriatic Sea. Fiume had belonged to Austria-Hungary, but now Italy claimed it as a spoil of war, and a delegation from Fiume had come to Rome in November 1918 to ask that Fiume be incorporated into Italy. Under Wilson's influence, however, the majority of the other Allies had agreed that Fiume was to go to the newly-created state of "The Kingdom of Serbs, Croats and Slovenes" (Jugoslavia) because that state had no deep water port in the area while the Italians had nearby Venice. There were also proposals put forward that Fiume might become a Free State as was planned for the former German city of Danzig on the Baltic Sea. "Free States," "plebiscites" and "mandates" were part of the new political rhetoric throughout post-war Europe.

BACK TO WORK AND MORE TROUBLES IN GERMANY

On January 7, Wilson and his party returned to Paris and its winter weather. Their hotels were cold and uncomfortable due to the shortage of coal. It was quite a change from sunny Italy. In Paris, Wilson was briefed by Col. House and others on the crisis in Berlin, the latest developments in Russia, and on Italy's growing concerns over Fiume. A tour of war-damaged areas in Belgium had been planned for Wilson, but it was canceled because of concerns for the problems at hand — and problems there were.

On the evening of January 9, all hell broke loose in Berlin. The Free Corps had arrived and began taking back the city street by street by force of arms. The first Free Corps to go into action was "Free Corps Regiment Potsdam," one of the very few such units well enough organized and equipped to take the field. It was bloody urban warfare and the first major clash between the German political right and the German political left. But the odds favored the Free Corps because most of their members were experienced war veterans, and with the Army's support, had acquired a smattering of artillery, machine guns, tanks, flame throwers, mortars, and other modern weapons. They also had an ally, the Berlin police force, which was adequately armed with light weapons, many of which had also been supplied by the Army.

The communists, on the other hand, had only their used army rifles. Then too, most of the communists were non-veterans and were poorly-trained and poorly-led, because the great majority of experienced officers and non-commissioned officers supported the political right. Within 24 hours the Free Corps and the German police began to gain the upper hand.

When the French and American units arrived, they were used to establish law and order in the areas outside the combat zones, thereby freeing up more freecorpsmen and police for action against the Reds.

By the 14th, the fighting was over and the Freecorpsmen and Berlin police were in control of the city and the Ebert government was saved. Liebknecht and Luxemburg were captured on the 15th. They were found by Freecorpsmen hiding in the home of a Jewish businessman, Siegfried Markussohn, and were murdered that same day. Hundreds of other communists were also summarily executed. Karl Radek, Lenin's representative, was jailed.

While the Reds were being put down in Berlin, Reds in the port city of Bremen in northwestern Germany suddenly sparked another revolution. On January 10, members and supporters of the German Communist Party (KPD) and the Independent Social Democrat Party (USPD), a radical spinoff of the Social Democrat Party (SPD), united to take over the city. They took control of the banks, newspapers, and harbor facilities — with the active support of the dock workers — and proclaimed an independent socialist republic to be known as the "Independent Socialist-Communist Republic of Bremen." And they renamed the city council the "Council of Peoples' Commissars." Here was another job for the Free Corps, but they were involved in Berlin or still being organized and were scattered throughout the country. In the meantime, the Council of Peoples' Commissars would have their way in Bremen.

In the Ruhr, there were troubles in the coal fields. Workers had taken over the coal mines, created a people's council, and declared an autonomous republic. This, too, would have to wait.

TURMOIL IN ITALY. MUSSOLINI FINDS AN ORGANIZATION.

In early January 1919, a militant group of Italian war veterans and civilians with extreme right-wing political sympathies created an organization called the "Adriti." This was a name used during the Great War for daring bands of Italian guerrillas who slipped behind enemy lines, disrupted enemy communications and supply efforts, and took no prisoners. Their exploits became famous, and everyone in Italy knew of the Adriti. Now the Adriti had re-emerged in a political form. And its members had uniforms, a flag, and an emblem. The uniforms consisted of black shirts, black fezzes or caps; their flag was black; and their emblem was the skull and crossbones. The Adriti's message to the people was that the democratic form of government was inadequate for Italy and that Italy needed strong centralized leadership.

Popular sentiment for such leadership was very strong in Italy and the organization grew very rapidly. The Adriti established its headquarters in Milan and by the end of January, it had grown into a national organization.

Then, on January 11, Adriti members took their first action. Wearing their uniforms, carrying daggers, and waving their flags, they marched into a hall in Milan in which Leonida Bissolati, a leading socialist, was to speak under the auspices of the Association for the League of Nations. Sitting in a box situated above the crowd was the newspaper editor Mussolini.

The Adriti totally disrupted the proceedings, and shouted slogans such as "Down with the Croat (Bissolati)!" and "Hurrah for Italian Dalmatia (the region on the eastern shore of the Adriatic Sea promised to Italy by the London Agreement of 1915)." The Adriti rushed the stage, brandishing their daggers and drove Bissolati from the hall. Fists flew and a brawl ensued and spread into the street. The Adriti then re-formed, linked arms, and marched together toward the Galleria Vittorio Emanuele, a famous Milan landmark. News of the brawl spread rapidly and crowds gathered along the route and cheered them on. Mussolini was excited and very impressed with the Adriti's actions and joined in the march to the Galleria. At the Galleria, speeches were made, daggers brandished, fists thrust into the air, and slogans shouted again and again. Then, as suddenly as it began, the Adriti disbanded — their point having been made. Mussolini was even more impressed.

The next day, and for several days thereafter, Mussolini's newspaper, *Il Popolo*, praised the Adriti, their daring exploit, and their political program. Mussolini had found an organization that was carrying forward a political philosophy almost identical to his own. In time, the two would come together.

Il Popolo had already taken up the cause for Italy's claims to Fiume and Dalmatia, and on January 13 published a document entitled *"Letter to the Dalmatians,"* written by Gabriele d'Annuncio, a well-known poet, a war hero and one of Italy's most outspoken proponents for Italy's claims. Mussolini's newspaper gave d'Annuncio substantial coverage and the Italian people, and indeed the world, would soon hear a lot more from both men.

Conditions in Italy were, by now, favoring the political right. The Red menace was seen as a threat to Italy as it was elsewhere in Europe. The Reds made no secret as to where their sentiments lay, their frightening slogans said it all: "Up the Revolution! Up the Soviets! Up the Spartacists! Up the Bolsheviki!"

To add to the woes of the Italian people, inflation was rising rapidly, there were shortages of food and other necessities of life, black markets had appeared, and speculation was rampant. Italy's middle class was rapidly becoming disillusioned with the squabbling and ineffective politicians in Rome and were becoming more and more sympathetic with radicals such as the Adriti. It was conditions and attitudes like these that brought *Il Popolo* a large influx of new subscribers.

In Paris, Clemenceau and Lloyd George were well aware of events in Italy and made an attempt to strengthen Orlando's position. They met on January 9, without Wilson, and offered Orlando's government a compromise settlement which was more advantageous to Italy than before. That being that Fiume, along with some additional territory, be made into a free state as well as the port city of Zara in Dalmatia — a city that Italy had hoped to acquire. Also, Clemenceau and Lloyd George offered Italy some small territorial concession in northern Albania. This proposal satisfied no one: the Italians, the leaders of the new Kingdom of Serbs, Croats and Slovenians and, least of all, Wilson, who was angered that he had not been consulted. But then too, Wilson had not consulted Clemenceau or Lloyd George when he issued his Fourteen Points.

THAT MESS IN THE MIDDLE EAST

On January 10, 1919, two months after the armistice, British forces occupied Baghdad, the largest city in Mesopotamia (Iraq). This after-the-fact military operation was a part of Britain's postwar planning for the Middle East.

During the war, British forces had conquered most of the Middle East from the Ottoman Empire. Those conquests included Palestine, The Lebanon, Syria, Kuwait, and the southern one-third of Mesopotamia. Now, the conquest of Baghdad gave them two-thirds of Mesopotamia. In northern Mesopotamia, the remaining third of the region were the Kurds, an indigenous non-Arab people, still quite primitive and politically backward. But, the Kurds had something the Allies wanted — oil.

The only country in the Middle East fully committed to the Allied cause was Hijaz, a long and narrow former province of the Ottoman Empire that stretched along the east coast of the Red Sea from Palestine to Yemen. Hijaz was ruled by Sharif (noble) Ibn Ali Husain of Mecca, the capital city and Islam's holiest city. Ottoman control in Hijaz had long been weak and Sharif Ali acted pretty much as he pleased.

Early in the war, Sharif Ali negotiated a deal with the British, whereby he would proclaim Hijaz as an independent nation and an ally of Britain in return for Britain's protection and support of his claims. The arrangement was agreed to and Hijaz joined the Allies. The British then sent a bright young army officer, T. E. Lawrence, to work with Sharif Ali's meager forces and he did an outstanding job. For this he gained the title "Lawrence of Arabia."

Sharif Ali's forces quickly laid siege to the city of Medina, north of Mecca and Islam's second holiest city. This action trapped some 7000 Turkish troops inside the city and kept them there — and out of action — for the duration of the war.

In their negotiation with Sharif Ali, the British had made vague promises that after the war, Sharif Ali would gain control over Palestine, Syria, and possibly The Lebanon and Mesopotamia.

Behind Sharif Ali's back, however, the British concluded a secret agreement with the French in early 1916, known as the Sykes-Picot Agreement, whereupon France would be given control over The Lebanon, Syria, and possibly parts of Palestine and Mesopotamia.

Meanwhile, in Hijaz, Sharif Ali proclaimed himself King and announced that the newly-conquered areas would soon be his.

To complicate matters even further in the Middle East, British Foreign Secretary Arthur Balfour made a public statement to the leaders of the world Zionist organization in November 1917, stating that Britain would favor the creation of a Jewish homeland in Palestine. At this point, the British had promised all or part of Palestine to three parties, the Hijazians, the French, and the Jews.

THE BALFOUR DECLARATION

The exact wording of the "Balfour Declaration" was only one sentence long: "His Majesty's Government views with favor the establishment in Palestine of a homeland for the Jewish people." That one sentence would bring on decades of problems.

The Balfour Declaration was, not surprisingly, most unwelcome in Mecca and, indeed, the entire Arab world. But, the British were pursuing their own interests and had motives which are explained below.

Then, to muddle the situation in the Middle East even further, the Bolsheviks, soon after they began their revolution in late 1917, made public the Sykes-Picot Agreement and several other secret agreements in an effort to discredit and embarrass the capitalist world. At that point, everyone learned that Britain had made conflicting promises with regard to dividing up the postwar Middle East. This was a great embarrassment to London and a matter of great concern to the French, the Jews, the Turks, and most of all, the Arabs. Also, many others around the world who had trusted Britain's word now had to re-examine that trust.

Now, in 1919, that mess in the Middle East had to be addressed, but not until the lands in question were firmly under Allied control. Hence, the advance on Baghdad.

OIL

In 1913, the British Navy made a momentous decision — to convert their navy, the world's largest, from coal-fired steam propulsion to oil-powered diesel propulsion. With this decision came the need for oiling stations around the world to service the fleet. Some of the British fleet's existing coaling stations could be converted, but new oiling stations had to be found. For a steam-powered navy, Britain could always provide their coaling stations with coal from Britain's own coal mines in Wales. But, the British Isles had no source of oil, and what oil was available in the various parts of the British Empire was not well-developed and not always in the right places. A large share of the Navy's oil needs could be supplied by Britain's traditional friend, the United States, but other sources were still needed. To this end, the British government created a "Petroleum Executive" in 1917 which was soon replaced by the "Petroleum Imperial Policy Committee" (PIPCo). PIPCo's mission was not only to see that the British Navy had an adequate and safe supply of oil, but that the entire British Empire would not be wanting in oil.

For the British, the securing of oil in the Mediterranean area was a problem because there were no developed sources for oil in the entire Mediterranean basin at that time. The closest oil sources were to the east near Mosul in Kurdish Mesopotamia and at the northern end of the Persian Gulf in southern Mesopotamia, Kuwait, and Persia. There, prospects looked promising to meet Britain's oil needs. Kuwait, formerly an Ottoman province, had been conquered by the British, and Persia had long been under the duel influences of Russia in the north and Britain in the south. Russia had little interest in Persia's oil because she had her own oil source in the Caucasus region. Therefore, the British rightfully believed that they could gain control of Persia's, Mesopotamia's, and Kuwait's oil and pipe it to the Mediterranean. The port of Haifa in Palestine was to be the terminus of the pipeline and the distribution point for British oil throughout the Mediterranean.

But, the pipeline to Haifa, and the port of Haifa itself, had to be secured. In British-controlled Mesopotamia, there was no major problem producing the oil and there was little danger seen to the pipeline in that it would cross very sparsely-inhabited desert areas to the west. The least secure section of the line would be in Palestine. Therefore, the British wanted to see a friendly and cooperative regime there. This was one of the main reasons for the Balfour Declaration. Haifa would be secure under the controls of the Jews, who were very experienced in world commerce and who would be forever grateful to Britain for giving them a homeland in Palestine. The Arab population of Palestine was, in London's opinion, not politically, culturally, or economically developed well enough and could not be expected to manage the distribution of the oil.

There was another reason why the British offered Palestine to the Zionists. During the Great War, the Turks, who controlled Palestine, launched a major offensive from Palestine into Egypt with the intent of capturing the Suez Canal. The British were able to stop the offensive, but at considerable expense in manpower and resources. Therefore, the British wanted to see Palestine in friendly hands as a protective measure for the Suez Canal.

THAT MESS IN RUSSIA

Soon after the Bolshevik Revolution started in November 1917 and its great threat to the rest of Europe was recognized, the Allies sent troops into Russia, ostensibly to prevent Allied war materials from falling into the hands of the Bolsheviks. The primary reason, however, was to help the Russian Whites defeat the Bolsheviks.

The Allied troops went into Russia where the supplies had gone in during the war. British, American, Italian, and Serbian forces went to Murmansk and Archangel in the north of Russia where they gained additional support from the Finns. In the Far East, American, Japanese, and Canadian forces went to Vladavostok and in the south of Russia, French, Romanian, Greek, and Polish troops went to the Black Sea port of Odessa and other areas in the Ukraine. In each place, the Allies established large and secure beachheads but did not attempt to advance inland. The Caucasus and the eastern part of the Ukraine were designated as British areas of control because of the strong British position in the Middle East. Unfortunate-

ly, the British never had the military or economic wherewithal to take control of these designated areas, but they were able to establish some controls in the southern Caucasian areas of Azerbaijan, Armenia, and Georgia.

Most of the supplies salvaged by the Allies in Russia were eventually turned over to the Whites, and additional new and surplus supplies flowed in for the Whites. Fortunately for the Allies, there were already strong Russian White forces at Odessa and in Siberia, while in the north at Murmansk and Archangel, Red forces were weak.

In the Ukraine, there was a large White army, known as the "Volunteer Army," under Gen. Anton I. Denikin, a former Tsarist officer, and in Siberia, the dominant White commander was Admiral Aleksandr Kolchak, a Tsarist naval officer and former commander of the Russian Black Sea Fleet. Kolchak established a subservient government, known as the "All Russian Government," in Omsk, some 500 miles east of the Ural Mountains (the dividing line between European and Asian Russia) and 1400 miles east of Moscow. From Omsk, Kolchak had proclaimed himself the "Supreme Ruler of Russia."

In the overall picture, the Whites were scattered, disunited, and operating under different leaders. The Reds, on the other hand, were more united because of geography and had one, very capable overall leader, Trotsky. Furthermore, the Whites were outnumbered by the Reds by about three to one.

This situation had remained fairly static until the end of 1918, by which time there were some 180,000 Allied troops in Russia.

Reliable news on what was happening in Russia was scarce because neither the Reds nor the Whites had sent formal delegations to Paris, nor did they acknowledge diplomatic missions anywhere in the world. There was one exception, however. The Bolsheviks had sent an unofficial mission to Stockholm, Sweden, which could be accessed by other countries when those countries thought it necessary and/or politically advantageous to do so.

The Whites had no united political agenda while the Reds had one that was well-structured and utopian-like. The Bolsheviks had a united government, had created a constitution in July 1918 and given themselves a name, "The Russian Soviet Federated Socialist Republic (RSFSR), and had made numerous and very appealing promises to the Russian people.

THE USSR

The RSFSR name lasted until 1923 when the four major Communist-controlled areas of the county, Russia, the Ukraine, Belorussia, and the federated republics of the Caucasus reorganized the na-

tion into the "Union of Soviet Socialist Republics" (USSR). This was the official name of the country all during World War II and, by that time, was comprised of 16 federated republics.

ENEMIES BECAME FRIENDS

In March 1918, the Bolsheviks signed a unilateral armistice with the Germans at the city of Brest-Litovsk, thus taking Russia out of the Great War and terminating that country's alliance with the Western Powers. Thereafter, the two parties collaborated to some degree. Now, with Germany defeated, that relationship was unknown but thought to still exist. Under various scenarios, it was widely believed that unofficial cooperation between the Germans and Bolsheviks was taking place and would only increase in the near future.

In Paris, it was painfully obvious that the peace delegates could do little or nothing about all of this.

CHAPTER 3
ON TO
VERSAILLES!

|||||||||||||||||||||||||||||||||||||||||||||||||||||||||||||||||||||||||||||||||||||||||||||||||||||||||||||

As the delegates to the forthcoming peace conference gathered in Paris, their presence was widely felt throughout the city. Hotel space became scarce and expensive, foreigners seemed to be everywhere, and the city ran day and night. Cafes and restaurants were crowded, especially the upscale cafes and restaurants because French cuisine was world famous and most of the delegates had generous expense allowances.

And, there were the uninvited. The writer John Dos Passos described the Paris scene thusly, "Around the edges of the delegations hovered all sorts of adventurers peddling oil concessions or manganese mines, pretenders to dukedoms and thrones, cranks with shortcuts to Utopia in their briefcases, secret agents, art dealers, rug salesmen, procurers and pimps... Restaurants and night clubs were packed. Taxis were forever at a premium. Business boomed."

War damage was still visible in some places in the city, having been caused by bombs dropped by the German's giant "Gotha" bombers and automobile-sized artillery shells fired into the city from 75 miles away by their "Big Bertha" railroad guns.

THE FIRST MEETING

On January 11, 1919, the first formal meeting of the Allied leaders of France, Britain, Italy, and the United States was held in Paris. The Japanese were not in attendance at this time, but they arrived the next day. This was not the opening of the peace conference, but a preliminary meeting to set an agenda and review positions. The participants at this meeting were designated as "The Supreme Council," a title that would be used throughout the peace negotiations.

A decision was quickly agreed to that the creation of the much-discussed League of Nations should be the first issued on the agenda. It was also agreed that recognition of the Bolshevik government would not be forthcoming from any of the major powers.

Four of the five primary representatives on the Council of Ten: seated left to right, Orlando, Lloyd George, Clemenceau, and Wilson. This photo shows how the major players at the Paris Peace Conference usually met in a small but ornate room, sometimes with a fireplace (it was cold in Paris), with or without aides and usually without the Japanese who attended only when matters of concern important to them were discussed.

Nor would the Russian Whites, who had sent a delegation to Versailles, be allowed to participate in the conference.

It was also unanimously agreed that the provinces of Alsace and Lorraine should be returned to France.

Since the peace conference would include more than thirty participating nations, it was agreed that a "Council of Ten" was to be organized to conduct the primary negotiations and then present them to the entire assembly. The Council of Ten would consist of two representatives each from France, Britain, the US, Italy, and Japan. These representatives would, of course, be the two leading members of their respective delegations. The primary

representatives on the Council were for France, Premier Clemenceau; for Britain, Prime Minister Lloyd George; for the US, President Wilson; for Italy, Premier Orlando; and for Japan, Prince Kimmuchi Saionji.

Wilson and Lloyd-George insisted that English and French be the official languages of the conference and they would have their way.

Other issues addressed was the Russian POWs still held by Germany and Austria-Hungary. Should they be repatriated to Russia or not? A committee was formed to study the problem. This was a precedent that would be repeated many times. Throughout the peace conference, some

60 committees would be formed to study specific problems.

Reparations were discussed, but it was learned that there were very wide disagreements on this subject so it was postponed until later.

French Marshal Ferdinand Foch, who had served as Supreme Allied Commander during the war, proposed that the Polish troops currently in France be sent to Poland to help the country ward off an invasion by the Bolsheviks. Wilson objected, saying that such an act could escalate the situation in Eastern Europe and might draw the Allies further into the Russian Civil War. At Clemenceau's suggestion, this question was also postponed.

"LET'S TRY FOCH" — AND NOT PETAIN!

Early in the war, Clemenceau was faced with the decision as to whom to nominate as the Supreme Allied Commander. He had two candidates, Generals Ferdinand Foch and Henri-Philippe Petain. He interviewed both men and upon making his decision later commented, "I found myself between two men, one of whom told me we were finished (Petain) and the other (Foch) who came and went like a mad man and who wanted to fight. I said to myself, `Let's try Foch!'"

Petain went on to serve as the Inspector-General of the Supreme War Council and acquired the rank of marshal, and later in the 1920s and 1930s served in several government posts.

In June 1940, as the military defeat of France became evident and Paris had fallen, Petain, out of desperation, was appointed Premier. He fled Paris and quickly sought an armistice with the Germans and Italians and accepted the terms presented to him.

When the French government re-established itself in the city of Vichy, the French Assembly voted itself and the

French constitution out of existence and passed all powers on to Petain. At this point, Petain became the absolute dictator of France taking the title "Head of State." He collaborated with the Axis Powers throughout the war and at war's end, he was charged with treason. He was tried, convicted, and sentenced to death by the de Gaulle government. His death sentence, however, was commuted to life imprisonment and he died at a villa on the Ile d'Yea, where he was held under house arrest, on July 23, 1951, at the age of 95.

There was yet another issue that had just happened that was of concern to the gentlemen at the meeting. Beginning on January 11, the day before the meeting, Romanian troops had invaded Transylvania, a large land area between Romania and Hungary that the two nations had fought over for centuries but which had been under Hungarian control since the Eleventh Century.

The Romanian government, an Allied nation, had been promised the area in the Treaty of 1916 with the Allies, which brought Romania into the war. Now, believing that they had the right to do so, the Romanians moved in and announced that they would annex the territory in accordance with that Treaty. This was a unilateral action taken by Romania without informing or consulting with the other Allies, and a very unwelcome issue for the peacemakers in Paris.

Another issue for the assembled peacemakers, and one with a sense of urgency, was that all of the major powers' armed forces were being scaled down and that decisions with regard to Germany had to be made while the Allies still had the power to enforce them.

Other issues concerned the revolutions, insurrections, and small wars that were currently taking place or were threatening. Also on the agenda was the severe food shortage that currently existed in much of Europe, the possibility of epidemics, the disrupted and unstable economic situation in Europe, refugees, housing, the disruption in transportation, and many other difficult issues.

TIME TO EAT
Clemenceau conducted most of the meetings and developed a unique way of ending them when it came time to eat. He would close the session, stand up, and walk out of the room, and he liked long lunch hours.

LUXEMBOURG
The Grand Duchy of Luxembourg declared its neutrality at the beginning of the war, but the Germans ignored it and still occupied the country. The Germans had long claimed that Luxembourg was a part of Germany's Zollverein (customs union) and that Germany had concessions and special rights in that country. Grand Duchess Marie Adelaide remained in the country and established a rather cordial relationship with the occupiers and did little to help the Allies.

When the war ended, the Allies and many Luxembourgers demanded her abdication and the Belgians made an attempt to annex the country. Demonstrations and riots broke out on January 9 and French troops rushed in to restore order. On January 12, with French troops patrolling her capital, Marie Adelaide abdicated in favor of and her sister, Charlotte. After experiencing this very unpleasant incident, Luxembourg became one of most peaceful places in Europe.

LUXEMBOURG IN WW II
When WW II started, Grand Duchess Charlotte was still Luxembourg's head

of state and had declared Luxembourg's neutrality as her sister had done. In May 1940, the Germans again ignored Luxembourg's neutrality and invaded and conquered the country; and Charlotte and members of her government fled to Lisbon, Portugal. She actively supported the Allied cause and broadcast daily to her subjects back home. Meanwhile, the Germans annexed the country.

When the war ended, Luxembourg regained its independence and Charlotte returned to her country amid widespread rejoicing. Charlotte served in her post until November 12, 1964, when, at the age of 68, she abdicated in favor of her son, Jean.

During the latter days of WW II, American troops liberated Luxembourg and the two countries established very friendly relations thereafter. One of America's great heros, Gen. George S. Patton, Jr., is buried in Luxembourg, along with many other fallen American servicemen.

THE UNITED STATES AND ITALY
On January 13, the day after their first formal meeting, Wilson told Orlando, once again, that he considered the 1915 Treaty of London no longer valid. By this action, Wilson set the United States on a collision course with Italy.

THE FLU
In early January, Wilson's most trusted advisor, Col. House, came down with a case of influenza and, by some accounts, almost died. House was just one of millions of victims who had been stricken by one of the most deadly flu epidemics ever known. The epidemic began in early 1918 and spread rapidly throughout the world. No one knew where it started, but nearly everyone blamed someone else; the French blamed the Spaniards, the

Spaniards blamed the French, the Americans blamed the Eastern Europeans, and British General Allenby, the hero of the Middle East campaign, blamed the retreating Turks. Germany was hard hit and lost tens of thousands of people. Estimates of those who died of the flu, worldwide, vary greatly from 70 million to 400 million people. In any case, the flu epidemic claimed many more lives than the Great War which was estimated to have caused only 8½ million deaths.

In January 1919, the threat of the flu epidemic was still a concern for everyone but, fortunately, it was on the decline and would die out in mid-1919 — but not before President Wilson, himself, caught the bug.

THAT MESS IN THE BALKANS

The Romanian invasion of Transylvania was just one incident that would stir the already volatile situation in Eastern Europe and the Balkans.

The Balkans had long been Europe's political and sociological basket case. Over the decades, the Ottoman Turks, who had controlled the area for centuries, were slowly beaten back and the local and very diverse peoples began fighting each other over territory and resources. The Balkan Peninsula, about the size of Texas, was home to a very diversified assortment of people. There were Greeks, Turks, Macedonians, Albanians, Montenegrans, Serbs, Bulgarians, Bosnians, Slovenes, Croats, Romanians and Hungarians. These people were further divided by religion. There were Roman Catholics, Greek Orthodox Christians, Bulgarian Orthodox Christians, Serbian Orthodox Christians, Romanian Orthodox Christians, various Protestant denominations, Bosnian Muslims, Turkish Muslims, Jews, and anti-religious communists. There were also many different languages spoken in the Balkans and two alphabets

used. Then, too, illiteracy was high and there was much poverty.

Furthermore, the larger nations that bordered the Balkans, Czarist Russia, Austria-Hungary, and Italy, all had had claims and interests there. Also, the British and French had their fingers in the Balkan pie.

All of this diversity and conflict had resulted in the First Balkan War (October 1912–May 1913) which saw Greece, Bulgaria, Montenegro, and Serbia fighting the Ottoman Turks. This war was followed within days by the Second Balkan War (June 1913–July 1913) which pitted Greece, the Ottoman Turks, Serbia, Montenegro, and Romania against Bulgaria.

When a Serbian Nationalist assassinated Arch-Duke Ferdinand of Austria-Hungary and his wife in Bosnia in August 1914, it appeared that the Third Balkan War was about to begin. This crisis, however, got out of control and resulted in the Great War. Everyone at Paris was well aware of the fact that the genesis of the Great War had been in the Balkans.

In December 1918, following the defeat of the Central Powers, the Serbs, Croats, and Slovenes united, with the blessing of the Allies, into one nation called the "Kingdom of Serbs, Croats, and Slovenes." The new kingdom soon gained the popular name of "Jugoslavia," after the local word "jugoslav," meaning pan-slav. Serbia, a staunch ally of Britain and France during the war, became the first among equals within the new kingdom. The Serbian king assumed the throne of the new kingdom and Belgrade, the capital of Serbia, became the capital of Jugoslavia.

Furthermore, the Dalmatian Coast on the east side of the Adriatic Sea, was made a part of the new kingdom, which infuriated the Italians. They thought that that area should rightfully be theirs as was agreed to in the secret Treaty of London of 1915. Understandably, this was a serious bone of contention between Italy and the new Kingdom on the one hand, and between Italy and the other Allied nations in Paris on the other.

Also, parts of Hungary, Romania, and Bulgaria were incorporated into the Kingdom, and those nations, too, could not reconcile themselves to their respective losses. Their resentments would linger for years. The new Kingdom was, therefore, surrounded by hostile neighbors and existed only under the protection of the western Allies.

YUGOSLAVIA

In 1929, the Kingdom of Serbs, Croats, and Slovenes would officially change its name to Yugoslavia.

In April 1941, during WW II, Yugoslavia was invaded by a coalition of Axis nations consisting of Germany, Italy, Hungary, Romania, and Bulgaria. The victors would then divide the country among themselves and Serbia and Croatia would become separate independent nations. Serbia became a vassal state under Axis domination and remained technically neutral, while Croatia became a member of Axis Alliance, declare war on the major Allies, including the US, and sent troops into the Soviet Union.

From the viewpoint of the optimists in Paris, the creation of Jugoslavia was one of the bright spots in the Balkans. In the view of the critics, it had the makings for the Fourth Balkan War.

The United States quickly extended diplomatic recognition to Jugoslavia in an effort to help stabilize the new country as well as to thwart Italian ambitions in the region. The French and British would not recognize Jugoslavia until June 1919.

BULGARIA

Bulgaria, like the other Central Powers, suffered a period of instability at the end of the war which was complicated by the many dynamic changes going on in the Balkans and the Red Scare coming from Russia. Bulgaria was seen by her neighbors as an aggressor nation and had gained the inglorious title "The Prussia of the Balkans."

Bulgaria's King Ferdinand, who had taken the country into the war, abdicated in October 1918 in favor of his 26 year-old son, Boris III. Ferdinand then retired on a large estate he owned in Germany.

The real power in Bulgaria was in the hands of the Premier, Todor Todorov, leader of the right-wing National Party, who cooperated with the young king.

BORIS AND HITLER

Boris III, who was half German, was still on the throne when WW II started. He was one of Hitler's favorite people in the Balkans and took Bulgaria into WW II — again as Germany's ally. Hitler often praised him and also spoke well of Ferdinand. Boris had his enemies, though, and he died under mysterious circumstances in August 1943.

ALBANIA

Another major area of conflict in the Balkans was Albania. Italy, Greece, and Jugoslavia had conflicting territorial claims on the country, and within Albania, where there was an active independence movement headed by Essad Pasha, who had unilaterally proclaimed himself Head of State. Essad Pasha took an Albanian delegation to Paris, hoping to be heard.

Albania was technically a monarchy, but its ruler, Prince William of Wied, a German, fled to Germany in 1914, abandoning the throne.

Albania had oil and for this reason, Lloyd George took interest in the country and sought out various members of the British nobility to serve as a replacement for Prince William. After contacting some 70 individuals, Lloyd George gave up. No one in Britain wanted to become the King of Albania.

The controversy over Albania would simmer for years, but in 1926, the Albanian nationalists would prevail and Albania would become an independent nation. Border areas, however, would still be in dispute.

ALBANIA DURING WORLD WAR II

In 1939, Italian forces invaded Albania and established it as a vassal state. The king of Albania, King Zog, was deposed but in theory, Albania remained an independent kingdom under the King of Italy and was governed by Albanians who were Italians and Fascist sympathizers. During the war, a multi-sided civil war erupted in the country between those who supported Italy, those who supported Zog, an aggressive coalition of Christian mountain people of the north who hated the Muslims in the south, and the communists. It would be the communists that would prevail.

When WW II ended, Albania become one of the first nations in Eastern Europe to adopt communism.

TROUBLES IN HUNGARY

Hungary, like Germany, was a defeated nation and was being treated very badly by the victorious Allies and by her neighbors. The new post-war Hungary had been split off from Austria, thus ending the Austro-Hungarian Empire which had existed since 1867. Hungary's neighbors claimed various pieces of Hungarian territory and had taken unilateral actions to occupy some of those areas. If Hungary lost all the land that was being claimed, the size of the country would be reduced from 125,000 Sq. Mi. to 35,000 Sq. Mi., and the population would diminish from 21 million to 8 million.

Unlike Germany, however, Hungary was a neo-feudal state with a large peasant population, wealthy and powerful landowners, the church, and a well-established aristocracy. Budapest was a fairly modern city, but the rest of the country was still quite primitive. There was a small but expanding middle class, heavy with Jews who comprised about 20% of the population and lived mostly in Budapest.

Hungary's economy was in shambles. There was run-away inflation, shortages of many things, a ruinous transportation system, and a near-collapsing civil administration. The army might, or might not, take orders from the government and Hungary had no ally or protector who would come to the country's aid — with the possible exception of Woodrow Wilson. His picture was everywhere in Budapest, along with the slogan, "A Wilson peace is the only peace for Hungary."

Hungary's fate was being debated at Paris along with the other Central Powers, but it was not top priority. The treaty with Germany and the creation of the League of Nations came first. Thus, the Hungarian leaders in Budapest had to await developments, as did the leaders of the other lesser Central Powers. In the meantime, the country, as with Germany, was blockaded by the Allies to induce the Hungarian Government to agree to the terms of its forthcoming peace treaty. As a result of these actions, Hungary was a place of great misery and was ripe for revolution.

As in Germany, the strength of the Hungarian communists was growing rapidly. Also, as in Germany, where Lenin had sent a special representative, Karl Radek,

Artist's conception of the Versailles Peace Conference. One British delegate called it a "riot in a parrot house."

to advance the cause of the revolution, he did likewise in Hungary by sending Bela Kun, a Hungarian exile and a dedicated communist. Kun, like Radek, was a Jew and with Lenin's political and financial backing, quickly rose to be the leading communist in Hungary.

GOING DRY

On January 19, 1919, in the United States, it was announced that the 18th Amendment to the Constitution, recently ratified by the states, would go into effect in January 1920. That Amendment prohibited the production, sale, and consumption of alcoholic beverages throughout the United States and its territories.

JANUARY 18, 1919 — THE BIG DAY

This day marked the opening of the peace conference. It began, not in the palace at

Versailles, but in the Salle de la Paix in the French Foreign Ministry on the Quai d'Orsay in Paris and was attended by 70 delegates from 27 Allied nations. Most of the meetings throughout the conference would be held in government offices and hotels of Paris and at the end of each week, a plenary meeting would be held of all nations to review the actions taken that week. For months to come, Paris would be the capital of the world.

The conference that began this day would officially be in session for one year and two days. The date chosen for the opening of the conference was not by happenstance. It was the 48th anniversary of the proclaiming of the German Empire (the Second Reich), by the German victors of the Franco-Prussian. That proclamation had been issued by the Germans at the Versailles Palace in the Hall of Mir-

rors. For the French, it was the beginning of retribution and there would be other dates that would be revisited.

French President Raymond Poincare gave the opening address and remembered that day. His opening remarks were "On this day, forty-eight years ago, the German Empire was proclaimed by an army of invasion in the Chateau at Versailles..." This left little doubt that the French saw the Great War, which they had won, as an extension of the Franco-Prussian War of 1870–71 which they had lost.

When Wilson spoke, he emphasized that the German people must be treated fairly lest they cause another war. This was the course of action he would consistently take throughout the negotiations and which would be counter to the attitudes projected by the French and, to some degree, the British and Italians.

The nations assembled that day represented about 75% of the world's population. Six of the nations, Britain, and her dominions, Canada, The Union of South Africa, Australia, and New Zealand, were likely to vote as a bloc. Clemenceau and others were not very pleased with this but could do little about it. The French had a huge empire, too, but they had no dominions. The Americans had no colonial empire but had a host of small and friendly nations — some called them vassal states — in Central America and the Caribbean that would likely support Wilson's positions.

While the great powers had stable governments, many of the other nations at the peace table did not. Some of the nations present were still in the process of forming governments and some had broken diplomatic relations with each other or were on very bad terms with one or more of the other participants.

Czarist Russia had been invited, but no one responded to the invitation.

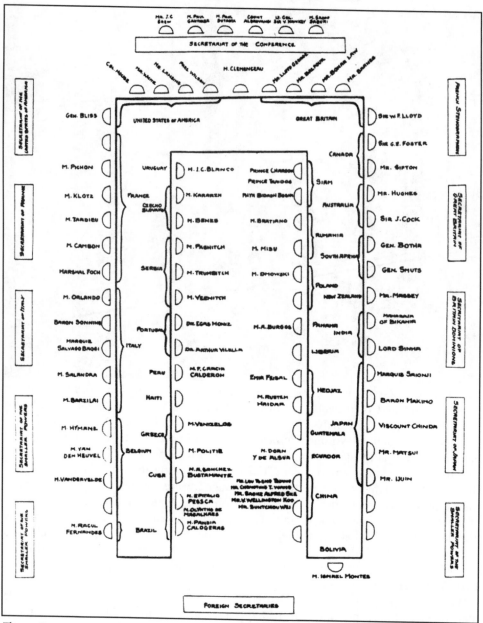

The seating arrangement at the Versailles Peace Conference.

Very little work was conducted that first day, and all eyes were on an event that was to happen the next day. On that day, by an interesting coincidence, democracy would come to Germany for the first time.

IN GERMANY, THEY VOTED

On January 19, amid all of the chaos in their country, the German people went to the polls in the first national election under the new republic. The purpose of the election was to select representatives to a National Assembly which would form an interim government and write a constitution. Turnout was good, there were no disturbances, and some 30 million people voted, out of 35 million eligible to vote. Also, for the first time in German history, women were allowed to vote.

The left-of-center Social Democrat Party was the biggest winner with 40% of the vote, or 165 seats in the Assembly. The Catholic Center Party was next with 90 seats, and another left-of-center party, the Liberal Democrat Party won 75 seats. From this, it was seen at Paris with much relief that the German people were demonstrating that they were moderate in the national politics and not polarized to the right or extreme left as many had feared. Neither the radical left nor the radical right gained many votes and those votes were nearly equal on both sides.

The German Communist Party, knowing it would do very poorly, and now without its two leaders, Liebknecht and Luxemburg, boycotted the election, calling it a bourgeois farce.

THE GERMAN NATIONALISTS UNITED WITH THE NAZIS

In the post-election negotiating that went on in Germany in January 1933, the German Nationalists, who had won 15% of the popular vote, united with the Nazi Party, who had won over 40% of the vote, to form a coalition government with Adolf Hitler as chancellor. Hitler came to power legally via the democratic process.

Friedrich Ebert, leader of the Social Democrats, formed a coalition government with the Catholic Center Party and the Liberal Democrat Party which, with their combined seats in the Assembly, created a strong majority. Ebert became

Chancellor and claimed that he now had a mandate from the German people and began cracking down on political extremists, which to most people, meant the communists.

He paid little attention to the right wing extremists, although on January 20, he had ordered the recently-formed Free Corps out of Berlin. Germany's right wing and military leaders understood the political necessity of this and did not interfere. As for the Free Corps, their leaving Berlin would have been ordered anyway — they were needed elsewhere.

Since there was still considerable turmoil and political instability in Berlin, Ebert moved his new government to the quiet and historic town of Weimar 135 miles southwest of the capital. Weimar was a beautiful town with a history of liberalism. From then on, the government of German was referred to as the "Weimar Republic" and it had a left-of-center image.

AND NOW — TROUBLES IN IRELAND

Ireland was an integral part of Great Britain, but nationalist fervor had been mounting there for many years. Now, with the new era of liberal thinking, the Irish people were stimulated anew in their desires for independence from Britain. The British, quite naturally, were totally opposed to losing this vital part of their empire and it became apparent that if Ireland were to be free, it would have to fight for that freedom.

Yet, the Irish were not united. Irish nationalism was strongest in the Catholic south where the leading advocate for independence was the Sinn Fein political party. In the predominantly Protestant north centered around Belfast, the sentiment for independence was very weak. Because of these differences, the local Irish leaders in Belfast were acting independently from the Irish leaders in Dublin.

In the south, though, there were demonstrations, strikes, boycotts, assassinations, and armed clashes. The future for Ireland looked bleak. Much of the violence was created by a recently-created and very secret organization known as the "Irish Republican Army" (IRA).

Then, on January 21, while the world's eyes were on Paris, and with Britain's armed forces being scaled down and committed to other parts of the world, the Irish acted. The Dial Eireann, Ireland's parliament, meeting in Dublin, proclaimed Ireland's independence. One of their first acts was to nominate a committee of three to go to Paris to plead Ireland's cause. This, however, was a political gesture only since two of the three people nominated were in jail, as were some of the members of the Dail Eireann itself. Lloyd George who was in Paris now had another burden on his shoulders and had to act. He was a busy man.

Wilson also gained a new worry. The large Irish-American minority in America — not long removed from their ancestral roots — almost unanimously supported Ireland's independence. And, the Irish-Americans usually voted for the Democrats. Wilson's dilemma was that he was in Paris negotiating the future of the world with Lloyd George and could not afford to alienate him or the other members of the British Empire at this critical time. Wilson, therefore, was in an untenable position and had only three options: support Irish independence, oppose Irish independence, or remain silent. He chose the latter and made excuses, saying that the Irish problem was in internal matter for Britain. Personally, Wilson revealed in private conversations that he had little sympathy for Irish independence.

Furthermore, Wilson's opponents back home were now in a position to say, "We told you so!" They pointed out that they had advised Wilson to remain in Washington where he could better manage such delicate situations as this. But, there he was, in Paris, face-to-face with Lloyd George.

THE LEAGUE OF NATIONS COMES INTO BEING

On January 25, 1919, the delegates to the peace conference held their second plenary meeting. The main issue on the agenda was the creation of a League of Nations. After suitable speeches were made, a vote was taken and it was unanimously agreed that the League should be created. Two days later it was agreed that the creation of the League of Nations would become an integral part of the peace agreement. Any nation accepting one would automatically accept the other. Herein was the seed for Wilson's eventual domestic catastrophe back home but this could not be foreseen at this point in time. A committee to work out the details of creating the organization and its covenant was formed with Wilson as its chairman. The main members of the committee were Lord Robert Cecil, representing Britain; Leon Bourgeois, representing France; Premier Orlando, representing Italy; and General Jan Christian Smuts of the Union of South Africa, representing the British Commonwealth. This small group met at the Hotel Murat in Paris where many of the delegations were staying.

BACK HOME

Back home in Britain, the soldiers were being discharged and unemployment had risen sharply in both England and Ireland. To help alleviate this problem, and to help Britain pay for the war, the Board of Trade, the government agency that regulated business affairs throughout the British Empire, declared that British firms could begin doing business in the areas that had recently come under British control. One of the first items of interest to the British businessmen was the oil of the Middle East.

In France, they were tallying up the cost of the war. It had cost the French Treasury 134 billion gold francs, a monumental sum. Furthermore, one out of every ten Frenchmen had been killed in the war. Three out of every ten young men, 18 to 28, had been killed and an additional 4,266,000 young men wounded. Many of these individuals would be wards of the state for the rest of their lives. The overall population of France was now less than before the war, even with the gain of some 200,000 new citizens from the newly-annexed provinces of Alsace and Lorraine. The overall population of France was estimated to be 39 million. Across the border in Germany, the population was 63 million and the German birth rate was rising.

IN 1939...

Due in part to these demographics, Germany would have twice as many men of military age (18–34) in 1939 as France.

Throughout France, there were calls to hang the Kaiser and the Germans were still referred to as "Huns," a barbarous nomadic Asian people who had invaded central Europe in the 4th and 5th centuries. Everyone in Europe knew of "Attila the Hun" and the Kaiser was seen as his modern-day equivalent.

Due in part to their tremendous loss of young men, France opened its doors to immigrants and thousands streamed in. In the coming years, France would accept more immigrants per capita than the US and would have the largest influx of immigrants of any western nation.

In the US, as in Britain, the soldiers and sailors were being discharged rapidly and unemployment was on the rise. With the sudden end of government war spending,

American industry was also in a state of flux and there were those in Washington who were proposing public work projects to fight the unemployment problem. Furthermore, inflation was beginning to take hold. Since 1914, food was up 84%, clothing 114%, and furniture 125%. This meant that the value of war bonds had diminished and workers' wages had not kept up. Here, in this latter situation, was a time bomb ready to explode.

And the American railroads were in trouble. Despite government control that had been imposed during the war, there had been major problems in transport during the war due to a lack of centralized control over the American rail system. Now, there were cries from Washington and elsewhere to nationalize the railroads as had been done in most European countries. The American labor unions strongly supported this plan. The Vanderbilts, Harrimans, and Flaglers, who would be shut out, began to use their vast fortunes and political clout to counter this trend.

During the war, a number of large government agencies had been set up to regulate such things as food, industrial production, investments, housing, telephones and telegraph services, shipping, sugar, lumber production, and other critical items of the economy. Now, they were being dismantled, which would add to the nation's unemployment statistics. Even with the government controls, some industrialists had made huge profits and were being accused of being "war profiteers." Political liberals, labor unions, Teddy Roosevelt Republicans, and a number of influential government leaders wanted to see the wartime agencies retained and restructured for peacetime. Herein lay another problem that would have to be postponed until President Wilson returned to Washington.

And Wilson's opponents would continue to cry out, "why isn't he here?"

Ignace Paderewski, considered to be one of the greatest concert pianists of all time, was elected premier of Poland and headed the Polish delegation in Paris.

Furthermore, social and economic mores were changing, some for the good and some for the bad. This curious mix included silk stockings, hemlines 6 inches above the floor, rouge, short hair, divorce, painted fingernails, cigarettes, cars, rumbleseats, muddy roads, airplanes, Jazz, radios, cellophane, cocktail parties, tourist cabins, zippers, crossword puzzles, Charlie Chaplin, Theda Bara, Jack Dempsey, psychoanalysis, auction bridge, the stock market, income tax, communists, and orientals flooding into the West Coast.

Back in Germany, there were life-and-death issues that made the situations in the Allied countries pale in comparison. There was a serious food shortages which the Germans blamed on the continuation of the Allied wartime blockade and was seen as a form of punishment imposed upon the German people by the Allies. Another uncomfortable situation for the Germans was that some 40 Allied army divisions were on German soil in the Rhineland and on three bridgeheads on the eastern bank of the river; one French, one British, and one American. For all Germans, the Rhine River was seen as Germany's last natural line of defense in the west and now it had been breached by three armies. At a moment's notice, these forces could surge into Germany. The American were well-liked, the British disliked, and the French hated.

Marshall Foch, who was always ready to fight the Germans again at any moment, had his military planners draw up six different plans for the Allies to stay on in the Rhineland indefinitely and eventually bring it under French military, and possibly, political control. This was known to the Germans and only added to the intense hatred that already existed.

When making monumental decisions, Foch claimed that he did not make them alone, but that he had help. He would spend hours at a time in religious meditation.

POLAND

Prior to the Great War, there was no Poland. It had been divided three ways a century and a half earlier among Germany, Austria-Hungary, and Czarist Russia. Now, Poland had been reconstructed by the Allies into one of the largest states in Eastern Europe and was a dedicated friend of the Allies. Most of the major Allied nations promptly recognized the new Polish state and sent ambassadors to Warsaw. And the Poles had sent a delegation to Paris which was warmly received. On January 18, 1919, the Poles held an election and elected the noted pianist and nationalist, Ignaz Paderewski, as their Premier. On January 26, another election was held to select delegates to a Constituent Assembly which would draw up a constitution. The election was a solid victory for the political right as well as for Poland's substantial anti-Semitic segment of society. The victory of the political right was seen as a positive sign in the West, because now Poland stood as a bulwark against the spread of Bolshevism into central Europe. Soon after his election, Paderewski left for Paris to head the Polish delegation there.

Premier Paderewski was something of a figurehead. His strength lay in the facts that he was an ardent nationalist, had high-level contacts in the west, and was adored by the Polish people. The real power in Poland rested with General Jozef Pilsudski, an experienced army officer that had fought in the Austro-Hungarian Army early in the war and later rose to command Polish forces in the German Army. As the war ended, Pilsudski formed the "Polish Provisional Government" and became its Head of State and converted his Polish forces into the fledgling, but rapidly growing and exceptionally loyal, Polish Army.

There was a third prominent Pole in the picture, Roman Dmowski, who headed the "Polish National Committee" in Paris and who had worked closely with the Allies during the war. With assistance from the French, Dmowski formed a small Polish army in France comprised primarily of Polish exiles. Therefore, when the war ended, Poland had two armies, one in Poland and one in France.

Dmowski, while something of a rival with Pilsudski, cooperated with the Allies who began making plans to send Dmovski's army to Poland to merge with Pilsudski's army, via the Baltic Sea and the new "Polish Corridor." The Allies strongly urged Dmovski to cooperate with Pilsudski, which he did, thus confirming Pilsudski as the dominant figure in the Polish political structure.

The creation of an Allied-oriented state of Poland was a bitter pill for the Germans. They were especially angry over the loss of German territory to the new state and especially the establishment of the Polish Corridor, a broad section of land cutting through the heart of Prussia to the Baltic Sea to give Poland an outlet to that body of water. They also saw Germany being encircled again by unfriendly states which had been one of the main reasons Germany went to war in 1914.

The Bolsheviks, too, were unhappy with the new Polish state. They saw Poland as a threat on their western border, especially since the announced aspiration of the Polish leaders in Warsaw was to reconstitute the Greater Poland that had existed in 1772. At that time, the Poles controlled parts of the Ukraine, Byelorussia, and Lithuania.

POLAND DISAPPEARED AGAIN DURING WW II

After Poland was conquered in late 1939 by a German invasion from the west and a Soviet invasion from the east, the country once again disappeared from the map. The Germans annexed most of the territory they had controlled in 1914, but they left a modest-sized enclave around the Polish cities of Warsaw, Lvov, and Lublin which was called "The General Government." This area was to be governed by Germany and serve as the reservation-like homeland for the Polish people. The General Government was also used as a temporary holding area for Jews who were to be "relocated to the east."

After the war ended, the Soviets kept the territory they had conquered in 1939 and, as compensation, Poland was given most of East Prussia, and their border with Germany was moved to the west to within 30 miles of Berlin.

To the north, the Lithuanians, like the eastern Poles, had lived for centuries under the Czars. They, however, were relatively well-educated and prosperous and had kept their Lithuanian culture intact. In centuries past, the Lithuanians and Poles had been seen as one people and had, working together, ruled large areas of eastern Europe. But now, those glories were past and the bonds between the two peoples had weakened considerably. The capital and largest city in Lithuania was Vilna and had a mixed population with more Poles than Lithuanians. Both the Poles and Lithuanians claimed the city as their own. In this respect, the Poles had an advantage in that it was Pilsudski's hometown and he wanted desperately to make it a part of Poland.

To insure the integrity of the new Poland, and to keep order, Pilsudski sent Polish troops as soon as possible into these former parts of Germany, Russia, Austria, and Lithuania.

The Western Allies disapproved of this action, but they could do little about it. In Paris, Wilson was most sympathetic toward the Poles position and said, "Paderewski's government is like a dike against disorder, and perhaps the only one possible."

Both the British and French sent missions to Poland to monitor and report on conditions there. One of the members of the French mission was Col. Charles de Gaulle.

THE NAZIS GAINED A POWERFUL ISSUE

In the late 1930s, the Nazis made a great issue out of the fact that many Germans had been forced to live in Poland because of the partition. They escalated this issue into a powerful propaganda weapon and ultimately used it to partially justify their invasion of Poland in 1939.

On southern Poland, there was a relatively small number of Czechs living inside territory claimed by Poland, but since both sides had armies, skirmishes occasionally occurred between Polish and Czechoslovak troops. The most bitterly contested areas was a small patch of territory known as the "Duchy of Teschen." This was a prosperous farming, industrial, and coal mining area and an important junction for north-south and east-west railroads in the region. The east-west railroad was a vital communications link between the Czechs and the Slovaks and the Czechoslovaks wanted desperately to control Teschen because of this and the area's other assets. The statistics on the population of Teschen favored Poland by about three to one, although exact numbers, like elsewhere in eastern Europe, were unreliable. The Czechs maintained that most of the Poles in Teschen were temporary citizens drawn to the area because of job opportunities. In Paris, there was a small Teschen delegation seeking independence based, in part, on the fact that there was a local administration in Teschen comprised of both Poles and Czechs and was functioning well. The Teschen delegation claimed that Teschen's problems were all being caused by outsiders. But this fact, and the Teschen delegation, were all but ignored by the major powers, although the peacemakers did set up another commission to study the Teschen situation. At one point, Lloyd George admitted he had never heard of Teschen until now.

In Paris, Dmowski presented Poland's case to the Council of Ten on January 29, 1919. Paderewski had not yet arrived. The Council listened with interest but made no decisions. They wanted to hear from Paderewski and, of course, Poland's neighbors. A few days later the Council formed yet another commission, "The Commission on Polish Affairs." This would be a busy group. They would meet more often than any other Paris-created commission.

THE US/ITALIAN CONTROVERSY WORSENED.

At the end of January, Wilson had a stormy meeting with Baron Sidney Sonnino, Orlando's foreign minister, over Italy's demands. It was reported that Sonnino lost his temper and told Wilson to stay out of European affairs. Clearly, there was trouble ahead.

CHAPTER 4
FEBRUARY
1919

|||||||||||||||||||||||||||||||||||||||||||||||||||||||||||||||||||||||||||||||||||||||||||||||||||||||||||||||||||||||||||||||||||

During February, Corporal Adolf Hitler was released from the hospital and returned to his adopted hometown of Munich. He was angry about Germany having lost the Great War and the sudden rise of the alien philosophy of communism and in the inroads it was making in German society. During his last days in the hospital, he wrote two poems, *"It Must Not Be!,"* a lament about defeated Germany, and *"Marxerei,"* which was filled with contempt for the German peoples' willingness to accept Marxism.

Still in the army, Hitler returned to the List Regiment barracks at the city's edge to await his next assignment. Time was heavy on his hands and he reported, years later in his book *Mein Kampf,* that one of his pleasures at this time was feeding scraps of bread to the mice that scampered across the barrack's floor.

The opportunity soon arrived to break his boredom. He volunteered to serve as a camp guard for Russian prisoners of war at the Lechfeld POW Camp at Traunstein.

There were over one million Russian prisoners of war in Germany which the Allies ordered not to be returned to Russia lest they join the Bolsheviks. During the war, the German leadership had made plans to form these men into an anti-Bolshevik force for use in Russia if and when needed. It never happened.

While at Lechfeld, Hitler kept up with events by reading the daily newspapers and wrote two more poems, both with patriotic themes.

VLASOV'S ARMY

During WW II, the Germans had over one million Russian prisoners of war again and did form an all-Russian army called the "Russian Army of Liberation." Its commander was General Andrei A. Vlasov and the organization was generally referred to as "Vlasov's Army." They saw some action on the eastern front against their former comrades, but they were never really trusted by the Germans. At the end of the war, most of them surrendered to the Western Allies but were forcefully repatriated to the Soviet Union. Virtually all of the officers were executed while the enlisted men were sent off to prison camps and gulags for lengthy sentences.

||||||||||||||||||||||||||||||||||||||||||||||||||||||||||||||||||||||||||||||||

In Russia, the Bolsheviks admitted to having executed 5496 "political criminals." Many in the West believed that the actual number was much higher and were surprised that the Bolsheviks would even admit to such actions. This announcement sent shivers through the veins of virtually every political leader in non-Russian Europe. Certainly, if the communists ever took over in their land, they too could be labeled as political criminals. Likewise, virtually everyone who gathered at Paris could fall into that category.

Herbert Hoover offered a suggestion — send them food — with the hope that is would have a calming effect on the Russian people and their leaders. This suggestion fell on deaf ears at Paris, and in Washington.

THE FIRST TWELVE DAYS IN FEBRUARY 1919

And behold, just as in the days of old, the seekers of aid and wisdom came forth to petition the wise and powerful kings for favors and recognition. It was a foregone conclusion that some would be rewarded and some not. Those who would be denied would go away unsatisfied, angry, and contemplating other ways to seek what they perceived to be rightfully theirs. This was what was beginning to happen at Paris and it was during February 1919 that some of the seeds of anger were sown.

In Paris, on February 3, Wilson's committee, charged with drafting the League of Nation's covenant, met for the first time in Col. House's suite of rooms at the Crillon Hotel in Paris. Hopes ran high.

In Russia, at this same time, the Red Army launched a major offensive into the Ukraine. The Ukraine was nominally independent, having attained its independence in early 1918 with Germany's help. Now the Germans were gone, and the Ukrainians had to defend themselves with their own small and ill-equipped army and fall back on the services of their erstwhile ally, the White Volunteer Army, commanded by General Denikin. Denikin's army was relatively large and well-armed, but it was spread very thinly throughout the Ukraine and southern Russia and its political goals and objectives were not clearly defined.

From London came a loud cry from Secretary of War Churchill for more Allied intervention in Russia and the Ukraine. Churchill suggested that the Allies raise an army of one million men and intervene in the Russian Civil War. His appeal fell upon a war-weary public and political leadership and was universally ignored. The people of Britain, and elsewhere in the West, had had enough of war. Lloyd George said of Churchill at this time that he "...has bolshevism on the brain."

The Red Army's advance into The Ukraine, orchestrated by Leon Trotsky, made rapid progress and, on February 3, the Reds captured the Ukrainian capital, Kiev. As the Reds spread out through the countryside, they seized large quantities of food from the Ukrainian peasants to feed their army and their workers back in their war factories in the north. The peasants, enraged but helpless, took out their anger on the local Jews, but this time, the Jews were in a position to strike back.

The Reds, having the need to keep order in the food-producing countryside, had recruited many Ukrainian Jews to serve in their secret police organization, the "CHEKA," an organization long known

"Comrade! Help me!" A Free Corps recruiting poster from Hamburg.

for its brutality. Seven of the top ten posts in the Ukrainian CHEKA were given to Jews and 80% of the rank and file were Jews. In this manner the Ukrainian Jews, were given the wherewithal to retaliate in kind, against their centuries-old torment-ers, the Ukrainian peasants. The scheme worked well. The CHEKA, using cruel and extreme measures, eventually restored or-der in the countryside but intense anger seethed in the breast of virtually every Ukrainian peasant. The CHEKA peace would not last long.

When these facts became known in the West, the ugly image of the Bolshe-viks/Jewish connection was considerably strengthened.

Most frightening of all to the Western-ers was the fact that the Bolshevik Revo-lution was spreading into the south of Russia. Heretofore, it had appeared that

it might be contained in Russia and the north. Now, this hope was rapidly fading.

In the north of Russia, there was some good news for the West. The Reds had launched an attack to capture the Arctic seaport of Archangel, held by American forces. But the Americans repulsed the attack and saved the port.

From Germany came another some-what positive headline. Three Free Corps had converged on the port of Bremen, which had been taken over by German Reds in January, and within a few days, liberated the city. Twenty-six Free Corps fighters were killed, 51 wounded, and 300 Reds killed and captured.

Troubles then erupted at Weimar. As the new German National Assembly convened in a local theater, local Red sympathizers, supported by mutinous and armed German soldiers, invaded the theater, disrupted the proceedings, and disarmed the small local Free Corps. For the next few days, the German govern-ment was paralyzed. Eventually, some 7000 Freecorpsmen converged on the city and, just as they had the month before in Berlin, charged into the city, ousted the Reds, and restored order. They then established a defensive perimeter around the area, and the Weimar Government was able to function safely under the pro-tection of the Free Corps.

On February 6, 1919, Friedrich Ebert was nominated by the National Assem-bly at Weimar for the post of President of the German Republic, an office cre-ated to replace the authority of the Kaiser. Nominated for the post of chancellor was Philipp Scheidemann, another leader of the Social Democratic Party. The Na-tional Assembly then began the task of creating a new constitution for the Ger-man Republic. On February 11, Ebert was confirmed as Germany's first President. The German President held most of the powers formerly held by the Kaiser; he was commander-in-chief of the German armed forces, and could appoint and dismiss chancellors, cabinet ministers, and military officers, but, unlike the Kaiser, he would, according to the early drafts of the new constitution, stand for popular election every seven years. Scheidemann was also confirmed as Chancellor and would have virtually the same powers as the chancellors who had served the Kaiser.

PRESIDENT HITLER

Hitler assumed the German presidency in 1934 after the death of President Paul von Hindenburg, a hero of the Great War and a great father-figure for the German people.

The year before, Chancellor Hitler had been empowered by the "Enabling Act" of March 1933 — following the Reichstag fire — which allowed him to "deviate" temporarily from the German Constitution and rule by decree. Hitler did just that. He "deviated" from the constitution by instructing the Nazi-controlled Reichstag to ignore the constitution and appoint him to the office of President. The obedient Reichstag promptly complied. Hitler refused to take the title "President," though, because of its association with democracies. Rather, he called himself "Head of State." At this point, Hitler was Head of State of Germany, Chancellor of Germany, and the leader (Fuehrer) of Germany's only legal political party, the Nazi Party. His position as the absolute dictator of Germany was, from this point on, unassailable.

Scheidemann formed a coalition left-of-center government and supported Ebert's former position on most issues which, in turn, brought him a considerable measure of popular support.

Also during this week, a demonstration against the shortage of food took place in Linz, Austria. It got out of hand and resulted in a short-lived, but bloody, riot. In Munich, Corporal Hitler followed these events very closely. Linz was his hometown.

Then too, on this date, February 6, a general strike broke out in the so-called Autonomous Republic of the Ruhr. It had been called by the local Workers' Councils and supported by Soldiers' Councils of the rebellious German 7th Army Corps to protest the Free Corps takeover of Bremen. This action created another urgent job for the Free Corps. Two of the Free Corps from Bremen rushed to the area and were joined by the Lichtschlag Free Corps, a large regimental-size unit. Together, the three Free Corps totaled some 2700 well-armed and disciplined men. Meanwhile, the local communists hastily formed a ragtag "Red Army" to defend their new republic. It proved to be no match for the Free Corps. Several pitched battles took place, the most intense being at Hervest-Dorten and Bottrop. Individuals were killed on both sides, but the Free Corps emerged victorious and the Autonomous Republic of the Ruhr was crushed.

Following this, the Free Corps converged on Gotha, Bremerhaven, and Cuxhaven, where strong and threatening communist groups existed. These cities were taken over by the Free Corps without bloodshed. Then, on February 9-10, Free Corps units moved into three more cities, the so-called "Republic of Oldenburg," and the cities of East Fresia and Wilhelmshaven where communist troubles brewed. Again, they were victorious and cleaned out the Reds.

In Hamburg, communists also threatened, but negotiation between the Red leaders there and representatives of the Weimar government were successful, and the central government's authority was restored in Hamburg without incident.

The Free Corps, buoyed by their string of victories had, by now, moved into the Baltic states from East Prussia to liberate those newly independent states from their Bolshevik oppressors. On February 8, Free Corps clashed with a small communist force in Kedainiai, Lithuania, and drove them from the city. It was a portent of things to come. The Free Corps would become very active in the Baltic states.

THE "WOBBLIES"

Meanwhile, as these incidents were taking place in Germany, a massive strike began in faraway Seattle, Washington, USA.

Seattle was well-known for being a "union town" and one of the biggest unions in the US, the "Industrial Workers of the World" ("Wobblies") was headquartered there. The leaders of this union were politically to the far left and, many thought, heavily influenced by communism. During the Great War, Wobblie membership had grown, and their coffers were full of cash, and they had already caused trouble. The most serious incident occurred in November 1916 when the Wobblies held a large rally in Everett, Washington, which turned into a confrontation and shoot-out between themselves, on the one hand, and the local police and vigilante groups on the other. Seven people were reported killed — although it was thought that the toll was much higher — and some 50 people injured. The incident became known as the "Everett Massacre" and was widely reported throughout the US and blamed on the Wobblies. By war's end, everyone in America knew of the Wobblies.

Now, in early February 1919, another Wobblie-directed strike began in a local Puget Sound shipyard and quickly escalated. The Wobblie leaders believing, with some justification, that they had the unions across the United States with them on the issues, called for a nationwide general strike, the first such call by a labor union in American history. The strike was to begin at 10:00 A.M. February 6, 1919. To the elected officials in Washington State, this action was seen as a Bolshevik-like tactic, and fears rose across the country that a communist revolution might be in the offing. The call for a general strike was dampened considerably when the American Federation of Labor (AFL), the nation's leading labor organization, refused to back it. But the Wobblie leaders were not deterred. At the appointed hour, tens of thousands of workers took to the streets of Seattle, marched on the city center, and took over many public buildings. Seattle was paralyzed. Labor disturbances also occurred in other American cities, but none of them were of this magnitude.

There was no help forthcoming from the Federal Government because, it was claimed by Wilson's opponents, the President was in Paris. Consequently, Seattle's mayor, Ole Hanson, jumped into the breach and deputized and armed some additional 2500 police deputies and prevailed upon the state governor to send him the Washington State Militia. With this support, Hanson boldly announced that he would accept nothing but "unconditional surrender" from the Wobblie leaders, and the "Battle of Seattle" was underway. The police and their deputies closed ranks, the Militia displayed its machine guns, and the labor rank and file began to back down slowly at first and then more rapidly. They disbursed and there was little or no bloodshed, but tensions were extreme and the confrontation lasted for five days. In the end, the Wobblie leadership called an end to the strike, but in the same breath, called their action a success and a very visible demonstration of the power of organized labor.

And, Ole Hanson was hailed as a national hero. He then took full advantage of his new notoriety and went on a nationwide speaking tour condemning unionism, communism, and the Wilson Administration. He was a much sought-after speaker and made a lot of money.

Hanson, however, had his enemies. In April 1919, a postal clerk discovered a bomb "big enough to blow out the entire side of the County-City Building" in Hanson's mail.

Throughout the US, the public's impression of the connection between leftist labor unions and communists was intensified, and, as a result, 32 states enacted laws against "criminal syndicalism," which forbade membership in any organization that preached revolution. The IWW was a main target for such laws.

THE GREEKS HAVE THEIR SAY AT PARIS

On February 4, 1919, Greek Premier Eleutherios Venizelos appeared before the Council of Ten to plead his country's case. Greece was one of the victorious Allies. There had been fighting in Greece and Greek troops had fought in other parts of the Balkans. And currently, Greek troops were engaged in the Ukraine as part of the Allied expeditionary force there. Furthermore, promises had been made to the Greeks that they would benefit from the dismantling of the Ottoman Empire and receive territory in European Turkey and in the Smyrna area of Asian Turkey on the eastern shore of the Aegean Sea. They were also promised territory from Bulgaria (an enemy power), in particular, the coastal area on the Aegean Sea known as Thrace. Furthermore, the Greeks expected territory from, or concessions in, neighboring Albania and Macedonia. Therefore, the Greeks now came to Paris to collect their rewards.

The Council of Ten was very receptive to Greece's acquiring Thrace and territory in Turkey, but with regards to Albania and Macedonia, the Italians and Jugoslavs had claims on some of territories in question. Lloyd George was particularly supportive of Greece because of the long-standing and friendly relations between Greece and Britain which had begun in 1827 when the British came to the aid of the Greeks during their fight for independence from the Turks.

The Italians on the Council of Ten were critical of Greece's claims, while the French and Americans kept open minds. The Japanese had little interest in the subject and remained mostly silent.

No firm decisions were made at this time, but it was a foregone conclusion that Greece deserved, and would receive, some of its demands. A few days later, the Council of Ten created yet another commission, "The Commission of Greek and Albanian Affairs."

GREECE IN WW II

During WW II, Greece was attacked by Italy, Germany, and Bulgaria. The British, once again, came to their aid, but the Axis Powers prevailed. The British evacuated the country, as did the Greek government which went into exile and continued to pursue the war. The Bulgarians re-acquired Thrace and the Italians gained territories in northern Greece and in the Aegean Sea.

After the war, Greece emerged again as a victor nation and re-acquired Thrace and the area taken by Italy. Unfortunately, Greece was at that time engaged in a bitter three-way civil war among the legitimate government in Athens, a nationalist rebel group in northwestern Greece, and a communists rebel group in the northeast.

THE CZECHS HAVE THEIR SAY AT PARIS

On February 5, 1919, Karel Kramar, Premier of Czechoslovakia and his Foreign Minister, Eduard Benes, appeared before the Council of Ten to plead their country's cause. Their main goal, above all else, was to secure full independence, a goal the Czechs had been seeking for some 400 years. Kramar and Benes received a warm reception because Czechoslovakia promised to be an emerging moderate democracy and one of the bright stars in Eastern Europe. The new nation was founded on democratic principles and the two major ethnic groups involved, the Czechs and Slovaks, had agreed to work toward the advancement of the new state. Furthermore, Tomas Masaryk, the country's founder and President, had spent many years in America and had an American wife. While still in the US, Masaryk had met with President Wilson in June 1918 when it was becoming evident that the Allies would win the war and the creation of the state of Czechoslovakia was almost a certainty. On September 3, 1918, the United States formally recognized Masaryk's "Czechoslovakian National Council" as a de-facto Allied government.

Czechoslovakia's borders were, by Eastern European standards, fairly well-decided. The two Czech provinces of Bohemia and Moravia, and the province of Slovakia, all carved out of the dismantled Austro-Hungarian Empire, had relatively well-defined ethnic borders. In the north, however, there was the dispute with Poland over Teschen and in the south there were territorial disputes with Hungary. But Hungary, a former enemy nation, had little support and sympathy in Paris.

At the western end of Czechoslovakia there was an a crescent-shaped area along the western border of Bohemia known as the Sudetenland. It, too, had been part of the Austro-Hungarian Empire and was populated by a mix of Germans and Czechs. The major powers in Paris had all agreed that this area should go to Czechoslovakia. During January 1919, Czech troops had moved into the Sudetenland to make good that commitment.

THE SUDETENLAND AND THE DISMANTLING OF CZECHOSLOVAKIA

When Hitler came to power in Germany in 1933, he confirmed one of his long-standing political goals, that being to bring all German-speaking people back to the Reich. This included the Germans in the Sudetenland. The Nazis pressed the issue with regard to the Sudetenland to the point where, in the Fall of 1938, they threatened to take the area by force of arms. Since Czechoslovakia had treaties of military alliance with Britain, France, and the Soviet Union, such a move could spark a new European war.

To prevent this, Prime Minister Neville Chamberlain of Britain, supported by Premier Edouard Daladier of France, proposed a negotiated settlement. Hitler agreed and the three met in Munich during September 1938 with Mussolini serving as mediator. It was agreed that Germany could have the Sudetenland in return for Hitler's promise that it would be his last territorial demand in Europe. Chamberlain, Daladier, and most of the world's leaders took Hitler at his word. Subsequently, German troops moved into the Sudetenland and the area was soon annexed to Germany.

This action negated Britain's and France's alliances with Czechoslovakia and left that country without the support of the West. As a result, the Czechoslovakian government in Prague fell and confusion and turmoil spread throughout the country. The Slovaks blamed the Czechs for the loss of the Sudetenland and threatening to secede

The three Husain brothers who were to play major roles in the events in the Middle East following the Great War. Seated right to left: Ali, the oldest and Crown Prince of Hijaz; Abdullah, the second son; and Faisal, the third son.

from their union. Matters worsened, a civil war threatened, and within a few months, German troops moved into Bohemia and Moravia, the Czech part of the country, to restore order. The Germans then declared these provinces a colonial protectorate under their care and allowed Slovakia to spin off as an independent state friendly to Germany. At this point, Czechoslovakia no longer existed.

Since the Czechs were the most westernized of all the Slavs and Czech industry so important to the German war effort, Hitler compromised his racial beliefs and agreed to a program to Germanize the Czech people over the years and eventually add them, along with Bohemia and Moravia, to the Third Reich.

After World War II, the victorious Allies reconstructed the Czechoslovak state and returned the Sudetenland. The German population of the area was then forced out by the Czechs.

The Sudetenland remains a part of the Czech Republic to this day and Slovakia has, once again, acquired its independence.

The French were more interested in Czechoslovakia than the others because they saw the new state as bulwark against the Bolsheviks and as an ally in any future confrontation with Germany. Lloyd George, however, took a disliking to Benes, privately calling him "the little French Jackal."

At the eastern end of Czechoslovakia, there was another disputed area, Ruthenia. The people of this small area were of Ukrainian blood, culture, and language, but their recent past and Catholic religion tied them to the Slovaks and Czechs. About 30% of the population were Poles

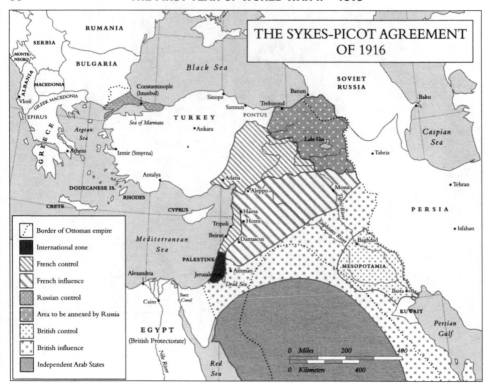

The infamous Sykes-Picot Agreement of 1916 in which the British and French divided the Middle East between themselves, disregarding Hijazi claims to much of the same area.

and 14% Jews. Ruthenia, which had been a part of Austria-Hungary, had declared its independence in November 1918 and formed a union with the Ukraine, but it was universally ignored. And the new government in Budapest claimed that Ruthenia was still a part of Hungary. On Ruthenia's northern border, there were sporadic clashes with the Poles over the oil fields near Lvov, and in the east, both Bolshevik and Russian White forces made occasional forays into Ruthenia. The Ruthenian delegates in Paris were divided and did not always speak with a united voice, but they did, in general, favor Ruthenia's union with Czechoslovakia.

The union of Ruthenia with Czechoslovakia would give the latter a border with another Allied nation, Romania. There was also talk in Paris of providing

Czechoslovakia with a corridor to the sea through Hungary and Jugoslavia.

There the Czechoslovak matters rested while the leaders in Paris addressed the multitude of other problems of the moment.

THE ARABS HAVE THEIR SAY AT PARIS

On February 6, 1919, Prince Faisal Husain appeared before the Council of Ten to plead the case for his country, Hijaz. Faisal was the third son of Ibn Ali Husain, ruler of Hijaz who claimed to be a direct descendent of the Prophet Mohammed. There was a second son, Abdullah, who had led pro-Allied Arab forces during the war and the first son, who was his father's heir, who had remained at his father's side in Mecca. The three brothers worked closely together and for the best interests of their family.

Faisal, a capable military leader, had led Hijaz's largest Arab military force and had fought with in British in Trans-Jordan, Palestine, and Syria. Also, Hijazi Arabs had made up the bulk of T. E. Lawrence's (Lawrence of Arabia's) force that had operated in the Aqaba area. T. E. Lawrence was now permanently attached to Faisal's delegation and was his constant companion, adviser, translator, and confidant. The expense of Faisal's delegation in Paris was also being paid by the British.

But then, there was the Sykes-Picot Agreement. Understandably, under this agreement, the French expected Lebanon and Syria to come under their influence and had managed to put in place members of Husain's delegation loyal to them. Thus, the issue of Syria and its adjacent areas became a major issue of disagreement among the British, French, and Hijazis in Paris. In the final analysis, the French were hostile to the Arabs, the British embarrassed, the Hijazis apprehensive, the Italians concerned about their own interests in the area, the Americans somewhat indifferent because the United States had not been at war with Turkey, and the Japanese, as usual, who remained silent.

As expected, Faisal asked the Council to live up the British promises and reject the Sykes-Picot Agreement.

And, as usual, his petition was heard and recorded, but no decisions were taken.

In public and on the surface, the French were openly cordial toward Faisal. He met with President Poincare, was awarded the French Legion of Honor for his part in the war, and was taken on an extended tour of the battlefields — some believed — to get him out of Paris. The French press was not as cordial, though. They attacked him as a puppet of the British, and, behind the scenes, French intelligence personnel

were reading his mail and monitoring his communications back to the Middle East. In all, Faisal's position in Paris was very weak.

And so it went in Paris. The next day another delegation appeared before the Council, and another the day after that, and so on.

THAT MESS IN EASTERN EUROPE

During the first two weeks of February, the remaining German troops in Eastern Europe withdrew and went home. This caused a huge power vacuum is the Baltic states, Poland, parts of Belorussia, and parts of the Ukraine. Into this vacuum now flowed a variety of feuding parties. The Poles were the most powerful of the contenders, because, thanks to Pilsudski, they had been able to put together a viable army. Pilsudski, however, could not gather in all of the armed Poles. There were Polish units serving with the Bolsheviks and with the Russian Whites.

The Polish Army became a legal entity only on February 26, 1919, when the Polish Sejm (parliament), which had been in existence for only four months, enacted the "Army Law." Heretofore, the units that would make up the new army were technically leaderless and wandering remnants of the German Army and/or Austro-Hungarian Army, trying to keep themselves fed and together as fighting units. In total, they numbered some 110,000, most of whom were experienced war veterans. On March 7, 1919, the Sejm introduced conscription and the Polish Army began to grow rapidly. By April, it numbered 170,000 and put a severe drain on the fragile Polish economy, consuming four-fifths of the country's national budget.

The Ukrainians, Lithuanians, and Latvians had also put together fledgling armies which now joined in the Eastern European vacuum. Also joining in were the Russian Whites, groups of roving anarchists dubbed "Greens," German freebooters and bandits.

The Bolsheviks were, of course, another contender but their forces in the area were very weak except in eastern Lithuania and western Belorussia. Because these areas were under the Red Army's control, in February Moscow designated the area as another soviet republic called "Litbel." It would last for two months.

Of major concern to the Poles and others of the region was the fact that Lenin had presented his Western Army with a military plan called, most unfortunately, "Target Vistula." The Vistula River ran through the heart of Poland and through the Polish capital, Warsaw. Clearly, judging from the name of the operation, it appeared that the Bolsheviks intended to conquer all, or most, of Poland. And if they conquered Poland, would Germany be next? In many ways, the Bolshevik leaders in Moscow were still political amateurs.

Offshore in the Baltic Sea, the British Navy ruled, but the Bolshevik Navy was powerful enough to cut off nearly all seaborne trade along the coast. This meant that virtually no Allied aid reached Lithuania and Latvia by sea. Aid could only come by land through Germany.

As the military vacuum evolved in Eastern Europe, Pilsudski's army was able to act quickly and establish a western frontier for Poland that included the major cities of Pinsk, Lvov, Chelm, and Brest-Litovsk. And all indications were that they intended to continue their advance when opportunities appeared. It was Pilsudski's contention, and announced goal, that Poland should rule these lands once again and that the peoples of the area would welcome Polish rule as opposed to Bolshevik rule.

In Paris and elsewhere, the Germans were strongly criticized for creating the military vacuum which now occurred, and in some quarters, it was seen as proof that there was a conspiracy developing between the Bolsheviks and the Germans. No one could forget that it was the Germans who had secretly transported Lenin and his entourage to Petrograd during the war and that the Bolshevik/German relationship might still be very strong.

Following the German pull out, military actions in the area were slow to develop because most of the contenders, except for the Poles, were ill-prepared to take action. Furthermore, the infrastructure, especially the railroads, was in disrepair and the muddy season was upon the land during March and April. When the warmer weather came, though, military activities increased, albeit slowly, and reports began to flow to the west which were often conflicting and incomplete. Also they were filled with unfamiliar, and sometimes difficult-to-pronounce, Slavic place names and surnames. Pilsudski was about the only individual who was well-known in the West. For the peacemakers in Paris, events in much of Eastern Europe were difficult to understand and to follow.

Food was also a major problem. This had been a part of Europe's grain belt but now the fields were abandoned and much of the food that was available flowed to the east to feed the Bolshevik armies and workers. There were also severe shortage of many other necessities of life, and crime and diseases went virtually unchecked.

Once again, Churchill's comment to Lloyd George that "...the quarrels of the pygmies have begun," was coming to pass.

ELSEWHERE IN EUROPE

On February 12, a women's suffrage conference began in Paris with delegations from many countries.

In Berlin, German police raided the office of Karl Radick, Lenin's representative in Berlin, and discovered plans for a

Bolshevik invasion of Germany. The plans called for an attack by Trotsky's Red Army to advance through Poland and into Germany. The offensive was to begin in the spring of 1919 and would be coordinated with the general communist insurrection, inside Germany, which would take place at that same time.

WILSON WINS ONE AND THEN LEAVES FOR HOME

On February 14, in Paris, the first draft of the Versailles Peace Treaty was published. It had many unanswered questions, and complaints, proposed changes, and amendments came in from all directions. One of the most stable and generally accepted proposals in the original draft was that the League of Nations would be created within the framework of the peace treaty with Germany. This was a great victory for President Wilson who had argued for this all along. It was also very significant in that it elevated the Paris peace treaty to an unprecedented international level. Since the League of Nations was to be an international organization, affecting every country on earth, the delegates at Paris now claimed the right to delve into the foreign relations, and even the domestic policies, of every nation. Needless to say, there were those political leaders around the world who deeply resented this intrusion into their affairs. As history would show, it would be very difficult for the League of Nations to become, in fact, an effective international peace organization.

The next day, Wilson sailed for home to sign important bills passed by Congress which was about to adjourn. He also had a task of informing the Senate on the progress being made in Paris and to address the many domestic issues that had arisen. He left Col. House in charge of the American delegation in Paris — a great slight to Secretary of State Lansing. Wilson was not completely out of touch with House as he crossed the Atlantic because the two could communicate by radio. Ever since the Titanic disaster of 1912, all American ocean-going ships were required, by law, to have ship-to-shore radios.

Wilson's absence created a lull that now came over the Council of Ten. With the first draft of the peace treaty published, the task of the Council members would now be to listen to those who wanted changes. In the next round a formal decision-making would not occur until Wilson returned. Lloyd George, however, thought Clemenceau would take full advantage of Wilson's absence. He told an aide "The old tiger (Clemenceau) wants the grizzly bear (Wilson) back in the Rocky Mountains before he starts tearing up the German hog."

Lloyd George, too, returned to London to address domestic issues and sign bills. He left Balfour in charge in Paris and was away from Paris for four weeks. Likewise, Orlando took the opportunity to return to Italy for brief periods.

THE UNITED NATIONS

When, after World War II, the United Nations was formed, it was done so within the framework of a separate international conference and not tied to any treaties. In this way, the various political leaders around the world could choose to participate or not. The political leaders of 1945 had learned a good lesson from their predecessors of 1919.

EVENTS CONTINUE

Wilson's departure and the lull at Paris had virtually no effect on world issues and events.

On the day of Wilson's departure, the American Legion Veterans Organization was formed in Paris.

On February 16, the British diplomat Mark Sykes, co-author of the controversial Sykes-Picot Agreement on the Mid East, died in Paris of the flu.

On the 17th, the German and Polish governments signed a unilateral armistice that awarded Poland a generous amount of German territory, including the controversial Polish corridor. Poland had not been a signatory to the general Allied/German armistice of November 11, 1918, therefore a separate armistice was called for. This armistice was seen in Germany as another terrible loss and would be a political issue for years to come. At this time, however, it had some merit in that it freed Polish forces to move to the east to confront the Bolshevik threat which, of course, was also a great concern to the Germans. Furthermore, it reduced the potential for armed conflict along the Germany-Polish border — conflicts that neither side wanted.

At 8:40 A.M. on the morning of February 19, a would-be assassin, Eugene Cottin, an anarchist and supporter of communism, fired ten shots at Premier Clemenceau who was on his way to a meeting with Balfour and Col. House. Three of the bullets hit their mark. Fortunately, Clemenceau's wounds were not life-threatening and the Old Tiger was able to return to work within eight days. One of the bullets was deemed too dangerous to remove so Clemenceau carried it in his body for the rest of his life. He also made jokes about Cottin's marksmanship. Cottin was convicted, sentenced to ten years, and was released in five.

Expressions of sympathy and support poured in from all quarters for Clemenceau. The Pope sent him his blessing, and the old anti-cleric returned the favor by sending his blessing to the Pope.

Also on the 19th, prominent black leaders from the United States and Africa, who had gathered in Paris hoping to be heard, announced the creation of a new organization, the "Pan-African Congress." The two leading members of the organization were the American W.E.B. DuBois and Blaise Diagne of Senegal, a French colony on the west coast of Africa. Diagne was the highest-ranking African in French politics and had been instrumental in raising Senegalese troops for the French Army during the war.

Fifty-seven delegates from fifteen countries and colonies attended. The focus of the new organization was a call upon the colonial rulers of their African colonies to improve the lot of their wards, and, at some time in the not-too-distant future, lead the people of Africa to self-determination. Here again was Wilson's Fourteen Points at work. W.E.B. DuBois met with Col. House, but nothing of significance was accomplished.

They had better luck with Clemenceau. He gave his formal approval of the Congress and saw to it that it got widespread publicity throughout France.

THE PAN-AFRICAN CONGRESS DURING AND AFTER WW II

The Pan-African Congress prospered and grew during the 1920s and 1930s and was a major voice for the African people during WW II. Its leaders supported the Allied cause while still calling for improved conditions for Africans and for the eventual self-determination of African nations. It also became an assembly point for the various African nationalist leaders that would emerge soon after the war and advance — sometimes with violence — the cause of African nationalism. Some of the prominent members of the Pan-African Congress who became strong leaders in the struggle for African independence were George Padmore of Trinidad, Kwame Nkrumah of

Gold Coast (Ghana), Nnamdi Azikiwe
of Nigeria, and Jomo Kenyatta of Kenya.
||||||||||||||||||||||||||||||||||||||||||||||||||||||||||||||||||||||||||||||||||||||

The next day, February 20, in the remote country of Afghanistan, the country's ruler, Emir Habibullah Kahn, was assassinated. Assassinations seemed to be in the air. A power struggle followed in which Habibullah Kahn's third son, 26-year-old Amanullah Khan, emerged as the new emir. Young Amanullah was known to be an ardent nationalist and an advocate of complete Afghan independence. This ran counter to a long-standing British and Czarist Russia agreement which had divided the country into British and Russian spheres of influence, with the end result being that the Afghan people were a divided and subject people. Now, with the Czar gone and Russia in state of turmoil, the future of Afghanistan was murky at best. Wilson's call within his Fourteen Points for self-determination by the people of such lands did not help matters. The Afghans, under the leadership of their new emir, were about to assert themselves and in the coming months the world would hear more about Afghanistan.

At Weimar, the German government passed a resolution on February 21 calling for the union of Germany and Austria and the name of that union to be the "Republic of Germany-Austria." In Austria, the proposal was looked upon with great favor. In the List Regiment barracks at Munich, Corporal Hitler welcomed the proposal unconditionally.

In Hungary, on February 21, the Karolyi government clamped down on the growing communist insurgency. The government closed all of the communist offices across the country and arrested hundreds of Hungarian communists and communist sympathizers including their leader, Bela Kun. This was not done peacefully. Some 30 people, including 7 policemen, were killed and many more injured.

Furthermore, this action was not successful. Thousands of Hungarians of all political persuasions were, by now, dissatisfied with conditions and the country began to slip into anarchy.

As with Afghanistan, the world would soon hear more about Hungary.

CHAPTER 5
GERMANY – JAPAN –
CHINA – KOREA

Kurt Eisner

SUDDEN UPHEAVAL IN BAVARIA

At 9:45 A.M. on February 21, Kurt Eisner, Chairman of the "Central Workers', Soldiers' and Peasant's Council of Bavaria" ("Central Soviet"), was assassinated by a lone gunman. Eisner, a Jew whose original name was Kamonowsky, was a leader of the leftist Independent Social Democratic Party, a radical offshoot of the Social Democratic Party.

Eisner had become Bavaria's most prominent political figure having led a successful leftist, non-Marxist revolution in Bavaria in November 1918 that ousted Bavaria's 750-year-old monarchy. At that time, Eisner proclaimed Bavaria a republic and became Bavaria's first premier.

Eisner's relationship with the Ebert government was not good. Soon after taking power, he produced documents that, he claimed, proved that Prussia had started the war and that Bavaria had had no hand in it. He also talked openly about severing relations with Prussia and seeking a separate peace with the Allies. Understandably, Eisner had many opponents in Prussia and other parts of the country and had earned the inglorious title "The Israelite Devil."

Upon taking power, Eisner promptly began applying socialist programs and his government soon ran out of money. As a result, government services began to fail, the economy faltered, and the citizens of Bavaria grew angry. On top of all this, there was a severe coal shortage in Munich and an estimated 40,000 unemployed. This anger took on a definitely anti-semitic tone with Eisner being the main target for the abuse.

This had been the political atmosphere in Munich when Corporal Hitler returned to join his regiment after having been released from the hospital.

Eisner's position became untenable and an election was held on January 12 in which Eisner and his followers were resoundingly defeated. Nevertheless, Eisner was able to remain in office for several more days before being forced to offer his resignation.

On the morning of February 21, he was on his way to address the Landtag (parliament) and formally submit his resignation. He never got there.

Eisner was gunned down by a disgruntled and deranged right-winger named Anton Count Arco-Valley who had recently been rejected for membership in the Thule Society. Rumors had it that Arco-Valley was part Jewish and in his twisted mind, saw Eisner as a target for his revenge.

Within minutes of the assassination, the Landtag was informed and its members went into a state of stunned confusion. As they slowly regained their composure, one of the Landtag's leaders, Erhard Auer, began making a speech eulogizing Eisner. As he finished, a stranger entered the assembly hall, calmly strolled down the aisle to the banister separating the speaker's rostrum from the delegates' seats, pulled out a rifle, steadied himself on the banister, and fired several shots at Auer. Auer was seriously wounded but survived. The stranger then strolled back up the aisle and fired several shots at various members scrambling for their lives. No one was hit. As the stranger exited the

building, an Army Major attempted to apprehend him but was shot dead with one rifle bullet to the head. The stranger then walked into the crowd that had gathered because of Eisner's assassination and disappeared. He was later identified as Alois Linder, an apprentice butcher. Linder fled to Austria, was later apprehended, extradited to Germany, tried, convicted, and served 14 years in prison.

With the assassination of Eisner and the attempted assassination of Auer, panic gripped the city. Jews thought a pogrom might be underway, and the political right thought it might be the beginning of a Red revolution.

The Social Democrat members of the Landtag, also fearing a possible revolution, fled Munich en masse to set up a loose government-in-exile in the small town of Bamburg.

With this and Eisner's assassination, Bavaria went into a sudden state of turmoil because a new chancellor had not yet been named. The leftists still had the political upper hand, but they were unable to decide on an immediate course of action. Soon, however, and in a show of leftist unity, they managed to have the Landtag temporarily dissolved and state affairs placed into the hands of the Central Soviet which would decide what course of action to take.

In the political vacuum that evolved, several individuals rose to the top: Ernst Toller, a twenty-five-year-old idealistic playwright and a Jew; and Erich Musham, an anarchist and cafe intellectual. Both were members of the Central Soviet which began to function informally under their leadership.

A new Chairman of the Central Soviet, Ernst Karl August Niekisch, was appointed but Toller and Musham held the real power. New cabinet members were also appointed which included several extreme radicals of the far left. Two of the most prominent were Dr. Franz Lipp, recently released from a mental institution, as Foreign Minister; and Gustav Landauer, an anarchist philosopher and a Jew, as Commissar of Public Instruction; and Silvio Gesell, as Minister of Finance.

When Landauer took office, and Bavaria once again had a functioning government, one of his first acts was to decree an immediate end to the study of history as it then existed. Landauer then ordered the rewriting of history from the proletarian point of view.

Silvio Gesell soon announced that it would be his goal to end the use of money.

Dr. Lipp was something else. He sent bizarre telegrams to his "friend," the Pope, and unilaterally declared war on Wurttemberg and Switzerland. Lipp was soon removed from office and taken back to the mental institution.

On February 26, with thousands of people attending the funeral, Eisner was buried. Numerous red flags were carried by the mourners and Catholic priests were forced, at gunpoint, to ring church bells for the fallen Eisner, who was an atheist.

In the chaotic days that followed, inflation soared, goods disappeared from store shelves, looting occurred, and the new Commissar of Housing decreed that the homes of wealthy people were to be confiscated by the government and converted into public housing. He also declared that all future homes built in Munich be of a standardized design with the living room built over the kitchen and bedroom. Of all the communist take-overs in Germany, this was, perhaps, the most bizarre.

THE GERMAN WORKERS' PARTY FORMS

During all of the turmoil in Munich, Anton Drexler's little discussion group, begun only the month before, had grown in membership but was still meeting in a beer hall.

On the evening of February 24, 1919, Drexler and his associates took a bold step. They declared themselves a political party with the name "German Workers' Party" (DAP). In this heady political atmosphere, the DAP was just one of several organizations that were popping up in Munich with political names and agendas.

The name, German Workers' Party, was deceiving in that it sounded like a leftist organization, which it was not. And due to its minuscule size and very limited resources, the DAP was not really a political party in the sense that it could field political candidates and take part in scheduled elections. Its main focus was still that of a discussion group with a far right political agenda and, at times, something of a carbon copy of the larger and better-known Thule Society.

The DAP had, however, made a significant enough impact to attract the attention of the competition. On March 3, the leftist press in Munich began condemning the DAP, calling them "the handymen of the Prussian aristocrats and militarists."

A MEETING WITH THE BOLSHEVIKS

The Allied leaders gathered at Paris tried to make contact with the Bolshevik leaders in Russia by suggesting a meeting in Turkey. The Bolsheviks, however, rejected the offer.

Wilson, though, following through with his Fourteen Points in which he offered a hand of friendship to the Bolsheviks, thought that a more determined effort was called for. He had little support for this in Paris, but he plowed ahead anyway. He offered to send an American delegation to Moscow to consult with the Bolsheviks' leadership, and that offer was accepted. To head the delegation, Wilson appointed an up-and-coming young diplomat, William

Bullitt. Bullitt's mission left for Moscow on February 22 while Wilson was at sea and returned with a somewhat glowing assessment of communist. Bullitt made a comment to the media that he had seen the future and "it works." He would live to regret these words.

Upon his return to Paris, almost no one wanted to meet with him and discuss his mission. The general feeling was that Bullitt was inexperienced and had been duped by the Bolsheviks. Lloyd George finally met with Bullitt over breakfast, but nothing came of the meeting. Even Wilson, considerably embarrassed by Bullitt's report, put off meeting with Bullitt for an inordinately long time, indicating, too, that he was not pleased with the mission's results. With this, Bullitt and his report faded into the background at Paris.

Bullitt resigned from the American Paris delegation in May, returned home an angry man. He testified before Lodge's Senate Foreign Relations Committee, speaking out against Wilson and the Versailles Treaty.

BULLITT'S RESURRECTION

The United States did not recognize the Soviet regime in Russia until 1934 when Franklin Roosevelt was President. As America's first ambassador to the communist state, Roosevelt selected William Bullitt. Bullitt served well in Moscow and then became Roosevelt's ambassador to France, another important post. Bullitt was in Paris in 1940 when the Germans captured the city. He returned to the United States and continued to receive Roosevelt's support, becoming the President's "roving ambassador."

JAPAN SPEAKS OUT

In the days just before Wilson left for home, the meetings within the Council of Ten with regard to the League of Nations were most intense. As now had become custom, the Japanese remained silent most of the time letting the Westerners take the lead. But then, the Japanese suddenly spoke out. They insisted that a clause be incorporated into the League of Nations' covenant, defining all of the races of the world to be equal and declaring that this was in keeping with the spirit of Wilson's Fourteen Points. Clearly, this was a bombshell for the British and the French. There was no way that these colonial masters could tell the multitudes of peoples within their empires that they were racially equal to their white European masters. The British were supported, most vehemently, by the Australian delegation headed by the country's Prime Minister, Billy Hughes. Hughes, a rough and tumble ex-dock worker, was one of the most outspoken delegates at Paris and was often rude and agitating. Australia had, at the time, a strong "White Australia" policy that excluded virtually all non-whites, especially Orientals, from settling in the country. Furthermore, Hughes and many Australians were angered by the fact that Japan had been accepted in Paris as one of the Big Five, whereas they, a white English-speaking nation with a much smaller population, had contributed much more to the war effort than Japan. Hughes was also an opponent of the Fourteen Points. He announced that if such a policy on racial equality was adopted, he would take the first ship back to Australia and that Australia would not become a member of the League.

This issue was so controversial that it was agreed that it should not be addressed at this time when the League Commission's chairman, Wilson, was about to leave for home. Besides, Wilson hated Hughes and had called him a "pestiferous varmint." Therefore, the equality issue was postponed. Eventually the white racists would have their way and no mention of racial equality was incorporated into the draft of the covenant.

JAPAN'S WAR EFFORT

In 1919, Japan was included as one of the members for the Council of Ten because of its contribution to the war effort in the Far East and the Pacific. Japan had conquered the lightly-defended German island possessions in the Pacific Ocean, North of the Equator, and had taken over the large German concession on the Shantung Peninsula in China. Germany's island possessions consisted of the Marshall, Mariana, Caroline, and Palau Island groups, and the island of Yap, a sum total of more than 100 islands. The Shantung Peninsula, which juts out from northern China into the Yellow Sea and in the direction of Japanese-controlled Korea, was one of the largest foreign concessions in China. It was very much like the British concession at Hong Kong, but much larger. It also was the home of Confucius and the scene of the Boxer Rebellion, and it had large coal deposits and other minerals. It had an estimated population of 30 million people which translated into numerous customers and an abundance of cheap laborers for whomever controlled the concession. On the southern side of the peninsula was the large seaport of Tsingtao (Qingdao) which had one of the best natural harbors in China. Furthermore, the Germans had poured a lot of money into the concession building railroads, opening mines, and improving harbor facilities. Naturally, the Japanese wanted to retain this valuable possession as a spoil of war.

But, Japan was a nation to be feared. It had had a meteoric rise to power from a feudal state in the 1850s to a modern industrial and military power by the end of the century. And, it had fought several wars, won all of them, and added greatly to its colonial territories. It had taken land from China, including the large island of Formosa (Taiwan) and the Ryukyu Islands, the largest of which is Okinawa. It had also been at war with Czarist Russia in 1904-05, a war which Japan started with a sneak attack on the Russian Pacific Fleet anchored at Port Arthur, China. The modern Japanese Navy managed to destroy both the Russian Pacific Fleet and the Baltic Fleet which came to replace it.

A NATION TO BE FEARED

The concept of Japan conquering other parts of the Far East was not new. In 1909 a book entitles *The Valor of Ignorance*, by Homer Lea, a well-educated American who served as a general in the army of Sun Yat-sen, predicted the eventual Japanese takeover of Southeast Asia. Lea predicted that the Japanese would, in time, conquer Manchuria, Hong Kong, French Indochina, Singapore, the Dutch East Indies, the Philippines, and parts of the US west coast. Douglas MacArthur was known to have read the book, as did many Japanese military officers.

Lea wrote another book in 1912 entitled *Day of the Saxon* in which he predicted the rise of Greater Germany based on national supremacy and ethnic purity.

JAPAN AND SNEAK ATTACKS

When the Japanese began planning their attack on Pearl Harbor, they had two precedents upon which to draw. The first was their sneak attack at Port Arthur which started the Russo-Japanese War of 1904-05. In that attack, fast Japanese destroyers suddenly steamed into the harbor at Port Arthur late in the afternoon on February 8, 1904, torpedoed the Russian ships at anchor, and then escaped under the cover of darkness. It was a magnificent military success. This attack gave Japan a large military advantage in the Far East and Japan eventually won the war.

The second precedent was the very successful British attack in November 1940, on the Italian Fleet anchored at the Italian Naval Base at Taranto in the heel of Italy. There, the British used their aircraft carriers and their antiquated, but reliable torpedo-carrying Swordfish biplanes (called "string bags"), and successfully decimated the Italian Fleet from the air. The Japanese, of course, learned of the attack and ordered their military attaches in Rome and London (Japan was still neutral) to gather up and send any and all information they could obtain on the Taranto attack to Tokyo. In the final analysis, the Japanese attack at Pearl Harbor was very much like the British attack at Taranto.

In the West, many felt that Japan was not a state that could be trusted. At the beginning of the war, the Japanese Army, many of whose officers had trained in Germany, tended to favor the Central Powers while the Japanese Navy supported the Allies.

The Japanese Navy's position prevailed, and Japan went to war against Germany and conquered the aforementioned German colonies in the Far East by November 1914. Then too, the Japanese government ruled out the use of Japanese troops in Europe, claiming that they were needed in the Far East, although they did send a naval squadron to operate with the western Allies in the Mediterranean, helped the British patrol the Indian Ocean, and loaned the British Navy a number of destroyers to help fight the German submarine menace. Furthermore, during the war, Japanese industry had expanded greatly from orders placed in Japan for war materials and now Japanese industrialists, in general, had the reputation of being war profiteers. Also, during the war,

the Japanese merchant fleet had doubled in size and was now a serious competitor to Europe's merchant marine fleets — not to mention being a great military asset in the event of war.

In Paris, many believed that Japan's military victories had been easy and that that country had taken advantage of the war to enhance its status as a world power. Others believed that Japan should not have been included in the Council of Ten.

Another concern for the Allies was that Japanese troops had entered Siberia as part of the Allied effort to contain the Bolsheviks, and there were fears in the West that the Japanese would never leave.

During the war, fears of Japan escalated in the United States. These fears were given a name that had long been used in Europe, the "Yellow Peril," and several popular novels were written by US authors around the possibility of the Japanese invading the United States. The powerful and politically right-wing Hearst newspaper empire, based in California, kept the fear of the Yellow Peril very much alive.

Another issue on the US west coast was that of Japanese immigration. It was widely believed by many in the west that it should be halted. To add to the problem, Japan had sold arms to, what many Americans considered to be the wrong side, in the Mexican Revolution. Furthermore, in the infamous, and fake, Zimmerman Letter that reportedly tried it entice Mexico into a war with the US, it was suggested that Mexico might seek an alliance with Japan to help achieve that goal.

In Japan, Japanese authors picked up on the undeclared literary war and produced novels and media articles concerning the same thing — a possible Japanese invasion of the United States. One popular novel was titled *Our Next War*.

Furthermore, rumors also circulated in the US that the Japanese military planners had extensive and detailed plans for the conquest of America's Pacific island possession and the Panama Canal and for an invasion of the US west coast. To many in America, as well as to many in Paris, Japan looked very much like an aggressor nation. The fact that Japan had militarily defeated and acquired territory from two European powers in the last 14 years was unnerving to virtually all European leaders who had colonial possessions and concessions in the Far East and the Pacific. The general consensus in Europe and the United States was, that if trouble were to occur in the Far East and/or the Pacific, the troublemaker would be Japan.

In Paris, there was little question of Japan's retaining control of the German islands in the Pacific, but the matter of Japan's acquisition of the huge German concession in Shantung was still an open question. The Japanese, of course, claimed that they had conquered it justly under wartime conditions, ousting the Germans from China and should inherit Germany's dominant position there. The Chinese, however, claimed that Shantung was, without question, Chinese territory and that it should be returned to China. In Paris very few supported the Japanese position but the unstable political situation in China provided for no clear-cut solution.

One possible solution to Japan's territorial ambitions was to grant that country's mandates over their conquests, mandates that would be overseen by the League of Nations and would, eventually, lead the mandated territories to self-determination. But the leaders in Paris were also divided on this issue. The US and Britain supported the idea, but France, South Africa, Australia, and New Zealand opposed it because the idea of granting a mandate to an Oriental race was repugnant to many.

To complicate the Shantung issue even further, Japan had concluded a secret treaty with China during the war which stated that Japan could conquer and take control of the German concession. Also, the secret agreement with Britain in which Japan was to acquire the German possessions north of the Equator, the Japanese interpreted it, too, to include Shantung. But wartime secret agreements, as we have seen, were widely discredited at Paris.

Both China and Japan conducted large-scale propaganda campaigns in Paris to promote their respective points of view. Both issued frequent news releases, gave interviews, made speeches, held dinners, and sought out high-level meetings with the Council Members and their top aides. To win sympathy, the Chinese made generous contributions to Belgium and France to help rebuild schools in the war-torn areas. The Japanese, for their part, began to soft peddle the racial issue but continued to stress the Shantung issue.

There was yet another issue with Japan. In Paris, there was much talk about America's Monroe Doctrine which established the US as the master power in North America, Central America, the Caribbean, and the northern rim of South America. Might not the Japanese claim the same privilege in their part of the world? This came to pass during WW II.

THE GREATER EAST ASIA CO-PROSPERITY SPHERE

Japan's primary war aim in WW II was to set up an economic bloc in East Asia and the Western Pacific very similar to the economic bloc the Americans enjoyed as a result of the Monroe Doctrine. The Japanese plan was to "liberate" the colonial lands in East Asia that belonged to the European Powers and the United States, set them up as independent states, and incorporate them into the economic bloc which they called "The Greater East Asia Co-prosperity Sphere." In the Co-prosperity Sphere, Japan would be the primary industrial power and everyone else would be Japan's captive customers and suppliers. And, the Japanese believed, these associate states would be forever grateful to Japan for having liberated them from their oppressive colonial masters and granting them independence.

THE JAPANESE RELOCATION OF WORLD WAR II

The relocation of the ethnic Japanese population on the US West Coast in 1942 had its roots in this time frame and the years before the Great War.

The great majority of the Japanese who came to America did not come to settle and start new lives as did the European immigrants who flooded into the East Coast. The Japanese, for the most part, came to earn money and return to Japan in their old age. Accordingly, they resisted integration and Americanization. Because of this, and the obvious racial and cultural differences, the ethnic Japanese were never really welcome or liked; at best they were tolerated. In the 1930s, when Japan conquered Manchuria and then attacked China, and committed a series of egregious atrocities, the respect of the American public for all Japanese, both overseas and local, declined to new lows.

When the Japanese attacked Pearl Harbor and invaded the American-controlled Philippines, this was the last straw. President Roosevelt issued an executive order requiring that they be removed, in total, from the West Coast and placed in relocation camps for the duration of the war.

The US was not the only country in the Western Hemisphere that mistrusted their ethnic Japanese. Canada, Mexico, and several South American countries also forced their ethnic Japanese into relocation camps. The Central American countries, in a series of negotiations with the US government, sent their ethnic Japanese to the US where they were incarcerated in three camps in Texas.

THAT MESS IN CHINA

In 1919, China had two governments and a host of warlords. One government, the successor to the old imperial government which ended in 1911, was in Peking (Beijing) and was very much a militaristic dictatorship headed by General Hsu Shih-chang. In Hsu's regime, there were many Chinese officials that were openly cooperating with the Japanese and rumors of bribes were widespread.

The other government, based in southern China at Canton, was known as the "Republic of China," and it had been founded by Dr. Sun Yat-sen in 1912. Sun's regime was dictatorial and totally opposed to cooperating with the Japanese.

Both governments were rather unstable and controlled only the immediate areas around their capitals. In the provinces, there were a number of warlords and in Tibet there was a religious regime under a holy man known as the "Dalai Lama." Tibet was technically a part of China, but the Dalai Lama's regime had acted independently for many years, much to the dismay of the Chinese. To complicate matters even further in China, a very large part of the Chinese population was illiterate and, due to the lack of communications, out of touch with events in their own country, and, of course, the world. One example of this was that after the five-year-old boy Emperor, Pu Yi, was ousted in Peking in 1911, it was months and even years before some of the rural peasants heard of it. Then too, foreigners were not safe in these areas, especially Europeans.

When the Great War started, the Peking regime declared war on the Central Powers and thus became a member of the Allies. The Canton government, however, proclaimed its neutrality and remained neutral throughout the war.

Even though Sun and Hsu were rivals, they managed to cooperate with each other during the war as far as the Allies were concerned. Neither had military forces to contribute to the war, but thousands of coolies were sent to Europe as laborers. Many of the Allied trenches that became the hallmark of the war were dug by these men. Casualties were relatively high among these men due to enemy shelling and disease. On one occasion, a ship carrying Chinese workers to Europe was torpedoed in the Mediterranean by a German submarine and some 500 died.

The Chinese delegation at the peace conference was composed of members from both the Peking and Canton regimes who, at times, were at odds with each other reflecting conditions back in China. It was also rumored that certain delegates were taking bribes from the Japanese. The members of the Chinese delegation were, however, firmly united on one issue, that being the return of Shantung.

On the racial issue, however, the Chinese and Japanese were united, but the Chinese did not press that issue as vigorously as did the Japanese.

The Chinese delegation also advocated the end of all foreign concessions in China and foreign controls over certain important railways and the collection of tariffs by foreigners — a measure that had been put in place by the British to combat rampant corruption. Success by the Chinese on these issues at Paris was unlikely, but the efforts of their delegation in Paris made for good propaganda back home.

KOREA

Here was another concern in the Far East that involved Japan. Japan had invaded and occupied Korea in 1905 during the Russo-Japanese War and then began a program of suppressing the Korean culture, language, and religion in favor of their Japanese counterparts. In 1910, Japan formally annexed Korea and renamed it Chosen. The Koreans deeply resented these things and there was both ongoing passive and armed resistance against the Japanese. Korean armed resistance operated out of bases in Manchuria, which was ruled by a local warlord, and an area in Siberia which was controlled by the Bolsheviks. Lenin saw a potential here and provided arms and training for the Korean rebels with the obvious hope that they would be receptive to communism. The Koreans had responded favorably to these communist overtures and had formed a political action group called the "Korean Workers' Union."

When the Japanese and Americans arrived in Siberia in September 1918, the Korean rebels joined the Bolsheviks in resisting the incursion. This put the Americans in the awkward position of fighting Koreans. The Bolshevik forces in Siberia, however, were weak and the Korean rebels even weaker and there were no major confrontations between the Americans and Koreans.

The Korean rebels continued to operate from Russian soil giving the Japanese a plausible excuse to remain in Siberia indefinitely to protect their national interests. This was a situation very unwelcome in the West.

In Paris, there was a small Korean delegation pleading for attention from the peacemakers, but it was all but ignored.

Then, on March 1, 1919, thirty-three prominent Korean cultural and religious leaders issued a statement proclaiming the independence of Korea. Demonstrations in support of the proclamation soon followed throughout Korea and the Japanese were forced to act. They began a brutal and thorough repression against the Korean people which lasted for several months. During that time, the Japanese killed several thousand Koreans and arrested tens of thousands more. Korean temples, schools, businesses, and private homes were destroyed or closed, and, in the process, the Japanese were condemned, world-wide, for their brutality.

The next month, the Korean leaders, by then in exile in Shanghai, China — a stronghold of Western influence — formed a Korean Provisional Government. Their program to liberate Korea was known as "The March 1 Movement" and found much favor in the West.

In Paris, the Japanese call for racial equality became even weaker because of their obvious maltreatment of the Koreans.

CHAPTER 6
EUROPE WITHOUT WILSON

||||||||||||||||||||||||||||||||||||||||||||||||||||||||||||||||||||||||||||||||||||||||||||||||||||||||||||||||||||||||||||||

On February 24, 1919, President Wilson's ship docked in Boston Harbor. The President was home — but some thought he had landed at the wrong place. Wilson's plan was to give a speech to the people of Boston and then travel to Washington by train. Boston, however, was the stronghold of his arch rival in the Senate, Henry Cabot Lodge. Wilson received a tumultuous reception, similar to those he had received in Europe, and during his stay the schools and many businesses were closed. Wilson made his speech before a huge audience touting the advantages of peace, the forthcoming peace treaties, and the League of Nations. It had little noticeable effect, however. The citizens of Boston were cheering their President but were listening to their Senator.

This was a portent of things to come. Wilson and Lodge had been at odds throughout the war. Lodge had been an interventionist early on; Wilson hesitated but finally called for war. Lodge wanted to march on to Berlin; Wilson accepted an armistice; Wilson wanted the US to take a leading role in a new world peace-keeping organization; Lodge believed in American power and American power alone; Lodge seemed to support the concept of a Rhineland buffer state; Wilson opposed it; Lodge believed that only democracies should be allowed to join the League of Nations; Wilson wanted every nation to be a member.

BACK IN WASHINGTON

While Wilson was still on the Atlantic, copies of the draft of the covenant of the League of Nations had been handed out in Washington. The President's opponents were well-prepared for his arrival.

Upon returning to the nation's capital, Wilson saw his new grandson for the first time. The child was sleeping and Wilson made the comical remark, "With his mouth open and his eyes shut, I predict he will make a Senator when he grows up." This remark eventually reached the Senate and was not appreciated.

Wilson was not without his strengths. The American public was generally in favor of the League of Nations, especially the states along the US East Coast. The Midwest and West were more withdrawn, but not openly against it. The South was a curious mix. Southern thought ran against any liberal ideal such as the League of Nations, but the southern political leaders were virtually all Democrats — "The Solid South" they had called it ever since the days of Reconstruction — and wanted to see a Democratic administration continue in Washington.

Then there was former Republican President William Howard Taft. He headed a bipartisan group called "The League to Enforce Peace," established in 1915, which had endorsed the concept of the League of Nations from its inception. This demonstrated that the Republicans were split on the issue.

Despite some recent setbacks, the American economy was still strong and had been so for several years. American farmers had also prospered. These were positive factors for the Wilson Administration.

On February 26, Wilson, at Col. House's suggestion, gave a White House dinner for the key members of Lodge's Senate Foreign Relations Committee. It did not go well and Wilson tended to blame House.

Soon after the dinner, a Republican senator from Connecticut commented to the press, "I feel as if I had been wandering with Alice in Wonderland and had tea with the Mad Hatter."

In the days that followed, the issues of the peace treaty and the League of Nations were debated in the Senate but no votes were taken. The Republicans were biding their time. A new Congress would come into being in early March and it would be solidly Republican. Then, votes would be taken. Before the adjournment of the current Congress, however, there was a sense of direction in the Senate. That was that a peace treaty should be signed first and then the League of Nations could be considered later. To this, Wilson replied with a resounding "No." Because of his intransigent attitude, the *Indianapolis Star* newspaper expressed what many Americans were coming to believe, "It is hard to escape the impression that President Wilson is riding for a fall."

THE RHINELAND BUFFER STATE

On February 25 (during Wilson's absence), the French issued a formal declaration stating that the future western boundary of Germany would be the Rhine River and that Allied forces would remain in the Rhineland and in the bridgeheads on the eastern bank of the river for an undetermined length of time. This strongly hinted at the possible creation of a future buffer state in the Rhineland. The timing of this announcement and Wilson's departure were no coincidence. The French plan for the buffer state had progressed to a point where the future state would be linked politically and militarily with France, Luxembourg, and Belgium.

Field Marshall Foch and his Deputy, Gen. Henri Petain, strongly supported this plan and there was strong public support for it throughout France. Public support was reinforced by the fact that throughout history, the French had considered the Rhine River as the dividing line between themselves and the barbarous people on the other side.

To woo the Rhinelanders over to the concept of a buffer state, various French leaders offered to drop the blockade on the Rhineland and to reduce, or possibly eliminate altogether, their share of German reparations. And, Clemenceau let it be know that he was willing to negotiate with the German government on lowering reparations in return for their acceptance of the buffer state.

Also, subtly but noticeable, the Rhineland Catholics, who had not always welcomed the rule of Protestants, were quietly told that in such a state, they would gain substantial politically power.

Alternative plans to a buffer state were also taking shape. One plan would turn the Rhineland into a demilitarized zone, whereas another called for a customs union that would favor France but leave the Rhineland a part of Germany. Still another plan called for the permanent occupation of the Rhineland by Allied troops or, perhaps, a permanent French military presence. The most radical plan of all called for the dismantling of all of Germany to its pre-Bismarck status which would restore the Rhineland's pre-Bismarckian independence along with that of the other German states.

Wilson's position at this point was to sidestep the Rhineland issue altogether and suggest that it be passed on to the League of Nations. He could rightfully see that the Rhineland issue was a no-win situation for the US. Lloyd George was also noncommittal on the issue and feared that a long-standing issue would be created between Germany and France as had been the case with Alsace-Lorraine which had kept the mutual hatred between the French and Germans alive for decades.

REDS AND FREE CORPS AGAIN

On that same day, February 25, Red factions in the German city of Halle called for a general strike which threw the city into a state of disorder and anarchy. Once again, the Free Corps were called to action. They marched into Halle on March 1 and restored order by force of arms. By now, the pattern had emerged that it was the Freed Corps, and no other organization in Germany, that was saving the nation from the Reds.

THEN CAME THE ARMENIANS

Back in Paris, it was the turn of the Armenians to appear before the Supreme Council. The day for their appearance, February 26, was chosen, in part, because Wilson was absent and the Americans had little interest in this remote area of the Caucasus.

Armenia had for centuries been an outpost of Christianity in a Muslim world and for this reason, and others, Armenia had a long history of support in the West, but a long-standing conflict with its Muslim neighbors. The Great War had brought many of these age-old feuds to the surface once again. When the war started, Armenia was a part of Czarist Russia and had the protection of the great Christian brothers to the North. Now the Czar was gone and Armenia was on its own threatened by its old enemies, Turkey, Azerbaijan, and Persia as well as by two new enemies, the Bolsheviks and the Russian Whites. Both wanted Armenia to remain a part of their respective post-revolution domains and opposed Armenian independence.

During the war, the Armenians suffered one of the greatest tragedies of the Twentieth Century — genocide. Several million Armenians lived in eastern Turkey and were seen by the Turks as an enemy people occupying Turkish land. As a result, the Turks carried out a wholesale massacre of these defenseless people. Estimates of the number of Armenians slaughtered range from 300,000 to 1.5 million. By any count, it was a horrible event and one that brought the Armenians world-wide sympathy and the Turks world-wide condemnation.

When Czarist Russia collapsed, the Armenians declared their independence in the spring of 1918, but this was all but ignored by the great powers.

Now, the Armenians were in Paris hoping to gain recognition of their independence, acquire compensation and territory for their losses, and gain the support of the victorious powers. The territory they asked for — which would come from Turkey, Persia, and other neighbors — was extensive and would contain many Muslims. Their largest claim was to the West, at Turkey's expense. The Armenians foresaw a Greater Armenia that stretched from their homeland in the Caucasus all the way to the Mediterranean coast. This was justified, in their view, by the Sykes-Picot Agreement which had promised Armenia an undefined portion of Turkish territory.

The Armenians also indicated that they would welcome a benevolent mandate for a brief period of time until they were capable of managing their own affairs. It was well-known that Armenia had been badly neglected by the Czarist government and its infrastructure was still quite primitive.

The idea of a mandate for Armenia was not new. It had been discussed for months. The thinking in Paris, fostered by both Britain and France, was that a mandate might be given to the Italians because the British and French were conspiring to keep the Italians out of the newly-won Arab lands to the South, but in Armenia, the Italians could be useful. There was also thinking that the Americans — the rich Americans — might take the Armenian mandate. In America several organizations, were collecting relief funds for the Armenians and there was a sizeable ethnic Armenian-American population that, it was generally believed, would be ever-grateful to the political party that helped bring about a truly independent Armenia.

From the British point of view, they wanted to see a strong Armenia to serve as a buffer state between the Bolsheviks and their interests in Mesopotamia and

India. The British might have taken the mandate if it were not the fact that their resources in the Middle East were already stretched to the limit. The British had good reason to fear for India. It was well known that the Bolsheviks hoped to find fertile ground in the colonial world for communism and Trotsky once said, "The road to London and Paris lies through Calcutta."

The Armenians, themselves, favored the idea of an American mandate and carried on an active campaign in Paris to bring it about. Wilson knew this and had expressed sympathies for the Armenians but had not formally committed himself one way or the other.

Oil was another factor. To the east of Armenia lay the rich oil fields of Baku, Azerbaijan, on the western coast of the Caspian Sea, and all of the Western world wanted to see that oil pass through friendly lands to the Armenian seaport of Batum on the eastern coast of the Black Sea and on to European markets.

THEN THERE WERE THE IRISH-AMERICANS

To most Irish-Americans, the events in Paris were secondary to those going on in Ireland. Since the draft of the League of Nations Covenant made no specific mention of Ireland, the question naturally arose, "Where does Wilson stand on Ireland?" As we have seen, Wilson tried to pass the question off as an internal matter within the British Empire but with little success.

During the first week in March, Wilson made a political sojourn to New York City, a stronghold of Irish-Americans, and on the agenda was a meeting with a group of Irish-Americans who called themselves "The Committee for Irish Independence." Wilson did not look forward to the meeting, but Irish Americans usually voted Democrat and Wilson was obliged to satisfy that constituency. Irish-Americans had opposed Wilson's call to enter the war in 1917 and, during the war, had demonstrated anti-British — and therefore pro-German — attitudes. Now, this committee, and others, were rabble-rousing the Irish-American community on Ireland's behalf and to the detriment of Britain. Also, some Congressmen and some prominent leaders of the Catholic Church were listening to their complaints. It must be remembered that, with regard to the latter, Wilson was a strong Presbyterian.

The meeting, which took place at the Metropolitan Opera House, was cordial but inconclusive. Afterward, Wilson expressed his true feelings toward the Irish-Americans by telling an aide that he was sorely tempted to tell the Irish-Americans "to go to hell."

Back in Washington, Congress was scheduled to recess on March 5 and the day before, during a late night session, Senator Lodge pulled a surprise maneuver by circulating a "round robin" (a letter of protest with the signatures thereon arranged in a circle so that no one individual headed the list). It called for a rejection of the League of Nations as currently formulated and that the creation of the organization be postponed and considered separately after a peace treaty with Germany had been created and signed. Thirty-nine of the ninety-six senators signed it; fifty-seven did not. This unofficial vote indicated that Wilson had substantial opposition in the Senate, because, as dictated by the the US Constitution, it required a two-thirds majority, or 64 votes, to ratify the treaty.

On March 5, Congress adjourned, Wilson signed a number of bills into law including a tax increase on corporations and people with large incomes, and then left again for Paris.

INTO THE AIR

The war brought about great advancements in aviation and had glamorized the airplane and made idols of some air aces: the Red Baron, Captain Eddie Richenbacher, Billie Mitchell, Herman Goering, Fiorello LaGuardia, and others.

The war also brought about great advancements in the mass production of aircraft. Germany, for example, built some 44,000 aircraft and 46,000 aircraft engines during the war in 35 aircraft plants and 26 engine plants.

During May 1918, while the war was still in progress, the US inaugurated the first air mail service in the country between New York City and Washington, DC. The pilots navigated their ways back and forth by following the railroad tracks.

In Britain, on March 1, 1919, the British government's newly-formed "Department of Civil Aviation" inaugurated its first regularly scheduled flight from Folkstone, England, to Cologne, Germany. Its purpose was to hasten the delivery of mail to the British occupation forces in the Rhineland. Soon afterwards, a new cabinet post was established by Lloyd George, "The Ministry of Transportation" and the Department of Civil Aviation became a part of it. Young Winston Churchill became its Minister.

Two days later, the Americans and Canadians created the first international mail service in North America with scheduled flights between Seattle, Washington, and Victoria British Columbia. The plans were built locally by the Boeing Aircraft Company of Seattle.

On March 4, 1919, the Italians began scheduled air service between Rome and Naples by dirigible.

The transportation of people by air was still in its infancy and, at times, risky, but there were those who were willing to take the risks. On one occasion in early 1919, A. T. Wilson, Britain's acting Civil Commissioner in Baghdad needed to rush to Paris and decided to fly. After four forced landings and utilizing two airplanes, he arrived in Paris shaken but intact.

There was another new phenomenon in the sky, "barnstorming." Surplus military aircraft were now on the market and cheap. Former military pilots and other adventurous souls, some of them women, saw that profits were to be made by demonstrating these new and fascinating machines to the public. They sharpened their skills and flew their planes doing daring and acrobatic aerial maneuvers, parachute jumps, and other awe-inspiring feats at fairs, on national holidays or anywhere an audience could be had. They also offered rides for those willing to pay. Flying was considered romantic by many and some of the pilots gained celebrity status. Also, there were popular songs written about flying.

In various parts of the world, air schools were popping up and airplane-to-airplane and airplane-to-automobile racing appeared. Needless to say, military aircraft was now an important weapon in every nation's arsenal as demonstrated by the events of the Great War. Paris and other cities had been bombed, and targets behind the lines, out of range of artillery, were hit. Aerial surveillance became important, the rapid transport of important people, orders and supplies was facilitated, submarines were located, and survivors at sea were found and rescued and on and on... The Allies also had airplanes under development that could reach Berlin, but the war ended before they were put into service. Berlin was never bombed.

As Air Minister, Winston Churchill saw the use of air power in controlling Britain's sprawling empire. In the latter case, he promoted the idea that remote and trouble spots could be quickly examined and reached and rebellious tribes and clans could be quickly attacked or otherwise intimidated by swooping aircraft, bombs, machine guns, and poison gas. Also, a tribe's horses and camels could be driven into a stampede if conditions were right.

GERMANY STARVING

The scarcity of food in Germany was still a pressing problem. Much of the entire blame for this fell squarely on the British naval blockade. And, it was winter, and fuel and, in some cases, housing, were in short supply. The German people were starving and freezing.

Hoover's food relief program was underway and helping to prevent the disaster from getting worse, but it was still not enough to feed all the people who were suffering. Hoover's agency admitted their own deficiencies and warned that some 200 million people throughout Europe were beyond their reach.

Ironically, food was readily available in other parts of the world and ships could be found to carry it to Europe. The US, Canada, Australia, New Zealand, and some of the South American countries — all traditional food exporters — were ready and willing to do business. But, politics and money problems got in the way. While much of the food was paid for by sympathetic nations and organizations, not all of it was. Germany was unable to buy large quantities of food because her credit was almost non-existent and she would have to pay with gold. The French, however, had laid claim to Germany's gold to pay reparations.

There were also those European businessmen who resented Hoover's efforts because they believed he was opening the door for the Americans to intrude into European markets that had traditionally been theirs. The peacemakers in Paris could do little so the matter rested and festered.

In the US, the attitude of helping Europe was mixed. In eastern Europe the situation was so muddled that the American public had trouble telling the good guys from the bad guys. Then too, hatred toward the Germans still lingered as a result of the powerful anti-German propaganda campaign fostered by the government during the war.

There were those in the US government and the private sector that wanted to help, but there were also a growing number of individuals who said that America had done enough to solve Europe's problems and should do no more. Isolationism was beginning to rise in America in several forms.

There were other agencies operating in Europe to help ease the food crisis, but Hoover's was by far the largest and most effective. Hoover's organization had offices in 32 countries, conducted soup kitchens, and fed millions of children daily. His organization had its own telegraph service, controlled some railways, supervised some mines (Hoover was a mining engineer), fought lice, and created special bathing facilities to maintain basic hygiene. Some of his operations were run by American soldiers. Travelers were closely watched and those who did not have "de-loused" certificates were seized and disinfected to prevent the spread of disease.

"LEBENSRAUM"

The hardships suffered by the German people during these times had a profound effect on German postwar thinking. Fundamentally, it was based on the belief that if Germany had had more land, it could have fed itself. Hitler and the Nazis seized upon this issue and made it a major part of their political rhetoric. They called it "Lebensraum" (living room) — that is, the acquisition of vast areas of land to make Germany self-sufficient in food and other essentials of life. This land, of course, could only come at the expense of Poland, Russia, and other eastern European nations, and would have to be taken by force.

In January 1933, in the depth of the Depression which had laid the Germans low for a second time, the concept of Lebensraum was very appealing to the German voters. It was a significant factor in the Nazis winning the election of November 1932 which led to Hitler's being installed as Chancellor on January 30, 1933.

And again, when Germany invaded the Soviet Union in June 1941, many Germans believed that the dream of Lebensraum was close at hand and that Hitler was the great savior who had brought it about.

TWO MORE PLEBISCITES

In Paris, during Wilson's absence, it was decided that Plebiscites should be conducted in two more areas. They were the three small enclaves along the Belgian/German border and in Schleswig-Holstein, the border area between German and Denmark where the population was split between Germans and Danes. Schleswig-Holstein had been forcibly incorporated into Bismarck's Germany in the 1800s and many of the residents, primarily the Danes, were angry that Germany had dragged them into the Great War.

With regard to Belgium, the three enclaves had long been disputed between Germany and Belgium and it now was Belgium's turn to prevail.

THE ZIONISTS ARE HEARD

Now, the Zionists got their time in the spotlight in Paris. Chaim Weizmann, the leading Zionist in Europe, appeared with his advisors before the Supreme Council. The subject, as all knew, was the prospect of a Jewish homeland in Palestine. It was not a unified group of men who addressed the Council this day. Two of Weizmann's advisors were French Zionists, forced upon him by the French government, and some of the members believed that the Zionists should take a go-slow approach to sending Jews to Palestine. Weizmann, on the other hand, wanted rapid and massive immigration into Palestine. Also, there were divisions within the Zionist organization as to which political faction should rule in the new homeland.

Nevertheless, they were all unified in the effort to make Palestine, or a major part of it, a Jewish homeland. That word "homeland" was generally used, but virtually everyone understood that it referred to a temporary situation and that a fully independent Jewish state was the ultimate goal.

Weizmann's argument centered upon the generally accepted fact that Palestine, whose borders had not yet been defined, was an empty and undeveloped land. In this respect, he was supported by a somewhat unreliable statistic that counted the population of Palestine at only 700,000 people — some of them Jews. Even if that statistic was too low and there were twice or three times as many people, it would still indicate that Palestine was a sparsely settled land. In this respect, there was a popular Zionist saying at the time, "The land without people for the people without land."

The Zionists had prepared a formal document entitled "Zionist Organization Statement on Palestine" dated February 3, 1919, that stated their position. And it was understood by all at the meeting that whoever resided in Palestine would have to have a mandatory power for some time to come. Here, the French stooges argued for a French mandate stressing that the French had had claims on the Holy Land since the time of the Crusades.

The British, however, had other thoughts. They wanted a friendly, cooperative, and relatively weak political entity on the eastern flank of the Suez Canal and a reliable and capable party to control Haifa, the terminus of the proposed oil pipeland from the Persian Gulf area. Furthermore, the British Army was occupying Palestine which gave Britain an advantage over all others.

The Organization Statement defined what the Zioinsts saw as the boundaries of the new Jewish Homeland. The northern boundary would include the southern portion of The Lebanon just south of the Litani River and including the seaport of Tyre, then run eastward, crossing the Jordan River, and turning south to include all of the arible land east of the Jordan. That eastern boundary would then run south of the Gulf of Aqaba parallelling, but not including, the Hijaz Railroad, the primary route for devout Muslims making their Haj to Mecca. The Organization Statement said, however, that the Zionists should have "free access" to the Railroad because on the Gulf of Aqaba, there would be enough coastline for the Zionists to build a seaport and a rail spur was needed to link up that seaport with the rest of Jewish Palestine. The southern border of Jewish Palestine would be the currently recognized border between Palestine and Egypt. The Zionists promised that Muslims living within their domain would he treated fairly and honorably. The only area of Palestine that would be totally in Arab hands would be the vast, and as yet undefined, desert area east of the railroad.

As for Jewish immigration into Palestine, the Statement recognized that the Homeland would not be large enough to accomodate a majority of the world's Jews, but that "Palestine can be made now, as it was in ancient times, the home of a prosperous population many times as numerous as that which now inhabits it." The Statement went on "... the land itself needs redemption. Much of it is left desolate... The Jews have adopted modern scientific methods and have shown themselves to be capable agriclturalists."

And the Statement continued "... the Jews of the world will make every effort to provide the vast sums of money that will be needed." The Statement also called for a Jewish university to be built in Jerusalem.

As for a mandate power, the Statement declared, "We ask that Great Britian shall act as Manditory to the League of Nations for Palestine...(because of the) peculiar relationship of England to the Jewish Palestinian problem. The return of the Jews to Zion has not only been a remarkable feature in English literature, but in the domain of statecraft it has played its part, beginning with the readmision of the Jews under Cromwell." The Homeland was referred to in the Statement as a "Jewish Commonwealth," a hint that the incorporation of a Jewish-controlled Palestine into the British Commonwealth of nations might be an option.

As for land, the Statement declared "... the Mandatory Power shall appoint a Commission with power to make a survey of the land and to schedule all lands that may be made available for close settlement, intensive cultivation, and public use... To propose measures for determining and registering titles of ownership of land... To propose measures for... compulsory purchase at a fair pre-war price and, further by making available all waste lands unoccupied and inadequately cultivated lands or land without legal owners and state lands... To propose measures whereby the Jewish Council may take over all lands available for close settlement and intensive cultivation...(and) to acquire and hold real estate."

AROUND THE WORLD

Early March, 1919, a cruel and powerful suppression of Korean resistance to Japanese rule began in Korea.

On March 1, the peace delegates at Paris recognized the new state of Finland as an independent nation. The Finns had declared their independence from Czarist Russia in 1918 and then became caught up in a civil war between communists and non-communist factions within their own country. The non-communists won the battle and Finland was now relatively stable and was invited to the peace table in Paris.

On March 2, 1919, the Bolsheviks created the "Communist Internationale" ("Comintern") at a convention in Moscow. Delegations from 35 nations were in attendance. Only five were from outside Russia and were made up mostly of emigres from those lands who had sought refuge in the newly-emerging communist state. Nevertheless, the creation of the Comintern was a bold challenge to the entire world in that it was now unmistakable that the Bolsheviks intended to export their revolution in an organized and aggressive manner. The constitution of the Comintern called for the spreading of communism "... by all available means, including force, the overthrow of the international bourgeoisie and the creation of an international Soviet as a transition stage to the complete abolition of the state."

Grigori Zinoviev became the Comintern's first president and Karl Radek, Lenin's man in Germany during the Sparticus Revolt, became the organization's Secretary. Both were Jews which added considerably to the world's growing anti-semitism.

A short time later, the Comintern commenced sending money and agents to communist organizations in Germany, Hungary, Britain, Bavaria, and other countries.

THE END OF THE COMINTERN

During World War II, during May 1943, with the Soviet Union in great crisis and desperately in need of aid from the Western Allies and a second front, Stalin terminated the Comintern as a goodwill gesture toward the West.

HEEDING THE CALL OF THE COMINTERN

In Germany, the labor scene was still unstable and dangerous and gave the leftist union leaders ample cause to take matters into their own hands. In January, unemployment in Germany was recorded as 180,000. In February, it rose to 250,000 and by March it reached 560,000.

On March 3, 1919, leftist unions in Berlin, heeding the call from Moscow, began another massive general strike within the city, their second in three months. It soon became violent as the strikers took over government offices and other elements of the city's infrastructure. Once again, the two million people of the city found themselves without utilities, transportation, or police protection.

From Weimar — safe and peaceful Weimar — the call went out again to the Free Corps to return to Berlin. The Free Corps, which were now better equipped and better organized, responded in large numbers. The equivalent of two full army division converged on the city with tanks, armored cars, artillery, flamethrowers, and, for the first time, air support. Two days of intense fighting erupted within the city and its surrounding areas, followed by several more days of mopping up as the powerful Free Corps broke the strike

and disbursed the strikers. By March 11, order had been restored in the city and some 600 Reds had been killed, including their leader, Leo Jogiches. Jogiches had been captured, beaten, and shot to death in the Alexanderplatz police headquarters. Jogiches' position was quickly filled by Paul Levi who vowed to fight on.

Since the creation of the German Communist Party in Berlin in December 1918, the Berlin communists had had three leaderships: Karl Liebknecht and Rosa Luxemburg serving as joint leaders, Leo Jogiches, and now Levi. Three of the four were Jews — Liebknecht was a Gentile — and the Free Corps had had to liberate Berlin twice. In Weimar, the leaders of the German government knew that their decision to flee Berliln had been a wise one.

BAVARIA SEEKS AN ALLIANCE

On March 3, the same day the communist-inspired strikes began in Berlin, the communist government of Bavaria informed the Soviets, through the Comintern, that it wanted to discuss a political, and possibly a military alliance, with Moscow. This would mean that Bavaria would likely secede from the German Federation and claim its independence.

THE FREE CORPS GROW

Throughout Germany, the Free Corps were expanding. That expansion was attained, in part, by the creation of auxiliary units known as "Einwohner Wehr" (Resident Defense Units). These were small reserve units that could be called upon when needed, usually in their own community. The Free Corps, however, were gaining an unsavory reputation and it was rumored that they were acting beyond the law and had even formed secret assassination squads. The image that they were, in fact, little more than right-wing thugs was growing. But, then too, many saw the communists as left-wing thugs. This brought forward the frightening prospect that the German people might be polarizing into class warfare.

In Weimar, the German government took steps to correct this. On March 6, 1919, the National Assembly, after much acrimonious debate, passed a law titled "Law for the Creation of a Provisional Reichswehr (army)." The law dissolved the old German Imperial Army and placed the command of the new army directly under the control of the German President, Ebert. Enlistment was voluntary for six or more years and the promotion of enlisted men to officers would be given strong consideration. General Hans von Seeckt, an experienced and very capable commander, was made Army Chief of Staff of the Reichswehr.

The Free Corps, estimated to be some 400,000-strong, would remain an unofficial addendum to the army but would be reduced to 200,000 members in order to get rid of many of the trouble-makers and to make the orgnization more manageable. The new Free Corps would be organizes into 20 brigades and distributed across Germany's seven military districts.

Some of the Freecorpsmen refused to join the Reichswehr and vowed to continue as — for want of a better word — mercenaries. Seeckt was unable to prevent this because there were no laws on the German books to do otherwise. Also, within the Reichswehr, there was some friction between former Free Corps officers and officers from the old Imperial Army. This friction would continue throughout the life of the Weimar Government and only serve to benefit the Allies.

WILSON RETURNS TO PARIS

On March 5, Wilson, his wife, and his doctor, left for Paris. This was not a happy occasion because Wilson had little in the way of domestic political support to take with him.

On March 6, 1919, while Wilson was on the high seas, the Council members in Paris announced that Geneva, Switzerland, would become the home of the League of Nations.

That same day, good news arrived from Siberia. Admiral Aleksandr Kolchak, commander of the Russian White forces there, launched a full-scale attack against the 2nd and 5th Red Armies, splitting them in two. Kolchak was now better armed than ever before with British and American arms shipped to him via the Trans-Siberian Railroad and the Pacific seaport of Vladivostok.

Within a week, Kolchak's forces crossed the Ural Mountains into European Russia and captured the important city of Ufa. Kolchak, however, was still 750 miles east of Moscow and had a difficult-to-defend 700 mile-long front. Nevertheless, Kolchak's victory raised hopes throughout the West that the Bolsheviks might yet be defeated.

On March 7, 1919, Col. House told Lloyd George that it looked very likely that the US would accept a mandate over Armenia and the borders of the new state of Czechoslovakia were approved. Since Czechoslovakia would acquire people and citizens from Germany, Hungary, and Austria, the Czechs had agreed to offer certain guarantees to these minorities and allow them to have representatives in the Czech government in Prague. Many individuals from the respective minorities were not happy with being incorporated into Czechoslovakia, but this discontent was muted because the alternative was to remain a part of Germany, Hungary, or Austria, all of which were unstable and threatened with revolution. The Czechs, however, would be true to their word and would allow the minorities to have a certain degree of automomy and their own representatives in the government.

On March 11, 1919, the Supreme Council in Paris voted to reduce the German Navy to 15,000 men. It was also agreed that the new German Army, the Reichswehr as the Germans now called it, would be only 100,000 strong. Two days later the British announced that they favored the sale of Germany submarines with the proceeds being distributed among the Allies.

On March 12, the desperate food shortage in Germany could no longer be ignored, and the Supreme Council agreed to allow some food to be supplied to the German people but that the German must pay for the food.

In Vienna, Austria, the Austrian legislature passed a new consitution and, at the same time, voted to seek union with Germany. In Munich, Corporal Hitler, still an Austrian citizen, was elated.

On March 13, 1919, Wilson's ship docked at Brest and he and his party boarded the train for Paris. This time, there was no cheering crowd with flags and banners.

CHAPTER 7
PARIS-USA-EGYPT-HUNGARY-
MIDDLE EAST

||||||||||||||||||||||||||||||||||||||||||||||||||||||||||||||||||||||||||||||||||||||||||||||||||||||||||||||||||||

WILSON IN PARIS THE SECOND TIME

Wilson and his party arrived in Paris on March 14, 1919, where a rented house awaited him. He would no longer reside in a hotel. Across the street was another rented house occupied by Lloyd George. Wilson soon became convinced that the French staff in his house were all spies.

His arrival was in deep contrast to that in December 1918 when he was greeted by throngs at the railroad station and cheering crowds along his way into Paris. This time, there were no great crowds and only a small French reception committee met him at the station.

By the time he arrived in Paris, Wilson had a heavy burden on his mind. His trusted advisor, Col. House, had met him at Brest and traveled with him to Paris giving him a detailed, but very discouraging, report on events in Paris during his absence. Most of the decisions that had been made by the Supreme Council met with Wilson's disapproval and Wilson tended to blame House. Reports from others tended to convince Wilson that House had been seduced by Clemenceau with flattery and occasional hugs.

Most damaging of all for Wilson was that he sensed that there was an effort afoot to delay the creation of, or possibly eliminate, the League of Nations.

Another issue was that Wilson was very disappointed that the size of the future German Army be set, without his consent, at 100,000 men. In time, however, he reluctantly agreed to it.

This was the beginning of the end of the close relationship between Wilson and House. The President is reported to have said to his wife, "House had given away everything I had won before I left."

Another problem that greeted the President was a memorandum from Marshall Foch repeating his demands that the peace treaty must specify heavy, but as yet undefined, reparations from Germany and that the Allies should occupy the Rhineland for a long period of time or, perhaps, set up the Rhineland as an independent buffer state between France and Germany.

Furthermore, there were renewed demands from the French that the German merchant fleet be turned over to them as partial payment for reparations.

These were old issues between the French and the Americans, but now they had resurfaced with a vengeance.

There was some positive news, however. In Germany, the communist regime in the state of Saxony had been overthrown and the state had come back under the control of the Social Democrats.

FAMILIARITY

By now, the Council members knew each other very well. At various times, they laughed and told jokes, discussed mundane issues, negotiated in all seriousness, got angry, shouted at each other and, on a few occasions, stormed out of the room. If they ever came to blows, it was not recorded, although it was reported that, at one point, Clemenceau challenged Lloyd George to a duel.

They would frequently gather in one of several relatively small rooms, at several locations, and sat in a circle with a few aides at their sides. Each had a small table. If the room had a fireplace, they would sit in a semi-circle in front of the fireplace and if it was a cold day, there would be a fire. Usually Wilson and Lloyd George would sit next to each other. They had a lot in common. They could converse without the benefit of a translator, they were both on the political left of center, and Wilson tended to bypass Lansing and Lloyd George tended to bypass Balfour. They had both won power due to splits in their political opposition, both entered the war reluctantly, and both had had problems with pacifists and anti-war supporters at home.

Balfour, who had his differences with just about everyone, was reported to have called Lloyd George, Clemenceau, and Wilson "Those three all-powerful, all-ignorant men..."

Orlando and the Japanese, when they were there, would usually sit next to each other. They had little in common. If the Council members sat in a semi-circle in front of a fireplace, Clemenceau would always be in the center. Otherwise, he floated around.

Many people witnessed their interactions and later wrote about them or made verbal comments. Clemenceau would often slouch in his chair and looked up at the ceiling with a bored expression. Some thought he dawdled and procrastinated. Wilson fidgeted in his chair and got up from time-to-time to stretch his legs. Lloyd George chatted in loud undertones with his aides and made jokes and witty comments.

At 5 P.M. they all had tea.

Wilson and Lloyd George spoke only English, while Clemenceau spoke French and English, but preferred to speak in French. Orlando spoke Italian and French, and the Japanese spoke only Japanese and had to rely totally on interpreters. When the conversation was in English, as it was most of the time, Orlando had to rely on an interpreter. This is significant in that, because of the language barrier, Orlando never had direct conversation with Wilson and/or Lloyd George and the Japanese never had direct conversations with anyone.

Clemenceau was described by John Maynard Keynes as "by far the most eminent member of the Council" and was also the oldest member at 78. He always wore white or gray gloves to cover a severe case of eczema on his hands. He coughed a lot and, according to Keynes, would "close his eyes with a air of fatigue when French interests were no longer involved in the discussion."

Keynes also noted that Clemenceau "spoke seldom" but when he did, it was "a short sentence, decisive or cynical (and) generally sufficient." When a question was posed to him, Clemenceau would often defer it to his aides whom he would allow to talk on endlessly.

Lloyd George was fifty-five years old, the youngest of the members and looked it. He was described as having baby blue eyes, a youthful exuberance, an alert mind, and a charming personality. He was a Welshman and had been a small town cobbler and a lay preacher but was now a liberal-turned-more-conservative politician and was often in the middle ground of negotiations between Clemenceau and Wilson. For this, he gained the title "the Negotiator." Lloyd George was, at times, late for their meetings and ill-prepared. He was also quicker then the others to change his position and tended to shift from one position to another quite easily. One observer labeled him "the Welsh chameleon." Lloyd George was also small in stature and was sometimes called "The Little Man" behind his back. Wilson stood half-a-head taller than his three European compatriots and a full head taller than the Japanese. This gave Wilson an aura of dominance.

It became noticeable that Lloyd George tended to back away from the fire-and-brimstone speeches he had made in December 1918 when he was running for re-election and seeking a mandate from the British people. He no longer spoke of hanging the Kaiser, making Germany pay outrageous reparations, and totally eliminating the German Navy so that Britain would remain the master of the seas. Lloyd George was also the least well-informed member of the group. On one occasion he said, "Who are the Slovaks?" — a people whose fate he was to take part in deciding. He made the mistake another time thinking that Kharkov, a large city in the Ukraine, was a Russian General. He also demonstrated that his knowledge of India, the jewel of the British Empire, was weak, and made no attempt to conceal the fact that he considered the Indians an inferior race. Lloyd George also gave indications that he would favor the US, in cooperation with the British Empire, becoming the world's future police force. Wilson and Lloyd George often dined together.

"The Crusader," that's what some people at the peace conference called Wilson because of his lofty idealism and boundless hope that a whole new world could be created by himself and his companions. He referred to his religious convictions often enough for the others to recognized, that they were a driving force in his decision-making. On one occasion Wilson said, "I believe in Divine Providence. If I did not, I would go crazy." And Wilson was poorly informed, to some degree, on such issues as European politics, age-old national ambitions and rivalries.

Wilson's mind lacked swiftness and he demonstrated, early on, his stubbornness and lack of adaptability on some major issues and even on some minor points. Col. House noticed this trait and wrote in his diary that his boss had "... a one-track mind and was sometimes inconsistent and clumsy in negotiations."

Lansing reported that Wilson had "... a sort of little chuckle or half-laugh which frequently interrupted his flow of language... It sounded almost apologetic." Lansing, General Bliss, and William Allen White, a noted journalist and member of the American delegation, were often ignored by Wilson. Behind their backs, the other members of the American staff called them "The Lesser Three."

John Maynard Keynes, who wrote prolifically of the peace conference, admired Wilson and his Fourteen Points, but he was quite critical of Wilson's negotiating skills. Keynes would write of Wilson: "He could take the high line, he could practice obstinacy; he could write Notes from Sinai or Olympus...," and " the President's slowness... was noteworthy," and "... ill-informed as to European conditions" and "... (Wilson was) liable, therefore, to defeat by the mere swiftness, apprehension, and agility of a Lloyd George," and "There can seldom have been a statesman of the first rank more incompetent than the President in the abilities of the council chamber," and "The President looked wiser when he was seated."

Wilson's health was a factor. At times, he looked pale and tired. He developed a nervous twitch on the left side of his face and, sometimes, and in the midst of a conversation, his left eye would rotate upward. Ike Hoover, the White House usher that served as Wilson's valet in Paris, reported that the President would often make decisions while lying in bed.

In public, Clemenceau and Lloyd George carried walking sticks but Wilson did not. All three wore top hats and Wilson sometimes wore gloves.

It was reported that, outside the Council room, Wilson could be quite charming and witty. He was at ease with women, playful at times, told folksy stories, loved gadgets and movies, made witticisms in Scottish, Irish and Southern Black accents and, on occasion, had a shot or two of whiskey at social gatherings.

Then there was Orlando — poor Orlando. He was handicapped by the language barrier and, as a result, he did not speak often.

Orlando was a short, square Sicilian, an eminent lawyer, a good orator, a man of genuine integrity, given to gesturing, and genuinely well-liked by the others. If it were not for Fiume and the 1915 Treaty of London, Orlando would have had a lot in common with Wilson. Lloyd George liked Orlando and said of him "... he had an attractive and amiable personality which made him an extremely pleasant man to do business with." Lloyd George, however, did not like Orlando's sidekick, Sonnino, saying "...Sonnino is hopeless." Apparently Orlando had his problems with Sonnino also, as the two could be heard at times arguing loudly in private.

Orlando was absolutely loyal to the Italian monarchy to the degree that some called him the King's "Flunky."

ORLANDO, THE SURVIVOR

Orlando, like Lloyd George, lived long enough to experience World War II. He was an opponent of Fascism and, in 1944, played a role in its demise and Mussolini's fall from power. By then, he was widely admired as an elder statement and, in the post-war years, served several terms in the Italian Senate. He died in 1952 at age 92.

Prince Kimmochi Saionji and his primary representative at the meetings, Baron Nobuaki Makino, were at so few meetings that opinions were not readily formed about them. They kept to themselves in Paris and were seldom seen in public — a trait common to Japanese politicians at the time. All agreed, however, that they were extremely polite. Col. House said of them that they were "silent, unemotional, watchful." Some of the American delegates called Saionji and Makino "the two Mikados."

Clemenceau, not surprisingly, was the most proficient at backbiting and name-calling. When it came to spiritual matters, this old mischief-maker was somewhere between non-religious and anti-religious and seemed to delight in criticizing Wilson, the son and grandson of Presbyterian ministers, in religious terms. At various times he said of Wilson, "We are going to have troubles with this Presbyterian," and, "How can I talk to a fellow who thinks himself the first man in 2000 years to know anything about peace on earth?" and, "Mr. Wilson bores me with his Fourteen Points. Why, God Almighty has only ten," and "Lloyd George believes himself to be Napoleon, but President Wilson believes himself to be Jesus Christ." Lloyd George picked up on this and once said, "Well, it was the best I could do, seated as I was between Jesus Christ and Napoleon Bonaparte." At another time Clemenceau complained that Wilson talked like Jesus Christ but acted like Lloyd George. Clemenceau liked Col. House and said to him on one occasion "... you are practical, I understand you but talking to Wilson is something like talking to Jesus Christ." Clemenceau laid another barb on Wilson one time saying, "He believed you could do everything by formulas and his Fourteen Points... the fourteen commandments of the most empty theory." In a stressful discussion on punishing Germany, Wilson said "Pray, Monsieur Clemenceau, have you ever been to Germany?" The Tiger's reply was, "No, sir! But twice in my lifetime, the Germans have been to France."

Keynes wrote of the differences between Wilson and Clemenceau saying, "Two rival schemes for the future policy of the world took the field — The Fourteen Points of the President and the Carthaginian Peace of M. Clemenceau."

Clemenceau even attacked his own. French President Raymond Poincare was one of his favored targets. Poincare was very Catholic and Clemenceau saw him as something of a lackey of the Church. They had had their differences in the past and the peace conference did not change

things. Clemenceau said of Poincare, "There are only two perfectly useless things in the world. One is the appendix and the other is Poincare." Poincare wrote in his diary that Clemenceau was a "madman, old moronic, vain man." When it came to Germany, however, Clemenceau and Poincare found common ground — they both hated the Germans.

And on America, Clemenceau said, "America is the only nation in history which miraculously has gone directly from barbarism to degeneration without the usual interval of civilization." Lloyd George also made uncomplimentary remarks about Wilson's religious beliefs and said of him that he had come to Europe to rescue the heathen Europeans with his "little sermonettes." Wilson used the phrase, "Well, my friends..," repeatedly and it became a private joke that when he used it, another of his sermonettes was coming. Wilson used the phrase so often that Clemenceau interrupted him on one occasion saying, "Mon Dieu! Don't use that again!"

The press was having a field day. There was plenty of gossip to write about and much of it was juicy. The French press became quite harsh on Wilson as his and Clemenceau's differences surfaced, and the French press seemed to delight in reporting criticisms of Wilson coming from his opponents in America, mostly, of course, from the Republicans.

The Italian press was also critical of Wilsons and the Japanese press occasionally attacked him.

In Britain, the press there attacked both Lloyd George and Wilson. One prominent journalist called Lloyd George "Wilson's puppy dog." Another said of Wilson, "He was the Messiah of the New Age, and his crucifixion was yet to come."

Each man had his own list of pet peeves which surfaced at times. Wilson attacked big banks, Lloyd George attacked landowners and the aristocracy, and Clemenceau attacked the church — any church.

In countries where tabloid newspapers were tolerated, they gave out fantastic reports — the peace conference was crashing — the League of Nations was dead — fist fights in the council chamber.

At Weimar, the German Foreign Ministry read the Allied newspapers carefully looking for divisions in the alliance. The German newspapers, on the other hand, followed only lightly the goings on in Paris. They were very painful for the German people to read.

IN SECRECY

The goings on in the council chamber in Paris were not the kind of events the council members wanted released to the media. Therefore, the details of the meetings were kept secret — or at least, as secret as possible. As a result, the news media felt starved of reliable information and were forced to rely on rumors, leaks, and, at times, pure fiction.

This, of course, was a direct violation of the first of Wilson's Fourteen Points: *"Open covenants of peace, openly arrived at..."*

EGYPT

During the second week in March, serious troubles erupted in Egypt, that land of magnificent ancient history and the very modern and much-needed Suez Canal.

At the beginning of the Great War, in 1914, Egypt was a part of the Ottoman Empire. Ottoman control was very weak and the British, who had firm control of the Suez Canal, quickly gained control over all of the country. They then proclaimed Egypt a protectorate to justify their sending troops into the country to protect it and the Canal. They also declared martial law in the country. As a protectorate, Egypt retained its own gov-

ernment and Sultan, and according to the accepted standard for protectorates would, one day, be granted its independence. But, under martial law the government and Sultan were virtually powerless. From the start, the British takeover was very much resented by the Egyptian people and now, with peace, they had begun demonstrating and speaking out.

One of the issues that complicated the relationship between the British and Egyptians was that the Sultan had proclaimed himself a "Caliph," a religious leader who speaks for all of Islam. This put the British in the delegate position of having to deal with an Islamic holy man as well as a head of state.

During the war, Egypt experienced a number of anti-British demonstrations, strikes, and protests and the Egyptian nationalist took full advantage of this. They organized into a fairly-well unified political party, the Wafd Party, under a popular leader, Saad Zaghlul. The primary aim of the Wafdists was to accomplish an early withdrawal of the British and early independence for Egypt. It was generally understood in Britain, and many other parts of the world, that when Egyptian independence eventually came, the British would still retain control of the Suez Canal because it was such a vital communication, economic, and military link within the huge British Empire. An example of what the future status of the Canal might be had been set by the Americans and the manner in which they had kept control of the Panama Canal. This understanding, however, was not necessarily shared by the Egyptians.

In January 1919, the Egyptian premier, Husayn Rushdi, formed a delegation he sent to Paris to meet with the British and discuss the independence and future of Egypt. Egypt had not declared war on the Central Powers but had contributed significantly to the Allied cause — often in the form of labor conscription and materials requisitioning. Now, the Egyptians believed they were due some rewards. The British, however, refused to meet with the delegation. Instead the British reconfirmed, as they had done before, that Egyptian independence was still forthcoming but that a time frame had not yet been set. This failure to open talks with the British forced the resignation of Rushdi, but the Sultan refused to accept his resignation as an affront to the British, so Rushdi stayed on as premier.

Demonstrations continued in Egypt, usually orchestrated by the Wafdists, and in early March these troubles suddenly escalated. The British now accused the Wafdists of having "Bolshevik tendencies" and on March 9, 1919, took action. They arrested Zaghlul and three other Wafd Party leaders and announced that they would be deported to Malta. The next day, the demonstrations escalated further and turned violent to the point where the British were hard pressed to maintain order. Clearly, an insurrection was in the offing. Out of desperation, the British dispatched General Sir Edmund Allenby, the hero of the British victories in the Middle East, to Egypt to take control of the situation. This gave credibility to the belief that the British would seek a military solution. Allenby was able to restore a semblance of order, but tensions were extremely high.

This was where the matter rested when the Supreme Council resumed it regular meetings in Paris. Eventually, the unrest in Egypt would re-ignite.

THE AMERICAN LEGION

There were many American Doughboys in France now with time on their hands waiting to be shipped home. Most of them were proud of what they had accomplished and wanted to keep alive the spirit and camaraderie they had gained. This resulted in the creating of a national veterans organization, "The American Legion," which eventually grew to be the largest veterans' organization in America.

"HOW YA GONNA KEEP 'EM DOWN ON THE FARM...

... after they've seen Paree?
How ya gonna keep 'em away from
    Broadway,
Jazzin' around, painting the town... ?"

It was spring in Paris. The magnolia and chestnut trees were blooming, there were children in the park, and hormones were flowing.

Paris was full of American men who had been without women for a long time. The Doughboys, passing through, could count their celibacy in years, while most of the Americans at the peace conference could count theirs in months. The top officials, of course, did not have this problem. They had been allowed to bring their female companions with them at government expense. Wilson had brought his wife and Lloyd George brought his mistress, Frances Stevenson.

Fortunately for all, the ladies of Paris came to the rescue of the male visitors in their city. At the upper levels of Paris society, there were receptions, dances, operas, concerts in the park, and parties, including a new and very suave type of party called the "cocktail party." Those who gave these high-level parties actively sought out famous and interesting guests such as Sarah Bernhardt, Paderewski (who was always asked to play the piano), the Queen of Romania, Herbert Hoover, Nancy Astor, Ruth Draper, Arnold Toynbee, and many others.

In the mid-range of society, there were the quaint little cafes and restaurants, bars, cabarets, the Folies Bergere, the Moulon Rouge, and the flirtatious encounters along the Champs Elysees. At the lower end of society, the ladies there also offered their unique services.

As a result, many American men left Paris with fond memories and, to a large degree, a new outlook on life.

A group of New York songwriters, Walter Donelson, Joe Young, and Sam M. Lewis, recognized this situation and wrote a song about it and it became a big hit.

"THE LAST TIME I SAW PARIS"

The fond memories and love of Paris lingered on through the years. In 1940, when Paris was lost to the Germans, another pair of New York songwriters expressed the sadness the Americans felt in another song. Oscar Hammerstein II and Jerome Kern wrote:

" The last time I saw Paris,
her heart was warm and gay...
No matter what they do to her,
I'll remember her that way."

Cover of the sheet music for the famous Great War song "How 'Ya Gonna Keep 'em Down on the Farm After They've Seen Paree?"

AN INVITATION TO THE FREE CORPS FROM THE LATVIANS

In the spring of 1919, the newly-independent government of Latvia, headed by Karlis Ulmanis, invited German Free Corps leaders to create a Free Corps in Latvia to protect the country from threats created by local communists and from the Bolsheviks who were involved in the Russian Civil War on Latvia's eastern border. Each Free Corps volunteer was promised 90 acres of land and Latvian citizenship for his services. Thousands of Freecorpsmen responded and a large Free Corps unit was formed in Latvia commanded by German General Rudiger von der Goltz. Members of the "Goltz Free Corps" wore German uniforms and had adopted the swastika as their symbol, which was painted in white on the front of each man's helmet.

Skirmishes erupted almost immediately between the Freecorpsmen and local Reds, with the Freecorpsmen usually gaining the upper hand. And the activities of Goltz' Free Corps spilled over into Lithuania to the south.

By April, the Goltz Free Corps had cleared much of the rural areas of Latvia and some areas in Lithuania and stood at the gates of Riga, the Latvian capital. But, the Free Corps had, at times, run amok and attacked non-Reds and innocent Latvian citizens for whatever reasons they wished.

Ulmanis and his government were appalled at this and soon realized that inviting the Free Corps to Latvia had been a grave mistake. The prospect now arose that the Germans might try to establish Latvia and part of Lithuania as a secure base of operations from which to attack Poland or even march on Berlin and establish a rival regime there to that at Weimar.

German acquisition of the Baltic states was not new. It must be remembered that during the Great War, the Germans had conquered the Baltic area from the Russians and re-named it Kurland with the intent of eventually annexing Kurland to Germany proper. Furthermore, this area, in times past, had been the heartland of the Hanseatic League, a loose confederation of German settlers and traders, which was controlled and protected by the German Teutonic Knights. Many officers and men in the Goltz Free Corps saw themselves as the successors to that noble order.

By now, however, a large segment of the Latvian population had turned against the Free Corps and there was every indication that they and the small Latvian army would fight them if they tried to take over Riga.

Out of desperation, Ulmanis petitioned the Allies in Paris to send Allied forces to protect Latvia, now, from both the Free Corps and the Bolsheviks.

In Paris, this petition was most unwelcome but the situation in Latvia was viewed with great alarm. The Allied were undecided on a course of action but did issue an immediate order to Goltz, through Weimar, not to occupy Riga. Goltz ignored the order, and on May 22, occupied the city and ousted the Ulmanis government. Goltz declared martial law in his new domain and began rounding up Reds and summarily executing them in batches of 50. Thousands more were jailed. He tempered his activities against non-communist Latvians because he now needed their support.

In both Berlin and Weimar, many German leaders were ecstatic over Goltz' success and saw that Germany now had a strong base of operations in the east — a base from which the German Army could operate if the Weimar government rejected the peace treaty and the war resumed.

In Paris, a temporary solution to the Latvian problem was found based on money. The Allies voted a 10 million pound credit to Ulmanis's government which, despite having been run out of

Riga, had remained intact, to finance and build up the Latvian armed forces. To help in this effort, the Allies sent a special military mission to Ulmanis headed by British General Sir Hubert Gough and encouraged the Latvians to seek volunteers from the neighboring Scandinavian countries. Furthermore, an Allied naval blockade of the Latvian ports was established to prevent supplies from German reaching the Free Corps. It was here that the matter rested until late June 1919.

LLOYD GEORGE'S OTHER PROBLEM

Apparently the relationship between Lloyd George and his mistress, Frances Stevenson, had its problems. While in Paris, Frances made this diary entry: "I know Stern (a gentleman friend) would marry me if I gave him the slightest encouragement and if he thought I would leave D (David Lloyd George). It is a great temptation in a way for although I don't love him (Stern) we are good friends and I know he would be very kind to me... But I can see that he (Lloyd George) would be unhappy if I left him, so I promised him I would not." D and Frances eventually married after D divorced his wife.

REVOLUTION IN HUNGARY

In Paris, a decision was made with regard to Hungary, that unhappiest of lands. The Commission that had been set up to advise the Supreme Council on Hungary presented its report. Part of the Commission's presentation included a map showing their recommendations for the new borders of Hungary which, it was claimed, were drawn along nationalistic lines. Unfortunately for the Hungarians, it drastically reduced the size of the country. The Commission also recognized Romania's recent conquest of Transylvania and recommended that a neutral zone be created, at Hungary's expense, in Transylvania between Hungary and Romania.

On March 18, 1919, the Council accepted the Commission's recommendations and Hungary was ordered to accept the decision and was given 10 days to comply.

This was a disaster for Count Michael Karolyi and his government in Budapest which had been a strong advocate of Wilson's Fourteen Points. Now, Karolyi's position was untenable and he resigned and fled the country. He was quickly replaced by Zsigmund Kunki, a leftist Social Democrat. In forming his cabinet, on March 20, Kunki released from jail the country's most prominent communist leader, Bela Kun, and made him a cabinet member. Kun had been in jail since February 21, 1919, following a Karolyi government crackdown on communists and other agitators. Kun quickly became the most prominent member of Kunki's government and demanded that the Communists and Social Democrats merge into one party to be known as "The United Socialist Party." Kunki approved and his government, now under Kun's influence, soon announced a Marxist agenda. And the country was renamed "The Hungarian Soviet Republic" and had 33 "commissars" which included Kun as Foreign Minister. On the 21st, Kun ousted Kunki in a bloodless coup and seized power. Waiting in the wings was a cadre of Russian communists who had come to Hungary with Kun under the guise of Red Cross workers. They had a large sum of money and were in radio contact with Lenin. The cadre now emerged from its cover, announced the creation of the "Communist Party of Hungary," created a party newspaper, and quickly implemented a whole program of communist schemes, some of them quite bizarre. In addition to the now-standard communist restructuring of society, the nationalization of industry, and the confiscation of bank deposits, they also confiscated theaters, apartment buildings, private art and stamp collections, private jewelry and furniture,

Bela Kun

and decreed the elimination of titles. Kun's regime cut taxes, gave substantial financial increases to the disabled veterans and the unemployed, introduced censorship, called for massive public housing projects, forbade the production and use of alcohol, began sex education in grade schools, began a program to standardize graves, and made regular bathing by every citizen compulsory.

In Paris, most delegates had never heard of Bela Kun.

WHO WAS BELA KUN?

Bela Kun was born into a non-practicing Jewish family in a small village in Transylvania. His father was a notary and a drunkard and Bela's early life was hard. Bela got a fairly good education in local Calvinist schools and became a radical, leftist-oriented journalist before the war and gained some notoriety. When the Great War started, he volunteered for duty in the Austro-Hungarian Army, served as an officer, fought in Russia, and was captured and converted to communism. He had natural leadership capabilities and was a good orator. With this, and his background as a journalist, he caught the attention of the Russian communist authorities. Kun was released from the POW camp, went to Moscow, and met with Lenin. Lenin was very impressed with Kun and appointed him the leaders of a Hungarian communist movement. Kun returned to Hungary with Lenin's blessing, gold, fake documents, a covey of undercover Russian associates, and a determination to spread the revolution. Upon arriving in Hungary, Kun issued a Red manifesto, organized strikes and demonstrations, was jailed by the police, beaten, and became something of a communist martyr.

Somewhat surprisingly, Kun's new communist government had broad support among the Hungarian people who saw it, not necessarily as a communist regime, but rather a communist and nationalist regime combined that would unite Hungary in the face of its adversaries. And to some, Kun, was seen as a messiah.

One of his first actions was to send a message to Lenin asking for advice and a treaty of alliance. His new government then sent out mixed messages to all Europeans. One message called for peace with the Allies, while another called upon the workers of Europe to revolt against their capitalist oppressors.

In neighboring Romania, Czechoslovakia, Austria, and Jugoslavia, there was alarm. In Paris there was indecision. Clemenceau wanted to arm the Romanians and give them a free hand. Lloyd George, Wilson, and Orlando did not know what to do. It was agreed, however, to send arms to Romania and possibly a mission of inquiry to Hungary.

THE MIDDLE EAST

The situation in the Middle East was still in turmoil. The British and French were still jockeying for position and arguing over the Sykes-Picot Agreement; the Italians wanted their share; the Americans offered suggestions; the Syrians, Lebanese, Kurds, and Arabs wanted their independence; the Turks were angry and searching for a leader; the Kurds and Persians feared the growing influence of the Arabs; the Shia feared the growing influence of the Sunnis; the Jews wanted Palestine; and the British wanted them to have it.

There were also the tribal leader who, under Turkish rule, were given considerable autonomy so long as they kept their areas peaceful and the people under their control continued to pay their taxes. Now, under the Europeans, this was changing which portended a plethora of mini-disputes throughout the Middle East for the Allies because they now had to negotiate individually with each tribal leader.

Syria and Lebanon were two of the major issues. The Sykes-Picot Agreement between Britain and France had promised Syria to France, but the British had conquered the country and its capital Damascus. Credit for the conquest of Damascus was awarded to T. E. Lawrence's Arab forces and to Prince Faisal of Hijaz which strengthened his claim to Syria at the expense of the French. British propaganda then went to work claiming that Faisal's forces, under the command of Lawrence and Allenby, were some 100,000-strong when, in reality, they were only several thousand. Lloyd George commented in private that this was "eastern arithmetic."

General Allenby, with London's approval, appointed Faisal military commander of the city, and Faisal promptly raised his flag over the main government buildings. Rumors soon circulated that it would not be long before Faisal would be proclaimed King of Syria. The British then pressured the French to accept Faisal as the leader of the Syrian government. But the French were not interested in having a British lackey in a country that was likely to become one of their mandates. The British warned the French, however, that the people of Syria, who were mostly Arabs, would be more loyal to Faisal than to them and that civil war was possible if Faisal was rejected. All the while, the British maintained a sizeable military force in Damascus which helped stabilize Faisal's regime. The British gave in on one concession, though, and had Faisal remove his flag in favor of the British Union Jack.

As for the coastal area of Syria, known as The Lebanon, there was no great disagreement — it would be under French although its boundaries were still undefined.

"Southern Syria" was another problem. The French and many Arabs counted northern Palestine (most of the land that the Zionists wanted) and the vast desert area east of the Jordan River that nobody really wanted, as part of Syria. The British, in contrast, considered northern Palestine as part of Palestine proper and, of course, the site of the future Jewish homeland that had been promised in the Balfour Declaration. The British also claimed that Palestine extended several hundred miles to the east of the Jordan River to the border with Mesopotamia.

On March 2, 1919, Wilson announced his support for a Jewish homeland in northern Palestine, thus throwing in his lot with the British and against the French and Arabs. This greatly strengthened the British position with regard to Palestine's borders.

In early March, Lloyd George produced a map that showed the British versions of the region. It awarded most of Syria to Faisal and The Lebanon to France. Clemenceau, not surprisingly, rejected the map and in private called Lloyd George "a cheat."

During the third week of March, Wilson suggested that the people of the region be allowed to vote on their future. Here again was his Fourteen Points at work. Clemenceau, confident that the people would welcome a French mandate, agreed. Lloyd George agreed, then had second thoughts, and stalled. He had good reason to stall. In The Lebanon, the Christian minority unilaterally declared its independence and its loyalty to France. And from Damascus came rumors that Arab opponents to Faisal's rule had grown in numbers and strength and were now criticizing Faisal for being too complacent with the French. This indicated that there might be serious political problems brewing among the Arab leaders in Syria. It was there the this troublesome matter rested until May.

In mid-March, the Italians added another factor to the uncertainty in the Middle East when Italian troops landed at Antalya on the southern coast of Turkey. From Rome came the explanation that the landing was in keeping with wartime agreements under which Italy would share in the occupation of Turkey. During the war, Italian troops had landed at several places along the Turkish coast, ostensibly to protect Italians and Italian property. As the war wound down, the Italian forces left except for the garrison at Marmaris opposite the Italian-controlled island of Rhodes.

In Paris, there was great concern with regard to this unilateral action by Italy and it was believed that the Italians would eventually march into Anatolia, the heartland of Turkey. Clemenceau, Lloyd George, and Wilson all publicly condemned the Italian action but could not agree on a course of action.

Here was yet another unpleasant issue between Italy and her wartime Allies.

CHAPTER 8
MUSSOLINI GOES INTO POLITICS–
BAVARIA GOES COMMUNIST

|||||||||||||||||||||||||||||||||||||||||||||||||||||||||||||||||||||||||||||||||||||||||||||||||||||||||||||||||||||||||||||||

TROUBLES IN INDIA

On March 21, 1919, following a series of local strikes and violent demonstrations, the British government introduced two anti-sedition laws with regard to India enabling British authorities to intern agitators without trial and gave judges the power to try cases without juries.

This would soon backfire. The Hindus, Muslims, and Sikhs, who had often been at odds with one another, now found a new unity in their hatred of the British. Mohandas Gandhi, a 50-year-old diminutive Cambridge-educated Hindu lawyer who headed India's largest political party, the "Indian National Congress Party" (Congress Party), now had a issue that would propel him, even more, into the forefront of Indian politics. The Congress Party was large and well-organized and advocated a policy calling for the eventual withdrawal of the British and Indian independence. The Party also advocated a nonviolent revolution against the British to accomplish this. This call had been heeded throughout India and took the form of work stoppages, demonstrations, boycotts, and other acts of passive resistance.

The Indians had a delegation at Paris, but it was considered a farce by most Indians because it was headed by a Briton, Edwin Montagu, Secretary of State for India, and had two Indian members who were considered to be under the influence of the British.

With the passage of the sedition laws and the general temperament of the people of India, there was trouble ahead for India.

MOHANDAS GANDHI

|||||||||||||||||||||||||||||||||||||||||||||||||||||||||||||||||||||||||||||||||||||||||||||||||||||||||||||||||||||||||||||||

When World War II started, Gandhi was the unchallenged leader of the Congress Party in India. He was 68 years old and had acquired the title "Mahatma" (Great Soul). And he was still seeking independence for India. At the outbreak of the war, Gandhi offered to cooperate with the British in their war effort in exchange for a promise of independence. The British refused and went about building a large Indian Army on their own that was used, with considerable success, in several theaters of war.

Gandhi continued his agitation. Since there was the possibility that the Japanese might invade India, he announced that he and his followers would continue their campaign of non-violence against the Japanese just as they had against the British. In 1942, when the British were struggling to survive against the Axis onslaught, the Congress Party issued the "Quit India" resolution which demanded an early withdrawal of the British and Indian independence. Gandhi was arrested and jailed again for this and other activities. While in jail, he went on a hunger strike which brought him notoriety and sympathy throughout the world. He was eventually released in May 1944 because of his frail health. In time, he regained his health and resumed his efforts to free India.

In 1947 India gained its independence, but it was a disappointment to Gandhi because the country was partitioned into two states, one Hindu and the other Muslim and civil strife followed. In 1948 he was assassinated by a militant Hindu. He was 79 years old.

The fasci, an ancient Roman symbol adopted by Mussolini when he formed his political party "Fasci Italiani di Combattimento." The word "fascism" comes from this symbol.

MUSSOLINI GOES INTO POLITICS

Up to now, Mussolini had been best known in Italy as the publisher of his well-received right wing newspaper . Understandably, he was deeply involved in Italian politics but had had no formal affiliation with any particular political party.

During the third week in March 1919, this changed. Mussolini and some 60 loyal followers, mostly veterans and some

of which were members of the militant Adriti organization that had been formed the month before, met in Milan to form a new political party known as "Fasci Italiani di Combattimento" (Italian Battle Fasci — FdC). The word *Fasci* came from the Latin word *"Fascio,"* meaning bundle of sheaths, and was an ancient Roman symbol which stood for strong, united, dictatorial, but benevolent, leadership. The Roman fasci consisted of an ax with reeds strapped around the handle and bound together by a red ribbon. The ax represented the Emperor, the reeds represented his advisors, and the red ribbon symbolized their unity with dictatorial authority over matters of life and death. The edge of the blade symbolized the Emperor's authority to make hard and permanent decisions.

Both the fasci and swastika in Germany were ancient symbols, but unlike the swastika, the fasci had always been a political symbol and, over the years, had been used by various political organizations and governments around the world — including the US government.

The new Fasci Italiani di Combattimento soon produced a political platform that was a mix of socialist and right wing ideals and called for the continuation of the constitutional monarchy. It also called for strong and militant workers' organization that would, in certain cases, be allowed to run their factories. The platform also supported Italy's territorial claims to South Tyrol, Dalmatia, and Fiume, and benefits for veterans and the elimination of the Senate in the Italian government, which was widely believed to be a tool of the rich and powerful. It also supported Wilson's Fourteen Points in general and especially where it benefited Italy. The platform went on calling for compulsory military service, the elimination of secret diplomacy, a census on the wealthy, the redistribution of land, a restructuring of Italians transportation (Italian trains were always late), a graduated income tax, an eight-hour work day, and sickness and old age benefits.

On the negative side, the platform called for the rejection of international socialism, democracy, and imperialism, and it admonished its followers to sabotage democratic elections whenever possible. Just how the party might come to power without elections was not made clear. Also, there was no mentioned of anything detrimental to the King or to the Italian royalty. Mussolini and his followers believed that they had indications that the King would be receptive to some, or perhaps all, of the party's agenda. The platform did call, however, for the elimination of titles of nobility.

The Party's platform was all-encompassing from the political left to the political right. Mussolini summed it up in an article in his newspaper on March 23, writing, "We allow ourselves the luxury of being aristocrats and democrats, conservatives and progressives, reactionaries and revolutionists, legalist or illegalist, depending on circumstances of time, place and situation..." The next day, *Il Popolo* sounded an ominous alarm; "... the next

attack by Bolshevism is imminent and will be directed against Milan, Turin, and Bologna..." — Italy's industrial heart land with its thousands upon thousands of workers.

With such a broad range of goals and a militant anti-communist stand, his party soon collected a broad range of supporters.

Mussolini went on to adopt a wide assortment of Party paraphernalia and customs, much of which had roots to Roman times. This included the outstretched straight-arm salute of the Romans and the counting of the years of the Party's existence in Roman numerals. Nineteen-nineteen was year I. They also adopted black shirts, fezzes, the dagger, a wide variety of flags, and banners and slogans, with their primary slogan being "Believe, Obey, Fight." Individual Party cells were to be created all over Italy and called "Fascis." Mussolini predicted, "In two months a thousand Fasci will have sprung up throughout all Italy." This was overly optimistic, but Fascis did begin to appear in mounting numbers.

The main enemies of Fascism were communists and international socialists. Concerted efforts would be made to convert willing and borderline socialists into Fascists (Mussolini had been an international socialist). Communists, however, were considered to be unredeemable.

And the Fascist party would have its own soldiers, the "Black Shirts" (the communists already had the "Red Shirts"). These paramilitary units were to protect Fascist meetings, property, individuals, meet the enemy in the streets, and do other necessary physical tasks as directed from above.

From its inception, the Fascist Party was a dictatorial organization with an acknowledged leader. That leader was, of course, Mussolini and he was simply called "Leader" *(Duce)*. The Party was also structured with a "Fascist Grand Council" whose duty was to advise the Duce on major issues and select a new leader when it became necessary.

IT WAS THE FASCIST GRAND COUNCIL THAT DID HIM IN

In July 1943, soon after the Allies invaded Sicily, the Grand Council convened in one of its very rare sessions to discuss the crisis. A vote of confidence on Mussolini's leadership was taken and he lost by a count of 19 to 7. He was then obliged, under his own Fascist rules and Italian law, to report to the King and submit his resignation as Premier. He did so and was immediately taken into protective custody by the King's guards.

SPRINGTIME IN PARIS AND ELSEWHERE

On March 24, 1919, the four principle members of the Supreme Council voted to oust the fifth member — Japan. It was not intended as an insult to Japan, but rather a streamlining of the Council's functions. The Japanese had participate in the Council meeting very infrequently and, in the opinion of the four other members, issues concerning Japan could be addressed as needed and Japan, of course, would be called upon to participated. So, the Big Five became the "Big Four." In Japan, there was great resentment.

The Big Four then surged on. On March 28, 1919, they agreed that there should not be a stated amount of German reparations written into the Versailles Peace Treaty. The four men could not agree on a sum in the first place and, secondly, it was feared, by all four, that any sum mentioned would be criticized by their political opponents at home as being either too large or too small, putting them on the political defensive from both directions.

Elsewhere, in the United States, an unknown physics professor, Dr. Robert Goddard of Clark University in Massachusetts, made a public statement predicting that rockets could be made to reach the moon. Most of the public passed this off with little interest, but in some military circles, alert officers recognized that if rockets could be made to reach the moon, they could be made to bombard an enemy at very great distances.

And from Holland on March 29, there came a statement from the exiled Kaiser. He said that he would commit suicide before he would stand trial before an Allied tribunal. This met with public approval and great respect in Germany.

During the last days of March, more food began to reach the German people, thanks to the efforts of Herbert Hoover's relief organization and a relaxation of the British blockade. More food was also reaching Austria where it was believed that a Bela Kun-type of revolution was brewing.

In the hotel meeting rooms and government offices in Paris, progress was being made on the forthcoming peace treaties with Austria, Hungary, Bulgaria, and Turkey. Much of the work was being done by lower level delegates with occasional supervision from the Big Four.

GOOD NEWS AND BAD NEWS FROM RUSSIA

One of the bits of good news with regard to Russia was a series of reports that the Bolsheviks were losing support among the leftists in the rest of Europe and elsewhere because of their excesses, cruelty, and social and economic failures in Russia. A good example of this was in Italy where many international socialists, that had originally supported the Bolsheviks, were now toying with the new type of socialism being proposed by Mussolini.

And, people continued to flee Russia. Eastern Europe was flooded with Russian refugees — most of them desperate and destitute. Here then, was a great social problem but also a ready pool of future anti-communist soldiers that might be recruited for a march back into Russia. And here too, was a political constituency that might serve and increase the anti-Bolshevik elements of Europe.

There were indications, too, that the Finns, who had won their freedom and were cooperating with the Allies, might launch an attack on Petrograd (St. Petersburg) which would take pressure off of the other fronts. It was also considered likely that the Finns would be supported in their attack by the small "Northwestern White Army" under General Nicoli N. Iudenich operating in the northern Baltic area. Iudenich had no love for the Finns and wanted Finland to become, once again, a part of the future Russian empire, but if the Finns attacked Petrograd from the north, he might then have the opportunity to sneak into the city from the south and capture it for himself.

ST. PETERSBURG — PETROGRAD — LENINGRAD

When the city at the mouth of the Neva River was built by Peter the Great in 1703, it was named St. Petersburg after his patron saint. During the Great War, that name sounded too Germanic to the Russians so the city was renamed Petrograd, a more Russian-sounding name. After Lenin died in 1924, the city was renamed again Leningrad. It still had that name during World War II and endured one of the longest and most dramatic sieges of the war.

In the Archangel area of northern Russian, the spring thaw had arrived. This enabled a small force of Kolchak's men to make contact with the British and White forces there. This was Kolchak's first contact with an Allied force in European Russian. In the southern part of European Russia, however, Kolchak's and Denikin's forces were still far apart.

In Paris, there was a growing school of thought that if food were shipped to the Russian people, it would cool their ardor for communism. Herbert Hoover was one of the strongest proponents of this. It was also hoped that, somehow, the Bolsheviks, with expressions of goodwill from the West such as this, might evolve into good democrats. Lloyd George and Wilson discussed these possibilities, which resulted in a plan of action being formulated in mid-April.

Now for the bad news.

Reports from Siberia indicated that Admiral Kolchak's forces were in very bad condition. His field commanders were stealing supplies from each other, sometimes at gun point; his government was riddled with corruption, his troops committed atrocities and summary executions, his rear was in shambles, and the Cossacks, who were supposed to be under his command, were disregarding his orders at will. Some of the Cossack bands took up banditry and the word "Cossack" had become synonymous with "renegade." Furthermore, the Cossacks were often seen with Japanese-made arms which, to many, was another indication that the Japanese were involved in ominous intrigues in Siberia.

Then too, the Western Allies in Russia had their problems. The morale of the Allied soldiers, never strong, was steadily declining. In the north and in Siberia, the Americans were seen as becoming neutral and indecisive. In Siberia, the Japanese were being seen as opportunists in that they continued to actively support and arm Kolchak while the other Allies began to have reservations. This suggested some sinister and secret relationship between the Japanese and Kolchak and might well have been the source of the Japanese-made arms acquired by the Cossacks.

In European Russia, most of the burden of supporting the Whites now fell on the shoulders of the British and French.

In the Ukraine, France's area of control, the French had had to do battle not only with the Bolsheviks but with Ukrainian Nationalists and anarchists. And on many occasions the French were outnumbered. French equipment and supplies arriving at Odessa often disappeared — stolen for the most part, by corrupt White officials and White officers. Because of this, the French refused to let White soldiers guard French supplies. This strained the relationship between the French and Denikin. Various White leaders and political factions at Odessa were now suggesting that the French should leave altogether. In Paris, this possibility was being given serious consideration.

Also in the Ukraine, the Jews, as ever, were persecuted by whomever chose to do so.

Another factor in the Ukraine was that Denikin had failed to gain the support of the Ukrainian peasants and his forces were, at times, engaged in fighting Ukrainian nationalists.

There was another event in Russia that was hard to determine if it was good or bad. In March, the communists held their Eighth Party Congress. Lenin and the other communists leaders confirmed that the Bolshevik Party was taking complete control of Russia's government and that, because of this, 1919 was to be proclaimed as "The Year of the Party." As a result, the bureaucracy was soaring and about half of the registered members of the Party had been given jobs in the government or in the military. This, and other actions, discredited Lenin's long-standing claim that the Bolsheviks would bring about true democracy. Only the most naive could continue to believe that communist Russia would be anything but an extreme left-wing dictatorship.

At the Party Congress, the leaders made loyalty to the Communist Party a major issue which was later seen as a preliminary to what happened next. Soon after the Congress ended, a purge of sorts began, which required every Party member to re-register and have his political ideals evaluated. Party membership was approaching an unwieldy 400,000. Eventually, about one in ten Party members had his memberships revoked.

IN PARIS — AGREEMENT AND CONTINUED DISAGREEMENT

In Paris, agreement was finally reached on the future makeup of the German armed forces. The German Army would be limited to 100,000 members, the Navy 15,000 members; there would be no air force, no dirigibles, no tanks, no armored cars, no heavy guns, no poison gas and, above all, no submarines.

Most of the existing weapons in German hands were to be destroyed, and fortifications along the east bank of the Rhine were to be dismantled. The importation of arms was to be prohibited and only a few German manufacturers were to be designated as arms makers. Veterans' organizations, police forces, private societies, and touring clubs would not be allowed to do anything of a military nature. Student cadet programs in high schools and universities would be discontinued and, finally, all military activities in Germany were to be supervised by an "Inter-Allied Commission of Control."

Another area of agreement in Paris was that an effort should be made to end the fighting between the Poles and the Ukrainians. It was agreed that an order should be sent to both sides to stop fighting. That order was sent but was totally ignored by both sides. So much for the influence Paris had in Eastern Europe.

In Italy, the issue over Fiume was still burning and the Italian delegation in Paris announced that if they were denied the city, they would withdraw from the peace conference.

And the issue of a buffer state in the Rhineland arose again. Here Foch and Clemenceau were united. They pointed out that both Great Britain and the United States were protected by the sea and that France was not. Lloyd George and Wilson listened politely but remained unconvinced.

Other major issues still on the table were reparations, the control of the Saar, a rich coal-mining area of the German-French Border, Belgium's claims, the revolution in Hungary, the armed clashes between Hungary and Romania, the Polish corridor, Danzig, and Shantung. Even the construction of a tunnel under the English Channel was discussed.

Some observed that Wilson seemed to be more fatigued than usual, suffered short-term memory loss, was irritable, and that the tick in his cheek had become more pronounced. Ray Baker, Wilson's Press Secretary, wrote, "I have never seen the President look so worn and tired."

FOOD, STRIKES AND OTHER EVENTS

In Germany, with more food reaching the people, the threat of famine diminished to some degree but did not disappear.

In both France and the US, there were waves of labor strikes. In the US alone, there were 175 strikes in progress. New York City was especially hard hit. The garment workers, transportation workers, cigar makers, and others were on strike. Observers reported that it was the greatest labor unrest in the city in living memory.

On March 31, 1919, another major communist-instigated strike began in Germany's Ruhr area.

On that same day, north of the Ruhr, the Workers' and Soldiers' Council that had ruled the German state of Hamburg since November 1918 was overthrown in a bloodless coup by a well-respected and moderate political leader, Werner von Melle. A local election was held and von Melle was elected as mayor of the city for the third time in his career. Hamburg was back in the fold.

In Paris, Clemenceau tended to disbelieve some of the reports coming out of Germany. He felt that the Germans were exaggerating the problems in order to gain concessions from the Allies.

THE SMUTS MISSION TO HUNGARY

On April 1, 1919, General Smuts left Paris on a special train heading from Hungary. He led a fact-finding mission that was to contact Bela Kun and ascertain, firsthand, what was happening in that country. Another aspect of the mission was to attempt to possibly establish a line of communications to Lenin. In Budapest, the Smuts' mission was seen as a hopeful sign that the peacemakers in Paris might be willing to recognized Kun's regime.

Smuts' train traveled through Switzerland and into Austria. They stopped at Vienna to learn the situation there and found it to be deplorable. Harold Nicholson, a British member of the mission, reported that the people of Vienna looked "dejected and ill-dressed." When the mission members went into the city, policemen were always present to protect them and crowds which followed them, constantly pleading for help from the West.

Smuts took pity on these poor souls and ordered the members of the mission not to purchase or consume any local food but to live on the army rations carried on the train. Smuts duly reported his findings in Vienna back to Paris.

Upon arriving in Budapest, Smuts and his entourage remained on the train which sat on a siding at the station. This sent the message that Bela Kun and the members of his government were obliged to go to Smuts — a diplomatic slight to a head of state in his own capital. Smuts' first impression of Kun was not good. One of Smuts' associates reported that Kun was "a small man of about 30: puffy white face and loose wet lips: shaven head: impression of red hair: shifty suspicious eyes: he has the face of a sulky and uncertain criminal. He has with him a little oily Jew — (wearing a) fur-coat rather moth eaten — stringy green tie — dirty collar. He is their Foreign Secretary."

Smuts discovered that Kun saw himself in the middle between two factions: his communist government which currently had a strong hold on the people, and the conservative old guard which controlled the army. Kun begged Smuts to come into town where suites awaited him at the city's best hotel and the Union Jack flew from its roof beside the tri-color flag of Hungary. The gesture would have shown, to some degree, Allied support for his regime. But Smuts refused and stayed on the train.

Kun wanted the Allies to modify Hungary's border with Romania in Hungary's favor and called for a conference of all parties involved in Hungarian issues and that that conference be held in either Vienna or Prague. Smuts responded by suggesting that Kun come to Paris and that an Allied-occupied buffer zone be established along the Hungarian-Romanian border. Kun accepted Smuts' proposals but with the condition that the Romanian Army withdraw from the border. Smuts rejected the proposal, saying that there "must be no reservations." Kun then expected Smuts to make a counter-proposal, but it never came. By now, Smuts had concluded that Kun's government would not last long and that the best course of action for the Allies was to do nothing. Within a few

hours, Smuts' train pulled out of the station and headed back to Paris. The parting was cordial, but the Hungarians were noticeably disappointed. The newspapers in Budapest, now communist-controlled, claimed that the Smuts visit amounted to de facto recognition of Kun's regime by the peace conference. They did not report that Smuts had left the country abruptly, but word of this leaked out and the people knew that the meeting had not gone well.

On April 10, Hungarian conservative counter-revolutionaries established a rival provisional government in the Hungarian city of Szeged, a large city in south-central Hungary 100 miles south of Budapest. The provisional government had French protection and its principle members were Count Julius Karolyi (brother of the former president), Count Stephen Bethien, Admiral Miklos Horthy, and Archduke Joseph. It would be Admiral Horthy who would soon come to dominate the new provisional government.

That same day, Romanian forces entered Hungary further north, ostensibly to forestall a Hungarian invasion of Transylvania. The real purpose was to prepare for a march on Budapest.

Another war was starting in Eastern Europe.

ALLIES EASE CONDITIONS ON AUSTRIA

Due in part to Smuts' reports from Vienna, the Allies eased their blockade of Austria. Soon, more food, clothing, and other items were appearing in the marketplaces and foreign loans and credits were being extended to the Austrian government. This trend would continue and Austria, seen as one of the most cooperative of the former Central Powers, would become the fourth largest recipient of Allied aid after Germany, Poland, and Belgium. A few days later, the Austrians took another step toward democracy by formally dissolving

Eamon de Valera, an American citizen and President of the Provisional Government of Ireland.

the monarchy and deposing Emperor Karl who had fled the country a few days earlier for exile in Switzerland. Austria thus became a constitutional republic.

AN IRISH-AMERICAN BECOME PRESIDENT OF IRELAND

From Ireland came word that the Irish rebels had elected a provisional president — an American. He was Eamon De Valera, who was born in New York City in 1882 and, therefore, an American citizen. De Valera was the son of a Spanish musician and an Irish woman and had been taken to Ireland as a youth. De Valera grew up considering himself Irish, and when he reached manhood, he became deeply involved in Ireland's struggle for independence. He became president of the Sinn Fein nationalist organization and was arrested several times. Now he was the president of a country that did not yet exist.

Soon, De Valera turned his attention to America. He went to Boston, a city with a large Irish-American population, set up an office and began to solicit money, support, and sympathy for Ireland's cause. One of De Valera's supporters was young Joseph Kennedy who would soon make his fame in both business and politics.

For Woodrow Wilson, here was another problem that awaited him when he returned home.

DANZIG

On April 1, 1919, the Big Four reached a decision on Danzig. It would become a free city but still would serve as Poland's main outlet to the sea. The free city would be administered by the League of Nations and the Poles would have special rights with regard to commerce, trade, and customs, and Warsaw would handle Danzig's foreign affairs.

In Poland, there was outrage. The Poles had demanded that Danzig be given to them in toto. It was reported that Premier Paderewski wept when he heard the news.

This news, also, came at a very bad time for the Poles. Their newly-created army was engaged in a bitter struggle with Bolshevik forces in the Lvov area. The Paris peacemakers had called for a cease-fire but both sides had ignored that call. Wilson referred to the Poles as "our troublesome friends."

DANZIG BETWEEN THE WARS

The loss of Danzig was skillfully used by the Nazis in their political propaganda and many Germans were receptive to it.

In the election of May 1933, the local Danzig Nazi Party gained more than half of the vote and established a Nazi administration very similar to that which had been established by the Nazis in Berlin four months earlier. Danzig thus became the world's second Nazi-controlled country.

DANZIG IN WWII

When the Germans invaded Poland in September 1939, they also invaded Danzig and re-annexed it to Germany.

At the end of the war, Danzig was captured by the Soviets who returned it to Poland. The Poles expelled virtually all of the German population and renamed the city Gdansk.

WILSON SICK: THE BIG THREE OF THE BIG FOUR CARRY ON

On April 2, 1919, it snowed in Paris. Tradition had it that this was a bad omen. On the evening of April 3, Dr. Cary T. Grayson, Wilson's personal physician, recorded that the President was suddenly "... seized with violent paroxysms of coughing which were so severe and frequent that it interfered with his breathing." Grayson was very concerned and ordered the President to bed immediately. Mrs. Wilson was also visibly shaken. One of their first thoughts was that the President had been poisoned. Wilson's temperature rose to 103 and he continued to experience severe coughing, along with vomiting and diarrhea. On April 5, Grayson confirmed that it was the flu and suggested that he might have caught it from Clemenceau's constant coughing.

A second American doctor, Edwin Weinstein, a neurologist, was called in and concluded that Wilson had suffered some brain damage. His report stated that Wilson "... sustained a lesion in the right cerebral hemisphere extending to include deeper structures in the limbic-reticular system... (and) he now had evidence of bilateral damage, a condition affecting emotional and social behavior."

Clemenceau, Lloyd George, and Orlando, however, could not wait for Wilson to recover and forged ahead. They met in Wilson's study with Wilson only a few rooms away. Col. House kept Wilson informed as best he could but it was questionable whether Wilson comprehended what was taking place. Some observers reported that Clemenceau and Lloyd George seemed to delight in Wilson's absence. House was unhappily aware of this and jokingly said to an aide that maybe "Clemenceau would pass on the germ to Lloyd George."

A recording secretary was brought into the study to record every detail for Wilson's benefit.

On April 5, the Council members made another decision — the war guilt clause. It would become Article 231 of the Versialles Peace Treaty and would read:

The Allied and Associated Governments affirm and Germany accepts the responsibility of Germany and her allies for causing all the loss and damage to which the Allied and Associated Governments and their nationals have been subjected as a consequence of the war imposed upon them by the aggression of Germany and her allies.

On Sunday, April 6, Wilson was better but not yet well enough to return to the meetings. Furthermore, he was very angry, believing that the others were taking advantage of his illness. The President sent word to his compatriots that only decisions that met with his satisfaction must be made or he would either go home or call for the negotiations on the subjects be brought into the open. To emphasize his threat of leaving, he ordered that his steamship, the *George Washington*, anchored at Brest, be made ready to leave on short notice. He also instructed that that order be made know to Clemenceau, Lloyd George, and Orlando. This action caused a sensation at the conference table but it brought results.

The response from the Big Three of the Big Four was a placating and cooperative statement that they would do all in their power to resolve these issues as soon as possible and in full cooperation with Wilson.

On April 7, Wilson got out of bed, got dressed, and went back to work. He did not make preparations to board the *George Washington* but neither did he order it to stand down. At this point, negotiations got back on track.

On April 11, the Big Four agreed that the new home of the League of Nations should be in Geneva, Switzerland. The Swiss were delighted.

THE FRENCH LEAVE RUSSIA

During the last days of March 1919, the decision was made by the French government to withdraw French forces from the Odessa area of the southern Ukraine. That evacuation began on April 1, 1919, and continued for several days. It was very poorly organized. There were not enough ships available and tens of thousands of civilians and Russian Whites who had hoped to leave with the French could not. They were left to their fate which would be most tragic.

For the Bolsheviks, this was seen as a great victory and the world took note. In early April, the new "Soviet Republic of the Ukraine" came into being.

THE SOVIET REPUBLIC OF BAVARIA

On March 30–31, thirty inches of snow fell in Munich and the city was virtually paralyzed. There was virtually no snow removal, and the populace became angry with the city administration.

The leftist clique that ruled in the city, which called themselves the "Central Soviet," was not satisfied either so they took action. They could do little about the snow, but on April 7, 1919, Bavaria became even more communist. On that day, there was another shakeup in Munich leadership, the extremists gained in power, and the "Soviet Republic of Bavaria" emerged. The new leaders formed a new three-man triumvirate and proclaimed themselves to be pure communists, whereas the members of the Central Soviet, in their opinion, had been less than pure. The members of the triumvirate were Eugen Levine, Tobias Axelrod, and Max Levien, all three Russian Jews.

The triumvirate soon began issuing a string of edicts arming workers, regulating the very limited food supply, nationalizing the press, confiscating all houses of four rooms or more, declaring free tuition to Munich's Ludwig Maximilian University, and more. They also announced that they would seek an alliance with Bela Kun in Hungary and the Bolsheviks in Russia. And too, they changed the flag of Bavaria to one of solid red.

At the List Regiment barracks on the outskirts of Munich, Corporal Hitler, who had just returned from duty as a guard at the Traunstien prisoner of war camp, watched these events with great anguish. In the political shakeup and the communists' takeover of the army, the regiment's officers had fled and the soldiers were on their own. Some of the men openly joined the Reds while those remaining stayed in the barracks and donned red arm bands for self-protection. Hitler was one of them. Later he claimed that he talked several of his comrades out of joining the marauding Red units.

At this same time, there was an attempted leftist coup in Dresden in the former Soviet state of Saxony. The coup was poorly organized and the "Free Corps Gorlitz" rushed in and restored order quickly and in a most brutal way. Dresden was saved, but Munich was lost.

DECISIONS IN PARIS

On April 8, 1919, the Big Four ruled out capital punishment for the Kaiser if he would ever be brought to trial.

On April 9, 1919, the French Assembly passed the French budget for the coming year. It depended heavily on reparation payments from Germany.

On April 11, 1919, the Japanese appeared before the Supreme Council, proposing an amendment to the Covenant of the League of Nations in the question of racial equality. It was not worded as strongly as before and simply asked for "the principle of equality of nations and just treatment of their nationals." The Japanese knew that the proposal would probably be rejected, but felt obliged to propose it for home consumption in Japan. Wilson, who was chairing the meeting, asked the Japanese to withdraw the proposal but they refused. A vote was then taken and the proposal was rejected.

During their meeting with the Big Four, the Japanese took the opportunity to press their claims, once again, to the Shantung concession in China. The Big Four sidestepped the issue and postponed making a decision. Before the meeting was over, the Japanese made veiled threats that they might leave the peace conference and/or not sign the peace treaty if their demands were not met.

On April 13, a decision was reached on the Saar based on Wilson's recommendations. German sovereignty over the region would be suspended for 15 years and the area would become a mandate of the League of Nations under French administration. France would also control the coal mines and their production, and retain their profits as part of Germany's reparations payments to France. After 15 years, a plebiscite would be taken to allow the people of the Saar to determine their own future.

THE SAAR

On January 13, 1935, the plebiscite was taken in the Saar under the watchful eye of the League of Nations and a temporary international military commission. Hitler had been Germany's Chancellor for two years and was growing in popularity throughout Germany. The vote was 90.35% in favor of rejoining Germany, and on the 17th, the League formally returned the Saar to German sovereignty. Hitler then traveled in the Saar and was greeted as a conquering liberator.

After WW II, the Saar became part of the American zone of occupation in Germany but there was no question of sovereignty or control of the coal mines. The Saar and its coal mines remained in German hands.

During the middle days of April, the subject of the Rhineland was hotly debated among the Big Four with Wilson and Clemenceau sometimes shouting at each other. In the end, it was Wilson's view that was accepted. The Rhineland would not be permanently occupied by the Allies. Rather, it would be occupied for 15 years by the French with withdrawals from certain areas in five years and from others in ten year.

THE RHINELAND BASTARDS

The French did eventually withdraw from the Rhineland, but they left behind a token of their occupation. Some of the French troops used in the occupation were black African colonials. As a result of fraternization, several hundred mulatto children were born to German women. These children became known throughout Germany as the "Rhineland Bastards" and were seen as a great embarrassment to many Germans and especially to the Nazis. Many in Germany thought that the French had deliberately used black troops to aggravate and punish the German people.

When the Nazis came to power in 1933, the Rhineland Bastards were coming of age and the Nazis ordered that they all — some 400 — be sterilized to prevent another generation of "racial contamination." This was made legal by the passage of a law entitled "Law for the Prevention of Offsprings with Hereditary Defects." These unfortunate individuals were then allowed to live out the remainder of their lives in Germany as they wished.

At the end of WW II, there were black African troops fighting for the French in Germany, but when the war ended, they were quickly withdrawn. The French did not want a repeat of what had happened in the 1920s and 1930s.

After the questions of the Saar and Rhineland were settled, Clemenceau made an unusual gesture to calm the waters of dissension between the Americans and French. He asked the French newspapers to stop attacking Wilson, as they had been doing for weeks. The editors complied and began printing only positive articles about Wilson and America.

Furthermore, the Big Four agreed that it was time to invite the Germans to Paris to hear the peace terms. Subsequently, the invitation was sent to Weimar.

CHAPTER 9
PROBLEMS STILL, BUT
HERE THEY COME!

|||||||||||||||||||||||||||||||||||||||||||||||||||||||||||||||||||||||||||||||||||||||||||||||||||||||||||||||||||||||||||

THAT MESS IN MEXICO

A bloody, multi-sided civil war had been raging in Mexico since 1910 and had spilled over into the US in 1916 when Pancho Villa, a bandit leader-turned-revolutionary, raided across the border into an American town, Columbus, NM, killing 16 Americans. Wilson was president at the time and sent an American Army expedition, under the command of General John J. Pershing, into Mexico to try to apprehend Villa. Pershing failed and Villa was still at large in 1919 and still seen as a threat to US border security. The failure to catch Villa was a great disappointment for Wilson, but a great enhancement for the reputation of General Pershing. The next year, when the US entered the war in Europe, Pershing was made commander of "American Expeditionary Force" (AEF) in France.

Then, on April 10, 1919, the revolution in Mexico took another turn. Emiliano Zapata, a popular revolutionary leader in the south of Mexico, was assassinated after having been tricked into attending a peace conference. Zapata's assassination had little effect on Mexican-American relations, but it served to demonstrate that America's southern neighbor was still very much of a problem and that there was little the US could do about it. Here was an old, and on-going, problem Wilson would face again when he returned home.

MORE TROUBLES IN INDIA — THE AMRITSAR MASSACRE

While the statesmen wrangled in Paris, events took a lurid turn in India. The unrest in the Punjab had continued as intensely as ever and the British were hard-pressed to maintain order.

On April 6, 1919, Gandhi called for a general strike throughout India but cautioned that it should be non-violent. On April 13, a large mob gathered in the city of Amritsar, the largest city in the Punjab and a holy city to the Sikhs. As their numbers grew, so did the threat of violence. To complicate matters, the Sikhs were conducting an annual pilgrimage in the city at this crucial time. The British Army commander in the area, Brigadier General Reginald E. Dyer, saw the threat and called out the troops to try to disperse the growing mob. Dyer's initial efforts were inadequate to handle the situation and the mob continue to grow and became even more aggressive. When Dyer learned that the mob had sacked the national bank and murdered the manager, attacked another bank, beat an English woman senseless in the street, and smashed and burned the telegraph office, Dyer ordered the troops, many of them Gurkhas, to shoot directly into the mob. The result was a massacre. Three hundred and seventy-eight people were killed and some 1200 wounded. Dyer declared martial law, refused to help the wounded, and then took punitive measures against the citizens of Amritsar which included, among other things, forcing a large number of innocent citizens to crawl down the street on their hands and knees wherein the English woman had been attacked.

When the world learned of this event, there was outrage and condemnation heaped upon the British governments in both England and India. The event has gone down in the history books as the "Amritsar Massacre."

Dyer was relieved of his post and an inquiry was conducted which concluded that Dyer had simply committed an error in judgment. A House of Commons investigation condemned the attack but Dyer was allowed to keep his rank. In London, one of the leading newspapers, The Morning Post, came to Dyer's aid and started a fund for his retirement. That fund eventually reached 26,000 pounds. Among the contributors was Rudyard Kipling, the man who had coined the phrase "the white man's burden."

The Morning Post came to Dyer's aid again by questioning whether Lord Edwin Montagu, a Jew and head of the Indian Colonial Office, was fit to continue in his job. In an editorial, the newspaper stated that the events at Amritsar seemed to be tinged with a "Bolshevik purpose." Thus, another link in the alleged Jewish-Bolshevik connection was forged.

AROUND THE WORLD AGAIN

On April 10, 1919, the Korean Provisional Government was formed in the French concession in Shanghai. Its leader was a revolutionary named Lee Dong Nyong. This, of course, was not a welcome event in Tokyo and further aggravated the already strained relations between France and Japan. It also gave the Japanese another excuse to continue their repressions against the Korean people.

In Latvia and Lithuania, there was an on-going multi-sided war among the Free Corps, the Latvian, the Lithuanians, the Poles, and the Bolsheviks. Later in the month, the Free Corps advanced northward into Estonia where it was reported that the Bolsheviks had taken refuge.

In neighboring Lithuania, to the south of Latvia, the Polish forces under General Pilsudski captured the disputed city of Vilna from the Bolsheviks on April 20 and then claimed the city and the surrounding territory for Poland. This was the ninth time the city of Vilna had changed hands in the last two years. This brought to an end the brief existence of Soviet republic, Litbel, that had consisted of Lithuania and Belorussia which had been created by the Bolsheviks in February 1919.

Flush with victory, the Poles then advanced eastward into Belorussia against the Reds.

Back in Lithuania, the leaders of the Lithuanian government, operating from Kaunas, 60 miles west of Vilna, were very devastated by the Polish annexation of Vilna and began plotting to strike back. Both sides appealed to Paris, and the Big Four attempted to draw a new boundary between Lithuania and Poland but neither side could agreed to it, and the result was another political stalemate. Lloyd George questioned whether on not Lithuania should even be independent, saying that it had a population only as large as his native Wales. Clemenceau wanted a viable Lithuania and feared that Poland might get too big if Lithuania and Poland were united. Poland's army, had by now, reached 200,000 troops and was still growing. It was firmly under the command of the very capable General Pilsudski who showed undeniable signs of wanting to continue enlarging Poland at the expense of her neighbors.

Yet, another argument persisted in Paris that a large and powerful Poland would be a bulwark against Bolshevism and that additional Polish troops would soon be needed to protect the soon-to-be-annexed Polish corridor.

From the far eastern part of European Russia came welcome news that Admiral Kolchak's forces had advanced some 100 miles to the west and were now in position to possibly link up with Denikin's forces in the Ukraine. No one knew it at the time, but this was to be Kolchak's high-water mark and there would be no linkup.

From Moscow, Lenin ordered his most loyal troops to converge on Kolchak's forces to stop their advance. Eventually, this would succeed.

That mess in eastern Europe continued.

In Milan, Italy, the home of Mussolini's newspaper and newly-formed Fascist Party, violent four-sided riots broke out which involved communists, socialists, the Italian Army, and Mussolini's Black Shirts. At this time, the Black Shirts took the opportunity to sack the offices of *Avanti*, the Socialist newspaper for which Mussolini once worked and which had given him the platform upon which he gained his first public notoriety.

In Paris, the magnolia and chestnut trees were blooming but the Supreme Council was still hard at work. They took care of some unfinished business which included, among other things, a visit by the Ethiopian delegation. The Ethiopians had territorial claims against the Italian colonies which bordered Ethiopia on two sides. So far, Ethiopian's claims had been all but ignored. And no decision was forthcoming from the council members now; they wanted no more problems with, or for, the Italians.

Another item of business concerned the Jews. Wilson was under pressure from American Jewish organizations who wanted a statement included in the peace accord protecting minorities. Wilson suggested the creation of yet another commission to address this issue. Lloyd George and Clemenceau agreed and the "Committee on New States and For the Protection of Minorities" was created and charged with drafting a "Bill of Rights" for minorities that could be incorporated into the final treaty.

On April 16, Lloyd George returned to London to report to Commons on the progress being made in Paris. The Prime Minister spoke in general and positive terms, taking great care not to reveal too many details that would benefit the Germans who were soon to arrive in Paris. His remarks were well-received and he took this opportunity of measured glory to lambast his opponents, especially Lord Northcliffe, publisher of the opposition newspaper, *The Daily Mail*. He said of the newspaper, "It is here today and jumping there tomorrow, and there the next day. I would as soon rely on a grasshopper."

In the state of Brunswick in Germany, political maneuvering brought to an end the brief reign of the Independent Social Democrat's leftist regime in that state. Sepp Oerter, who held the title Chairman of the Council of People's Commissars, resigned and was replaced by a Social Democrat, Heinrich Otto Jasper, who took the title Chairman of the Cabinet. Brunswick was now back in the fold.

THE ITALIANS LEAVE PARIS

On April 19, 1919, and again on April 20 — Easter Sunday — the Big Four met in Wilson's study and discussed, once again, the question of Italy's territorial claims. They were extensive. Italy demanded significant border adjustments in the Alps with Austria; the seaport of Fiume which was 40 miles southeast of Treste on the eastern shore of the Istria Peninsula; a long stretch of land on the eastern shore of the Adriatic Sea known as Dalmatia; many of the offshore Dalmatian islands; broad influence in Albania; broad influence in the Aegean Sea; concessions in Asia Minor from the Turks; and territorial adjustments in their favor in colonial Africa. In support of these claims, they presented the promises made in the Treaty of London of 1915, which brought Italy into the war on the Allied side, as well as various formal and informal conversations and understandings they had with the Allies thereafter.

Clemenceau, Lloyd George, and Wilson, for a variety of reasons, were not willing to grant so many and so extensive concessions to Italy, and they had communicated this to the Italians in earlier meetings. Still, the Italians persisted, because Orlando's premiership was on the line at home and he had to return to Italy with some sort of gains. Otherwise, his government would, almost certainly, fall.

Orlando and Sonnino's domestic situation carried little weight with the others, however, they all had problems back home.

One, and only one, area of agreement was reached. It regarded the adjustment in Italy's Alpine border centering on the South Tyrol. This was an area on the southern slope of the Alps which, geographically, should be Italian. It also contained the important Brenner Pass over which Italy had been invaded for centuries, and awarding it to Italy would give that country an added measure of security along its northern border. Unfortunately, about half of the population was German who did not want to live under the Italians. But, by now, giving away Germans had become commonplace and no concession was made with regard to this area. The Italians would acquire South Tyrol.

THE BRENNER PASS

It was at the Brenner Pass that Hitler and Mussolini held several of their meetings before and during WW II.

After Mussolini's government collapsed in 1943 and the Germans rescued him, one of their demands was that South Tyrol be returned to Austria — then a part of Germany. This was done and Mussolini was powerless to prevent it.

After the end of WW II, South Tyrol was returned to Italy.

Wilson led the counterattack against the Italians' other territorial demands because the US had not been a party to the Treaty of London and was not bound by it. Wilson's position was that the emergence of the new state of Jugoslavia showed great promise in toning down the dangerous, and age-old, conflicts in the Balkans. After all, it was there that the Great War had started. Therefore, Wilson argued,

Jugoslavia's new and fragile government in Belgrade had to be supported and the country had to have a viable outlet to the sea. Italy's claims on Fiume and Dalmatia would strip Jugoslavia of any such opportunity.

Then there was the three-way dispute over Albania where Jugoslavia, Greece, and Italy all had claims. And in the Aegean Sea and Asia Minor, Italy's claim conflicted with those of Greece, France, and Turkey. Giving Italy all, or even part of these concessions would stir up a political hornet's nest in the region and could possibly ignite yet another Balkan war.

Clemenceau tended to side with Wilson because it was to France's advantage to have a formidable, and friendly, state on Italy's eastern border.

The discussion over Italy's claims became very heated and the always argumentative Sonnino, became so abusive that, at one point, Wilson asked Orlando to remove him from the room.

The argument centered on the city of Fiume, the largest and most modern seaport in the northern part of Jugoslavia. Fiume had been a part of Austria-Hungary before the war and had modern rail links into Central Europe and a well-developed harbor. Orlando argued that there were 30,000 Italians in the city and that it should go to Italy. Wilson sarcastically quipped that there were over a million Italians in New York City and asked Orlando if he intended to annex that city.

Italy had, as yet, not recognized the new state of Jugoslavia, claiming the country had ongoing conflicts with Italy in the Balkans and that Jugoslavia would contain large numbers of Slovenes and Croats who had fought against Italy in the war, and, the Italians believed, would do so again if given the opportunity.

The argument went on and on with Orlando and Sonnino making their demands and their three compatriots holding their ground. Orlando eventually threatened to leave Paris if his demands were not met and got very emotional. At one point, his eyes teared up and he began to sob. Wilson tried to console him, Lloyd George asked Italy to make one more sacrifice for world peace, and Clemenceau glared with cynicism.

By the end of the day, there was still no agreement but much bitterness.

Wilson then had a brainstorm. He would go over Orlando's head directly to the Italian people. After all, they had welcomed him with open arms during his trip to Italy in January. Maybe they would listen to him now. Orlando and Sonnino remained silent, knowing that it was a very naive idea and would probably fail and might, very well, provide additional support for them at home.

On April 23, 1919, Wilson issued his appeal, via the news media, to the Italian people, calling on them to remember what they had already gained: to embrace Jugoslavia as an Allied nation, support world peace, and consider minority rights. In Italy, the people read the newspapers and laughed.

The next day, Orlando and Sonnino met again with the other members of the Council, but the outcome was the same. That evening Orlando left for Italy by train. Sonnino followed a few days later. The Big Four was now the Big Three. Some were beginning to speculate that, considering Wilson's problems with the US Senate, there might soon be a Big Two.

In Italy, Wilson's message was seen as a great insult and acted as a unifying force in a country fraught with divisions. Orlando was right, Wilson's attempt had failed miserably and the Italian people had found a new unifying force, their hatred for Wilson.

When Orlando arrived in Rome, he was greeted with cheers, large crowds shouting "Down with Wilson", the ringing of church bells, and patriotic leaflets being spread over the city by airplanes. *Il Popolo d'Italia* and other voices from the right condemned Wilson and began advocating the takeover of Fiume by force.

In the Italian Assembly, a vote of confidence was taken on the Orlando government and it passed by 382 to 40. Wilson had saved Orlando.

And the Belgians, who were unhappy over their share of reparations, announced at this time that they, too, might leave Paris.

In Paris, one newspaper headline read "CHAOS." And chaos it was. In addition to the issues with Italy, Jugoslavia, Belgium, eastern Europe, there were still major and unresolved issues with Japan, China, Turkey, the Middle East, and in Africa. This led some cynics to claim that the peace conference, itself, was doomed. At the Quai d'Orsay, the conference secretariat, convinced that Italy would not sign the peace treaty, began working feverishly to remove references to Italy from the draft of the peace treaty. Behind the scenes, however, low level contacts were maintained with the Italians in an attempt to get them to come back to Paris.

The greatest concern in Paris now was that the Germans were coming and might well find the peace conference in great disarray.

Clemenceau then made the somewhat bewildering announcement that the Austrians had been invited to Paris in mid-May to discuss their peace treaty. What would the Austrians find when they arrived?

Wilson, vengeful that the Italians had rejected his counsel, announced that a $25 million credit promised to the Italians would now be postponed. Lloyd George hinted at compromise and it was well-known by now that the Big Three

had some major problems on their hands. The newspaper was right — Chaos!

On April 25, 1919, the first contingent of the German delegation arrived in Paris and in Bavaria, several Free Corps were assembling around communist-controlled Munich.

HITLER AND CHRIST

On April 20, 1919, Hitler turned 30. In later years he would boast that both he and Christ began their missions for mankind at the age of 30.

AND NOW — SHANTUNG

In Paris, the Big Three took up the issue of Shantung once again. On April 21 and 22, the Japanese presented their arguments for yet another time to the three wise men. They also made an outright threat — no Shantung — no League of Nations.

On the 23rd, the Chinese presented their arguments. And they, too, made a threat — no Shantung — no peace treaty.

The Big Three discussed the issue for several days and concluded that there was no good solution to this problem, and that they would have to choose between losing Japan or China in the peace process. The Big Three had succeeded in reaching an agreement of sorts with the Japanese in that they could take over the economic aspects of the concession but could not annex it to Japan. This, in theory, left Shantung a part of China. But, between now and that vague and indeterminate date when Shantung would revert to the Chinese, it would be a Japanese concession.

And, yet another problem loomed. A plenary session of the entire peace conference had been scheduled at the Versailles Palace for the afternoon of April 28 to vote on the Covenant of the League of Nations. With Italy absent, the Big Three did not want to have either China or Japan absent too. So, they agreed to postpone announcing their final agreement on Shantung until after the session.

On the 28th, the plenary session met as planned and the League of Nations was unanimously approved. Makino made a bland speech in which he made no threats and did not mention the absence of a racial equality clause. It was a good sign. But there was also a bad sign coming from the Far East. While the Japanese delegate were placating the members of the peace conference in Paris, the Japanese Army was ruthlessly suppressing yet another rebellion in Korea.

THE LEAGUE OF NATIONS' COVENANT

The League of Nations' Covenant, which was agreed to this date, outlined the general functions of the League of Nations. It stipulated that nations signing the agreement of April 28, 1919, were all members of the League and that additional countries could be admitted by a two-thirds vote of the General Assembly. All members agreed to extend mutual protection against aggression, to submit disputes to arbitration or inquiry, and to abstain from war for at least three months after an arbitration award had been made.

All existing treaties which had terms incompatible with those in the Covenant became abrogated and had to be revised or canceled. And, all future treaties had to comply with the League's regulations and had to be registered with the League and made public.

The League would focus on the problems of disarmament, labor legislation, health problems, international administration, and other world issues.

The permanent Secretariat and the General Assembly would be located in Geneva, Switzerland, and the League's first Secretary-General would be Sir Eric Drummond of Great Britain. The permanent Secretariat would consist of nine members, five of them permanent and four selected on a rotating basis from the General Assembly. The five permanent members would be Britain, France, Italy, Japan, and the US. The first four temporary members would be Belgium, Brazil, Greece, and Spain.

In the General Assembly, all members would have one vote each.

The League of Nations Covenant would become an integral part of the peace treaty with Germany and would become effective in January 1920.

A FINAL DECISION ON SHANTUNG, AND CHINA LEAVES

Immediately following the creation of the League of Nations, the Big Three made the formal announcement that Shantung would go to Japan under the terms agreed to. Few were happy with the decision and the Chinese were outraged.

Wilson was one of those opposed to giving Shantung to the Japanese, because the US had had long-standing, and relatively good, relations with China. And, Wilson had a domestic problem with regard to the ethnic Japanese living in the US. For several years, there had been a growing popular resentment toward the ethnic Japanese in the US because of their ever-increasing numbers and their reluctance to assimilate. This attitude was especially strong in California. Before and during the war, thousands of Japanese had immigrated to the West Coast to find employment and the people of the West Coast deeply resented the influx of these very foreign intruders. They already had tens of thousands of Chinese who had come to California during and after the Gold Rush days. Some efforts had been taken to stem the flow of all Orientals, but they continued to come. By siding with Japan, Wilson and the Democrat Party would, almost certainly, lose some degree of political support from the voters on the west coast.

But, Wilson gave in. Before he relented, however, he obtained a promise from the Japanese that they would, at some unspecified time in the future, return the area to China.

Upon learning of the Shantung decision by the Council, the Chinese delegation announced that it would make good its threat and leave the conference and would not sign the peace treaty with Germany. Within days, the entire Chinese delegation had left Paris.

ANOTHER BLOW FOR THE CHINESE

Little note was taken in Paris, but the Chinese had just suffered another defeat, this time at the hands of the Bolsheviks. When the Bolshevik Revolution started, the Chinese took advantage of Russia's weakness and occupied Outer Mongolia (Mongolia), a large flat, cold, barren, sparsely-settled area between Northern China and Russian Siberia. The Chinese had long considered Mongolia as a part of Greater China, but during April, Bolshevik forces invaded Outer Mongolia and expelled all of the Chinese representatives and administrators. Within a few years, the Bolsheviks would allow the Mongolians to declare their independence.

WE'D BETTER LOOK TO THE SOUTH AND NOT TO SIBERIA

Outer Mongolia, the land of Genghis Khan and Kublai Khan, would eventually become the world's second Communist country in 1924 and assume the name "Mongolian People's Republic." In 1932, the Japanese gained control of Manchuria, Mongolia's neighbor to the east, and declared it to be an independent country and renamed it "Manchukuo." If fact, both Mongolia and Manchukuo were puppet states of their respective mentors.

During the summer of 1939, a border dispute erupted between Mongolia and Manchukuo at a remote location known as Khalkhin Gol. The Soviets rushed in some of their best forces to support Mongolia's claim, and the Japanese did likewise for the Manchukuoans. In a series of clashes, which included tanks, heavy artillery, and aircraft, the Soviets resoundingly defeated the Japanese and settled the border dispute in Mongolia's favor. Back in Tokyo, the Japanese leadership realized that the Soviet ground forces were far superior to their own and that if Japan was to expand, it would not be wise to do so at Russia's expense. Rather, it would be best to expand into Southeast Asia. On December 7, 1941, that drive to the south began.

"CORPORAL HITLER, YOU ARE UNDER ARREST"

On April 27, 1919, according to a account later given by Hitler, three men arrived at the List Barracks in Munich to arrest him. Hitler later said of the encounter, "Faced with my levelled carbine, the three scoundrels lacked the necessary courage and marched off as they had come." Many people believe that the accuracy and content of this event are in question.

HERE THEY COME!

On the 28th, as the Allied nations voted on the League of Nations, a special train left Berlin heading for Paris. Aboard were 160 members of the German delegation. Count Ulrich von Brockdorff-Rantzau, Germany's Foreign Minister, headed the delegation. Brockdorff-Rantzau, a socialist, had been an outspoken critic of German war policies and had, early on, urged a negotiated settlement. Now he would have his day.

This is what the Germans saw from the windows of their train as it traveled trough the battlefields of France. There was nothing like it in Germany.

Also aboard the train were representatives of the Big Three that would brief the Germans on what to expect in Paris. The Germans had already announced that their position at Paris would be based on Wilson's Fourteen Points, but the Allied representatives aboard the train insisted that the Germans would be compelled to sign the treaty pretty much as it was written.

The Germans also held out hope that, judging from reports coming out of Paris, that their might be a last-minute split among the Allies that would benefit Germany.

THE NAZIS, TOO, HOPED FOR AN ALLIED SPLIT

During the last months of WW II, the German leaders perceived what they came to believe was the beginning of a split between the Western Allies and the Soviet Union that would benefit Germany. It didn't happen — at least not at that time. During the latter months of 1945, however, the Cold War began to unfold and East Germany eventually became a separate communist state while West Germany became a western-style democratic state. Neither of the two Germanies were punished as had been the case in 1919. So the Nazi leaders were right, there was a split coming, but it came too late to benefit them.

The train traveled rapidly through Germany and Belgium, but when it reached the French border and came under the control of the French railway officials, it was ordered to slow to 15 mph. On this leg of the journey, the train passed through some of most heavily damaged areas of northern France. At some badly damaged villages, the train was ordered to stop altogether for a brief period. The French wanted the Germans to have a good look. There was nothing like it in Germany.

When the Germans' train reached Paris, the highest Allied official to meet them at the station was a French colonel. There were hoards of photographers, a large and unfriendly crowd, and waiting buses. The Germans were taken, unceremoniously, to the Hotel des Reservoirs, an old but very upscale hotel. In 1871, the French peace commission that had gone to Berlin to seek peace terms from the Germans resided in this hotel after they returned to Paris.

The Germans' luggage was dumped in the courtyard of the hotel and the delegates had to find their bags and carry them to their rooms. No self-respecting French bellman wanted to carry the Germans' luggage.

Armed guards were plentiful around the hotel and in full view of both the Germans and the crowds. An area in an adjacent park had been cordoned off with barbed wire and the Germans were allowed to stroll there. The Germans made frequent use of the park because is was a place where the Germans felt they could speak freely to each other because they believed their hotel rooms were bugged. When holding meetings in the hotel, the Germans usually played music in the background to thwart the Allied interlopers. They had brought their own wind-up gramophones and records to Paris for this purpose.

In time, the crowds disappeared and the Germans ventured further afield: shopping, sight-seeing, taking motoring trips into the surrounding countryside, and bird watching. There was, however, virtually no fraternization with the French people.

There was little formal contact between the Germans and the members of the peace conference except that the Germans were told they would receive the final draft of the peace treaty on May 7. In the meantime, they would have to wait at their hotel.

CHAPTER 10
MORE
MESSES

||||||||||||||||||||||||||||||||||||||||||||||||||||||||||||||||||||||||||||||||||||||||||||||||||||||||

THOSE DAMNABLE RUSSIANS

During April, there were serious troubles in Russia. In Siberia, some 25,000 peasants and workers banded together in a communist-inspired rebellion against Admiral Kolchak's corrupt regime. The rebellion spread over such a wide area that Kolchak was hard-pressed to maintain order and had to take troops from his frontlines to do so. And the Cossacks, once again, were running wild.

Kolchak's forces were unable to restore order in some areas, simply because of the immense size of Siberia. In those areas the rebellion continued to flourish and the communists became well-entrenched.

Instead of making some concessions to the workers and peasants in an effort to make peace, Kolchak continued to insist that the question of reforms and Russia's future be postponed until after "peace" was restored. In Paris, Kolchak was beginning to be seen by the peacemakers as politically inept.

Also in Paris, the concept of politically isolating Russia from the rest of the world began to take hold. This would include building up Russia's neighbors militarily and politically to support that containment. Some western leaders, however, including Churchill, warned that such a policy would throw the Bolsheviks into the arms of the Germans.

In Paris, the Hoover plan to send food to Russia was reviewed once again. Low level contacts were made with the Bolsheviks offering food in exchange for a containment of their revolution. Lenin was not interested and the plan fell apart. After that, the peacemakers shook their heads, not knowing what to do next with those damnable Russians.

THAT MESS IN TURKEY

In the spring of 1919, the Paris peacemakers turned their attentions to the former Ottoman Empire, also known as Turkey, which was now on the Allies' chopping block. There was little sympathy in Paris for this ancient and decrepit Muslim nation that had become so corrupt and had plagued Christian Europe for so many centuries. The country was now prostrate and defenseless and almost everyone wanted a piece of its remains. The Greeks wanted all of European Turkey, known as Thrace, including the capital city of Constantinople. They also wanted parts of western Turkey in the area of Smyrna. The Italians wanted parts of southwestern and southern Turkey and had already landed troops at Antalya. King Faisal and his fledgling Arab government in Syria wanted parts of southern Turkey, while the French wanted a small slice of southern Turkey at Alexandretta which they hoped to add to their future mandated territories of The Lebanon and Syria. They also wanted a more encompassing "sphere of influence" in southern Turkey which stretched deep into Anatolia, the Turkish heartland in the interior of the country.

In the east, the Armenians had laid claim to a huge slice of Turkey and the Kurds — the poor and struggling Kurds — harbored a pipe dream that one day there might be an independent Kurdistan comprised of lands taken from Turkey, Mesopotamia, and Persia. In the West, however, the Kurds had little support. The Kurds were an ethnic nationality, many of them still nomadic, and within their own culture they spoke different languages; had different religions; had no history of unity or independence; had no great leaders except for Saladin; and had a history of being an unruly people. Some observers compared the Kurds to the American Indians of the Wild West.

In Constantinople, Sultan Mehmet VI was still the titular head of the nation but, in fact, was a prisoner in his own palace. The city was occupied by Allied troops and the Sultan could do only what the Allied powers allowed him to do. The Sultan had very few friends in Paris and for years had been seen as an evil person and the head of an outrageously corrupt regime.

The Allied occupiers had divided Constantinople into occupation zones and each zone was run, more or less, independently from the others.

Furthermore, Constantinople was crowded with defeated Turkish soldiers and some 100,000 homeless refugees. All of these people competed with the local population for food, fuel, and status. Black markets and crime flourished in the city as did wild rumors of all sorts.

The population of Constantinople was only about half-Turkish with the other half being a mix of foreigners, including many Jews. The Greek population of Constantinople was a dominant force in that they had long-controlled much of the city's commerce and still did. The presence of a large contingent of British warships in the harbor was also a constant irritation to not only the Turks, but to the other Allied occupiers.

Taking all of these things into consideration, the city, and much of Turkey, was a hotbed of discontent and the Allied occupiers were well aware that a political vacuum existed throughout Turkey which did not bode well for their future dealings with this country.

Another thorny issue in Turkey was an international concession arrangement known as the "Capitulations." This started in the 1500s and allowed certain foreigners special rights in Turkey, including being exempt from the Turkish judicial system and from paying Turkish taxes. The Capitulations had long been resented by the Turks and their leaders.

To resolve some of the problems in Turkey, there was talk in Paris of awarding mandates over the most vital parts of the country, including the Straits. There was also talk of a mandate over a revived and enlarged Armenia might, or might not, include generous areas of eastern Turkey. The British and French, who would have more than enough mandates to manage, agreed that the US might be a suitable mandatory power in some of these areas. The US had not been at war with Turkey and would, therefore, not be seen by the Turks as a former enemy, but rather a neutral, benevolent and rich overseer, and a country that had no Capitulations.

Another factor in the Turkish puzzle was a Turkish peace movement that had sprung up in Constantinople calling itself the "Wilsonian Principles Society" which sought a just peace for Turkey based on Wilson's Fourteen Points.

Wilson and his advisors were not enthusiastic about the idea of taking Turkish mandates, but neither did they reject it. This was an issue that Wilson would have to discuss with the leaders of Congress before any firm decisions could be made. Furthermore, others had to be consulted, including the Greeks and Armenians.

The debate over an American mandate, however, went on in Paris and one of the strongest proponents for this idea was Clemenceau. On one occasion, when Wilson and Clemenceau were discussing a possible US mandate for European Turkey and Constantinople, Clemenceau quipped, "When you cease to be President, we will make you Grand Turk." Wilson was not amused.

STARVATION

Reports had been reaching Paris for some time about the never-ending food shortages in Germany and elsewhere. Some of those reports came from Allied forces stationed in the Rhineland and were believed to be very credible. The reports stated that in some German communities such things as meat, rice, coffee, and coal were unavailable — even from the black marketeers. Diseases were spreading, including typhus, and child mortality rates were increasing. In Vienna, Austria, it was especially bad. People were killing policemen's horses for the meat. Pope Benedict XV pleaded with the Allies to end the blockades and conclude a rapid peace treaty.

Unemployment was rising rapidly, too. In Berlin alone there had been 180,000 unemployed in January; 250,000 in February; and 560,000 by the end of March.

Finally, these things began to have an impact on the peace delegates. Even the old warhorse, Winston Churchill, was concerned. He wrote of this time that there was a real danger of "... the entire collapse of the vital structure of German social and national life under the pressures of hunger and malnutrition."

Herbert Hoover, who had been pleading all along for more aid for his food program, was now given authorization to increase food shipments to Poland, Czechoslovakia, Romania, and Austria, but not to Germany or Hungary.

MUNICH LIBERATED

By the last week of April 1919, some 30,000 Freecorpsmen had surrounded Munich. They were commanded by Colonel Franz von Epp, a professional army officer who sported a mini-mustache much like the one Hitler would soon adopt. And, one of Epp's units, the Erhardt Brigade, had swastikas painted on their helmets. Supporting the Free Corps was a new volunteer force of 9000 men calling itself the "White Guards of Capitalism."

Epp's force was very formidable compared to the Bavarian Red Army which had been hastily put together by those now in power. Before attacking, the Free Corps leaders employed a number of aircraft, piloted by out-of-work former German Army pilots to soften up the Reds. These former comrades of the Red Baron and Hermann Goering bombed selected targets and strafed anyone in the open whom they considered to be the enemy. The Reds had virtually no defenses against this relatively new military tactic except for their rifles and pistols.

Then, on April 30, the Free Corps attacked. For the next 72 hours, there was violent and bloody warfare within the city. Since the Freecorpsmen saw the Reds as traitors to Germany and defenders of an alien Asiatic ideology, there was little quarter given. As the Free Corps moved into the city, many local citizens came forth and volunteered to help them. One of the volunteers was Rudolph Hess, a thrice-wounded German Army veteran. He helped man a howitzer and subsequently received his fourth combat wound.

Most of the city was eventually secured by the Freecorpsmen, but pockets of Reds held out for another week. Most Reds, however, melted into the populace or fled to outlying districts. When it was over, the bodies of over one thousand Reds — no one bothered to make an exact count — were thrown unceremoniously into mass graves. Many were the victims of summary executions.

At the List Barracks, the officers returned and things returned to normal. Corporal Hitler had remained in the barracks during the fighting and let events play out around him.

When the local courts began functioning again, Corporal Hitler was called upon to testify against some of his comrades who had joined the Reds. He made a good witness. One eyewitness reported that Hitler's testimony was "mercilessly exact." Some of the men Hitler testified against were executed.

FRITZ KUHN

One of the members of Epp's Brigade was Fritz Kuhn. Khun would later immigrate to the US and eventually become the leader of the America's largest pro-Nazi organization "The German-American Bund."

MAY DAY

For some years, May 1 had been recognized by workers, labor leaders, socialists, and others on the political left as their day. May 1, 1919 was no exception.

In Moscow, Lenin gave a rousing speech in Red Square, praising the revolution and his Bolshevik comrades for their ongoing efforts. In his speech he said, "The working class is celebrating its holiday freely and openly not only in Soviet Russia, but also in Soviet Bavaria." Word had not yet reached Lenin that Soviet Bavaria was in its death throes.

In Paris, the citizens and the peace delegates witnessed a number of larger-than-usual pro-labor demonstration. But Clemenceau and the police were ready. They were out in force and heavily armed, and French Army units were held in ready reserve. The city virtually shut down as merchants locked their doors, fearing the worst. Clashes occurred but they were quickly brought under control by the police. During the day, however, two people were killed and some 700 injured. Also in Paris, the newly-arrived German delegation spent May Day in a quiet and subdued manner at their hotel.

In communist Hungary, there were celebrations, the like of which had seldom been seen. Bela Kun was in his glory.

In the US, there were May Day celebrations in many cities but not in all. In cities where May Day was celebrated, there were fiery speeches praising the glories of the labor movement and socialism. Red flags were plentiful. Some city authorities, fearful of unrest, refused to issue parade permits and took other measures to keep the celebrants subdued. In other cities, the police were out in numbers and in a few places there were self-styled vigilante groups and posses ready to take action.

In New York City, a mob of ex-servicemen in uniform burst into the offices of the socialist newspaper, "*The Call*," terrorized the employees, ransacked the files, and destroyed equipment. In San Diego, a vigilante mob beat up a member of the Wobblies who tried to give a speech, and in Cleveland clashes resulted in two deaths and scores of injuries.

These antics tended to further polarize the American people toward or against the labor movements — mostly against. The American people had learned to hate the Germans during the war and now many of them had a new devil to hate. Also, since socialism was seen as a thing of foreigners, immigrants were now a notch or two higher on the list of suspicious elements of society.

In Munich, Germany, where the city's leftist community was now virtually nonexistent, the Free Corps held a parade, marched in goose-step, and were joined by Corporal Hitler. At the Cathedral there were high Masses of thanksgiving. Under the Reds, the Cathedral had been taken over and declared a "revolutionary temple."

OTHER EVENTS DURING THE FIRST WEEK OF MAY 1919

On May 2, the Italians sent several warships to the port of Smyrna on the west coast of Turkey. Wilson was outraged by this act and spoke of sending American warships to oust the Italians. Having been resoundingly rejected by the Italian people and with Orlando and Sonnino having left Paris, Wilson had little love now for the Italians. Similarly, Clemenceau and Lloyd George were also concerned and they met together once again to address the problem. The result was, that the Greeks, who were now more acceptable to the peacemakers than the Italians, were to be encouraged to send troops to the Smyrna area and occupy the city and the surrounding territory. This was based on a secret treaty that Britain, France, and Tsarist Russia had made with the Greeks in January 1915 in which they promised Greece part of the Smyrna area.

The Greeks readily accepted the invitation and began making preparations for an amphibious invasion at Smyrna. There was also talk in Paris that the Greeks might be permitted to take over the Turkish capital of Constantinople. The Italians were not told of these decision by the Big Three.

Now Finland! The Bolsheviks had never accepted Finland's declaration of independence from the Russia Empire in December 1917 and on April 30 launched a half-hearted attempt to invade and reconquer the country. The Finns had seen this possibility coming and had prepared a small but determined army under General Karl Mannerheim, a very capable and experienced Finnish officer who had served in the Tsar's Army. The Finns asked Sweden for help, but the Swedes refused. They then turned to the Germans who agreed to help. By the time of the Bolshevik attack, there were some 12,000 German army troops in Finland ready to defend the country.

The Bolsheviks had misjudged the situation badly, and when they clashed with these two very determined organizations, the Bolsheviks were quickly defeated. By May 2, 1919, it was all over. Mannerheim and his German allies had saved Finland.

MANNERHEIM IN WW II

Mannerheim became Finland's greatest hero and was called upon again to defend Finland against the Soviets during the Winter War of 1939/40 — another war over disputed territory. The Finns lost and the Soviets regained all of the territory that the Finns had taken in 1919 and more.

When the Germans invaded the Soviet Union in June 1941, the Finns joined in the war on the side of Germany in an attempt to regain what they had lost. Here again, Mannerheim commanded Finnish forces. But again, the Finns lost and the Soviets took still more Finnish territory.

Mannerheim's image remained the country's great hero and in 1944 he became Finland's president. He negotiated a peace treaty with the Soviets in September 1944 and Finland dropped out of WW II. Mannerheim remained president until March 1946 when he resigned because of ill health. He died soon afterwards.

CHINA, MAY 4, 1919 — A MOVEMENT

News traveled very slowly in China, but by Sunday May 4, 1919, every urban Chinese knew the horrible truth. China's wartime Allies had awarded the valuable German concession of Shantung to the Japanese. This would mean that the Japanese would replace the Germans on Chinese soil. As if directed by some unseen hand, the Chinese people erupted en masse. Led in many places by students, hordes of people poured into the streets of China and public places, like Tienamen Square in Peking, and railed against the Allies, Japan, and the two Chinese governments who had let such a terrible thing happen. In Peking, the Japanese ambassador fell into the hands of the rioters and was severely beaten. In the International Settlements throughout China, westerners huddled in their compounds fearing for their lives. Memories of the horrible Boxer Rebellion came to the fore and civil war was possible. In Shanghai, ongoing talks between the Peking and Canton governments broke down, and the Peking government announced that it would not sign the Versailles Treaty unless the decision on Shantung was reversed. The Canton government took a wait-and-see attitude.

Throughout China, May 4th became known as "National Humiliation Day." The Chinese people had finally become unified and they had a whole host of new enemies — Japan, the western democracies, the peacemakers at Paris, and almost all foreigners.

Taking part in the May 4th demonstrations were the library assistant, Mao Tse-tung, and a 21-year-old university student, Chou En-lai. They were among the millions who had now lost faith in democracies, military dictatorships, Europeans, Japanese, and Americans. Mao, Chou, and many others soon began to look toward that new utopian ideology of the north — communism. Heretofore, communist influence in China had been weak, but as of May 4th, a new day began to dawn for the Reds. In time, communism would grow in China and its leaders would remember this day by naming one of their most powerful political movements after it, "The May 4th Movement."

In 1920, the Chinese communist would organize into a political party but they would backdate the inception of their party to May 4, 1919.

MAY 4TH IN PARIS, SOME WORK, THEN A PICNIC

As the globe slowly turned and it became Sunday, May 4th, in Paris, reports from China were coming in, but their meaning was not yet clear. For the Big Three it was another day of business. They met briefly and made some last-minute decisions concerning the German peace treaty. Their last order of business that day was to direct that the treaty be sent to the printer and ordered that it be read to the entire peace delegation at Versailles, as well as to the Germans, on May 6. The Big Three then departed. Lloyd George went off to Fontainebleau for a picnic with his lady friend.

"WE ARE COMING BACK"

In Rome, it was decided that it was in Italy's best interest that Orlando and Sonnino return to Paris and become a part of the peace settlement. Otherwise, Italy would have to make a separate peace with Germany and apply, at some time in the future, for membership in the League of Nations. It was therefore announced, on May 5, that the Italians would return to Paris. Orlando and Sonnino left that afternoon.

In Paris, this caused the conference's secretariat and the printers another major problem. Now, all references to Italy in the treaty had to be re-inserted — and fast. These people began working around the clock.

Most Italians realized that signing the treaty was necessary, but their anger toward their former allies did not subside. Italian newspapers remained as vindictive as ever toward France, Britain, and Wilson — not the US, but Wilson. A disturbing report came from Fiume that four French soldiers had been lynched by an angry mob.

Before he departed, Orlando said to a few of his aides that his days as premier were now numbered.

When Orlando and Sonnino arrived in Paris, they learned of the decision to allow Greek forces to invade and occupy the Smyrna area of Turkey. This was yet another slap in the face for the Italians. The Supreme Council, now the Big Four once again, took a vote on the Smyrna issue. It was three to one in favor of proceeding with the planned invasion.

OFF TO THE HALL OF MIRRORS ONCE AGAIN

On May 7, all of the peace delegations and the Germans met again at the Versailles Palace to hear the first reading of the Treaty. It now had an official name, the "Conditions of Peace." Andre Tardieu, a leading member of the French Assembly and one of Clemenceau's closest aides, read the lengthy document in French. Many who did not understand French simply dozed off. Those who did understand French could not possibly have absorbed the 440 articles that they now heard for the first time. This was not a document for light reading.

The next day, the German translation of the treaty was finished and rushed to the Germans' hotel. Soon, the Germans knew what they faced. Their emotions ran the full gamut: anger, hatred, frustration, depression, fear, and revenge. Some of the German delegates got drunk and the French newspapers escalated their escapade into an orgy. When the treaty reached Weimar and Berlin, reactions were the same. The Treaty was published in virtually every German newspapers and the public reactions were predictable. There were large-scale demonstrations in the streets and other forms of protest throughout Germany.

At the Americans' hotel in Paris, there were a number of low-level delegates who threatened to resign but most were talked out of it. One of the resignations accepted was that of William C. Bullitt.

Then the paperwork began in Paris. The Big Four had insisted that all communications between themselves and the Germans be in writing. The German delegation broke itself down into committees, each charged with examining certain sections of the Treaty. And, as might be expected, they had questions — lots of questions. Therefore, a steady stream of correspondence began to flow between the German delegation and the Supreme Council, and between the German delegation and Weimar. The Germans' messages to the Supreme Council frequently quoted Wilson's Fourteen Points. The Council passed this torrent of paperwork on to their committees that had helped formulate the decisions recorded in the treaty. Bureaucracy was at work — big time. But, the Big Four were deeply involved. Wilson personally typed out some of the responses and all responses to the Germans were signed by Clemenceau.

The Big Four had decreed that only a synopsis of the Treaty be released to the Allied press and that the full text not be released until after the Germans had signed. This gave rise in many quarters to the question of what it was that the Big Four was trying to hide?

As the Germans' questions and counter-proposals, and the Council's replies, flew back and forth, they were printed in the world's press. This would go on daily for more than two weeks.

ALSO IN THE NEWSPAPERS--

On May 10, 1919, an announcement came from Moscow that Lenin's government would now begin a program called "Subbotniki," or days of work without money. Communist ideology decreed that when pure communism was in place, there would be no need for money. Each would contribute according to his ability and each would take according to his need. Now, this revolutionary program was to be phased in a day or two at a time over the next several years. Railroad workers were to lead the way, then workers at zoos and other public services. Lenin called it the "actual beginning of communism."

Also on May 10, Brigadier General Douglas MacArthur was appointed head of West Point Military Academy.

In New England the telephone operators, mostly all women, were on strike demanding better wages.

Throughout the US, the newspapers were full of stories about individuals who had made excessive war profits during the Great War.

DADDY WARBUCKS

The stories about war profiteers died slowly. In 1925 a popular comic strip began in the US entitled "Little Orphan Annie" in which a war profiteer, "Daddy Warbucks," adopted an orphaned girl somewhat out of guilt.

On May 13, the legitimate Social Democrat Bavarian government of Johannes Hoffmann, a Social Democrat, returned to Munich from its refuge at Bamberg. A few days later, the Free Corps left the city. Bavaria was back in the German fold.

On May 13, the Big Four redrew the map of Turkey giving Greece, France, Italy, Armenia, and the US pieces of the pie. Wilson spoke optimistically of America's role in Turkey as one of the mandate powers. No territory was awarded to the Syrians or the Kurds.

This was an issue that had not been given much forethought in Paris and it suddenly appeared to many people that the announced partition of Turkey had been a major mistake. Among them were the powerful British leader, Arthur Balfour, and several leading members of the British military. They told Lloyd George that the plan for the partitioning of Turkey was unworkable and militarily unwise. Adding to this descent was a litany of objections from all over the Muslim worlds with the main theme being that it smacked of a modern-day Crusade of Christians attempting to take control of Muslim lands.

The Big Four had no good response to all this and, on May 19, canceled the partition plan. This showed, once again, that the wise men of Paris were not really so wise and that they were not very much in touch with conditions in the Middle East. As a result, the future of Turkey was back on the table.

JIHAD!

On May 10, the new, young, and ambitious ruler of Afghanistan, Emir Amanullah Kahn, declared a jihad (holy war) against the British and called upon the Muslims of India to rise up against the colonial infidels. To back up his jihad, Amanullah ordered his army to invade India to support the forthcoming uprising. No sooner had Amanullah's army crossed the Kyber Pass into India than it encountered a much stronger British force. There was a brief battle and the Afghans were chased back into Afghanistan within a few days.

Amanullah had made a monumental error in judgment but neither he nor the British wanted to pursue the issue any further so a settlement was quickly reached and this neo-comical episode became known as the "Third Afghan War." In a way, Amanullah came out ahead because the treaty recognized Afghanistan as an independent country no longer tied to Britain.

In Muslim India, there was no great response to Amanullah's call for jihad.

GREEKS LAND AT SMYRNA IN WESTERN TURKEY

On May 15, 1919, Greek forces, as authorized by Three of the Big Four in Paris, landed three army divisions on the western coast of Turkey in the Smyrna area. This was the culmination of a centuries-old dream for the Greeks.

There was little opposition except for a brief fire fight at the Turkish Army barracks. The Turkish soldiers soon surrendered and the Greeks took control of the city. The Greek populace then turned out en masse to cheer and greet their fellow countrymen. As a countermeasure, Turkish citizens roamed the streets, beating on drums and shouting anti-Greek slogans. It was a tense but peaceful atmosphere for a short while, and then it turned ugly. Looting and other acts of violence began and the city virtually shut down.

The Turkish troops in the Smyrna area regained some military order and a number of clashes ensued. The Turks, however, were demoralized, outnumbered, and outgunned. In the end, between 300 and 400 Turks were killed. The Greeks lost about 100 men.

The Greeks fanned out into the surrounding countryside and more armed clashes occurred, but in every case, the Greeks prevailed.

In Constantinople, Turkish crowds marched through the streets carrying black flag and shouting defiance. It was reported that the Sultan wept when he heard of the landing.

The Sultan no longer had an army, but he still had the semblance of a general staff and dispatched one of Turkey's great war heroes, General Mustapha Kemal, the hero of Gallipoli, to confront the Greek invasion. The British, surprisingly, supported this decision. They were anxious to see that their rivals, Greece, France, and Italy did not become too strong in Turkey. They supplied Kemal and his

Secretary of the Navy, Josephus Daniels, and Assistant Secretary of the Navy, Franklin D. Roosevelt, were strong supporters of the Navy's historic flight. Here, they pose with the Navy flyers involved. Daniels and Roosevelt are in the front row wearing straw hats, Daniels to the left, Roosevelt to the right.

small party with British visas to leave occupied Constantinople and sail off into the Black Sea. The British were also glad to see Kemal leave the city because he was a potential rallying point around whom the discontented Turks of Constantinople might gather.

On May 19, Kemal and his party landed at the Black Sea port of Samsun, 300 miles east of Constantinople and set up their headquarters. In later years, May 19 would become a Turkish national holiday. In Paris, the peace delegates knew noth-

ing of these events and would not know for some time.

At Samsun, Kemal was in the Turkish heartland that had not been occupied by any of the Allied powers and, therefore, he had a free hand to function and he began, at once, to rebuild a Turkish army for the purpose of ousting the Greeks from Smyrna. Kemal and his associates made no secret that they would also, when able, oust any other foreign interlopers who sought to occupy Turkish land. Volunteers flocked to his cause and by June, he would be ready to act.

IN EASTERN EUROPE

In Eastern Europe, it seemed that everyone was at war with someone. The Romanians and Czechs were fighting the Hungarians, the Finns and their German allies were fighting the Bolsheviks, the Poles were fighting the Lithuanians, Czechs, and Bolsheviks, and the German Free Corps were pursuing their own interests in the Baltic states.

On May 18, 1919, Lenin's government added to the list of disasters by declaring war on Romania over their dispute with regard to the border region known as Bessarabia (Moldavia). This did not bode well for Romania because, now, the Romanians had to fight on two fronts — the Bolsheviks in the east and the communist Hungarians in the west.

BESSARABIA — BACK AND FORTH

Bessarabia would eventually be acquired by the Romanians during this period, but in 1939/40, it would be taken back by the Soviet Union which, at the time, was cooperating with Nazi Germany. Then, in June 1941, Romania joined Germany in the invasion of the Soviet Union and recovered Bessarabia. In 1944/45, the Soviets reconquered Bessarabia and it, once again, became a part of the Soviet Union. When the Soviet Union collapsed in the late 1980s, Bessarabia proclaimed its independence and is now known as Moldavia.

WHAT? SOME GOOD NEWS?

While the world's political leaders were struggling, with great difficulties, to bring fourth a new era of peace, the world's engineers and aviators were bringing forth a new era of transportation and global communications.

The development of bigger and better aircraft continued its wartime pace because it was seen as a wave of the future and there was money to be made in the process.

The Americans had begun regular air service in a few selected areas and, during May, a US Navy Curtiss NC-4 flying boat flew from Newfoundland to the Azores and on to Lisbon, Portugal. This proved that trans-Atlantic air travel was now possible.

US Secretary of the Navy, Josephus Daniels, and his Assistant Secretary, Franklin D. Roosevelt, were strong proponents of this undertaking.

In naval circles, plans were being made to build ships from which aircraft could take off and land. During the Great War, some ships were capable of launching aircraft, but landing on ships was still untested. These new ships of the future were given the very practical name — aircraft carriers.

CHAPTER 11
ON THE HORIZON –
THE TREATY

|||||||||||||||||||||||||||||||||||||||||||||||||||||||||||||||||||||||||||||||||||||||||||||||||||||||||||||||

WILSON LISTENS AGAIN TO THE JEWS

Jewish groups from the US, Britain, France, and elsewhere had sent a delegation to Paris called the "Comite des Delegations Juives." Their mission, of course, was to secure the promised Jewish homeland in Palestine and obtain some international commitment with regard to the civil rights of Jews. One of the leading members of the Comite was an American Jew, Louis Marshall, who chaired the Comite's pivotal human rights sub-committee.

Now, with the treaty under wraps, Wilson had the time to listen to more of the petitioners such as Marshall. Meeting with the Jews was high on Wilson's list because American Jews had, traditionally, supported the Democrat Party.

The Jewish delegation in Paris had appeared before the Supreme Council in February but now, on May 16, 1919, Wilson met with Marshall and his aides alone at the President's residence. As expected, Marshall asked for Wilson's support on their various issues. Wilson had already come out in support of the Jewish homeland in Palestine, but he reminded his guests that this was primarily an issue that had to be resolved with the British, and possibly, the League of Nations.

Pogroms in eastern Europe had been much in the news over the last few months and Marshall asked for Wilson's help. He agreed to send a fact-finding commission to eastern Europe to report on the situation and to recommend actions that might be taken. This would become the "Morgenthau Mission."

Marshall's group asked Wilson for his support in allowing the world Jewish community the right to petition the League of Nations. The President was not sympathetic with this issue, because it would open the door for any and all minorities scattered around the world to bring their respective problems to the League and involve the League in the internal affairs of the nations in question. Undoubtedly, Wilson was mindful of the rebellion in Ireland. Marshall also asked for Wilson's support for the American Jewish Congress, but here again, he made no outright commitment.

TURKEY

On May 14, 1919, Wilson told the other members of the Council that the US would be willing to take a mandate in Turkey, subject to the approval of the US Senate. Details about the mandate were yet to be worked out, but the area would be substantial. It would most likely stretch from the Black Sea to the Mediterranean. Critics speculated then and later, that this was just a ploy by Wilson to satisfy Lloyd George because Wilson certainly knew that the Republican-controlled Senate, growing more and more isolationist, would almost certainly reject the idea.

On May 17, 1919, a delegation of high-ranking Indian Muslims barged in, uninvited, upon the Big Four at their meeting, demanding that Turkey not be partitioned. This unorthodox procedure had its effect, especially on Lloyd George. With the Indians now becoming involved in the Turkish issue, Lloyd George grudgingly concluded that Turkey ought not be partitioned. He wanted no troubles in India, the jewel of the British Empire, and the campground of Gandhi and his followers. Lloyd George, therefore, arranged to have a Turkish delegation, headed by the Aga Kahn, a progressive and respected leader of the Muslim Ismaili Sect, come before the Big Four and present their case. Unfortunately, Clemenceau disagreed with this and on May 21 had a violent argument with Lloyd George over this issue, and the issues in the Middle East in general. One observer said that the exchange was so heated that Clemenceau challenged Lloyd George to a duel. In any case, Lloyd George then backed down and the decision on Turkey's future was put off once again. It was agreed, however, to leave the Sultan in command of his rump government in Constantinople.

Mustafa Kemal (later to be known as "Ataturk")

Turkey had now become a major problem in Paris and London — and it would get bigger.

While the Allied leaders were contemplating Turkey's fate, Mustafa Kemal was doing something about it at Samsun. His efforts to build a new Turkish army were paying big dividends — big enough that he no longer needed the Sultan. The Sultan learned of these developments and ordered Kemal to return to Constantinople. Kemal's response was to resign from the Sultan's army and ignore the Sultan's order. At this point, Turkey had two political regimes, the Sultan's all-but-powerless government in Constantinople and Kemal's rapidly expanding military and political organization at Samsun. The Sultan was not altogether unhappy with these events. He could see that Kemal was doing what he could not do, and, in the end, there still might be a place for him as Sultan or at least as caliph.

FORTY-TWO DIVISIONS

In Paris, on May 20, 1919, it became known, almost certainly on purpose, that Foch had given the order to his army to have forty-two divisions readied for a possible invasion of Germany. It was also reported that the British were reviewing their blockade policy. These were obvious ploys to induce the Germans to sign the peace treaty.

RUSSIA

In northern Russia, the Finns and their erstwhile ally, Iudenich's White Army, were closing in on Petrograd from both the north and the south. Iudenich's White Army was small in comparison to Kolchak's White Army in Siberia and Denikin's White Army in the south, but Iudenich had British tanks and the Bolsheviks had little defense against them. Lenin sent his close aide, Joseph Stalin, to the city to head the city's defense with orders to hold the city at all cost. The Bolshevik defenders were, eventually, able to hold the city, although it took months, and Stalin's star rose considerably within the Bolshevik hierarchy.

"HOLD THE CITY AT ALL COSTS"

In the Fall of 1941, it was the Germans who were besieging Petrograd, then called Leningrad, and it was Stalin that sent orders to the city's defenders to hold at all costs. They did, and again, Stalin gained laurels.

Lenin and Trotsky saw that Kolchak's army in Siberia was falling apart and sent some of their best troops to the area to hasten its demise. By the end of the month, several well-armed Communist Party units, consisting of some 20,000 party members, were in action, along with about 60,000 reliable worker/soldiers

and 3000 Komsomol (Communist Youth Groups). Kolchak's forces would prove to be no match for such an adversary.

From Paris came a measure of support for the beleaguered Kolchak. The Allies extended partial recognition to his government and offered military support in exchange for a promise that, after the war, Russia would become democratic. Kolchak's reply to Paris was somewhat garbled, but he appeared to have accepted the proposal. Unfortunately for both Paris and Kolchak, however, the situation in Siberia was so bad and the area so remote that there was nothing Paris could do to offset the fact that Kolchak's forces were now losing the war.

Wilson was at his wit's end with regard to Russia. He made the comment, "They can stew in their own juices until circumstances make them wiser."

MUSSOLINI AND ROSSI

On May 24–25, 1919, the Fasci di Combattimento held its second formal meeting in Milan. Benito Mussolini and Cesar Rossi, a typesetter with Mussolini's newspaper, were appointed joint leaders of the party. Mussolini, of course, was the dominant member of the duo. The Fascists were also having second thoughts regarding some of their more radical demands. At the meeting, they dropped their demand that the Italian Senate be disbanded and adjusted some of their other platform issues so that the party could be more acceptable to the voters in the forthcoming local elections. In this regard, Mussolini urged his followers not to be too conservative and not to forget the needs of the workers. In an attempt to gain workers' support, he urged that a tax of up to 85% be placed on excess war profits.

As for the Papacy, the Fascists softened their rhetoric with regard to religious involvement in politics but still called for the confiscation of church lands. And, the thorny issue on the redistribution of land to the peasants was postponed because the party needed money and a substantial portion of their money came from wealthy landowners.

At this time, discussions on womens' rights was a major issue in government circles in Rome. On this issue, the Fascists came out in support of women voting, holding public office, and obtaining divorces.

On other issues, the party passed a resolution stating that the 1915 Treaty of London did, in fact, promise Fiume to Italy and that Italy should make an effort to draw closer to other Mediterranean nations and away from the "western plutocratic nations."

The party also affirmed Italy's need for colonial expansion. To almost everyone in Italy, this meant Ethiopia, Tunisia, and Corsica.

On June 6, 1919, the resolutions taken in Milan were printed in *Il Popolo* in a seventeen-point program which became the Fascist Party's formal platform. Whereas Wilson had had fourteen points and Lloyd George had had six points during his election campaign of December 1918, Mussolini now had seventeen points. Ideological programs were in the air.

In the streets of Italy, it was ugly. Leftist-sponsored strikes were everywhere. During the month of May, there were 316 strikes called in Italy — more than ten a day and some of them quite bizarre. In one strike, priests of the Basilica of Loreto stopped performing the liturgy, demanding more pay. Naturally, there were clashes with police and rival organizations which resulted in deaths and people being injured. If Italy had become one of the victors of the Great War, it was not evident in their streets.

During this time, *Il Popolo* supported many of the strikes while, at the same time, condemning the Socialists and communists. They also attacked the government on many issues.

The Fascist Party was growing, but not at the rate Mussolini had predicted in March when he said, "In two months a thousand Fasci will have sprung up throughout Italy." But, there were solid gains with strong Fascists organizations having sprung up in Genoa, Verona, Naples, Parma, Bologna, and Florence.

PARIS: THE GERMAN COUNTER-PROPOSAL

On May 29, 1919, the Germans presented their counter-proposal to the peacemakers in writing as required. It consisted for some 65,000 words and had been printed by their own printers and typesetters brought from Germany for that purpose.

The Germans' principle contentions were that the proposed treaty was one of violence and not of justice. They objected to the declaration that Germany had been responsible for the war and that, in any case, the war had been conducted by the Kaiser's government which was now defunct and had been replaced by a democratic government of the people. Given this fact, the Germans demanded that the new government be allowed to join the League of Nations immediately.

On disarmament, the Germans agreed to disarm, so long as it was part of a world-wide disarmament program. The German government had planned on keeping an army of some 400,000 men which included tanks, aircraft, and other modern weapons. The reductions in the size of the future German armed forces called for in the treaty were extremely disappointing to the Germans.

The Germans also objected strongly to the demands that Danzig, the Polish Corridor, the Saar, Memel, and Upper Silesia be taken from Germany. Instead, they demanded that before any territory was detached from Germany, a plebiscite be taken in each to determine the wishes of the people involved. This was also to include Alsace and Lorraine.

As for the coal shortage in France, the Germans offered to supply France with coal until such time that the French coal mines were back in operation.

In the east, the Germans offered to make the ports of Danzig, Memel, and Konigsburg into free ports so that Poland would have access to the sea but Germany would still own, control, and administer those ports.

With regard to the German colonies, the Germans agreed to give up Shantung, but they argued that a special commission be set up to hear Germany's position with regard to any future mandates over the other German colonies.

The Germans agreed to pay reparations in the amount of $25 billion over a yet-to-be-determined period of time, but without interest. They also demanded that any asset, such as railroads, mines, and merchant vessels taken from Germany be credited against the $25 billion and that the value of the German Navy, which had been turned over to the Allies, also be a credit against that sum.

As for the union between Germany and Austria, the Germans stated they would no longer pursue that union.

The German counter-proposal was made public and the peacemakers began to review it in fine details. They would reply on June 16.

INDEPENDENCE FOR THE RHINELAND

On June 1, 1919, trouble erupted at Wiesbaden in the German Rhineland when an organized group of Rhinelanders, seeking independence for their state, attempted to seize the city's government offices. The coup leaders demanded independence for the Rhineland because, they claimed, it had been forced into Imperial Germany by Bismarck in 1870 against the will of the people. The new nation would, henceforth, be known as the "Rhineland Republic." The putsch failed, and it soon became obvious that the French had had a hand in the matter.

In Paris, Wilson and Lloyd George were very upset with the French for their support of the Rhineland rebels and made public statements criticizing the French for their actions.

BOMBINGS IN AMERICA

On the evening of June 2, 1919, a powerful bomb went off in front of the home of Attorney General A. Mitchell Palmer that destroyed the front of his house. Palmer and his family were not hurt. As the government's top law enforcement officer, Palmer was looked upon by the country's leftists as their #1 villain.

One of the first to arrive at the bombing scene was Franklin Roosevelt and his wife, Eleanor, who lived nearby and were returning home from a dinner engagement. The area was strewn with anarchist literature, obviously deposited by the bomber who, inexplicably, blew himself up, apparently by accident in the blast.

That same night, bombs went off at the homes of a judge in New York, the major of Cleveland, two local politicians in Massachusetts, an industrialist in Patterson, NJ, an immigration office in Pittsburgh, and a Catholic church in Philadelphia. Obviously, it was a grand conspiracy perpetrated by the militant left.

This was the second time Palmer had been targeted by bombers. In April, 16 brown paper parcel bombs were discovered by a New York City postal clerk, one of which had Palmer's name on it.

Palmer used the conspiracy to his advantage and was able to get a half million dollar appropriation from Congress to expand the Justice Department's program to root out radicals and bring them to justice. A young and up-and-coming law enforcement officer, J. Edgar Hoover, became one of the top officials in the new program.

J. EDGAR HOOVER

The Justice Department's anti-radical group would later be named the Federal Bureau of Investigation (FBI) and Hoover would become its head in 1924. He served in that position throughout WW II and into the early years of the Cold War.

THE GERMAN COUNTER-PROPOSAL REVIEWED

In Paris, there was a great flurry of activity as the Big Four reviewed the German counter-proposal. Lloyd George brought his entire cabinet to Paris which, of course, included Winston Churchill.

Clemenceau consulted his cabinet and other governmental and military leaders.

Wilson called the entire American delegation into a conference at Hotel Crillon. It was the first time that all 38 of the members had met at one time. Methodically, Wilson asked each member for his views on the issue. Much to Wilson's displeasure, there was no clear consensus on a course of action and a considerable amount of criticism of the peace treaty as it was written. Wilson, seeing that this meeting would be of little value, soon ordered it adjourned. For all of the members of the Big Four, these next few days would not be easy.

THE OTHER PEACE TREATIES AND THE OTHER ISSUES

While the major players at Paris debated the German counter-proposal, their subordinates began work on the treaties with Austria, Hungary and Bulgaria.

On June 2, the Austrians saw the draft of their peace treaty for the first time.

Many of the articles in it were identical to those in the treaty with Germany. There was, however, no article placing war guilt on the Austrians, and the borders with Italy and Jugoslavia were not yet fixed. A date for the treaty's signing was set by the Allied leaders for July.

When the terms of the Austrian treaty were made known, the Vienna government called for three days of mourning.

On June 3, 1919, the Big Four addressed the thorny issue of Upper Selesia, the area on the eastern border of Germany that was to be given to Poland. The issue of a plebiscite, which the Germans had demanded, had been previously debated in Paris but without resolution. Now, it was time for a decision. It was fairly obvious that if such a plebiscite were carried out, the area's population, which was overwhelmingly German, would vote to remain with Germany. Nevertheless, both Wilson and Lloyd George favored a plebiscite and offered to send American and British troops to supervise it. Clemenceau, however, was bitterly opposed and unbending. Thus, once again, the decision was postponed on the flimsy excuse that the question should be delayed until such time when it could be reasonably assured that such a plebiscite would be fair and equitable. When that time would come, no one could say. When Paderewski learned of this, he was livid. Pilsudski who, by now had little faith in the political leaders in Paris, could see only a military solution.

In the US, on June 4, the House of Representatives passed a bill calling for a constitutional amendment to provide for women suffrage. The vote was 304 to 84 and the bill was then passed on to the 48 states for ratification and that ratification would proceed rapidly. This would be accomplished in time for the November 1920 Presidential election.

That same day, American Marines landed in the Central American country of Costa Rica. They had been requested by the Costa Rican government which feared an invasion from neighboring Nicaragua.

US Marines were already in Haiti, since 1915, and the Dominican Republic since May 1916. Furthermore, Washington was keeping a watchful eye on Cuba, where Cuba's corrupt President, Mario Garcia Mendocal, who had profited greatly during the war, was facing a possible insurrection. Cuba, however, had declared war on Germany in April 1917 immediately after the US declared war and, in its own unique war, contributed to the war effort. As a result, Mendocal's indiscretions had been tolerated. But now, the war was over, and American business interests wanted to do business in Cuba in an orderly and acceptable manner.

On June 6, Finland escalated its war with Russia. The Finns now wanted Karelia, the land east of the Finnish heartland which was populated by the Karelian people, who were ethnically related to the Finns. Karelia also included the important all-weather seaport of Murmansk and the mineral-rich Kola Peninsula. This action, taken by Finland, is not surprising because the bulk of the Bolshevik forces in the north were defending Petrograd which left Karelia only lightly defended. There was no action taken in Paris to condemn Finland.

On June 7, the noted economist, John Maynard Keynes, resigned from the British peace delegation and the British Treasury in protest over the pending peace treaty. He would go on to write a book entitled "*The Economic Consequences of the Peace* (1919)" which would became one of the most prestigious and detailed condemnations of the Versailles Peace Treaty of its day.

On June 8, the British unveiled the world's largest bomber. It had three wings, a long range, and could carry four tons of bombs. Bombing raids deep into German would soon be feasible. This contention was backed up on June 15, when British and American flyers flew another British-made aircraft, a Vickers biplane, from Newfoundland to Ireland, a distance of 1900 miles. This was another large aircraft for its day and such aircraft could easily be converted into bombers. The German leaders could not help but take note of these events. The bombing of Berlin and other German cities to the east was now possible.

On June 9, in Washington, Senator William Borah (R-Idaho), a staunch isolationist, prohibitionist, and supporter of the income tax, read the entire German peace treaty to the US Senate. The entire text had not yet been released to the Senate by the Wilson Administration, but Borah had obtained a copy surreptitiously from a reporter of the *Chicago Tribune*. There was plenty in the treaty that the Borah's fellow senators did not want to hear.

BORAH AND LINDBERGH

Borah would serve in the Senate for some 33 years and would remain a staunch isolationist all that time. In the late 1930s and early 1940s, when WW II loomed, he became a close associate of fellow isolationist, Charles Lindbergh, and advocated that the US stay out of all foreign wars. On December 7, 1941, he was forced to alter his views.

Also on June 9, a massive strike in the French steel industry began.

And in Russia on this date, Trotsky's Red Army captured the major city of Ufa, east of Moscow, from Kolchak's forces. In the days that followed, the Reds forced Kolchak's Whites to retreat over the Ural Mountains and back into Siberia.

On June 16, there was a communist-inspired riot in Vienna and eight people were killed.

And in Paris, the German delegation left the city to return to Weimar to discuss the peace treaty, firsthand, with the German leaders. On their way from their hotel to the train station, their automobiles were stoned by the locals and the Paris police had to protect them all along the way.

BELA KUN IN TROUBLE IN HUNGARY

From Hungary came reports showing that Foch's prediction that Bela Kun's government was incompetent were coming true. Hungary's treasury was now empty, but Kun's government ignored that and simply printed more money and, as a result, inflation soared. They also continued to force communist ideology on the Hungarian people, and in their zeal, confiscated the personal property of priests and other religious leaders. This action greatly angered many people in the country that were deeply religious. Kun's government had, by now, confiscated all of the large landed estates, but had made little or no effort to redistribute the land to the peasants. Opponents to these and other measures, now branded "Counter-revolutionaries" by the Kun government, were being arrested by the hundreds and some of the more aggressive communists "enforcement squad" has become vigilantes and bandits. One of their favorite tactics was to burst into middle class homes, usually at night, search for contraband and drag the guilty parties off to one of the many revolutionary courts which almost always found them guilty on the spot and sentenced them to jail. On June 7, a report reached Paris that Kun's Red Army had hanged some 300 people in western Hungary.

In Paris, the Big Four could not agree on what to do. Clemenceau wanted to send Allied troops to Hungary but Lloyd George wanted to impose economic sanctions. By now, the Romanians and Czechs had entered the fray and it was they who resolved the turmoil in Hungary.

The Big Four did, however, send another cease-fire order to Hungary, Romania, and Czechoslovakia on June 12 and further ordered the Romanians, who were advancing on Budapest, not to occupy the city. The telegram further stated that the Big Four would not recognize any borders established by force of arms.

Kun replied to the cease-fire order declaring that his government would cease-fire if Romania and Czechoslovakia would do likewise. This was most unlikely because the Romanians and Czechs believed they had the upper hand and the Western powers were paralyzed by indecision.

Bela Kun had no friends but Lenin, and Lenin was not in a position to help. Kun, however, manufactured a friend, the "Slovak Soviet Republic." For some time the Hungarians had occupied a small area in southern Slovakia, the eastern half of Czechoslovakia, and Kun had encouraged his supports there to declare the area an independent county. On June 16, they complied. The Slovak Soviet Republic would last three weeks.

Along with the growing disgust with communism in Hungary and elsewhere in eastern Europe, anti-Semitism rose to a new height. Anti-Semitism was especially strong in Budapest which turned many Hungarians against Kun's "Jewish" government. They began calling it the "Jewish Conspiracy," a phrase that was very likely inspired by the Protocols book.

TO SIGN OR NOT TO SIGN

At Weimar, the Scheideman government was in crisis. When the German delegation from Paris arrived, Brockdorff-

Rantzau went immediately to the Grand Ducal Palace to consult with Chancellor Scheideman and his cabinet. The gut feeling of virtually every member of the government was not to sign such a horrible treaty, but when the alternatives were considered, there were few options. Vocal opinions came forth from all directions. The German Army officer corps emphasized, again, that they could have won the war, or at least, reached a stalemate which would have brought about a more generous peace. The army leaders further implied that the Weimar government was made up of cowardly civilians. Such rhetoric demonstrated that the German military was not all that loyal to the government and that a military takeover was possible. Out of self-defense, some of the members of the government demanded that the generals put their claims in writing and state whether or not they were now in a position to defend German against a renewed Allied attack. The generals countered with several plans. One of the most feasible was for German forces to draw back to the Elbe River and make a last stand. This plan had some merit because Allied forces in the west were down to 39 divisions as compared to 198 divisions in November 1918.

And what if the Poles and/or the Czechs attacked from the east? This was a question no one in Germany could answer. The chaos in Poland reduced the chances of an attack from Poland, but the Czechs, on the other hand, had built up their forces along the German border and gave every indication that they would participate in an Allied invasion of Germany.

It was not surprising, then, that the German cabinet was deadlocked. On June 19, a vote was taken and it was seven to seven. The question was passed on to the National Assembly, but they too, could not reach a conclusion.

It was obvious to all that if the treaty were signed, the Scheideman government would fall, and very likely, President Ebert as well. Under such a scenario, Defense Minister Gustav Noske, a tough and crude politician with a recently-acquired reputation as a peacemaker because of his efforts in defusing the German Navy's mutiny in late 1918, offered his services as Germany's dictator. And it was rumored that Noske had the support of the Free Corps. Noske, however, had few supporters at Weimar or within the German population. The time was not yet right for a dictator.

NOSKE – 1933

In February 1933, following the turmoil created in Germany by the Reichstag fire and the possibility of civil war, some military leaders called again for Noske to become Germany's dictator. This, of course, did not happen. It was Chancellor Hitler who jumped into the breach and fulfilled that role.

State leaders were surveyed. The states of Bavaria, Saxony, Wurttemberg, Baden and Hesse favored signing. Most of the others did not or could not make up their minds. There was the distinct possibility that some states might sign the treaty on their own and others might not. Once again, the possibility of Germany fragmenting into a number of separate political entities surfaced.

The right-wing political parties opposed signing while the left-wing parties generally favored signing.

And there was grasping at straws. Some foresaw a split between the Allies over the spoils to be had, and/or between the Allied leaders in Paris if the prospect of a renewed war became imminent.

Surmounting all of this was the ugly prospect of civil war within Germany itself, or a communist uprising, or general strikes, and a continuation of the blockade, or of any combination of these things.

Von Hindenburg remained aloof and non-committal, and to some observers, seemed to be in a "dreamlike passivity" uttering monarchist phrases. It was reported that he had said that it might be better to die as an honorable soldier fighting in the field rather than accept such a disgraceful peace. In the end, however, he made no hard decision. It was the duty of the politicians to decide, not the country's military leaders. This was a good sign that Hindenburg and the army were not planning a coup.

And there was a time limit which had been imposed by the Allies — June 24, 1919.

On June 19, the Scheideman government resigned but Ebert remained at this post as the nation's President. Brockdorff-Rantzau also resigned and dropped out of politics for several years.

BROCKDORFF-RANTZAU TURNED TO THE RUSSIANS

In 1922, Brockdorff-Rantzau became Germany's ambassador to Moscow and was instrumental in arranging the secret arrangement under which German pilots and officers were trained in Russia.

Within hours, a new Chancellor was chosen. He was Gustav Bauer, an Austrian by birth, and one who favored signing. Bauer, like Scheideman, was a Social Democrat. These were reassuring signs. At least there would not be a split or a radical change in Germany's political leadership nor would there be a dictator.

ITALY–BRITAIN–THE CAUCASUS–TURKEY–FRANCE

The falling of governments was in the air. In Italy, Orlando's government also fell and Francisco Nitti, a neo-isolationist, was asked by the King to form a new government. He offered a program that concentrated on Italy's internal problems with international problems becoming secondary. As an example, there had been talk that Italian troops might be sent to the Caucasus region to replace the hard-pressed British troops there. Nitti put an end to this, saying that Italy would no longer consider the idea.

Then too, the British were losing interest in the Caucasus. Lloyd George now strongly opposed any thought of Britain taking a mandate over any part of that region.

As for Turkey, Nitti had little incentive to keep Italian troops in the southwestern part of the country because there were frequent clashes with the Greeks to the north. With time, the Italians would withdraw from Turkey.

About this time, Marshal Foch visited the Allied troops in the Rhineland, urging them to be ready to march into Germany. The first such action was scheduled, if need be, for 6:45 P.M. on the 24th — the day of the deadline.

On June 21, the German sailors aboard the impounded German warships at Scapa Flow in the Orkney Islands off the northern coast of Scotland scuttled their ships under the noses of their British overseers. It was a gallant and suicidal act of defiance but it changed nothing. In Paris, Colonel House noted in his diary, "Everyone is laughing at the British Admiralty."

FINALLY, AN AGREEMENT AT WEIMAR

The mental carnage went on at Weimar for a few more days, but on the 23rd, the

Bauer government announced that Germany would sign.

When the telegram reached Paris, Wilson, Clemenceau, and Lloyd George were meeting in Wilson's study. They were overjoyed and promptly adjourned the meeting without further discussion.

IS ANYONE SATISFIED?

Around the world the extent of the Versailles Peace Treaty was being realized and there was a great international polarization. Leftist and neutral government generally supported it, while countries like Austria, Jugoslavia, Japan, and China opposed it. Hungary, Austria, and Bulgaria opposed it because it portended what was in store for them. Whatever the opinion was from the isolated Turkish Sultan, it did not get beyond the palace walls.

In Italy, the new Nitti government was struggling to gain support but with little success. The Italian people were hurting badly and law and order continued to break down. There was looting and strikes, and a group of Red radicals had proclaimed a soviet republic in Florence.

At this time, Mussolini and d'Annunzio were attending a veteran's convention in Rome and were approached by high-level military officers with an interesting message. That was that if they intended to carry out a coup against the government, the Army would not interfere. This was very reliable information because it was well known that the head of the army, Emanuale-Filiberto, Duke of Aosta and the King's cousin, was very unhappy with the new Nitti government. Mussolini and d'Annunzio returned home with this message burning in their minds.

TO HELL WITH PARIS

On June 19, 1919, Mustafa Kemal, no longer a general in the Sultan's army but now an independent political leader, founded the Turkish National Congress with the overriding mission of saving Turkey from partition by the foreigners. The crises going on in Paris and Weimar were of little interest to him. It was the Allied partition of Turkey that had become his cause and a major cause for most of the Turkish people. To advance that cause, Kemal was raising a fast-growing and very willing army. As the first order of business for his new organization, Kemal announced the start of the Turkish national resistance movement against the Greeks in western Turkey. Of all the interlopers, the Greeks were the most hated.

In London, after studying the issues, Churchill advocated establishing a friendly relationship with Kemal, but Lloyd George opposed it. In his mind, Turkey was still the enemy, and a state of war still existed between Britain and Turkey.

SOUTH AND EAST OF TURKEY

In the Arab lands of the Middle East, troubles continued unabated. In Mesopotamia, British rule had become very unpopular. The British had promised to create a civil government, but their pace was too slow for many Mesopotamians. From Damascus came a call from Prince Faisal to unite Mesopotamia with his realm in Syria and his father's regime in Hijaz. This would created the long-dream-of Greater Arabia. In London, the India Office was gravely concerned that granting political controls to the Muslims in the Middle East would incite the Muslims in India to demand the same.

Also, there were reports that Faisal was working at cross purposes with the Allies. He was making nationalist-oriented speeches and it was rumored that he was conspiring with the Egyptians for a common front against the British, and that he was talking to the Turks about the possible union of Syria, Lebanon, and Turkey. In Syria's capital, Damascus, British troops were actually in control but

Faisal was given a relatively free hand to pursue his political goals. Reports sent to London, however, by the local British military leaders stated that their meager forces could be overwhelmed if an Arab revolution broke out.

During June 1919, Faisal called for elections to form a Syrian National Assembly. Those elections were held in Syria and in northern Palestine, which both Faisal and the French considered part of Syria. As a result, the new Syrian National Assembly, when it came into being, had delegates from Palestine.

And Germany still had a hand in the Middle East. During the war, the Germans had created the "Pan-Islamic Propaganda Bureau" to foster anti-British and anti-French sentiments in the region. The Bureau continued to function after the war and its message was still the same, much to the annoyance to the British and French.

The British Army in the Middle East was now down to 312,000 troops from a high of over one million at the end of the war. And the majority of them were Indian troops with a large minority of them being Muslims. Many of these troops were stationed in northern Persia along the borders with Christian Armenia and Muslim Azerbaijan and in position to go to the aid of those countries if they were threatened by either the Bolsheviks or Turks. However, the prospects of ordering Hindu and Muslim Indians to protect Christians, and Hindus to protect Muslims in Azerbaijan, and/or Indian Muslims to oppose Turkish Muslims, made for a situation that was highly unpredictable. On the other hand, if called upon the defend against the Bolsheviks, there would be little question.

And then there was oil. In the latter days of the war, British troops had moved into the southern Causacus as a part of the Allied effort to contain the Bolsheviks. In the process, British interests gained control of the area's developing oil and manganese resources and, since then, profited from the export of those items. There was hope among many people in the region that the Americans would accept a mandate over Armenia and that American troops could then replace the British troops. This, as had been seen, would be very unlikely.

Despite the uncertainties in the Caucasus, the British position in the Middle East was developing fairly well and Lloyd George was pleased with the progress being made. On the positive side of the ledger was the fact that Mesopotamia was relatively secure; the British had the dominant military forces in the Persian Gulf area, they controlling most of the Persian Gulf oil, Persia was not causing any major problem, and most of Palestine was firmly in British hands which gave protection to the Suez Canal. And, with the help of the Jews, there was the promise of a stable westernized political entity in the region and a safe terminus for the Persian Gulf oil which would soon be flowing to Haifa.

Since an American mandates over Armenia and parts of Turkey were still on the table, Wilson sent a "Commission of Inquiry" to the area to learn more about what was happening there. The Commission was headed by Charles Crane, a Chicago plumbing supply manufacturer, and Henry King, President of Oberlin College. The Commission travelled about talking mainly to Arab leaders and was given little support from the British and French who, for the most part, resented the Commission's presence in their domains. Crane and King soon found that the Arabs, overwhelmingly, wanted immediate independence and "emphatically" opposed the creation of a Jewish homeland in Palestine. These things were totally incompatible with the plans of the Big Three for the Middle East and Crane and King were apprehensive about American involvement there.

The Commission's report, therefore, was negative and became an embarrassment to Wilson and his compatriots in Paris. Accordingly, it was shelved and not released to the public. It was released, eventually, in 1922 under the Harding Administration by which time the prospects of the US taking a mandate in the Middle East was a dead issue.

This was Wilson's second failed mission in several months, the first being Bullitt's mission to Russia.

THE BATTLE OF TURABA

Turaba? Where's Turaba? Reports of this conflict sent many people in Paris to their maps of the Middle East. Turaba is an oasis town in the Arabian Desert about 110 miles east of Mecca and it was here that an issue on the future of the Arabian Peninsula was determined.

The Kingdom of Hijaz, a stronghold of orthodox Sunni Muslims, and the Wahabis, a militant religious clan led by Ibn Saud and based in Riyadh, 400 miles to the east, had been at war for years. During the turmoil of the Great War, both sides had acquired caches of modern British weapons. Ibn Saud's ambition was to control as much of the Arabian Peninsula as he could and, at the same time, spread his Wahabi religion. The capture of Islam's two holiest cities, Mecca and Medina, both in Hijaz, would be a tremendous advancement in his cause.

Saud had marched his forces across the barren desert with the intent of taking those cities and ousting the Hashimite clan headed by King Husain Ibn Ali. It was at Turaba that the two forces met. The Wahabis were commanded personally by Ibn Saud and the Hijazian forces were commanded by Prince Abdullah, the second son of the King. In a surprise and bloody attack, Saud's forces overwhelmed and routed Abdullah's forces and almost captured Abdullah himself.

He was wounded and forced to flee into the desert at the last minute, clad only in his nightshirt. With the Hijazian army in shambles, the Wahabis now had the upper hand and it appeared to be only a matter of time before Saud conquered all of Hijaz. This battle, and those which would follow, shattered the dream of Husain's family of building a pan-Arab empire in the Middle East under their control.

This development was also a setback for the British because they had been able to exercise some controls over the Hijazians. Ibn Saud, however, was a loose cannon.

Abdullah never lived down his defeat at Turaba and became the butt of jokes and ridicule throughout the Middle East.

SAUDI OIL

Hijaz disappeared from the map in 1925 and became a part of Saudi Arabia. In the early 1930s, it was realized that Saudi Arabia had one of the world's largest oil reserves located on the eastern shore of the Arabian Peninsula (not in Hijaz). Ibn Saud was firmly in power in Riyadh and needed western technology to develop those oil resources, but he was suspicious of all of the European powers and their long history of taking over countries such as Saudi Arabia and turning them into protectorates or colonies. This fear opened the door for the US which, since its inception, had had an anti-colonial policy. Riyadh and Washington found common ground, and the Americans eventually won the major oil concessions in Saudi Arabia in 1933.

The Saudi-American oil deal cemented relations between the US and Saudi Arabia, and through the US, with the western Allies when WW II started. Ibn Saud was still on the throne at that time and maintained close relations with both the US and Britain during the war although his country remained neutral until early 1945. At that time, the Saudi government declared war on Germany in order to become a founding member of the United Nations and to have a seat at the peace table. This had been arranged in January 1945 when President Roosevelt, during his trip to Yalta, met with Ibn Saud aboard an American warship in the Great Bitter Lake of Egypt. The meeting went fairly well. The only issue of concern was the Jewish homeland in Palestine and Saud suggested that the Jews be given land in Germany. Nevertheless, Roosevelt said of Saud at the time that he is a "... great and good friend."

Jozef Pilsudski

HIGH POINT FOR THE RUSSIAN WHITES AND THE POLES

There were encouraging reports from Russia. In the Ukraine and southern Russia, Denikin's forces were marching northward. On June 23, his forces took Belgorod and a few days later, Kharkov. On the 30th, Ekaterinslav fell as well as the major city of Tsaritsyn on the Volga, and Denikin claimed to have captured 40,000 Reds and two armored trains named the "Lenin" and the "Trotsky." His announced target, now, was none other than Moscow.

From the Polish front, now some 500 miles in length, came reports that the Poles had dismantled the Soviet Republic of Litbel and that large parts of both Lithuania and Belorussia were now under Polish control.

It was the Poles' plan that Vilna would become a part of Poland and the city's Polish University, closed for a hundred years, would be reopened. The rest of Lithuania would become independent, but closely allied with Poland as had been the case in centuries past. Lithuania's capital would become the city of Kaunas, 60 miles northwest of Vilna.

In Moscow, Lenin was very upset over these losses and wanted them back. He would have his chance in August 1920.

But now, in June, 1919, Pilsudski's forces were very formidable, having been recently strengthened by the arrival of some 50,000 trained and well-equipped Polish soldiers from France. These troops were under the command of Polish General Jozef Haller, an experienced and very capable leader. The French had sent them by ship to Odessa and they then marched overland, through territory controlled by the Whites, to Poland. A short time later, another 10,000 Polish soldier, who had been in the Tsar's army, arrived at Gdansk from Siberia. The acquisition of these two forces gave Pilsudski the advantage in manpower over the Bolsheviks that opposed him.

Now, under Polish control, both the Lithuanians and the Belorussians se delegations to Paris to cooperate with Paderewski's Polish delegation.

In Siberia, however, Kolchak's forces were in retreat and the picture was very bleak. A report from the US ambassador to Japan reached Washington and stated that Kolchak had by now "... failed to command the confidence of anybody in Siberia..."

So this was the high point for the anti-Bolshevik forces in Russia and the Baltic region. From here on, the Bolsheviks would rebound and begin to win the Russian Revolution.

IN AMERICA, HUNGARY AND GERMANY

On June 20, 1919, there was a race riot in Chicago. Three people were killed.

On June 24, Bela Kun's regime in Hungary adopted a new constitution which officially established communism as the nation's form of government.

On June 25, there was a brief, but unsuccessful, communist-inspired revolt in Hamburg.

On June 26, there was an unsuccessful assassination attempt on Bela Kun in Budapest.

That same day, there was another lynching in the US at Ellisville, Mississippi. *The New York Times* reported that it was "orderly." Lynching were a part of the American scene. During the war there had been some 200. And, during the war, tens of thousands of southern Negroes moved north to take jobs in the war industry and the tradition of lynching followed.

In the US Senate, the Republicans re-issued a resolution that had first been proposed in December 1918 and revised in May 1919. It asked the President to give "... reasons for sending US soldiers to Siberia, what duties are there to be performed by these soldiers, (and) how long they are to remain..." The document was sent to the White House and was on Wilson's desk when he returned.

In Paris, the British, Americans, and French signed the draft of a new treaty of alliance that called for Britain and the US to come to the military aid of France if she were attacked again by Germany. The draft treaty was subject to the approval of the American and French Senates and the British House of Lords.

CHAPTER 12
THE VERSAILLES TREATY-
SIGNED, SEALED, & DELIVERED

‖‖‖

JUNE 28, 1919

It was a fine day at Versailles and everything was ready. Flowers had been planted, the lawns were manicured, the streets were immaculate, the arrival areas cordoned off, the news reporters and photographers were at their stations, and the police were plentiful and very visible, as were vendors selling souvenirs of this great event.

It was no coincidence that June 28, 1919, was the fifth anniversary of the assassination of Austrian Arch Duke Ferdinand and his wife in Sarajevo, the event which started the Great War.

Crowds had gathered to watch the show and they would not be disappointed. Some of the people had come from Paris by special trains placed in service just for the event.

Just after noon, the limousines began to arrive. The members of the various delegations stepped out, waved to the crowds, and the cameras flashed, making photographs that would appear on the front pages of newspaper back home. Secretary Lansing was the first of the Americans to arrive early at 1:45 P.M. Clemenceau entered the Hall at 2:20 P.M., and Wilson arrived with his wife and daughter at 2:50. And, the movie cameras were rolling. This was the first time a major international treaty had been filmed in this manner. A group of French veterans of the Franco-Prussian War served as an honor guard and stood in the exact spot where the Prussian guardsmen had stood during the French surrender in 1871.

After they had made known their arrival to the press and cameras, the delegates strolled into the cavernous palace. As they passed through the doorway, a brilliantly-uniformed French Guard of Honor presented arms for each delegation. The delegates then ascended the marble staircase which had been the entrance to the Queen's Apartments and the Hall of Peace which then led into the famous Hall of Mirrors.

Other individuals who were not delegates, but who would be admitted to the Hall of Mirrors, had to present tickets to identify themselves as participants. Some of the tickets had been scalped at exorbitant prices.

The Germans entered the palace unceremoniously through an obscure doorway.

At 2:30 P.M. a group of forty-five French, British, and American soldiers — fifteen from each country — arrived and took up positions inside the Hall of Mirrors. All of the French soldiers had been wounded in the war and Clemenceau went up to each one and shook his hand. Also at 2:30 P.M., the German news correspondents arrived and were directed to the correspondents' section where they were positioned at the rear of the other assembled newsmen.

In the Hall of Mirrors, the U-shaped table was ready with the places set and marked for each delegation. At the open end of the U-shaped table was a small table with two chairs. This is where the Germans would sit. Clemenceau had taken personal charge of all of the arrangements and his great hatred for the Germans was apparent.

When all of the delegates were in their places, there were still two seats vacant — China. And, of course, at the small table, those chairs were vacant.

It was estimated that about 1000 people would witness the signing in the Hall of Mirrors which measured 240 feet long by 35 feet wide. Obviously, it would be standing room only for most of them. Of that number, only about 15 were women.

Printed programs were provided, listing the names of all those who would sign.

In the minutes leading up to the formal opening, there was an active scurrying about as the program holders sought out ˄me of those listed for their autographs.

˄

˄menceau who was to chair the ˄t to his seat and called the

meeting to order promptly at 2:45 P.M. He sat at the head of the U-shaped table with the major Allied and Associated Powers delegates to his right and left and the smaller nations seated along the arms of the U. Clemenceau made a brief opening statement in French and then ordered, "Faites entrer les Allemandes" (Bring in the Germans). There was absolute silence as Dr. Hermann Muller, Germany's newly-appointed Foreign Minister, and Dr. Johannes Bell, the Colonial Minister, entered the Hall and walked to the small table. As they approached, they avoided eye-to-eye contact with any of the delegates. Everyone remained seated as they entered. Observers said that the two gentlemen looked pale and very nervous. When the Germans reached their chairs, they bowed slightly toward Clemenceau and then took their seats. It was 3:07 P.M.

Muller and Bell had come to Paris on the same slow train that the German delegation had used in May so they, too, had been given a firsthand look at the devastation the war had caused to France. On the table in front of Clemenceau lay the one and only official copy of the treaty. It was enclosed in a ornate leather case. The various seals of the signatories had been affixed to the treaty beforehand to save time and each signer would sign next to his seal. The Germans would be the first to sign.

Wild rumors had circulated, predicting that the two Germans would sign the treaty and then commit suicide in front of all of the delegates. Other rumors stated that they would try to assassinate Clemenceau and/or Lloyd George or that they would bring a bomb into the Hall and set it off. None of this was true. The only accoutrements the Germans carried were their papers and their own pens. They refused to sign the treaty with French pens.

When the Germans were seated, Clemenceau spoke briefly again in French saying, "An agreement has been reached upon the conditions of the treaty of peace... The signatures about to be given constitute an irrevocable engagement to carry out loyally and faithfully in their entirety all the conditions that have been decided upon. I therefore have the honor of asking Messieurs, the German plenipotentiaries, to approach to affix their signatures to the treaty before me." Clemenceau's remarks were translated into German.

The Germans then rose and approached the table to sign the treaty. To the German's annoyance, the pen they had selected did not work. Col. House stepped forward and offered his pen which the Germans accepted. The Versailles Treaty was signed by the Germans with an American pen. It was 3:12 P.M. The Germans also signed a second document, a protocol covering changes in the document and an agreement with regard to Poland. As the Germans began signing, the clicking of still cameras and the humming of movie cameras rose to a new height.

The day of reckoning! The German delegates, in the chair in front of Clemenceau, sign the Versailles Peace Treaty. To Clemenceau's right is Wilson and to his left is Lloyd George.

After signing, the Germans returned to their small table and sat while the others signed. Next to sign were Wilson, Lansing, House, Bliss, and White. They signed at 3:49 P.M. Lloyd George then signed followed by Balfour, Lord Milner, and Bonar Law. Clemenceau then signed followed by Pichon, Klotz, Tardieu, and Cambon. Then, the Italians signed, then the Japanese, and so on down the line.

A box of old-fashioned goose quills were available for those dignitaries who wished to sign this important treaty in the old and traditional manner.

A long line formed of those waiting to sign. The people in the Hall began to chat quietly. Some of the delegates approached the Germans for their autographs. Wilson, Lloyd George, and others thought this was in bad taste.

When Prime Minister Smuts signed for the Union of South Africa, there was a noticeable murmur in the Hall. It was well-known that he had declared that he would sign only under protest and that the treaty, in his opinion, was unsatisfactory.

Upon a signal given by someone in the Hall, the guns of nearby St. Cyr Military Academy began to fire. Then, more distant guns began to fire. In the streets, the crowds began to cheer and celebrate.

After the last delegate had signed, Clemenceau spoke again saying, "Messieurs, all the signatures have been given. The signature of the condition of peace between the Allied and Associated Powers and the German Republic is an accomplished fact. The session is adjourned."

The Germans rose quickly from their seats and left the Hall, under escort, through a side door. Outside, they passed through a large and silent crowd of onlookers and soldiers who protected their route to their waiting automobiles back to

Paris. Within hours, they left the city by train.

But, the work of the Allied and Associated Powers delegates was not yet done. Two more agreements, each resting on separate small tables, were to be signed. The first treaty was entitled "Treaty between France and Great Britain (Treaty of Guarantee) 28 June 1919" and was a protocol declaring that Britain would come to the aid of France militarily if France were again attacked by Germany. Article two provided for the United States to come to the aid of France only if this treaty was ratified by the US Senate.

This Treaty also spelled out additional details on the administration of the Rhineland agreed to by the Big Three.

The second treaty was entitled "Treaty between the Allied and Associated Powers and Poland and the protection of minorities, 28 June 1919." This treaty guaranteed the civil rights and protection under the laws of Poland for all minorities within Poland including Germans, Jews, Ukrainians, Russians, Belorussians, Lithuanians, and others. It was also intended to serve as a prerequisite to the future recognition of the Polish state and was designed to be a model for future treaties which were to be concluded with Czechoslovakia, Jugoslavia, Romania, and Greece.

For the signing of this treaty, Premier Paderewski and his associate, Roman Dmowski, were ushered into the Hall of Mirrors to sign for Poland. They had not been parties to the German peace treaty because Poland had not been at war with Germany.

After the documents were signed, the delegates began milling about the hall congratulating each other, gathering more autographs, and making small talk. Wilson, Clemenceau, and Lloyd George joined in.

Other American dignitaries who witnessed the signing were Herbert Hoover; Bernard Baruch; Vance McCormick; Henry Morgenthau; John W. Davis, US Ambassador to Britain; Hugh C. Wallace, the US Ambassador to France, and a number of the dignitaries' wives.

The Big Three then went out onto the terrace and were cheered by the enthusiastic crowds. Soldiers had to hold them back. Chants of "Vive Clemenceau," "Vive Wilson," and "Vive Lloyd George" were heard over and over. Overhead, a formation of Allied warplanes appeared. All the while, the cannons continued booming in the distance. The three gentlemen then strolled across the lawn. Clemenceau appeared to be somewhat confused and it was reported that he had tears in his eyes.

They strolled on a prearranged path around the grounds of the palace, primarily from fountain to fountain, and thereby led a planned and dignified exit procession for themselves and for all of the other delegates who followed. Eventually the Big Three got into a large, closed automobile which took them back to Paris. The car had been bathed in flowers placed upon it by well-wishers.

SEALED

The Versailles Peace Treaty consisted of 440 Articles with the English language version being 268 pages. It created the League of Nations, dictated the terms of peace with Germany and, in the process, reduced Germany to a third-rate power. And, historians usually agree, it was a major factor in causing World War II.

The first 26 Articles of the Treaty created and defined the League of Nations. Article 1 read, "The original Members of the League of Nations shall be the signatories which are named in the Annex of the Covenant and also such of those other States named in the Annex as shall accede without reservation to this Covenant."

THE UNITED NATIONS

When the United Nations was formed after WW II, only those nations that had been at war with one of more of the Axis nations could become charter members and there were no connections in forming the United Nations with any of the peace treaties.

Article 11 defined what the League was to do in case of war. Its opening lines read "Any war or threat of war, whether immediately affecting any of the Members of the League or not, is hereby declared a matter of concern for the whole League, and the League shall take any action that may be deemed wise and effectual to safeguard the peace of nations."

Article 16 was the "sanctions" Article. It read, "Should any Member of the League resort to war... it shall, ipso facto, be deemed to have committed an act of war against all other Members of the League, which hereby undertake immediately to the severance of all trade or financial relations...(and the offending member) may be declared to be no longer a Member of the League..."

Article 21, at Wilson's insistence, specifically exempted the Monroe Doctrine from the other obligations of the League. The article read, "Nothing in this Covenant shall be deemed to affect the validity of international engagements, such as treaties of arbitration or regional understandings like the Monroe Doctrine, for securing the maintenance of peace."

Article 22 established the mandates and spoke of the backward peoples in Central Africa, the Pacific and "advanced" Arabs in the Middle East.

Article 23 addressed matters of labor, drugs, arms trade, freedom of movement, and diseases.

Article 27 through 41, the first articles following the establishment of the creation of the League, established the boundaries of Germany and East Prussia with Belgium, Holland, Luxembourg, France, Switzerland, Austria, Czechoslovakia, Lithuania and some, but not all, with Poland. The boundary with Denmark, it had been agreed, would be decided by plebiscite at a later date.

Despite losing 13% of its territory, Germany remained the second largest country in Europe after Russia and had the good fortune that German territory had remained virtually unscathed during the war.

Articles 42, 43, and 44 called for the demilitarization of the Rhineland.

Articles 45 through 50 addressed the decision made with regard to the Saar and defined the plebiscite that was to be taken there 15 years hence. These were among the most lengthy articles in the treaty with 39 sub-articles.

Articles 51 through 79 returned Alsace and Lorraine to France and detailed all of the conditions applying thereto including French control over the Rhine River.

Articles 80 through 98 guaranteed the independence of Austria, Czechoslovakia, and Poland and detailed all of the conditions applying thereto.

Article 99 gave the East Prussian seaport of Memel to Lithuania.

MEMEL AND HITLER'S PROMISES

Memel and its surrounding area (Memelland), at the extreme eastern end of the East Prussian coastline and at the mouth of the Niemen River, was given to Lithuania to provide that newly-independent country with a modern seaport. It had a population of 140,000 people with German comprising a considerable majority.

Since the situation in Lithuania was unstable, Memel was placed under a French administration that governed under a League of Nations mandate and would function until removed by the League.

In January 1923, an uprising of the Lithuanian population, supported by the Lithuanian Army, ousted the French. Protests were forthcoming from Paris and elsewhere, but the parties involved accepted the fait accompli. In December 1923, Memel was formally recognized by an international treaty to be an autonomous region within Lithuania. Tensions, however, remained high between the Germans and Lithuanians.

During the early 1930s, the local Nazis gained considerable power within Memel. In an election in December 1938, the Memel Nazis won 26 of Memel's 29 city council seats and promptly petitioned Hitler to re-annex Memel back into the Reich. Hitler agreed, and on March 23, 1939, German troops marched into Memel unopposed and reclaimed the city for Germany.

At this point, the world realized that Hitler's promises were worthless because six months earlier, on September 30, 1938, he made the promise to Britain and France at the Munich Conference that if Germany were given the Czechoslovakian Sudetenland, it would be his last territorial demand in Europe. The British and French accepted Hitler's promise and the Sudetenland was taken from Czechoslovakia and given to Germany. At the time, the Munich Agreement was hailed as having saved the peace of Europe from a second Great War and that Hitler had been neutralized. Now, with the German takeover at Memel, the world knew otherwise.

In October 1944, with the Red Army rapidly approaching from the east and the city badly damaged, the German population began to flee the city en masse. On January 28, 1945, the Soviets occupied the city. It was later renamed "Klaipeda" and awarded to the Lithuanian Soviet Socialist Republic. The few remaining Germans in the city were expelled and ordered not to return.

IIIIIIIIIIIIIIIIIIIIIIIIIIIIIIIIIIIIIIIIIIIIIIIIIIIIIIIIIIIIIIIIIIIIIIIIIIIIIIIIIIIIIII

Articles 100 through 108 made Danzig a Free City and defined its relationships with Poland and Germany.

Articles 109 through 114 detailed the conditions under which the planned plebiscite were to be taken in Schleswig, the area between Germany and Denmark.

Article 115 required the fortifications on the German island of Heligoland in the North Sea be removed.

Articles 116, 117, and 433 dismantled the German conquests in the East during the war and required Germany to "... accept definitely the abrogation of the Brest-Litovsk Treaties and all other treaties, conventions, and agreements entered into by her with the Maximalist Government of Russia." Germany was also required to recognize the independence of all nations that might evolve whose territories were once a part of Tsarist Russia.

Articles 118 through 154 stripped Germany of her colonies and nullified German claims in other parts of the colonial world.

Article 155 required Germany to "... recognize and accept all arrangements which the Allied and Associated Powers may make with Turkey and Bulgaria..."

Articles 156 through 158 gave the German concession of Shantung in China to Japan.

Articles 159 through 202 put the very repressive and highly resented military limits on Germany. The German Army would be reduced to 100,000 men and the Navy to 16,5000. There would be no air force, General Staff or military conscription, and no military academies. Warships would be limited to 10,000 tons (about the size of cruisers). Above all, Germany would not be allowed to have submarines which had been much vilified during the war and at Paris because of the unscrupulous way in which they attacked their victims and cost the lives of innocent civilians. Some likened the use of submarines to the use of poison gas. Ten of the German submarines were, however, given to France and the others were scrapped out.

THE 100,000 MAN FRENCH ARMY

When France was defeated in WW II and forced to sign an armistice with Germany, Hitler specifically ordered that the French Army in metropolitan France be reduced to 100,000 men. French forces in the colonies were to be maintained, for the most part, at existing levels so that France could continue to protect her empire.

Furthermore, the German armed forces would be forbidden to have tanks, armored cars, heavy artillery, poison gas, military aircraft of any kind, and zeppelins. All aircraft not handed over to the Allies was to be destroyed.

No commercial aircraft was to be built in Germany until July 1, 1920. This was seen by the Germans as a maneuver for the commercial air lines of the Allied nations to grab up the most lucrative air routes in Europe.

The amounts of small arms Germany was allowed to have was spelled out in great detail. As for ammunition, the Germans could have only enough to sustain their army in about ten days of combat.

Germany's army was to be an all-volunteer force with enlisted men serving up to 12 years and officers up to 25. Once these men were discharged, they could not join military reserve units. Veterans' organizations that had any tie to the German government were forbidden.

All coastal fortifications in Germany within 30 miles of the coast were to be dismantled.

Articles 203 through 210 established the "Inter-Allied Commissions of Control" that would monitor Germany's compliance with the treaty.

Article 211 required Germany to modify, within three months, its existing laws to comply with the conditions in the treaty.

Article 212 declared that certain provisions of the armistice of November 11, 1918, and the Protocol of April 4, 1919, remained in force.

Article 213 required Germany to cooperate with the League of Nations but did not offer membership.

Articles 214 through 226 dealt with the questions of prisoners of war and graves.

Articles 227 through 230 called for the arraignment of certain German leaders, including the Kaiser, for "Supreme offenses against international morality and the security of treaties." Some 900 individuals had been identified as possible war criminals, but in the end, only a few were tried and convicted.

Article 231 was the infamous "war guilt" clause which, to many victims of Germany's aggression, justified the harshness encompassed in the treaty and satisfied their needs for revenge.

The article read, "The Allied and Associated Governments affirm and Germany accepts the responsibility of Germany and her allies for causing all the loss and damage to which the Allied and Associated Government and their nationals have been subjected as a consequence of the war imposed upon them by the aggression of Germany and her allies."

There were many things that had happened in the last four years to justify such a statement in the eyes of the treaty-makers. It must be remembered that the Great War was the worst war in modern history and had killed and maimed millions of people and cost billions of dollars. It must also be remembered that it was Germany's declaration of war on Russia in 1914 — at a time when there was still time for negotiations — that started the chain reaction which activated alliances which brought France, Britain, Belgium, their colonies, Austria-Hungary, Serbia, and other nations into the war. That war, by any count, was truly a world war. It must also be remembered that the war had been fought, almost entirely, on soil other than Germany's, and that the Germans were the first to use poison gas, launched attacks on Christian holidays, carried out the indiscriminate bombing and shelling of the civilian population in large metropolitan areas, and were the first to use incendiary bombs on such targets. All the while, the Germany civilian population remained virtually unharmed.

Then too, the war aims of the Germans were out-and-out aggression as demonstrated by the crushing peace terms they laid upon the Russians with the Treaty of Brest-Litovsk (March 1918) and the gigantic amount of land they grabbed in the east. Furthermore, the Germans planned to dismantle Belgium and very likely would have created a new buffer state between themselves and France out of French and Belgian territory. And lastly, it was the Germans who secretly transported Lenin and his entourage to Petrograd for the purpose of destabilizing the new revolutionary and democratic regime that formed there after the fall of the Tsar. Now, many believed, Lenin had replaced the Kaiser as the world's enemy number one — and the Germans had made it happen. It is no wonder then, that mercy was in very short supply in Paris and at the Versailles Palace on June 28, 1919.

Also, every politician at the peace conference was mindful of the fact that if he appeared to be soft on Germany, he would have had to explain himself to his constituents back home and at the next election.

Articles 232 through 244 expanded on Germany's war guilt and discussed at length how and with what Germany would pay reparations. The instructions given here were very detailed. An interesting example is this requirement stated that Germany had to replace the livestock it had taken or destroyed during the war. The Versailles Peace Treaty demanded that Germany deliver to France "500 stallions, 30,000 fillies and mares, 2000 bulls, 90,000 milk cows, 1000 rams, 100,000 sheep and 10,000 goats. Lesser quantities of livestock were to be delivered to Belgium.

Germany was also required to deliver to France seven million tons of coal each year for ten years and lesser amounts to Belgium, Italy, and Luxembourg for the same period.

Throughout the lengthy details establishing conditions of payment there were to be made, no total cost figures or time limits were stated.

One reason for this, it was publicly stated, was that the Germans had to first accept the war guilt by signing the treaty before intense discussions on reparations could begin. This was, for the most part, legal mumbo-jumbo which allowed the politicians to avoid setting figures that would, back home, set off intense debates as to their being too soft or too harsh.

The German people were divided on many issues, but Articles 231 through 244 gave them a common cause for continuing their hatred toward the western Allies.

Article 245 required Germany to "... restore to the French government the trophies, archives, historical souvenirs or works of art carried away from France by German authorities in the course of the war of 1870-1871 and during the last war."

Article 246 was self-explanatory. It read "... Germany will restore to His Majesty the King of Hedjaz the original Koran of the Caliph Othman, which was removed from Medina by the Turkish authorities and is stated to have been presented to the ex-Emperor William II (the Kaiser)." This article also demanded "Germany will hand over to His Britannic Majesty's Government the skull of the Sultan Mkwawa which was removed from the Protectorate of German East Africa and taken to Germany."

Article 247 required the Germans to turn over to the Reparations Commission certain "... manuscripts, incunabula, printed books, maps and objects of collections corresponding in number and value to those destroyed in the burning by Germany of the Library of Louvain." And certain works of art were to be returned to Belgium.

Articles 248 and 249 stated the Germany must not "...export or dispose of gold..." without permission from the Reparations Commission, and these articles required Germany to pay all of the Allied occupation costs in the Rhineland.

Articles 250 through 263 detailed a wide range of financial obligations Germany was to accept.

Articles 264 through 270 dealt with economic and commercial matters and with regard to customs regulations duties and restrictions.

Articles 271 through 312 dealt with shipping, unfair competition, treatment of nationals of Allied and Associated Powers, existing treaties, international debts, property rights and interests, contracts, legal judgements, insurance, investments, and industrial property.

Articles 313 through 320 dealt with air services inside Germany giving the Allied Powers full access to German air space, air fields, navigational systems, etc. Allies commercial airlines were to be given "most favored nation" status inside German air space. These controls would last until January 1, 1923.

Articles 321 through 386 addressed waterways, railroads, navigation, ports, rivers, and international transport and gave the Allies extensive controls over these assets.

Articles 387 through 427 set up an international labor organization to be called the "International Labor Office" (ILO) as a part of the League of Nations with every member of the League being a member of the organization. In these articles, the line of reasoning strayed from the matter of making peace with Germany into the world of international relationships. These articles stipulated that the members must meet at least once a year and that at least one member of each delegation was to be a woman.

Article 396 outlined the functions of the ILO; "The functions of the International Labor Office shall include the collection and distribution of information on all subjects relating to the international adjustment of conditions of industrial and labor..." In other words, this would be a League of Nations watch dog agency over questions regarding labor and industry on an international scale.

Washington, DC was designated as the site for the first annual meeting of the ILO and the following issues would be addressed: the eight-hour day or the forty-eight hour week, unemployment, women's employment, maternity benefits for women employees, night employment, health concerns, the employment of children, a minimum age of employment, and the "Extension and application of the International Conventions adopted at Berne in 1906 on the prohibition of night work for women employed in industry and the prohibition of the use of white phosphorous in the manufacture of matches."

Articles 428 through 432 further defined the occupation and future demilitarization of the Rhineland. Article 428 read, "As a guarantee for the execution of the present Treaty by Germany, the German territory situated to the west of the Rhine, together with the bridgeheads (on the eastern bank), will be occupied by Allied and Associated troops for a period of fifteen years from the coming into force of the present Treaty." That would be until 1934. The Articles went on to explain that a partial withdrawal of Allied troops would occur in five years and again in ten years "If the conditions of the present Treaty are faithfully carried out by Germany." Article 430 warned that if "... the Reparations Commission finds that Germany refuses to observe the whole or part of her obligations under the present Treaty with regards to reparation, the whole or part of the areas specified... will be reoccupied immediately by the Allied and Associated forces." In other words, the Germans had to buy back their Rhineland.

Pressuring Germany to pay reparations would not be an issue with the US since the Americans demanded no reparations. They did, however, expect that war loans be repaid. All told, foreign nations owed the US government some $7 billion and half again that much to US banks.

Article 433 ordered Germany to accept definitely the "... abrogation of the Brest-Litovsk Treaty," to remove all German troops from the east, "... to abstain from all requisitions and seizures and from any coercive measures... and shall in no way interfere with such measures for the national defense as may be adopted by the Provisional Governments of Estonia, Latvia and Lithuania."

Articles 434 and 435 required Germany to recognize the future countries carved out of the territories of the former Aus-

tro-Hungarian Empire and the Ottoman Empire and to "...recognize the guarantees stipulated by the...Act of November 20, 1815 (The Congress of Vienna)..."

Article 436 read, "The High contracting Parties declare and place on record that they have taken note of the Treaty signed by the Government of the French Republic of July 17, 1918, with His Serene Highness the Prince of Monaco defining the relations between France and the Principality."

Article 437 addressed a procedural matter with regard to "... the Chairman of any Commission established by the present Treaty..."

Article 438 read in part "The Allied and Associated Powers agree that where Christian religious missions were being maintained by German societies or persons in territory belonging to them...(they) shall continue to be devoted to missionary purposes."

Article 439 read in part "... Germany undertakes not to put forward directly or indirectly against any Allied or Associate Power... any pecuniary claim based on events which occurred at any time before the coming into force of the present Treaty."

Article 440 ended the Treaty unceremoniously by decreeing that Germany would accept and recognize "... all decrees and orders concerning German ships and goods and all orders related to the payment of costs made my any Prize Court of any of the Allied or Associated Powers..."

DELIVERED

The last paragraph of the Treaty read "Done at Versailles, the twenty-eighth day of June, one thousand nine hundred and nineteen, in a single copy which will remain deposited in the archives of the French Republic, and of which authenticated copies will be transmitted to each of the Signatory Powers."

The ceremony at Versailles lasted just over 45 minutes and it was the last meeting between Clemenceau, Lloyd George, Wilson, and the other major players on the Supreme Council. They had met 145 times in 168 days.

MULLER AND BELL

One might think that, by signing the Versailles Peace Treaty, Drs. Muller and Bell had severely damaged their future political careers. This was not the case. Both were prominent members of the German Social Democrat Party which continued, all through the 1920s, to be a major factor in German politics. And, as would most parties, the Social Democrats protected their own. Muller remained Germany's Foreign Minister until June 1920 and in June 1928 became Chancellor of Germany. He died in 1931.

Bell remained a cabinet member as long as Muller and acquired another cabinet post in 1926, that of Minister of Justice.

When the Nazis came to power, however, his political career came to an end. Bell survived WW II and died in 1949.

TOO MANY DOCTORS

Hitler was of the opinion that non-medical doctoral degrees, such as those held by Muller and Bell, were too easy to come by in German society, and that they gave the recipients undeserved prestige and status. In Hitler's Germany, non-medical doctoral degrees would become more difficult to obtain.

Ironically, one of Hitler's closest associates, Joseph Goebbels, had a doctoral degree in Drama and Romantic Studies from the University of Heidelberg and was regularly referred to as "Dr. Goebbels." Behind his back he was called "The Little Doctor."

THE YEA-SAYERS AND THE NAY-SAYERS

The signing of the Versailles Peace Treaty brought to the people of the world a measure of hope that they had never known. Here, after centuries of wars and conflicts, was a plan to end war and bring about perpetual peace. There were plenty of public officials, church leaders, professionals of every ilk, labor leaders, leaders of womens' organizations, educators, philosophers, industrialists, workers, and peasants who wanted it to work and praised it in glowing terms.

And almost everyone who signed the treaty, with the exception of a few individuals such as Smuts, spoke well of it, at least at first. Furthermore, almost every news media outlet in the world gave the Peace Treaty their support and reports came from various learned sources, claiming that this new and modern interpretation of international relations, as well as modern technological advances, now made war impossible.

But would it work? The Versailles Peace Treaty had plenty of enemies: Germany, Austria, Hungary, Bulgaria, Turkey, China, Japan, most of eastern Europe and, of course, the communists who had their own plan for world peace.

Then there were many individuals who participated in the creation of the Peace Treaty and the League of Nations who thought that their efforts at Paris were doomed to fail. These people became the nay-sayers and some of the yea-sayers would, eventually become nay-sayers. Some of their comments are recorded herewith:

Marshal Ferdinand Foch: "This is not peace; it is an armistice for 20 years," and

"Kaiser Wilhelm lost the war... Clemenceau lost the peace," and "The next time, remember, the Germans will make no mistake. They will break through into Northern France and seize the Channel ports as a base of operations against England."

To show his disapproval of the Treaty, Foch did not attend the signing at Versailles. He remained at his headquarters in the Rhineland.

Clemenceau: "Yes, this treaty will bring us burdens, troubles, miseries, difficulties and will continue for long years," and "There are (still) 20 million too many Germans."

Lloyd George: "Well, we shall have to do the same thing all over again in 25 years and at three times the cost," and "You may strip Germany of her colonies, reduce her armaments... to that of a fifth rate power... in the end... she will find means of extracting retribution on her conquerors."

Wilson: "I am convinced that if this peace is not made on the highest principle of justice, it will be swept away... in less than a generation. If it is any other sort of peace... there will follow not mere conflict but cataclysm," and "If I were a German, I think I should not sign it."

Former German Chancellor Philipp Scheidemann: "This treaty is... unacceptable, impossible of execution."

Jan Christian Smuts: "I am not enamored of our so-called peace terms... Sometimes they appear to have been conceived more in a spirit of making war than of making peace," and "And so, instead of making peace, we have made war, and are going to reduce Europe to ruin."

Churchill: "The economic clauses in the Treaty were malignant and silly... The multitude remained plunged in ignorance of the simplest economic facts, and their leaders, seeking their vote, did not undeceive them."

Col. House: "If after establishing the League, we are stupid as to let Germany train and arm a large army and again become a menace to the world, we would deserve the fate which such folly would bring upon us."

US Secretary of State Lansing: "It must be admitted in honesty that the League is an instrument of the mighty to check the normal growth of national power and national aspirations among those who have been rendered impotent by defeat. Examine the Treaty and you will find peoples delivered against their wills into the hands of those whom they hate, while their economic resources are torn from them and given to others," and "The terms of the peace appear immeasurably harsh and humiliating, while many of them are incapable of performance."

Senator Philander Knox: "...not a treaty but a truce."

Walter Rathenau, newly-appointed German Minister of Reconstruction and Germany's former wartime munitions chief: "They have destroyed or taken your weapons, but these weapons would, in any case, have become obsolete before the next war. That war will be fought with brand-new ones..."

Economist *John Maynard Keynes*: "The Allies are sowing hatred for the future; they are piling up agony, not for the Germans, but for themselves," and "European history is but a prizefight, of which France had won this round...certainly not the last...the day (will come) when she (Germany) will again hurl at France her greater numbers and her superior resources and technical skills...," and of the League of Nations "... a body merely for wasting time."

The Archbishop of Canterbury: "... very uncomfortable."

US Supreme Court Justice Charles Evans Hughes: "There has never been a time so pregnant with opportunities for future discord," and "New territorial adjustments, the establishment of new States and new international agreements... will undoubtedly carry with them the seeds of dissension."

Admiral Sir John Fisher of the British Admiralty: "Every damn fool knows that every war begins where the last one left off."

Hindenburg: "... as a soldier I can only prefer honorable defeat to a disgraceful peace," and "As long as there is mankind there will be wars. Only dreamers believe otherwise."

Hitler: "I think that a peace which lasts for more then 25 years is harmful to a nation. People... sometimes need regeneration by a little blood-letting."

Of all the Nay-sayers, Foch was the most accurate. His prediction of an "... armistice for 20 years" played out to be 20 years, two months, and three days: from June 28, 1919, the day the Versailles Peace Treaty was signed, to September 1, 1939, the day the German invaded Poland starting World War II.

A NEW NAME

In Germany the Treaty of Versailles quickly acquired some new names. It was frequently referred to as "The peace of violence," and more often, simply the *"Diktat."*

THE PEACE TREATY WITH GERMANY AFTER WW II

The peace treaty with Germany after WW II was not signed until September 12, 1990 — after communism had collapsed in the Soviet Union and the Cold War had come to an end. Between the end of the war and that time, there were two Germanies, the Federal Republic of Germany (West Germany) and the German Democratic Republic (East Germany) and no one wanted to make peace with only half of Germany.

The Peace Treaty of 1990 was altogether different from that of 1919. It was held in Moscow; there were only six participants: one each from West Germany and East Germany, the US, Soviet Union, France, and Britain, and there was no connection made between the Treaty and the United Nations, as had been the case with the League of Nations in 1919. No heads of state were present and all matters were handled by the foreign ministers of the six states.

The new Treaty, of course, paved the way for the two Germanies to reunite into one sovereign state.

The other Allied powers of WW II were expected to conclude their respective peace treaties separately with the two Germanies or the united Germany.

CHAPTER 13
JULY 1919 –
THE HONEYMOON

||||||||||||||||||||||||||||||||||||||||||||||||||||||||||||||||||||||||||||||||||||||||||||||||||||||||||||||||||||||||||||||||||

If the Versailles Peace Treaty ever had a honeymoon, it was in July 1919, and it was brief. Around the globe, there were still problems aplenty. By one count, there were 23 wars, revolutions, and armed conflicts going on around the world.

Within a few days after the signing, the various delegations at Paris returned to their homes and Paris was no longer the capital of the world. The Supreme Council continued to function in Paris but with lower level personnel at its helm.

IN THE US

On July 1, 1919, the United States of America went dry. The Eighteenth Amendment to the Constitution went into effect, decreeing that prohibition was the law of the land. It was illegal to produce, sell, or consume alcoholic beverages — and the drys declared that there would be no major problem with enforcement and that it was, as many believed, the beginning of "The American Journey to Utopia."

Utopia is in the mind of the beholder and for many American working men, it was a good cold glass of beer at the end of a day's labor. Beer was a part of his life and the unions were behind him. A group of New York labor unions came together to threaten a strike over the issue. Their battle cry was, "No beer, no work."

The next day there was a report of a hijacking of a truckload of now illegal booze, and from the West Coast came a report of the suicide of a California vintner. New York Congressman, Fiorello LaGuardia, who was known for his wit, commented that it would take 250,000 policemen to enforce prohibition and another 250,000 to police the policemen.

At the annual AF of L national convention, the delegates voted overwhelmingly against prohibition. Gone were the days during the war when beer and pretzels were seen as "German" and were to be avoided. Now they were an elements of an individual's civil rights.

Wilson was on his way home and there was great enthusiasm among the American people that he brought with him a plan for permanent peace. The polls showed this to be true. Although the detail of the Versailles Peace Treaty were vague to most Americans, it was the hour of the yea-sayers. The nay-sayers were studying the document and biding their time. Thirty state governors and legislatures had announced that they favored joining the League of Nations. In Washington, the Senate watchers reported that out of the 96 Senators, there were only 14 Republicans and four Democrats who had announced their unalterable opposition to the Versailles Peace Treaty — a total of only 18. It would take 32 "no" votes to prevent ratification so ratification, seemed very possible.

By now, most of the American soldiers were home and looking for work. The only sizeable force overseas was the American occupation force in the Rhineland which consisted of some 15,000 men.

The creation of the Versailles Peace Treaty and the League of Nations was seen by American liberals as the beginning of a new era in American politics. Praise was heaped on Wilson, the Versailles Peace Treaty and the League, and serious efforts began to continue the ball rolling in the liberal direction. There was talk of a national health plan, nationalizing the railroads, and creating ever-stronger labor unions. This thinking attracted many young Americans and in Britain and France there were similar happenings. It was a good time for the world's liberals.

As would be expected, the political right opposed these things and became more vocal so as not to be drowned out by the liberals. When Wilson arrived, he would have an American constituency that was noticeably more polarized than when he left for Paris in December 1918.

An anti-prohibition cartoon. The frowning, disgruntled, unshaven character seen here, with scraggly hair, a top hat, an old-fashioned coat, would become a common cartoon figure in anti-prohibition cartoons and would be seen time and again throughout the Prohibition Era.

Col. House saw trouble ahead with regard to ratification and urged Wilson to be ready to make compromises. The President did not want to hear such things and gradually came to the conclusion that House's advice was no longer welcome. On the issue of compromise, House was sounded his swan song.

Lloyd George, now back in London, foresaw Wilson's coming problems and his less-than-successful efforts at Paris. He commented to a friend "Well, Wilson has gone back home with a bundle of assignats (worthless money issued during the French Revolution). I have returned with a pocket full of sovereigns in the shape of German colonies, Mesopotamia, etc. Everyone to his taste."

On the positive side for the Americans, the US had replaced Britain as the world's financial center due to the enormous sums of money owed to the US by debtor nations as a result of the war. This looked good on the books, but collecting the money was a very different matter.

Economist John Maynard Keynes acknowledged America's financial contribution to the Allied war effort when he wrote, "After the United States came into the war her financial assistance was lavish and unstinted, and without this assistance the Allies could never have won the war...." He also wrote that lending more money to Europe was a risky business "If I had influence at the United States Treasury, I would not lend a penny to a single one of the present Governments in Europe."

In virtually every American heart, there was pride that it had been the Americans — so it was believed — that had won the war. It was America that supplied the Allies with weapons and it was the American doughboys that stopped the German advance on Paris, broke the Germans' will to continue the war, and were pushing them back into Germany when their government declared for peace. Yes, there was pride, but a large segment of the population was asking whether or not it was worth it. And, this segment of the population was growing. They were the vanguards of the American isolationist movement.

THE FASCIST MANIFESTO

In Italy, on July 1, 1919, *Il Popolo* published the Fascist Party's Manifesto which formalized the party's political platform that had been worked out in recent weeks. The Manifesto called for universal suffrage for both men and women aged 18 and over, proportional representation in the Italian Assembly, autonomy for local governments, the disbanding of the Senate and the government's political police force, the creation of a purely defensive army, the confiscation of church property, a prohibition against speculating in the stock market, retirement at age 55, an eight-hour day, a minimum wage, and

a progressive tax on capital that would rise to 85% on war profits. In the world of Italian politics, this was a curious thing — a mix of both liberal and conservative political objectives.

THE MIDDLE-EAST STILL BOILING

In Damascus, Syria, on July 2, Prince Faisal had called his followers together in a national congress, under the watchful eyes of the British occupation administration, to decide on Syria's future. Resolutions coming out of the congress called for immediate independence for Syria, or, if that was not possible, a mandate under either the British or Americans. A mandate under the French was totally unacceptable. A short time before, Faisal had met with Felix Frankfurter, a representative of the American Zionists and reached a tentative agreement that his government would not press claim to the northern part of Palestine that would infringe on the future homeland for the Jewish people and which the French had, all along, claimed was a part of Greater Syria. This surprising development was welcomed by the Americans and the British, but, of course, not by the French. The end result was an increase in tensions between the US and Britain on the one hand, and France, on the other.

It was also widely understood by Faisal and his supporters that Damascus would, one day, become the capital of a large all-Arab nation in the Middle-East that, at its greatest extent, would include Syria, The Lebanon, Mesopotamia, Palestine east of the Jordan River, and Hijaz.

To complicate matters further, Arab units continued to carry out hit-and-run attacks against the French in various parts of Syria. Only in the parts under British control, were the French safe.

In The Lebanon, the French were in full control and the Lebanese people were generally friendly toward the French. This gave indication that the partition of Greater Syria was very possible and that The Lebanon could become a separate political entity and under a French mandate.

And then there was Persia (Iran). During the war, after the fall of the Tsar, the British had moved into Persia to secure it from the Bolsheviks and replace the Tsarist Russian influence that had been in place for decades. It was one of several measures taken by the British in the Middle-East to protect India, their wartime conquests in the Middle-East, and the oil. This action made Persia a de facto protectorate under British control. The British had also managed to keep Persia neutral throughout the war, but things had not gone well. The country's top leader, Shah Sultan Ahmad, was only in his early twenties and was inexperienced and incompetent in matters of state. He had allowed his government to become racked with corruption and his country's economy to deteriorate badly. The British had little interest in spending additional men and resources to make it otherwise. Their main concern was that the country remain quiescent and not become a threat to the British position in the surrounding territories.

As for Persia's oil, it had been discovered in southwestern Persia by the British in 1908. In 1912, British investors formed an oil company which soon dominated the oil production of the region and eventually became known as the Anglo-Persian Oil Co. (APOC). The timing was most fortunate because the next year the British Admiralty made the decision to convert the British Navy from coal-generated steam propulsion to that of oil-powered diesels.

Obviously, from the British perspective, here was a situation that would require a permanent British presence in Persia.

Next door, in Mesopotamia (Iraq), the British had their hands full and then some. They had given priority to Mesopotamia over Persia because of its more strategic location and because, it too, had oil in the Mosul region of northern Mesopotamia, and that oil was much closer than Persia's oil to the Mediterranean where the British Navy needed it most.

One of the major problems in Mesopotamia was that the local leaders were not united as to the future of Mesopotamia and were often at odds with each other as well as with the British. Under Turkish rule, Mesopotamia consisted of three separate provinces which had been ruled by the Turks with a heavy hand. Now, the local leaders who emerged in this region were inexperienced and disunited. In the south, the very religious and politically unsophisticated Shiite Muslims were in the majority; in the center of the country around Baghdad, the more secular and progressive Sunni Muslims ruled; and in the north were the often rebellious and politically backward Kurds. Also interspersed throughout Mesopotamia were Jews and Christians.

The end result was that Mesopotamia would continue to be a problem area for the British and that a democratic society with meaningful elections would remain a thing of the future.

FLYING ACROSS THE OCEAN

On July 2, 1919, the British dirigible R-34 left Edinburgh, Scotland, for Atlantic City, NJ. Many believed that dirigibles would be the wave of the future for long-range air transportation. They were definitely safer and more reliable than winged aircraft, but they were slow. R-34 landed at Hazelhurst Aviation Field near New York City on the 6th after four days in the air. It remained there to be available to make a fly-over New York City when Wilson's ship arrived. Then, R-34 flew on to Atlantic City and from there back to Scotland. With prevailing westerly winds, the trip back to Scotland took only three days.

A NEW FLAG

In Weimar, the German National Assembly adopted a new German national flag consisting of three horizontal bars, black at the top, red in the center, and gold on the bottom. Those colors were based on the flag used during the German revolution of 1848. The new flag replaced the red, white, and black flag of the Kaiser's era. Many objected to the change and one of those was Corporal Hitler. When he designed the Nazi Party flag a year later, he used the Kaiser's colors: a black swastika on a round white background in a field of red.

FLAGS

When the Nazis came to power, they made their party's swastika flag the national flag of Germany. After WW II, both the West German Government and the East German government reverted to the black, red, and gold flag of 1919. Both were identical except that the East German flag had a communist coat of arms in the red panel.

STALIN UP, TROTSKY DOWN

On July 3, 1919, a political event of significance took place in Moscow. In the political in-fighting that took place around Lenin, Stalin was able to maneuver enough of his people into the seats of the all-important "Revolutionary War Council" so that he held the majority of the votes. This was the agency of the Soviet government that was running the war. Trotsky had been, and remained, the Council's chairman, but now Stalin began running important segments of the war from behind the scenes. Within a few days, Trotsky offered to resign, but Lenin ordered him to stay on. This created a very unhealthy atmosphere within the Council. Stalin and Trotsky were at war with each other and were now forced to engage in daily contact at the highest levels of the Soviet government. It was a very unhealthy situation.

A new plan for an attack against Denikin in the south, proposed by Stalin, soon emerged. Lenin approved it and by doing so, propelled Stalin into a higher position within the Soviet hierarchy than Trotsky. Stalin up, Trotsky down.

Ironically, the same day Stalin gained control of the War Council, Denikin, who was headquartered in the city of Tsaritsyn on the Volga River, activated a plan of his own — that being to march on Moscow. He called it the "Moscow Directive." On July 3, Denikin attended a Solemn High Mass at Tsaritsyn's Cathedral, reviewed his troops, and announced that the attack would begin at once.

Fighting around Tsaritsyn was not new. It had been going on with considerable intensity since the fall of 1918. To some, Tsaritsyn was called the "Red Verdun."

TSARITSYN/STALINGRAD

Denikin's plan would fail miserably within a few weeks and his defeat would become Stalin's victory. Tsaritsyn would eventually be captured by the Bolsheviks and would, after Stalin came to power, be renamed Stalingrad.

VOROSHILOV AND BUDENNYI

To meet Denikin's challenge from Tsaritsyn, Stalin was able to put two of his most loyal associates in control of the military operations there, Generals Semen Budennyi and Klement Voroshilov. They, along with Stalin, emerged as heroes of the conflict and remained closely associated with each other from that point on. Both Budennyi and Voroshilov escaped the Stalin purges of the late 1930s and played major roles in WW II.

||||||||||||||||||||||||||||||||||||||||||||||||||||||||||||||||||||||||||||||||||||||||||

SLOVAK SOVIET REPUBLIC KAPUT

On July 7, 1919, the Czechoslovakian army, cooperating with the Romanians in the invasion of Hungary, recaptured the southern part of Slovakia that had been occupied earlier by the Hungarians and had been, in mid-June, proclaimed as the Slovak Soviet Republic.

As a result, Bela Kun lost the only ally he had other than Lenin.

WILSON AND ANOTHER GLORIOUS OCCASION

On July 8, Wilson and his party arrived in New York City to a tremendous ovation and a massive welcoming ceremony. He and his party then boarded a train and a few hours later arrived in Washington around midnight. There too, was a tremendous ovation — in the middle of the night. It was estimated that some 100,000 people turned out for the occasion. Wilson could only believe that he had the strong support of the American people for his Peace Treaty and his League of Nations. This would be an important factor in his thinking for months to come.

When he arose on the morning of the 9th, he was greeting with the good news that the German government had ratified the Versailles Peace Treaty.

The next day, Wilson personally presented the Peace Treaty to the US Senate and, as he often did, invoked Divine guidance by saying "...it has come about by no plan of our conceiving but by the hand of God....". There were, however, those in the Senate who believed otherwise and it was well known by now that it would be a mighty task to get the Republican-dominated Senate to ratify the Treaty. But, the events of the past few days could not be

Senator Henry Cabot Lodge of Massachusetts.

discounted. Wilson knew he was admired and was optimistic.

At this point in time, the US Senate was divided into three factions: most of the Democrats favored immediate ratification; a bipartisan group of Senators, led by Henry Cabot Lodge of Massachusetts, favored participating in the League of Nations, but with reservations to protect certain American interests; and there were the "irreconcilable" who demanded complete rejection. This latter group had three well-known and outspoken leaders, Hiram Johnson of California, William Borah of Idaho, and Robert La Follette of Wisconsin.

At the end of the week, the Wilsons escaped the summer heat of Washington for a while by sailing down the Potomac River on the presidential yacht. Observers said Wilson looked tired. A short time later, Wilson took to his bed for several days. Dr. Grayson reported that it was a touch

The two most aggressive "irreconcilable," Senators Hiram Johnson of California (left) and William E. Borah of Idaho (right).

Anatolia. It also put Kemal in a position to create his own Turkish government. The Sultan remained under house arrest in his palace.

On July 12, 1919, following the German ratification of the Versailles Peace Treaty, the British Navy lifted its blockade of German seaborne trade. It had been in effect since 1914. The blockade had been very successful but had become a very detrimental factor for long-term British/German relations.

The Allied blockade against the Bolsheviks, however, remained in place.

THE BLOCKADE OF WW II

When WW II began, the British Navy, along with the French Navy, blockaded Germany once again. The blockade succeeded in shutting down Germany's overseas trade, but the Germans had, by then, made political and military gains in eastern Europe which gave them sources for food, supplies, and oil (in Romania) that the Kaiser's Germany did not have.

of dysentery. Several months later, after Wilson's health failed, some believed that he had suffered a mild stroke at this time.

AND SO IT CONTINUED AROUND THE WORLD

On July 8, 1919, the German state of Coberg ended its union with the state of Saxe. That union had been created in the chaos of November 1918. Now both were separate states, once again, within the German federation and that federation was still noticeably unstable.

On July 11, 1919, the Sultan of Turkey officially declared Mustafa Kemal a rebel and ordered his arrest. This was very unlikely but this action served to create the final break between the Sultan's regime in Constantinople and Kemal's regime in

On July 13, 1919, race riots broke out in two counties in Texas.

On July 14, the Wilson administration announced that trade with Germany could resume.

Two days later, with the US armed forces rapidly scaling down, the administration announced plans to create a 440,000-man National Guard.

In Russia, Trotsky's Army — and now Stalin's Army too — had crossed the Ural Mountains into Siberia in late June and, by now, captured the city of Zlatovsk. The cities of Cheliabinsk and Omsk, the latter being Adm. Kolchak's capital, were now in danger and Adm. Kolchak's forces were still disintegrating. Kolchak soon began

A British sentry before the Imperial Palace in Constantinople.

moving his capital to Irkusk, 1500 miles to the east of Omsk.

In Finland, on July 17, 1919, the Finnish government approved a new constitution that made the country into a democratic republic. This was a much-needed victory for the western world.

AND NOW THE AUSTRIANS

In Paris, on the 20th, the Allied representatives on the Supreme Council gave the Austrians their peace terms. Many features were the same as those in the treaty with Germany but not nearly so severe. The Peace Treaty awarded South Tyrol, the Trentino area, the Istria Peninsula, and the former Austrian seaport of Trieste to Italy. No mention was made of Fiume.

Austria was also obliged to recognize the new surrounding countries that had been wholly or partially carved out of the former Austro-Hungarian Empire. They were Czechoslovakia, Hungary, Poland, and Jugoslavia.

The Austrian army was to be reduced to 30,000 men and the Austrian government had to pay an unspecified amount of reparations over a thirty year period.

And Austria was forbidden to seek union with Germany except with the consent of the Council of the League of Nations.

AND SO IT CONTINUED...

A short time later, the Bulgarians were summoned to Paris. Their Peace Treaty was not yet ready and they would have to wait until September.

On the 21st the British House of Lords ratified the Versailles Peace Treaty. At this time also, Parliament ratified the Treaty of Guarantee on the condition that the US Senate also ratified it. This treaty, it will be remembered, was signed at Versailles the same day the Versailles Treaty was signed and obligated Britain and the US to come to France's aid if that country was attacked again by Germany.

YOU ARE ON YOUR OWN, FRENCHY

The US Senate did not ratify the Treaty of Guarantee so the British ratification was null and void. From the French point of view, this was another betrayal by their wartime Allies. If Germany attacked again, France was on its own.

On the 21st, the dirigible "Wing Fool," making a demonstration run over Chicago, exploded suddenly and crashed through a bank skylight, killing a dozen people. The dirigible was filled with very explosive hydrogen gas. A few days later, leaders in the US aviation industry announced that they were considering using non-explosive helium gas to provide the lift in dirigibles rather than hydrogen.

DIRIGIBLES IN WW II

The only country to use dirigibles to any extent during WW II was the United States because the US had the world's only naturally available source for helium which was in western Texas. Dirigibles were used extensively by the US Navy to patrol for enemy submarines off the American coasts.

The US supplied helium to some of the other Allies who used it in such applications as barrage balloons. The Axis Powers had no source of natural helium and therefore used hydrogen in all of their lighter-than-air equipment.

In France on July 21, the radical leftist trade union *"Confederation Generale du Travail,"* (CGT) which had objected to French policies in Russia, threatened to call a general strike over those issues. Similar trade unions in Britain and Italy openly supported the CGT, and indicated that they might also call for general strikes in support of the CGT. Clemenceau, with

many other issues on his hands, avoided this catastrophe by making generous concessions to the CGT including firing his unpopular Minister of Supply. This action by the trade unions clearly indicated that the leftists were strong and well-organized in western Europe and that they could force their wills on elected governments.

On the 24th, a report came from Russia stating that the heretofore Russian White units at Archangel, an area controlled by the Allies, mutinied and joined the Bolsheviks.

That same day there was a race riot in Washington, DC, with six killed and about a hundred injured.

At this time, there was yet another march on Berlin. German General Hermann von Hofman, an outspoken opponent of the Versailles Peace Treaty, ordered his troops to march on Berlin to put down a non-existence Red revolt. His apparent intent was to take over the government offices in Berlin and establish a rival German government to that at Weimar. Other army officers learned of Hofman's lot and were able to stop it, but not before some of Hofman's troops had reached the outskirts of the city. This was the third upheaval in the city of Berlin since January 1919.

Also on July 27, a race riot, accompanied by numerous acts of arson, broke out in Chicago and continued until August 2. The White House authorized the use of federal troops to help quell the riot. In the melee, 38 people were killed, 537 injured, and a thousand or more left homeless.

On July 29, the Italian and Greek governments signed a treaty over the future division of Turkey. The Greeks agreed to acknowledge an Italian protectorate over Albania and Italian claims in western Turkey, while the Italians agreed to support Greek claims in Thrace and Epirus.

On July 31, the Weimar government adopted the new constitution with a vote of 262 to 75. It was much like Bismarck's constitution but with a Reich President instead of a Kaiser. The President was to be elected by popular vote every seven years and a democratic political structure would be guaranteed, whereby deputies to the Reichstag would be elected by popular vote and a Chancellor selected thereafter. For the political right and many others who had lived under, and supported, the neo-dictatorial regime of the Kaiser, this new form of government, in their opinion, would be flawed and unstable. It opened the door to an unlimited number of political parties and organizations operating within Germany and the likelihood that every government would be a coalition government formed by several parties on the basis of compromise and behind-the-scenes bargaining. This was, by now, the dominant form of democratic government in western Europe and it did have its flaws. It was also seen as a concession to the Western Allies that would result in a permanent politically and militarily weak Germany.

On the other hand, the constitution had in it the elements for creating a dictatorship. Article 25 gave the President authority to dissolve the National Assembly (Reichstag) and Article 48 further gave the President the authority to take command of the German armed forces, use them as he saw fit, and rule by decree.

HITLER USED ARTICLE 48 TO START WWII

By 1939, Hitler had legally absorbed the constitutional offices of both Chancellor and President. Furthermore, he had been given the "Enabling Act" by the Reichstag in 1934, following the Reichstag fire, that authorized him, as Chancellor, to "deviate from the constitution." These acts made Hitler the absolute and uncontested dictator of Germany. Therefore, in September 1939, he had the legal authority, under Article 48, to declare war on Poland without seeking anyone's approval.

PRESIDENT DOENITZ USED ARTICLE 48 TO END WWII IN EUROPE

In his political testament during the last days of his life, Hitler transferred his office of the Presidency to Admiral Karl Doenitz, the Supreme Commander of the German Navy. The transfer was effective upon Hitler's death. This legally authorized Doenitz to use Article 48 to surrender to the Allies.

The Weimar constitution had remained in effect from its inception to the end of WW II, but Hitler had, through the Enabling Act, deviated from it many times.

As a result of the new constitution, Friedreich Ebert, already serving as Germany's President, now had his authority defined and legitimized. On August 11, Ebert signed the new constitution putting it into effect, thereby completing the restructuring of Germany from a monarchy to a republic.

Also on the 31st, Senator Lodge's Foreign Relations Committee began public hearing on the Versailles Peace Treaty. This was a grandstand play by Lodge to bring this issue before the public under the careful guidance of his committee. The hearings would go on for six weeks.

FREE CORPS LEAVES LATVIA

Several months earlier, the new Latvian government had invited the German Free Corps to come to their country to protect them from the Bolsheviks. Now, with the Versailles Peace Treaty having been signed and ratified by the Weimar government, the Germans were obliged to withdraw any and all of their armed forces from all three of the Baltic states. This was not altogether unwelcome by the Latvians because some of the Freecorpsmen had become unruly and turned into renegades.

The leaders in Paris abhorred what had happened in the Baltic states and, in late July, ordered the Weimar government to remove all German forces from that part of Europe by the end of August. If Weimar refused, the Allies threatened to re-instate the naval blockade of Germany. With this, the Ebert government ordered the Free Corps to return to Germany.

The leaders in Weimar, too, wanted to see the power of the Free Corps broken in the Baltic region because it posed a threat to their government in an area that was not under Weimar's control.

General von der Gothz, commander of the Free Corps in Latvia, grudgingly obeyed Weimar and ordered his troops to return to Germany, which most of them did. Some, however, disobeyed Goltz's orders and remained in the Baltic region, continuing their free-booting ways. Not surprisingly, law and order in the Baltic states suffered as Latvians, Lithuanians and Estonians now had to deal with the renegade Germans as well as the Bolshevik threat, and in Lithuania's case, the Polish threat. Fortunately for the Baltic peoples, they had time to deal with these problems because the Bolshevik threat had subsided due to the demands put on the Red Army elsewhere. All knew, however, that this would only be temporary.

During July 1919, the US Jewish Committee, headed by Henry Morgenthau, who had been the US Ambassador to Turkey during the war, went to Poland to discuss the treatment of Polish Jews with the Polish government. Their trip was labeled as a fact-finding mission, but it was also intended to warn the Polish government that maltreatment of Polish Jews would not be tolerated by the US and could adversely affect Polish/American relations.

HENRY MORGENTHAU'S SON

Henry Morgenthau, Jr. followed in his father's footsteps and became an important figure in the Democrat Party. He became a friend of, and close advisor to, Franklin Roosevelt and served in Roosevelt's cabinet as Secretary of the Treasury from 1934 through 1945.

Also during the month, the Weimar government offered to send German laborers and materials to France to help rebuild France's war torn infrastructure. The cost of this would become a credit against Germany future reparations due France. The French government rejected the offer because French firms and laborers wanted the work. Also, former German soldiers would not be welcome in France and Clemenceau had no interest in helping alleviate Germany's unemployment problem.

RUSSIA BEGAN TO WOO CHINA

Having lost Shantung to Japan and refusing to sign the Versailles Peae Treaty, China was now politically isolated in the world community. Not surprisingly, the Bolsheviks saw China as fertile ground for their revolution. China had no strong pro-Bolshevik movement within the country, so the Bolsheviks had to work, from the outside, to find, help organize, and support their scattered followers in China. To soften their way into China, Lenin's government voluntarily agreed during July to give up all Russian concessions in China. This included the Russian naval base at Port Arthur and some economic concessions including the control of several important rail lines. Both the Peking and Canton governments welcomed the offer.

In China, Mao Tse-tung, the former library assistant, began publishing a monthly and very leftist magazine called "Hsiang-hiang p'ing-lun." One of the first articles to appear in the magazine was entitled "The Great Union of the Popular Masses."

Mao would go on to publish more periodicals and books and would, eventually, succumb to the wooing ways of the Bolsheviks.

Parallels can be drawn between Mao and Mussolini in that both used their writing and publishing skills to lead them to power.

HUNGARY

In Hungary, the Romanian invasion advanced steadily toward Budapest. Bela Kun's "Peoples' Army" had launched a spirited counterattack at the Tisza River, 100 km east of Budapest, but it had failed. Now, the Romanians used the Tisza River attack as justification to continue their advance on Budapest and flaunting the cease-fire demands coming from the west. Some of Bela Kun's units saw the handwriting on the wall and changed sides. Bela Kun's days were numbered.

CHAPTER 14
THE VERSAILLES PEACE TREATY
SINKS IN

||||||||||||||||||||||||||||||||||||||||||||||||||||||||||||||||||||||||||||||||||||||||||||||||||||||||||||||||||||||||||||||||||

The Versailles honeymoon, if there ever was one, ended in August. By then, the politicians, ordinary people, pundits, military leaders, business leaders et al had had time to read the Treaty and the League of Nations Covenant and began to digest their meanings. The Treaty was so voluminous that virtually everyone who read it could find something in it that they did not like. But this was the document the world would be expected to abide by for the foreseeable future.

Whereas the Versailles Treaty was fairly clear-cut and understandable, the League of Nations Covenant was not.

In the US, the American government had never been involved in such an organization before so its long-term effects were vague and its obligations perplexing. Understandably, this made many people suspicious of its purpose and how it would affect the US.

Around the world, many people had already made up their minds. The communists and socialists opposed both the Versailles Treaty and the League of Nations; they had their own plans for world peace. Right-wingers did not like them because of the many liberal ideals contained in both; Jews did not like them because there was no mention of a Jewish state or equal rights; the Irish had the same complaint; colonialists saw troubles ahead; colonial nationalists saw nothing in them for their causes; the Germans, Turks, Hungarians and Bulgarians saw their former enemies now running the world; and the Chinese (one-fourth of the world's population) saw the continuation of Western oppression in their country as demonstrated by the decision on Shantung.

Knowledgeable and important people began to speak out against the Treaty and/or the League. John Maynard Keynes had an opinion and would later write of the League, saying that it was "... a body merely for wasting time." Senator Borah of Idaho called the League "The greatest triumph for English (not American) diplomacy in three centuries." Senator Lodge called it a "deformed experiment" and "dangerous internationalism."

In the US, the world's melting pot, opposition mirrored that shown around the world. Jewish-Americans, Irish-Americans, German-Americans, Chinese-Americans, Italian-Americans, and other hyphenated Americans often reflected the negative attitudes for their former mother countries.

The growing number of isolationists saw the Treaty and the League as the ultimate embodiment of all they opposed, racists saw them as sinister devices to pollute the blood on the white race, and Republicans saw them as valuable political ammunition for the forthcoming presidential elections in November 1920.

While the world's leaders and intellectuals studied words on pieces of paper, wars, revolutions, armed conflicts, and anger continued among nations — some of them League members.

ON TO BUDAPEST

During the first days of August, the Romanian Army advanced steadily toward Budapest while the Czechoslovak Army continued its operations against Bela Kun's forces in the north.

Finally, Bela Kun found his position in Budapest untenable and fled the country. His regime had lasted 133 days. On August 3, the Romanians entered Budapest and soon allowed Gyula Piedl, a leader of the Hungarian Social Democratic Party, to form a new government.

Piedl, however, was overthrown by a coup on August 6 and another government was formed under Istvan Friedrich, a businessman and former deputy minister of defense under the Karolyi government. Upon conquering Budapest, the decades of hatred by the Romanians for the Hungarians came into full bloom with the Romanians having their way. For the next three months, the Romanians conducted a nightmare of pillage and looting of stores, homes, businesses, hospitals, churches, and anything else that had value.

Bela Kun and eight of his associates and their families made it to Austria where they were given temporary asylum in the annex of the Seinhof lunatic asylum. Those Hungarian communists left behind were not so lucky. Most of the members of his government were arrested and several were executed.

BELA KUN IN DEFEAT

Kun eventually left Austria for Russia in a prisoner exchange. He became a leading figure in the Comintern, and, in the years that followed, was sent as a communist operative to Germany, Austria, and Czechoslovakia. In the late 1930s, Kun got caught up in the Stalin purges, was accused of being a Trotskyite, arrested, tried, convicted, and executed.

THEY ARE YOURS AGAIN

On August 1 in the US, the government terminated many of its wartime controls over the economy. Telephones, telegraphs, railroads, ocean shipping, and shipbuilding were returned to their owners. There was a string attached, though, that being that the owners could not increase prices and rates for four months.

The railroad owners now were under more public scrutiny than ever before because the government had run the railroads more efficiently and safer than they had before the war. This fact was not lost on labor leaders and those who wanted to nationalize the railroads. The next day, the US rail workers went on strike, demanding nationalization of the railroads and profit-sharing for the employees.

MARCHING INTO AUGUST

On August 4, the US Senate proposed 38 amendments to the Versailles Treaty.

President Wilson was opposed to every one of them.

At Petrograd, the military situation there had reached a stalemate. The Finns and Iudenich's Northwestern White Army had been unable to take the city, and, in a counterattack against Iudenich's forces, the Bolsheviks had retaken the city of Iamburg south of Petrograd. Stalin's defenses had proven to be too formidable to crack. Yet, the Bolsheviks wanted peace so they proposed a settlement: they would recognize Estonian independence if Iudenich would give up the city of Pskov and withdraw his forces into Estonia where they would be disbanded. The Estonians were ecstatic about the offer, but it would mean the demise of Iudenich's army. Iudenich objected, and decided to take unilateral action and hold his position in Russia east of the Estonian border. Therefore, the fighting in northwestern Russia would continue.

On August 8, 1919, Belgium ratified the Versailles Treaty.

That same day, Wilson addressed a joint session of Congress on spiraling costs, wages, and strikes. The President was now deeply immersed in domestic issues which had been festering since his departure for Europe in December 1918. And labor problems were at the forefront. Foreign affairs had been put aside temporarily while the Senate and public wrestled with the Treaty and the League and decided on their respective courses of action. In Washington it was hot and sultry as it always is in August. This sapped energy and shortened tempers.

On the 9th, the British and Persians reached an agreement concerning the future of Persia. Sultan Ahmed, age 21, a respected member of the faded Kadjor dynasty, was recognized as Shah (head of state) under British tutelage. Unbeknownst to the Persian people, the Shah received a secret payment of 130,000 British pounds in the deal. Publicly, the British confirmed Persia's independence and promised to build railroads and roads, provide loans, organize state finances, help the nation create a viable army, and collect customs duties which, heretofore, had been the prerogative of entrenched and very corrupt customs officials. The British would also conduct Persia's military and foreign affairs, making the country a de facto protectorate.

Unfortunately, strong opposition to the agreement soon arose within Persia and the Majlis (parliament) refused to convene to ratify the agreement.

PERSIA (IRAN) IN WW II

Sultan Ahmed ruled until October 1925 when he was overthrown by a military coup headed by General Mohammed Reza Khan who then became Shah. Reza Khan was still in power when WW II began and openly cooperate with the Axis Powers. In August 1941, British and Soviet troops invaded Iran, deposed Reza Khan, and installed his son, Mohammed Reza Pahlavi, in this place. Pahlavi cooperated with the Allies during and after WW II and ruled until January 1979 when he, himself, was overthrown by religious zealots who established an Islamic Republic.

In Europe, Herbert Hoover, the American saint, lost some of his luster by stating that the US had done enough for the Europeans and it was time for the Europeans to address their own problems. This was received in Europe with great anguish because there were still many people without adequate supplies of food and other necessities of life. But, all knew that the generosity of the Americans was only temporary. One astute observer, John Maynard Keynes, bucked the trend and expressed gratitude for what the Americans had done. He wrote "Europe... should never forget the extraordinary assistance afforded her during the first six months of 1919 through the agency of Mr. Hoover and the American Relief Committee."

There were others who were not so kind and wanted the American dole to continue.

POLITICS USA

On August 6, Secretary of State Lansing appeared before Senator Lodge's Foreign Relations Committee. His testimony was a great disappointment to the President who had expected him to defend the Peace Treaty and the League of Nations. Instead, Lansing claimed to know little of the Treaty and the League because Wilson had not kept him well-informed in Paris. In a barb directed at Wilson, Lansing said that the League was "... negotiated largely by the President, who alone of the American delegation would be able to reveal details of the discussions."

On the 19th, Wilson, in an unusual breach of convention, met with the Senator Lodge's Senate Foreign Relations Committee and personally urged ratification of the Versailles Treaty as it was written and with no amendments. It was a waste of time. Four days later, the Committee began voting on the proposed amendments to the Treaty and it was almost certain that some of them would be adapted by the Senate.

One of the most important issues was the Shantung question. It was being hotly debated in the US press which, almost universally, supported China's position. Japan's Emperor was being compared to the Kaiser, Japan was seen as an aggressor, and China was hailed as a Christian outpost in the Far East. Hatred of the Japanese was, as ever, most intense on the West Coast due, in part, to their own actions. Most of the Japanese immigrants

had remained aloof, and secretive and refused all attempts to be Americanized. The Chinese, however, were slowly taking on American ways, learning English, and some of them were converting to Christianity — but not the Japanese.

For each and every senator, this posed a problem. If he voted to ratify the Peace Treaty as written which awarded Shantung to Japan, he would be put on the defensive at the next election to explain his vote. Voting against ratification would be safer.

On August 23, Lodge's Foreign Relations Committee recommended that Shantung be given back to China and that the treaty be amended in that respect.

It was about this time that Wilson concluded that dealing with Lodge and his committee was futile and that he would have to go over their heads and appeal directly to the American people. This was a most unusual undertaking for an American President, but then, had he not been widely acclaimed as a conquering hero and great statesman wherever he went? It was easy for Wilson to believe that the people were with him.

On August 27, 1919, the White House announced that President Wilson would make a trip, by train, through the country seeking the people's support of the Versailles Treaty and the League of Nations. The trip would begin on September 4 from Washington and would take the President and his party all the way to the Pacific coast. All told, it would cover over 10,000 miles and require more than 30 speeches by the President. Privately, Mrs. Wilson was apprehensive about the trip because of the President's health, but her concerns were overruled. Wilson, himself, knew that his health was not good and on at least one occasion spoke of dying for the cause. All agreed that Dr. Grayson should accompany Wilson on the trip.

GREENWICH VILLAGE, NEW YORK

Greenwich Village had, since the end of the Civil War, been a gathering place for avant garde American liberals. During 1919, it became even more so. Small leftist organizations and newspapers sprang up, soap box orators held forth on street corners, and there were calls for socialism, support for the Bolsheviks in Russia, and free love. Poetry, plays, songs, novels, and works of art were the products created in the Village for export, and noisy and opinionated crowds frequently gathered at coffee houses and bars where leftist politics was thick in the air. Some establishments of note were The Golden Swan, a saloon; The Liberal Club on MacDougal St.; the Washington Square Book Shop; and Polly Holladay's, a basement restaurant.

The elite of the American liberals lived in, or frequented, the Village. May of them would become well-known; Emma Goldman, John Reed, Big Bill Heywood, Theodore Dreiser, Eugene O'Neill, Dorothy Day, Margaret Sanger, Henrietta Rodman, Dr. A. A. Brill, Max Eastman, Mabel Dodge, Daniel Aaron, and Mike Gold. In the Village, in comparison to the rest of New York City, there was a disproportionate number of Jews and suicides.

To outsiders, the Village was looked on with amusement, disdain, and sometimes fear. If ever there was to be a Bolshevik Revolution in America, it would very likely start here. And the residents of the Village were often seen by outsiders and people who were trying to make it in life without really working.

LABOR USA

It was a long hot summer for the men and women in the factories, mills, mines, and fields of America. Prices were rising, while wages, in their opinion, were not keeping pace. Prohibition was on the land and the working man was having to cope with not having his tall cold one after work at the local pub or even in his own kitchen. And the politicians were hotly debating international issues in Washington without much concern for the plight of the working people of America. As labor discontent mounted, so did the prospects of more strikes.

In the steel industry, the "National Committee for the Organization of the Iron and Steel Industry" (NCOISI) had, in July, petitioned the steel barons, among other things, to replace the 68-hour work week and the much-hated rotating 12-hour shifts. This system was structured so that, at certain times, men had to work 24 hours straight. The NCOISI leaders asked for a 48-hour week, 8-hour shifts, and increasing wages to keep up with the cost of living.

The NCOISI had grown rapidly within the steel industry, and, by this time, claimed over 100,000 members — a great number of them immigrants. Almost all of them lived in hovels without plumbing and electricity, and, in some cases, in decrepit company-owned towns. About 12 percent of the NCOISI member were Negroes that had come up from the South during the war and did not want to return.

The steel barons delayed, and delayed again. From their point of view, the NCOISI was a collection of rabble led by socialists and communists. And there was some credibility to this. William Z. Foster, leader of the union, was well-known for his extreme leftist views and would, in the 1920s, become Chairman of the American Communist Party. Then too, there was the IWW, the Wobblies, out West who had caused all that trouble during the war. Their activities had tainted the whole labor movement.

The NCOISI set a strike deadline — September 22, 1919.

In Chicago, the Socialist Party of American held its annual meeting, but it ended in chaos as two factions fought for control of the Party. As a result, at the end of August 1919, both factions formed communist parties, the "American Communist Party" and the "Communist Labor Party." One of the founding members of the Communist Labor Party was John Reed, a relatively well-known journalist who had witnessed the Bolshevik Revolution in Petrograd in November 1917 and had written a good-selling book about it entitled *Ten Days that Shook the World*. Reed took it upon himself to apply for membership for his party in the Comintern. He had also acquired an honorary title among his leftist friends — "the wonder boy of Greenwich Village."

The relationships between the two communist parties and organized labor was not yet clear, but, in Washington and elsewhere, the worst was suspected. Both parties had many immigrants as members and some critics claimed that only about 10% of their memberships used English as their first language.

The gulf between workers and management in the steel industry was, by now, extremely wide and it is not surprising that virtually no progress was being made on the issues.

But the NCOISI had its strengths. Samuel Gompers, the highly respected head of the American Federation of Labor (AF of L) had given the organization his support and, in addition, popular support for labor was growing among the general public as it was revealed how decrepit the working and living conditions were for the steel industry's workers.

Labor was also making progress in other fields. In New York City, the actors formed a union, the "Actors' Equity Association," and they had caught the President's ear in that he made favorable comments about the new organization. On August 25, Wilson tried to cool down the labor issue by calling for a moratorium on strikes and predicting a drop in consumer prices. In this effort, Wilson found a friend in Samuel Gompers. On the 28th, Gompers called upon the striking railroad workers to call off their strike in order to give the government time to address the problem of rising costs. Two days later, Gompers spoke out again, urging the US Senate to ratify the Peace Treaty because it contained guarantees that would protect the international rights of workers. At the same time, Gompers also criticized Lodge and his committee for attempts to water down the Treaty. Gompers was proving to be a voice of reason.

TROUBLES IN FIUME

During the month of August, the Italians reached an agreement of sorts with the French and British. Italy's new premier, Francesco Nitti, found common ground with Clemenceau and Lloyd George under which Italy would renounce it claims in Dalmatia in favor of Jugoslavia, in return for Fiume not going to Jugoslavia, but becoming an independent city state — like Danzig — under League of Nations supervision. The agreement was then sent off to Washington for Wilson's approval which would, considering Wilson's strained relations with the Italians, give him an opportunity to improve that relationship.

Not surprisingly, this arrangement was totally unacceptable to a large segment of the Italian population and especially the political right. Behind the scenes, various groups were plotting to take action of their own and Mussolini was deeply involved.

During the last week in August, 1919, the troubles in Fiume took another turn for the worst. Since the end of the war, the city had been occupied by a joint British-French-Italian force and relations between these troops had not been good, reflecting the goings-on in Paris. During

June, the French and Italian soldiers had gotten into a series of brawls. An Allied commission of inquiry was convened and its decision was that the Italians were to blame and, as a result, ordered the Italian military contingent to leave the city. On August 31, they departed leaving Fiume, and its Italian citizenry, under British and French control.

Mussolini's *Il Popolo* was one of the many Italian newspapers that railed against this great insult. And the situation in Fiume would soon get worse.

ANOTHER LOOK AT THAT MESS IN RUSSIA

In the preceding weeks, things had gone from bad to worse for Kolchak in Siberia. His forces were disintegrating, abandoning their weapons or changing sides in large numbers. An eyewitness reported from Omsk, which was being abandoned, saying "... people are packing suitcases and the poor openly rejoice and wait for the Bolsheviks to arrive." And as the situation disintegrated, there were more pogroms against the Jews. One in Ekaterinburg reportedly claimed 2000 lives.

During August, Clemenceau asked Wilson to send more American troops to Siberia to help Kolchak. This was not received well in Washington, especially since the French had recently pulled out of the Ukraine. The reply from Washington was negative.

About this time, another request was made of the Americans from the British. Lloyd George asked Wilson to send units of the American Navy to help with the Allied blockade operating in the Baltic Sea. This request, too, was denied.

Opponents of the League of Nations in the US pointed out that these sorts of requests might become commonplace if the US joined the League.

And from Canada came word that the Canadian government would pull its small force out of Siberia. Ottawa had had enough.

On the 13th, however, the Wilson Administration took some positive action and authorized the shipping of surplus American arms to the Russian Whites.

In the western part of Russia, the Poles and Bolsheviks were still at it. Their respective fronts were long and weak but the Poles had just received a welcome gift from the peacemakers in Paris, in that with the conclusion of the Versailles Treaty, thousands of Polish troops had now been freed from the German border and could now be sent to the east to fight the Bolsheviks. This paid dividends because on August 8, the Poles captured the major city of Minsk and the Reds retreated further to the east.

To the north, the Poles were still in conflict with the Lithuanians and the issues there were still in doubt. During August, Weimar ordered the withdrawal of the last of the German forces in Lithuania, and out of desperation, the Lithuanians began negotiating with the Bolsheviks for help against the Poles.

And in western Poland, there was more trouble with Germany. In Upper Selesia, an area scheduled for a future plebiscite, a Polish uprising occurred which was supported by the Warsaw government. On August 18, local Poles seized the area's mines, its most valuable assets, and claimed them for Poland. This left the plebiscite and the area's future very much in doubt and created another problem for the Allies in Paris.

THE DOWN-SIZING OF THE GERMAN ARMY

After the armistice in November 1918, the German Army had been reduced to some 400,000 men and it was there that the German leaders hoped it would stay. But the Versailles Treaty dashed this hope, and now, the new army, to be known as the "Reichswehr" (National Militia), had to be reduced to 100,000 and the German economy had to absorb another 300,000 employment-seeking men.

REICHSWEHR BECAME THE WEHRMACHT

The new German Army continued to be called the Reichswehr until 1935 when Chancellor Hitler decreed that its name be changed to "*Wehrmacht*" (Defense Power).

The failure of the Ebert government, in not having prevented such a catastrophe, widened the already existing gulf between the German political leaders and military leaders. Some saw the possibilities of a military coup or even a civil war.

The army leaders, however, had to comply with the Diktat because relatively strong Allied forces were poised in the Rhineland ready to invade Germany at any time. And the German army was in no condition to prevent it.

The German military leaders now had to determine whom to keep and whom to let go. This was a fairly simple decision for the military leaders as well as the political leaders. Only those individuals who had been the most loyal, obedient, and politically reliable would be retained. Most of the mutinous sailors and soldiers from the days of the armistice had already been released and now those who were known, or suspected, of having leftist political leanings, or were troublemakers or disciplinary problems, would be the next to go.

For those who remained in the army, it was a desirable thing, given the condition of the German economy and job prospects on the outside.

Corporal Adolf Hitler met all of the necessary requirements, without question, and was one of those retained.

The mechanics of restructuring the German Army were complex. The number of, size of, and makeup of the old army units had to be adjusted and nearly every officer and enlisted man had to be reassigned. In the interim, most of the troops were idle and bored. And there were complaints. The new Weimar constitution required every officer to take a loyalty oath to the new republic. To many of those whom had, for years, served the Kaiser, this was repugnant. Also the new German flag was disliked in many quarters of the army as were the proposed changes in uniforms, regimental colors, and other military accoutrements. On such issues, the Ebert government threaded lightly and let things happen at their own pace.

Men who had served honorably in the Free Corps were given top priority to re-enlist and many did. In some cases, Free Corps units were inducted into the new army as complete units. For example, Maercker's Free Corps became the new 16th Brigade.

On the other hand, a relatively large number of Freecorpsmen who had not been offered re-enlistment were now unemployed and resentful — and they were coming together. Soon, a new political organization was created, known as the "National Union" with a membership top heavy with ex-Freecorpsmen. The creation of such an organization was no earth-shaking event in Germany by now because political organizations were still popping up all over the country. To many, however, the National Union was different. It could become a breeding ground for a military takeover.

CORPORAL HITLER BECOMES A "V-MAN"

In Munich, the Reds were gone, but the political scene was still turbulent. Street corner and beer hall orators were common sights, and many of them still preached leftist doctrines while others called for the restoration of the monarchy and still others attacked Jews and other minorities. One eyewitness reported, "There is nothing so stupid that it would not have found thousands of willing believers in Munich." Ben Hecht, an American reporter, sent a message to his editor in Chicago saying, "Germany is having a nervous breakdown. There is nothing sane to report."

The Munich authorities estimated that there were over 50 political parties, associations, and groups operating in Bavaria. One of them was the German Workers' Party (DAP).

As part of its reorganization, and in an effort to cope with this politically volatile situation, the intelligence branch of the Bavarian Army created a new political unit called the "Abteilung I b/p." This unit was given three tasks: weed out left-wingers in the army, monitor the many political parties and groups that had emerged in Bavaria, and provide a pool of speakers to espouse the army's political views whenever the occasion presented itself. Members of this unit would become known as "Vertrauensmann" (Trustee) or "V-men." Corporal Hitler was one of the first to be selected. Some of the others selected had been Freecorpsmen.

In Hitler's file was a document that aided in his being selected. It was from his commanding officer at the Lechfeld POW Camp. It read in part "Herr Hitler... is a born peoples' speaker, and by his fanaticism and his crowd appeal he clearly compels the attention of his listeners, and makes them think his way." Hitler knew of this report and was buoyed up by it. He composed an article criticizing horse racing and Jews and sent it to the racist newspaper "Munchener Beobachter." It was rejected.

As part of their training, the V-men attended a two-day lecture at the University of Munich given by a right-wing professor of History, Professor Karl von Muller, a Rhodes Scholar who had studied at Oxford. Hitler and most of the others were inspired by Muller's views. In their free moments, the students discussed the contents of the lectures among themselves. In such a situation, Corporal Hitler was in his element. He relished the opportunity to speak to a small captive audience and expounded on the Professor's lecture at length in his own words. And, his listeners responded very well to what he had to say. Muller noticed what was happening and later said that Hitler's listeners seemed to be "spellbound," and added, "I had the peculiar feeling that their excitement was derived from him and at the same time, they were inspiring him."

Muller was so impressed with Hitler's speaking ability that he called it to the attention of the Abteilung's commander, Captain Karl Mayr. Mayr attended the second session and, like Muller, was equally impressed with this oratorically gifted corporal. Subsequently, Mayr personally interviewed Hitler and assigned him to one of Abteilung's more important missions, that of talking to former German prisoners of war who were returning from Russia and whom, the Army feared, had been tainted by communism. They were housed at Camp Lechfeld, now a transit camp established for such individuals. Only the best speakers could be sent to Camp Lechfeld. Mayr attended some of Hitler's lectures at the camp and became even more impressed with his oratorical skills and ability to persuade his listeners. As a result, Hitler became one of the favored members of the Abteilung and was regularly assigned to carry out some of the unit's most important tasks.

In his book, Mein Kampf, Hitler wrote of this time "... all at once I was offered an opportunity of speaking before a larger audience; and the things that I had always presumed from pure feeling without knowing it was now corroborated: I could speak."

Corporal Hitler had always loved the army, and now the army loved him. It was a happy union that would last for years to come.

At this time, another individual entered the picture that would be of great benefit to Hitler. He was Dietrich Eckart, a dapper, well-educated, intelligent, socially connected member of the German upper class and twenty-one years older than Hitler. Eckart was a member of the Thule Society, very anti-Semitic and founder and publisher of a right-wing weekly newspaper called "*Auf gut Deutsch*" (In plain German). One of Eckart's employees was Alfred Rosenberg who had been a member of the DAP since January 1919 and had preached its glories to Eckart.

Eckart was impressed and joined the DAP in August. He and Rosenberg would be on hand when Hitler appeared several weeks later. Eckart, like the other members of the Party, would be quick to recognized Hitler's unique talents. So when Hitler joined the party, Eckart befriend him, educated him in social graces, taught him how to dress, and introduced him to influential individuals who were supportive of the Party. In a way, it would became a father/son relationship with Hitler being the great benefactor.

PALESTINE — "A RANKING THORN"

In London, some of the British leaders were giving second thoughts to accepting a mandate over Palestine. The original thought was, of course, that British control of Palestine would protect the Suez Canal as well as the all-important oil pipeline terminus at Haifa. But now, there were new developments. Weizmann, who was still in London, was putting pressure on the British government to set up a political and military administration in Palestine that was friendly to the Zionists. This was seen as a forerunner to a complete, and early, Zionist takeover of Palestine. Weizmann also wanted included in Palestine large parts of the political no-man's-land east of the Jordan River, especially those areas which could be irrigated. Some of the British leaders supported this, but, on the other hand, there were those in London who believed that Weizmann was asking for too much.

Furthermore, there were rumblings from the Arabs that a Jewish takeover of Palestine would be totally unacceptable. Lloyd George was undecided, but Lord George Curzon, the British foreign secretary, had made up his mind. On August 20, he wrote a memorandum to Balfour which began, "Personally, I am so convinced that Palestine will be a ranking thorn in the flesh of whoever is charged with its Mandate that I would withdraw from this responsibility while we yet can."

A DECISION ON SYRIA

During August the British and French reached an agreement on Syria. Under pressure from France, and with problems mounting at home, Lloyd George decided to get out of Syria. He agreed to an arrangement whereby the French would have the western part of the country, The Lebanon, and Faisal and his Arabs the eastern part with their capital at Damascus. The withdrawal of all British forces from Syria was set for November. This agreement met both promises made to the French (under the Sykes-Picot Agreement) and Arabs during the war. Syria would come under French influence and the Arabs would have their chance to establish an independent nation in Syria. It would then be up to the French to deal with the Arabs in Syria while the British dealt with the Arabs in neighboring Palestine and Mesopotamia.

AND NOW, A PEACE TREATY WITH TURKEY

During August, Lloyd George and Clemenceau agreed that they should now begin to give serious thoughts to the peace treaty with Turkey.

There was a very large problem, however. The government of Turkey with whom Britain and France had been at war was the Sultan's government which, by now, ruled only a very small part of the country. The real power in Turkey rested with Kemal and his rival organization in central Turkey, and Kemal could not be expected to adhere to any peace treaty signed by the Sultan.

This had been confirmed in late July when Kemal and his followers held a congress at Erzurum in eastern Turkey and formalized their political position. Kemal had not yet formed a rival government, but it was clear that he was in a position to create one at any time. Furthermore, from Kemal's viewpoint, holding back on forming a rival government would put pressure on the Allies to moderate their peace terms with the Sultan.

Kemal's group made several declarations from the Erzurum Congress: that Turkey was not be partitioned, nor any part of it become a protectorate of a foreign power; that if the Sultan's government was unable to come to reasonable terms with the Allies, they reserved the right to form a "temporary" government to deal with the Allies to seek better terms.

A committee of nine people, with Kemal as its chair, was formed to pursue this action and the demands of the Erzurum Congress were published. The leaders in London and Paris realized that a peace treaty with the Sultan would be only a sideshow compared to the real issues that existed in Turkey.

CHAPTER 15
SEPTEMBER 1919 — TRAGEDY IN THE MAKING

||||||||||||||||||||||||||||||||||||||||||||||||||||||||||||||||||||||||||||||||||||||||||||||||||||||||||

OFF TO SEE THE PEOPLE

On September 4, 1919, President Wilson left Washington on his train to take his message to the people. Wilson and his immediate party traveled in a private car named the "Mayflower" which had a speaking platform at the rear. It was the last car on the train and in other cars were some 100 reporters, photographers, service personnel, and presidential aides

On the day he left, he complained about having terrible headaches.

The First stops were Columbus, Ohio, on the 5th, Indianapolis on the 7th, then onto St. Louis, Kansas City, Des Moines, and points west.

Two days earlier, Congress passed a bill forbidding railroad strikes. This provided Wilson with one less worry.

On September 10, two of Wilson's most bitter enemies, Senators Borah and Johnson, departed on a nationwide tour of their own to present their views to the American public.

THE BOSTON POLICE STRIKE

In Boston, labor troubles had been brewing within the police force for a long time over wages and working conditions. The Boston police force, heavily Irish, was grossly underpaid in comparison with those in other large cities. The policemen formed a union which received a charter from Gompers' AF of L and then the policemen did the unthinkable — they went on strike. Although there was no federal law against it, the people of America were outraged to learn that such a critical agency, constituted for the public good and supported by tax money, would betray the public trust in such a manner. Needless to say, the 1500 striking policemen of Boston had very little public support.

The strike was seen by many, not as a contest between labor and management, but rather a betrayal of labor against the public good. It was widely compared to the unpatriotic strikes carried out by the Wobblies during the war and it did not bode well for the American labor movement. Also, because the Boston Police Force had so many Irish members, the strike took on anti-Irish and anti-Catholic undertones.

The day the strike began, Gompers urged negotiations but the Republican governor of Massachusetts, Calvin Coolidge, would have none of it. He sent an angry telegram to Gompers saying, "There is no right to strike against the public safety by anyone, anywhere, any time."

Almost immediately criminal activities and looting began in the city. The night of September 9/10 was hellish. A hastily-assembled force of non-striking policemen was overwhelmed and the criminal mayhem continued throughout the 10th. On the 11th, Coolidge ordered the entire Massachusetts National Guard to take over police duties in Boston. Coolidge made it known that he had every intention of breaking the strike.

In the national press, the Boston policemen were vilified and labeled "agents of Lenin," "Bolsheviks," and "deserters." But in Boston the battle lines were drawn. The Boston firemen struck in sympathy with the police and the streetcar workers, also unionized, threatened to strike, as did the unionized phone workers.

On the 15th, Boston officials began hiring new policemen to replace those on strike.

Before it was over, the Boston police strike would have far-reaching consequences for labor relations in America. Some states began to consider, and eventually passed, laws allowing "yellow dog" contracts, the right of an employer to hire a worker only after that worker agreed not to join a union.

Samuel Gompers, upon returning from an international conference, publicly scolded the Boston police for their actions.

Not surprisingly, the strike collapsed as the Boston officials found plenty of men ready to take the place of the strikers. Some of the strikers asked to be re-instated but were rejected. All-in-all, it was a major defeat for organized labor.

Emerging from the fray as a hero, and thrust onto the national stage, was Governor Calvin Coolidge. More would be heard from this gentleman and some were saying that here was a man with presidential possibilities.

LABOR RELATIONS IN THE US AND ITS CONNECTION TO THE REDS

Since the end of the war, labor relations in the US had gone from good to bad. Labor had been widely praised for its very important role in winning the war, but now labor was seen as greedy and tainted by the Reds.

In the US Senate, the Senate's Judiciary Sub-Committee began a probe into radical influences upon labor. This committee had a track record, because during the war it had successfully exposed German propaganda and subversive activities in the US. So now, this august body had the public's and the media's attention. Witnesses were called and the testimony was juicy. Various individuals claimed that the Reds had infiltrated into high positions in the labor unions and that there were bizarre secret plans which, among other things, included the creation of a free love society and the liquidation of white collar workers and people with higher education. Many union officials were eagerly "exposed" by committee witnesses. One such individual was L. C. Martens, head of the "Russian Soviet Bureau" in New York City, which was a strong supporter of the American unionism. Martens was labeled as Lenin's man in America and others who sympathize with labor were called "parlor pinks."

The American newspapers had a grand time with all the material being generated by the sub-committee.

THE PEACE TREATY WITH AUSTRIA

There was news again from Paris. On September 10, the peace treaty between 27 Allied nations and Austria was signed. It had 381 articles and would be known as the "Treaty of St. Germain" because it was signed in that suburb of Paris.

The treaty forced Austria to recognize the independence of several states that had previously been within, or parts of, the Austro-Hungarian Empire. These included Czechoslovakia, Hungary, Poland, and Jugoslavia. These and other territorial concessions reduced the Austrian population to seven million from nearly twice that before the war. Now, one third of Austria's total population now lived in Vienna.

The Austrian army was reduced to 30,000 men and the ships of the former Austro-Hungarian Navy were confiscated by the Allies, leaving the Austrians with only a small number of patrol boats with which to patrol the Danube River. And, like the Versailles Peace Treaty, Austria was to pay an unspecified amount of reparations over a period of thirty years.

Also under the treaty, union with Germany was forbidden without the consent of the Council of the League of Nations. And, the treaty stipulated that the country should now be known as the "Republic of Austria." The Austrians had wanted it to be named "German Austria." The treaty contained eight clauses protecting minorities and it was an open secret that they pertained to Austria's Jews.

Restrictions on Austrian commerce and financial matters were similar to those required of Germany. The Danube River was put under international control and Czechoslovakia, to the north, was granted transit rights across Austria in order to have access to Italian and Jugoslavian seaports on the Adriatic Sea.

In Munich, Corporal Hitler, still an Austrian citizen, was livid when he read the treaty. Not only had his adopted land, Germany, been raped by the Allies, but now the land of his birth had been defiled as well.

Signing the treaty for the US was Frank Polk, Undersecretary of State; Henry White, Ambassador Extraordinary and Plenipotentiary; and General Tasker Bliss.

A SEPARATE PEACE WITH AUSTRIA

Because the US Senate failed to ratify the Versailles Treaty, this treaty also went unratified. In 1921, the US made a separate peace with Austria.

BACK IN THE USA

President Wilson was crossing the Midwest. His days consisted of an endless string of speeches, dinners, receptions, and parades.

And as expected, the American media gave him full coverage. In one of his first speeches, Wilson said with regard to the Senate's refusal to ratify the Treaty, "I can predict with absolute certainty that within another generation there will be another world war," and "What the Germans used (in this war) were toys as compared with what would be used in the next war." In St. Louis, he told his audience, "Peace partnership (through the League of Nations) or armed isolation is our choice." In Chicago, the crowds were noticeably hostile. To add to his woes, his Secretary of State, Robert Lansing, made a speech in Washington critical of the League of Nations. Also, Senator Lodge called William Bullitt to testify before his Committee, knowing that Bullitt would denounce the Wilson administration because of the shoddy way he had been treated in Paris. Bullitt's performance before the Committee lived up to Lodge's expectations.

On the 11th, the Lodge's Foreign Relations Committee sent the Versailles Peace Treaty on to the Senate for ratification. The Committee recommended 45 amendments and four reservations. Five of the amendments would nullify the controversial Shantung agreement.

In New York City, it was a mixed bag. Eamon de Valera made a speech denouncing Wilson for his stand on the Irish issue and, on the 10th, the city put on a grand ticker-tape parade down Broadway to welcome home Gen. Pershing and 25,000 Doughboys. Also in New York City, they were starting the World Series of Baseball. It would be learned later that its outcome had been rigged.

On the 17th, Pershing and his Doughboys paraded again, this time in Washington, DC, down Pennsylvania Avenue.

During September, Herbert Hoover also returned home to a hero's welcome. His mission of mercy was about to end. During its existence, Hoover's organization had fed some 300 million people in 21 countries in Europe and the Middle-East.

Hoover had a lot of friends now, and they began to promote him as a possible presidential candidate for the November 1920 elections. Also, with Hoover's full cooperation, his supporters were able to keep his food program going in a new form called the "European Children's Fund," which was supported by private funds and the sale of "Food Draft Packets." The program lasted until 1921.

CARE PACKAGES

After WW II, a similar program evolved which began the sending of "Care Packages." These were modeled after the Food Draft Packets of 1919.

HONDURAS, IRELAND, GERMANY, CHINA, SYRIA, AND THE LEBANON

On September 11, 1919, American Marines landed in the Central American nation of Honduras to prevent a civil war. Negotiations were successful and law and order were restored. It was the Monroe Doctrine at work once again.

The next day, British forces seized the headquarters of Sinn Fein in Ireland and shut down the Dail Eireann, the Irish parliament. This action was taken after Irish mobs had killed several policemen and soldiers and stole their weapons. To increase security in Ireland, the British began pouring in more troops. And from across the Atlantic came sympathy and money pouring into Ireland from the Irish-American.

On September 15, China, which had refused to sign the Versailles Treaty, reached an agreement with Germany that hostilities between them had ended and that a peace treaty would be negotiated. That treaty was signed in October 1921.

Also on September 15, the British formally relinquished all interest in a mandate over Syria and The Lebanon to the French. Nothing was said about Arab interests in those areas.

THE MARCH ON FIUME

In Italy, the Italians did it their way. On September 11, 1919, a nationwide farm strike erupted with tenant farmers and some war veterans and army deserters seizing land from their owners. The leadership of the strike was a curious mix. While many of the strikers carried red flags, some of the leaders were respected Roman Catholics with strong leftist political leanings who had gained the title "White Bolsheviks." In the countryside law and order broke down in places and there was banditry.

That same day, the strike was upstaged by the poet-activist, Gabriele d'Annunzio, who set out with about 200 Adriti and other loyal followers to march on, and seize, Fiume. Some 700 soldiers sent by the Italian government in Rome to stop him, mutinied and joined him instead. And along the way, others joined the march.

Before leaving for his march, d'Annunzio sent a wire to his dear friend, Mussolini. It read in part, "My dear comrade, the die is cast, I am setting out. Tomorrow I will seize Fiume, sword in hand. May the God of Italy stand by us." The wire was signed "I embrace you, Gabriele d'Annunzio."

D'Annunzio led his force, now over a 1000, into the disputed city on the 12th. They seized control of the cities administrative offices while the British and French administrators stood idly by. D'Annunzio then took personal control of the city. In Fiume and throughout Italy, the people were ecstatic. Church bells rang, sirens wailed and people danced in the streets.

In Rome the government was paralyzed. To oppose such actions would be political suicide, while to support them would cause grave international consequences. D'Annunzio called upon the Rome government to immediately annex Fiume, but, under such circumstances, that was unthinkable.

The seizure of Fiume was seen, by some, as the first step in Italy, seizing all of Dalmatia which had been promised to Italy in the Treaty of London of 1915.

Upon securing Fiume, d'Annunzio sent another telegram to Mussolini. "My dear Mussolini, I have risked all, I have given all, I have conquered, I am the master of Fiume... if the Italians had the spirit of the Fiumese, we should be the rulers of the world...." Mussolini wrote back, "The Italian government is not in Rome but in Fiume. It is that government to which we owe obedience."

Then, d'Annunzio wrote and published a manifesto that glorified his conquest

D'Annunzio speaking to the citizens of Fiume from his balcony. Note that he had a shaved head. Mussolini would later adopt the same hair style and often spoke from balconies.

and ended with the slogan, "Either Italy or death!"

The Allies were outraged by D'Annunzio's actions and by Rome's inactions and promptly set up a naval blockade of the city. It proved to be ineffective because the Italians found ways to get around it. Meanwhile, the Allied troops in Fiume were confined to their barracks and, therefore, neutralized.

In the next days and weeks, there were victory parades, ceremonies, parties, and other merriment in the city. D'Annunzio spoke frequently to his people and his every word was reported in the Italian press.

Auturo Toscanini, the famous conductor, joined in the festivities and brought his orchestra to Fiume to play concerts; Guliermo Marconi, the inventor of wireless radio, visited the city, as did other famous personalities.

D'Annunzio wrote the city's constitution and divided the city into ten "Corporations" according to professions. The purpose of this was to avoid class conflicts and labor disputes. In each of the Corporations, the leaders of their respective professions ruled under the guidance of the city's *"Commandante"* — d'Annunzio.

In the coming weeks, d'Annunzio's paramilitary force grew to some 7000 and eventually to 20,000, and there was talk of marching on Rome. D'Annunzio, however, had become a political pariah and found himself along on the world stage. No legitimate regime in the world could possibly condone his actions.

This did not stop d'Annunzio from formulating foreign policies. He made contact with other rebel organizations of the world, the Bolsheviks; Egyptian nationalist, Sinn Fein in Ireland; and various factions within the new state of Jugoslavia which were opposed to Belgrade's rule.

With time, the carnival atmosphere in the city turned bizarre. There were increases in drunkenness, free love, gambling, prostitution, gangs, and an increase in venereal diseases. Priests demanded the right to marry and people began to dress in outlandish fashion. Fezzes became popular as did shaved heads, large mustaches, and long beards.

International trade, the life blood of Fiume, plummeted and the economy of the city deteriorated rapidly. D'Annunzio's paramilitary forces took to looting and piracy to sustain themselves.

The farmers' strike that started it all ran its course, but produced some results. The Nitti government issued a decree legalizing the seizure of some lands and granted amnesty to army deserters who had taken part in the strike and the takeover of Fiume.

The seizure of Fiume encouraged various rebellious groups all over Italy to come out in the open, hold protest meetings and rallies, make speeches, and produce anti-government and anti-Allied publications and the like. Clearly, d'Annunzio's seizure of Fiume further destabilized the already fragile political scene in Italy. The crime rate throughout Italy rose, children of wealthy families were given bodyguards to prevent kidnapping, and Nitti rode about in an armored car and saw traitors and coup-planning rebels in every shadow. Mussolini was dismayed at what was happening and his newspaper began condemning the leftists and radicals for their rebellious and hurtful actions. He was careful, though, not to condemn d'Annunzio. This courageous reversal of policy was seen by many as a voice of reason. *Il Popolo* also called for Nitti to resign which many people now saw as necessary.

Mussolini was now being listened to by many more people and they began to like what he said. And as for Mussolini, he was learning about marches and the politics of action.

THE MARCH ON ROME

In late October 1922, Mussolini organized and carried out a successful march on Rome similar to d'Annunzio's march on Fiume. Mussolini then took control of the government and avoided some of the mistakes that d'Annunzio had made. Mussolini proclaimed himself Italy's premier, became a dictator, and served as such until his fall in 1943.

Nitti sent General Pietro Badoglio, second in command of the Italian Army, to negotiate with d'Annunzio. The talks failed. Then, under Nitti's order, Badoglio set up a land blockade around Fiume, but, like the Allied naval blockade, he had little effect. Badoglio, however, was able to keep a line of communication open between the Nitti government in Rome and d'Annunzio in Fiume

BADOGLIO

||||||||||||||||||||||||||||||||||||||||||||||||||||||||||||||||||||||||||||||||

After Mussolini's fall from power in September 1943, General Badoglio signed the surrender documents under which Italy accepted unconditional surrender. He then headed an interim government that cooperated fully with the Allies.

||||||||||||||||||||||||||||||||||||||||||||||||||||||||||||||||||||||||||||||||

In Fiume, the position of the British and French troops in the city was now untenable but nonetheless, on the 22nd, the Nitti government asked that they wrest Fiume from d'Annunzio. London and Paris refused and the Allied troops were soon withdrawn. At that point, Fiume belonged totally to d'Annunzio.

In the US, the actions at Fiume made nationwide headlines and became a closely watched issue. Senator Lodge and other political leaders who had large Italian-American constituencies openly supported d'Annunzio. Lodge compared the situation in Fiume to America's demands for New Orleans in the early 1800s.

In some large cities with sizeable Italian-American populations, local political leaders called upon Wilson to support d'Annunzio.

These efforts had little impact and were seen for what they really were — local politics.

THE CONGRESS AT SIVAS

In Turkey, Kemal and his followers held another conference, this time at Sivas, in east-central Turkey, to publicize their views on Turkey's future in view of the pending peace treaty with the Allies. At the conclusion of the meeting, which ended September 11, the congress published a five-point bulletin stating in points #1 and #2 that the partition of Turkey would not be tolerated and that if the Sultan's government in Constantinople agreed to any such partitions, that decision would not be accepted. Point #3 called upon foreign nations to recognize the "national independence and totality" of Turkey and consider offering economic, industrial, and technical assistance. Point #4 called upon the Sultan's government to implement a nationwide "Committee of Representatives" to determine Turkey's future. Point #5 announced the creation of a defense committee whose immediate mission would be to preserve the integrity of Turkey. The committee was called the "Anatolian and Rumelian Legal Defense Associations" and claimed that all "existing national organizations" would be subsidiaries of the Association. Point #5 indicated that Kemal would be prepared to enforce his political positions with military action.

Obviously, this was a warning and a threat to both the Allies and the Sultan and that, in the final analysis, he could form a rebel government at any time.

V-MAN HITLER SENT TO REPORT ON THE GERMAN WORKERS' PARTY (DAP)

While d'Annunzio was making headlines in Italy, V-man Hitler was given an assignment. He was to start attending the public meetings of the small political group known as the German Workers' Party (DAP), a right-wing political organization of about 40 members. Currently, they met monthly in a back room of the Sternecker Brewery in Munich. Hitler was instructed to wear civilian clothes, observe what was going on, and report to his superior officer, Captain Mayr, on the Party's political stance and its other activities.

The first meeting Hitler attended was on the evening of Friday September 12, 1919, in the serving room of the Sternecker Brewery. No one knew it at the time, but this happenstance meeting would, have far-reaching consequences on the history of Germany, the world and the Twentieth Century. There were 45 people in attendance.

The guest register of that day showed that there was one doctor, four businessmen, a chemist, two bank employees, two engineers, a writer, 16 laborers (Drexel's co-workers), six soldiers (one of which was Hitler) and five students. The others were party officials and members.

Hitler wore a dark blue suit and had recently clipped his full-lip mustache into a little brush no wider then his nose. He signed the register and gave his profession as being a *"Gefreiter Munchen 2. I. Rgt.,"* a lance corporal of the Second Infantry Regiment.

Corporal Hitler fit well into this atmosphere. At this time in his life, he drank beer, smoked cigarettes, and was becoming very interested in politics.

NO SMOKING AROUND THE FUEHRER

In later life, Hitler gave up smoking and became violently opposed to it. When he gained the authority to do so, he ordered that no one was to smoke in his presence. He continued to drink beer, although sparingly. He also drank a little wine and liked to put several teaspoons of sugar in his glass.

The format for the DAP meetings was that First Chairman, Karl Harrer, opened the meeting and made the necessary and appropriate announcements. Sitting at the same table were Second Chairman, Drexler, and the other four members of the executive committee. The minutes from the last meeting were read and other business was taken care of.

There was usually an invited speaker and this night's speaker was Gottfried Feder, 36 years old, a successful engineer who had developed his own construction company and had been an advisor to Prince Otto of Bavaria. He was also the brother-in-law of Professor Karl von Muller who had conducted the indoctrination classes for the V-men at Munich University. Apparently, there was some connection between this relationship and Hitler's being ordered to attend the meeting. Hitler did not know it, but his immediate superior, Captain Mayr, had the authority to funnel secret army funds to organizations such as this and was considering doing just that. Therefore, Mayr would be very interested in Hitler's report.

Feder's expertise, so he claimed, was in finance and he specialized in right-wing financial theories and programs. The title of this speech was "How and By What Means Can One Abolish Capitalism?" Feder identified himself as being a national socialist, an anti-Semite, and an anti-communist. In his speech, he pointed out that there were two kinds of capitalism, good and bad. The good type consisted of tangible assets such as mines, factories, railroads, and machines. The bad kind was money that was used for loans which, in turn, created "interest slavery" for the people. The worst kind of money was international capitalism which had been created by, and was now run by, the Jews.

"THE ROTHSCHILDS"

The image of the Jews being very strong in financial matters in Europe stemmed from the Rothschild family, a Jewish family which, in the late 1700s and early 1800s, controlled much of Europe's banking and other financial activities.

The influence of the Rothschild family had waned with time, but the image of Jewish control of European financial matters was still very strong.

Feder recommended that Jews in Germany be forbidden to be lawyers, judges, or teachers, but allowed that they could have representation in the Reichstag, but only in proportion to their numbers. As for land, Feder proposed that the state should own the great majority of the nation's acreage and prohibit the sale of private lands. Hitler listened with interest and recognized some of the same things that he had heard in Muller's lectures. In all, he liked what he heard.

After the speaker had finished, it was customary to have an open discussion and anyone could speak. Hitler had been instructed not to participate in the discussions, but only to make mental notes for his report. He listened to several speakers, then one member of the group got up and suggested that Bavaria should secede from the German federation and join Austria. This was more than the corporal could take. He took to the floor and in a masterful and powerful rebuff took the position that Bavaria was, and should remain, a vital part of Germany and should remain in the German federation. He declared that a "Greater Germany," not a weaker one, was the nation's only hope and that Austria should eventually be brought into the Greater Germany. Drexler and others took note of the stranger's exceptional speaking ability and enthusiasm and watched his performance with great interest. Drexler was reported to have said to a fellow committeeman "This one had a big mouth! We could use him!"

Hitler, years later, would claim that he shamed the speaker so much that he left the room "like a wet poodle."

When the meeting broke up, Drexler approached Hitler, congratulated him on his excellent speech, and handed him a 40-page booklet that he, himself, had written, entitled, *"My Political Awakening: From the Diary of a German Socialist Worker."*

Hitler then returned to his quarters, put the booklet aside, thinking it unimportant and went to bed. He could not sleep so he rose and began glancing at the booklet. Hitler soon discovered that the message conveyed in the booklet was that a well-planned form of national socialism for Germany was possible and far superior to the often unpalatable international brotherhood of the working class which was the hallmark of almost all other socialist organizations. The booklet claimed that the working class should aspire to rise into the middle class until there was no more working class but rather a "National Union of Citizens." To achieve these aims, democracy should be done away with and a national government created that was strong, dictatorial, and benevolent. Throughout the booklet, Drexler used the phrase "national socialism" which was not his own, but one that was being used with increasing frequency at this time. The booklet also claimed that the Jews and the Freemasons were responsible for many of Germany's troubles and that these problems should be forcefully addressed. Hitler was very impressed by the booklet and his opinion of the German Workers' Party was now greatly enhanced. He had discovered the DAP, just as Mussolini had discovered the Adriti several months earlier.

Hitler's first impression of the DAP was not good, however. He would later write that the DAP was "Political club life of the lowest sort; aside from a few broad paragraphs, the party had no full program, no membership cards, no office, not even a miserable rubber stamp." And they kept their meager treasury and important papers in a cigar box. A few days later, Hitler received a postcard stating that he had been accepted for membership in the Party, even though he had not shown any interest in joining. He was somewhat taken aback by the presumptuousness of the DAP's leaders, but he was also curious. The postcard asked Hitler to attend the next public meeting at the Altes Rosenbad Tavern to be received as a member.

Hitler informed Captain Mayr of the offer and Mayr advised Hitler to accept it. Obviously, it would be very beneficial for the army to have an operative inside this right-wing political organization.

Mayr read Hitler's report with great interest and on September 16, 1919, gave Corporal Hitler another task, that being to compose a letter to be given to Alfred Gemlich, another V-man, on his (Hitler's) thoughts on how the Jewish question should be handled.

Hitler followed orders and, in a lengthy letter which was to be one of Hitler's earliest writings on the subject, he wrote that the Jews had brought about "the racial tuberculoses of nations," and that he rejected anti-Semitism on "purely emotional grounds," which had led to pogroms. Instead, he favored a program of "anti¬Semitism of reason" which should be defined by national legislation in which "Its ultimate goal... must unalterably be the elimination of the Jews altogether."

AND THEY WENT TO BERLIN

On September 15, the first contingent of 70 Allied officers of the Inter-Allied Commission of Control, defined by the Versailles Treaty, arrived in Berlin. Their task was to monitor the German government's compliance with the Versailles Peace Treaty and to oversee the dismantling of Germany's armaments industry. Knowing that they would receive a very cool reception, they got off their train at a small station outside Berlin and drove, inconspicuously, into the city. Everyone knew, however, that they had arrived and one of the Berlin newspapers called them "our unwelcome guests." The newspapers in Munich and other German cities also reported their arrival with negative and derogatory commentary.

STEEL STRIKE IN THE US

On September 22, steel workers throughout the US walked off the job as they had threatened. The strike, which involved some 250,000 workers, was well-organized by NCOISI and managed personally by William Z. Foster. It was the largest strike in US history to date. By the end of the week, additional walkouts sent the number of strikers to over 365,000. Ninety percent of the American steel industry was shut down.

It was obvious that the leaders in the steel industry had greatly underestimated the power of organized labor. But they fought back. They promptly labeled the union leaders as radicals, socialists, and Bolsheviks, and played the immigration card, calling the many immigrant steel workers dupes of the radical left, especially the eastern Europeans. With this approach, they found a measure of popular support from many Americans who had an innate fear of the Reds, and who, it was widely believed, were mostly eastern Europeans. The steel barons vowed to break the strike and called in non-union workers, including many Negroes, to take the places of the strikers.

In Gary, Indiana, a major steel city, there were riots and the Indiana State Militia was called out to restore order. They failed to cope with the problem, so the US Army took over and declared martial law. Army troops were also sent to Pittsburgh, Pennsylvania, where tensions were high. And in Pennsylvania, the State Police openly cooperated with steel management.

As other segments of the US economy began to suffer, sentiments shifted from the workers to the steel companies. The press followed suit and the Wilson Administration began to take a stand in favor of the steel industry. The union was poorly funded and the strikers soon fell on very hard times. Their jobs were being taken by "scabs;" therefore, the NCOISI could offer them no money or benefits and they had little support in the halls of government. For many of them, there was no other alternative but to continue the strike. And continue it did. The strike would go on until January 1920.

DISASTER IN PUEBLO — WILSON STRICKEN

The cross-country trip had been very hard on President Wilson and his headaches had gotten worse. After leaving Los Angeles on the leg home, Mrs. Wilson later wrote, "He grew thinner and the headaches increased in duration and in intensity until he was almost blind during attacks."

On September 23, he spoke at the Mormon Tabernacle in Salt Lake City to an audience of some 15,000. Mrs. Wilson wrote that he perspired profusely. The party then went on to Cheyenne and then Denver. On September 25, Wilson spoke for the 40th time in Pueblo, Colorado. Late that night, as the train headed east, he collapsed in his private car. He remained conscious, but the left side of his body became partially paralyzed and the left side of his face drooped. He could still speak and walk, but with difficulty. The next morning he arose and was able to shave and dress himself but Dr. Grayson realized what was happening that the President had had a stroke. Grayson, Mrs. Wilson, and Joseph Tumulty, Wilson's secretary, agreed that the President could

not carry on and that the remainder of the trip had to be canceled. Wilson objected, but as the train approached Wichita, he gave in. Upon reaching Wichita, the train stopped and Tumulty spoke to the local officials and explained, in very general terms, that the President was sick and had to return to Washington, 1700 miles to the east.

When news of the trip being canceled was released, the public was aghast and wild rumors began to circulate; Wilson was dead, he had had a nervous breakdown, he had gone insane, there had been an assassination attempt, he had syphilis…

Upon arriving in Washington on the 27th, Wilson was able to walk from the train to the waiting cars. He smiled and waved to the crowd and photographers. This dispelled many of the worst rumors.

When he got to the White House, he went into seclusion and witnesses reported that he seemed confused and wandered about. And, his headaches were still intense. Wilson tried to keep up his normal routine as much as possible but it was not to be. His symptoms continued. At night, Mrs. Wilson checked on him about every hour.

BRITISH PULL OUT OF SYRIA

On September 13, Lloyd George's government announced that British forces would be withdrawn from Syria in November.

Then, on September 25, a disturbing report reached London from General Allenby's headquarters in the Middle East. It stated that Prince Faisal of Syria and the Zionist leader, Weizmann, had met on two occasions unbeknownst to the British. According to the report, Weizmann had instigated the meetings and offered Faisal money and advisors in exchange for Faisal's support of Zionist ambitions in Palestine. It was also reported that Weizmann claimed he might be able to get France to drop her claims to the

Syrian hinterland. Faisal countered by suggesting that the Zionists come out in the open and support Arab claims against France. At this point, the talks floundered, but the reaction in London was predictable; both Weizmann and Faisal were conducting their own respective foreign policies without consulting their primary benefactor, Britain. Curzon commented at this time that it would be "fatal" if Faisal's regime would be "run by the Zionists." In London, the general attitude grew that it would be better to have the French in Syria than the Zionists.

Lloyd George and Clemenceau met to discuss the Syrian issue and agreed that the British would pull out of Damascus and the French could do what they wished with Faisal. After additional talks, it was agreed that Britain would, in exchange for pulling out of Syria, acquire political control over the Mosul area of Mesopotamia, but would share the area's oil with the French. The dispute between the British and French over the border between northern Palestine and Syria was not resolved at this time and would not be until 1922.

As might be expected, Faisal objected bitterly to the British withdrawal. The British response was to suggest that Faisal open talks with the French. Unfortunately, Faisal had few options but to do as the British suggested. Therefore, the Prince went to Paris to negotiate with Clemenceau. Officially, he received a glamorous welcome although the French press was somewhat critical of Faisal and his Damascus government. As part of the pomp and ceremony, Faisal presented Clemenceau with several fine Arabian horses.

Faisal's meeting with Clemenceau, though, was most unglamorous. Faisal was told bluntly that as long as he could maintain order in Damascus he could rule, and if problems arose, he should call upon the French for help. This was an old ploy used by all of the colonial powers in their negotiations with native regimes. At the first signs of troubles or public disorders, the colonial power would then have the justification to take over the country in question and proclaiming it as a protectorate. This was the way colonial empires were built.

FROM RUSSIA

In the south of Russia, the White forces under Denikin had been thrown into retreat. As the Whites withdrew, the local populace took out revenge on those who had helped the Whites because that rule had often been brutal and corrupt. It was a bloody month in southern Russia.

In Siberia, Kolchak finally concluded that he needed a political agenda and, on September 26, called for the redistribution of land. This had little effect. Time was running out for Kolchak.

Because of Kolchak's problems, the Allies had a problem of their own in Siberia. There were 60,000 Japanese troops in Siberia and only 8500 Americans, 1400 Italians, and 1000 French. The dilemma for the Westerners was that if they pulled out, they would leave the field open to the Japanese and, given Japan's aggressive tendencies, might create a situation in which Japan could gain permanent control over parts of Siberia.

In northern European Russia, the story was entirely different. On the 27th, the British and American troops began, as planned, to pull out of Archangel and Murmansk to avoid another Russian winter. In London and Washington, little was said of this matter because it demonstrated the Allies' overall failure in Russia. Red Army units quickly occupied the abandoned areas and proclaimed that northern Russia was now theirs.

On the Polish front, the Reds were still very weak, and the Poles continued to take advantage of the situation. Polish troops had advanced steadily into Belorussia and the Ukraine. At the time, the Polish Army stood at an impressive 540,000 soldiers, and Pilsudski wanted more. In Paris, Polish Premier Paderewski made a proposal to the French and British that they help Poland acquire an additional 500,000 soldiers and, in return, the Poles would march on Moscow and eliminate the Lenin government. He reminded them that the Poles had taken Moscow once before — in 1610.

Such an undertaking would cost the Western Allies a great sum of money and resources and neither Clemenceau nor Lloyd George wanted to underwrite such a scheme. Furthermore, they were very skeptical about the Pole's ability to take Moscow.

On September 15, Paderewski's plan was officially rejected.

While these talks were underway in Paris, Pilsudski sent a delegation to Denikin in an effort to create an alliance between their two forces. Advancing Polish forces had recently made contact with Denikin's forces in the Ukraine and Pilsudski hoped to create some sort of alliance with Denikin. Pilsudski's price was that Poland would remain free and independent. Denikin rejected this and stood by his long-standing claim that the eastern portion of Poland should be reincorporated into the post-revolutionary Russia as it had been under the Tsars. On this point, the talks broke down.

Pilsudski then sought out an alternative alliance with Semen Petlura, a Ukrainian warlord who ruled in what was known as the "West Ukrainian Republic," which bordered Poland on the southeast. An agreement was reached in which their forces would cooperate with each other against the Reds and that Poland would recognize the West Ukrainian Republic, and Petlura would recognize an independent Poland. It was also agreed that they would divide the spoils of their future conquests.

This was a risky undertaking for Pilsudski. Petlura's forces were little more than an organized gang of bandits who operated under the guise of Ukrainian nationalism. They were despised by the people because of their harsh and corrupt rule. Not surprisingly, Petlura had no allies anywhere - except now for Poland. Petlura's reliability was also very much in question. At various time, he had fought against the Reds, then against Denikin's Whites and more recently against Ukrainian Reds, and always against Jews wherever he found them. It was well-known that Petlura allowed, and even encouraged, pogroms. Petlura also had an extreme political agenda. It called for the nationalization of almost everything of value in his domain under a dictatorial regime which he, of course, would head. In some quarters, the Pilsudski/Petlura agreement was seen as an alliance between a saint and a devil.

But Pilsudski was not through. Since July, he had made overtures to the Bolsheviks in an effort to reach some sort of understanding. Lenin did not reject the offer because he saw that he might gain some advantages from such talks and could, at least, buy time. Therefore, negotiations got under.

And then there was the Petrograd front. On September 28, Iudenich's Northwestern White Army launched another offensive along the southern shore of the Gulf of Finland in as attempt to take Petrograd. Iudenich was not satisfied with the new and friendlier relationship between the Bolsheviks and Estonia and would try again to settle the issues on his own terms. Stalin, who had saved Petrograd once, was now obliged to do it again.

ARMIES EVERYWHERE

In the turbulent Baltic area, adjacent to and south of Iudenich's Army, there were armies everywhere. Estonia, Latvia, Lithuania, and Poland had armies, the main Bolshevik forces in the area were the XV and XVI Red Armies, and the German-controlled "Baltikum Army" which was comprised of remnants of the German Free Corps were operating as Latvian mercenaries. The officers and men of the Baltikum Army were more loyal to the Baltikum's commander, German General Colmar von der Goltz, than to the Riga government. To many, it was seen as a renegade German army that could charge off into any of several directions, including the possibility that it could even become a powerful German force that could move back into Germany to support a right-wing revolution.

Other, and smaller armies, were operating in the Baltic which included the "Bermondt-Avalon" White Army, operating in Latvia, and the "Lieven" White Army, operating on the Kurland Peninsula. In such an atmosphere, alliances were constantly changing and reports flowed to the West of battles, the purpose of which were not fully understood and taking place in such strange and unfamiliar locations as Dunaburg, Dvinsk, Polotsk, Baranowicze, Luniniec, Morzyr, Sarny, Shepetovka, and Kamenets Podolsk.

IN OTHER PLACES

In France, political opposition against Clemenceau was mounting. There was an election scheduled for November 16 and Poincare and Foch had joined forces in an effort to oust Clemenceau. The Premier also had enemies on both the left and right who were preparing for that November day.

At this time, the Supreme Council in Paris ordered that a plebiscite be conducted in the disputed enclave of Teschen on the Polish/Czechoslovak border. This would be a difficult task because the residents of Teschen had been fighting with each other for months and there was no signs that it could be stopped in order to take a plebiscite.

Throughout Europe the book *Protocols of the Elders of Zion* was still selling well. It was now available in Japanese. It was also selling well in the US.

And another book had appeared that swept through Europe and the Western world, *The Decline of the West*, by school teacher Oswald Spengler. It predicted the fall of western culture due to the forces at work and that it could only be prevented by reordering society into a better-disciplined and cohesive body obedient to an authoritarian state. Corporal Hitler could have written this book. The book followed Nietzsche's philosophy and was hailed by many intellectuals, especially in Germany.

After gaining notoriety, Spengler published a political pamphlet entitled "The Prussian Spirit of Socialism," in which he claimed that socialism was the next logical step to the advancement of society but not along Marxist or democratic lines. Instead, he suggested that that order be developed along the time-honored, and benevolent, Prussian model. Corporal Hitler could have written this pamphlet too.

In Munich, Anton Drexler received a letter from a political ally, Walter Riehl, head of the Austrian National Socialist Party. Riehl suggested that Drexler change the name of his party from the German Workers' Party (DAP) to the "National Socialist German Workers' Party" (NSDAP). Drexler began to give the idea serious consideration.

In Hungary, things were not going well. The Romanians were collecting a form of reparations by confiscating locomotives, rail cars, automobiles, livestock, food, carpets, phones, and shoes. The Romanians justified their actions on the grounds that this was their due because they had saved the Hungarian people from the communists.

In Paris, the peace treaty with Hungary was in limbo until conditions settled down in Budapest. In London, John Maynard Keynes began writing his book *The Economic Consequences of the Peace* which would prove to be a book of accurate prophecies of things to come.

On the last day of the month, the Weimar government announced that the German army would be restructured according to the Versailles Diktat. In the interim an *"Ubergangsheer"* (Transitional Army) would be created to serve as Germany's army. All of this would be done very slowly. However, the new *"Reichswehr"* would not become operational until January 1921.

CHAPTER 16
WILSON DOWN, HITLER UP
BOLSHEVIKS UP

||||||||||||||||||||||||||||||||||||||||||||||||||||||||||||||||||||||||||||||||||||||||||||||||||||

PRESIDENT WILSON'S CONDITION WORSENS

On the morning of October 2, 1919, Mrs. Wilson found the President unconscious on the floor of the White House bathroom and immediately summoned Dr. Grayson. Together, they got him back to his bed. Grayson discovered that the President had had a massive stroke and was paralyzed on the left side of his body. He called in several consulting doctors who confirmed that diagnosis. All were greatly concerned that the stroke might be fatal or that it might adversely affect Wilson's mental abilities.

After a brief time, when it was clear that the stroke would not be fatal, Mrs. Wilson and Grayson made the decision to keep the President's condition secret, even from the White House staff. The only staff member allowed to see the President was Irwin "Ike" Hoover, the President's usher, whom Mrs. Wilson trusted completely. Mrs. Wilson and Grayson then began a program of "protecting" the President from the outside world and the constant flow of stressful and controversial information that would normally have reached him. Both hoped that the President would make a partial recovery relatively soon. Dr. Grayson, with Mrs. Wilson's encouragement, ordered that no one should see the President except for their children, other doctors and nurses, and Ike Hoover.

Rumors about the President soon spread within the White House and caught the attention of reporters who spread them to the news media. The secret was out. The President was very, very sick. An announcement then came from the White House that the President was, in fact, sick, suffering from "nervous exhaustion."

On the 4th, Grayson noticed a slight improvement in the President and the next day he announced it to the press.

With the President incapacitated, however, Attorney General A. Mitchell Palmer, Lansing, and Tumulty began a very close association with each other in an effort to serve in the President's stead. Of the three, Palmer soon emerged as the dominant member.

On the 6th, Secretary of State Lansing convened a cabinet meeting in the President's absence. Before doing so, he phoned Dr. Grayson to get information on the President's condition. Grayson downplayed Wilson's condition and never mentioned the word "paralyzed." This response did not match the many rumors that were circulating, so Lansing and the others were still in the dark about Wilson's latest condition.

IN EUROPE ONCE MORE

On October 5, the still-powerful Italian Socialists began holding a convention in Italy. On the 8th, they made the startling announcement that they would support Lenin's Comintern with its mission to spread communism worldwide. With this act, the Italian Socialists moved to the extreme left and accentuated the political polarization that had already taken place in Italy.

In Florence, the Fascists were also meeting, but because of their newness and relatively small size, did not attract much attention. Mussolini dominated the proceedings and claimed that his organization had grown substantially. He said that there were now 148 branches with a membership of 45,000. In reality, there were only 56 branches and 17,000 members, but still an impressive number considering the short time the Fascist Party had been in existence.

To the Fascists, d'Annunzio was the hero of the hour and Premier Nitti was the villain. There was also criticism of the King and the monarchy and Mussolini said in one of his speeches that "the monarchy has undoubtedly outlived its usefulness." Some of the more radical members of the movement called for the ouster of the

Pope and the "devaticanization" of Rome but this was voted down.

The primary purpose of the meeting was to prepare for a coming national election and Mussolini needed to fire up the troops. He was realistic, though, realizing that his Party's prospects at the polls were very weak. He said, "We Fascists should realize that we stand alone… and if we are few, it must be remembered that we have been in being only six months."

As a part of their activities, and to gain more attention, the Fascists held a parade in Florence with uniformed men marching in formations, mock-armored cars, rockets being fired into the air, and Mussolini standing prominently in a reviewing stand. Some of the Italian newspapers picked up the story and the Fascists got a measure of publicity Mussolini had hoped for.

In Bulgaria, on October 6, 1919, a new leftist government came to power under Alexander Stamboliski, leader of the Peasant Party. Stamboliski had been an opponent to Bulgaria's entry into the war and was imprisoned throughout the war.

Now, as Premier, he took revenge on his opponents. All of the members of the Bulgarian War Cabinet were arrested and charged with the crime of dragging Bulgaria into the war. They were tried, convicted, fined, and given heavy prison sentences. Stamboliski also embarked on an extensive reform program which called for the confiscation of crown lands, church lands, and estates over 75 acres for redistribution to the peasants. He also shut down the universities pending revisions of the curriculum and imposed censorship on the press.

In the diplomatic arena, he sought reconciliation with Jugoslavia and broke up the wartime Bulgarian-supported Macedonian Revolutionary Organization (IMRO) that had fought against the Allies in Macedonia.

The western Allies were not all that pleased with Stamboliski's coming to power and his reform measures, but at least his government came to power peacefully and it was much more moderate than the government Bela Kun had created in Hungary. Also, it would be the Stamboliski government with whom the Allies would have to negotiate a peace treaty.

On the 17th, the Austrian Assembly ratified the Treaty of St. Germaine with the stipulation that it would become effective on July 17, 1920.

BALFOUR OUT — CURZON IN

On October 27, Balfour resigned as Foreign Secretary from Lloyd George's cabinet and was replaced by Curzon. This represented a significant change in British foreign policies because Balfour and Curzon had often disagreed. Whereas Balfour was an internationalist and ardent supporter of empire, Curzon was more of an isolationist. Harold Nicolson once said of Curzon, "His ideal world would have been one in which England never intervened in Europe and Europe never intervened in Africa or Asia." Curzon particularly disliked the French and had a low opinion of all foreigners in general. With this change, Lloyd George now had to deal with another curmudgeon.

The differences between Balfour and Curzon were dramatized by the issues in Palestine. The very controversial Balfour Declaration had now lost its creator and the implementation of that agreement was in the hands of Curzon who had, at times, questioned the wisdom of that agreement. In the past, Curzon had suggested that an international organization be formed to address the issues in Palestine in order to relieve Britain of what looked to be the beginning of a never-ending problem there between the Jews and the Arabs.

Curzon's concerns were highlighted at this time because renewed violence was occurring in Palestine between Jewish settlers and Bedouin tribes in upper Galilee, a no-man's land claimed by France as part of Syria and Britain as part of Palestine. Also, in Jerusalem, anti-Zionist agitation was turning into anti-British agitation, and, in the overall picture, Britain's staunch support of the Zionists, personified by Balfour, was undermining Britain's position in Syria and elsewhere in the Muslim world.

Then there was Turkey. Curzon had little love for the Turks but even less for the Greeks. He believed that the authority given to the Greeks at Paris to invade Smyrma was one of the greatest mistakes of the peace conference. On this issue, however, Curzon was in total disagreement with Lloyd George who had supported the Greek initiative in Paris. One of Curzon's first acts was to send a secret emissary to Kemal to obtain his views on a peace treaty. Curzon saw Kemal as the greatest threat in the Middle East and had repeatedly warned against turning Kemal into an enemy of the West.

There was now a parallel between the US and Britain. In both countries, the chief executive had a director of foreign affairs with whom they often disagreed.

Also in Britain, the British Army had been greatly reduced from its wartime strength. Winston Churchill who, by now, was well-known for his arch conservative views and colorful rhetoric, was quoted as saying in public that "the army had melted away."

GERMANS ORDERED OUT OF THE BALTIC

On October 8, 1919, the Allied Powers ordered the German government to withdraw the German forces operating independently in Latvia as mercenaries and the Germans willingly complied. This would be the end of the Baltikum Army which had been proved to be an embarrassment to Weimar. That Army had gone from bad to very bad. It had driven the Bolsheviks out of Latvia, but then turned on the Latvians themselves and even threatened to take over the country. Understandably, the Allies did not want this to happen, thus the order to Weimar.

The Baltikum's commander, General von der Goltz, objected to the order from Germany, but without the German government's support, his army was doomed. Von der Goltz announced that he would obey the order and began making plans to withdraw his forces back into Germany.

With the Germans moving out of Latvia, Poland's Pilsudski jumped into the military vacuum and offered to be Latvia's protector. This would constitute a de facto recognition to the Latvian government by Poland. From Pilsudski's viewpoint, there were several advantages. Poland needed allies and Latvia was strategically situated to assist Poland on its northern border in that Lithuania, Poland's adversary, was now sandwiched between Latvia to the north and Poland to the south. The Poles also offered to support any claims that the Latvians might have against the Lithuanians.

In Lithuania there was fear and indecision. So far, during 1919, Lithuania had had four different government. The existing government, headed by Ernestas Galvanauskas, assumed power on October 15, 1919, and was no more stable than the last. It would remain in office only until June 1920.

IN THE US AGAIN

On October 1, there was a race riot in Elaine, Arkansas.

On October 8, the wartime ban on Germans immigrating to the US was lifted.

On the 10th, President Wilson sat up in bed for the first time since his stroke. Now the rumors said that he would be back to work soon, but other rumors continued,

saying that he was permanently disabled. By now, the leadership of the Democrat Party had agreed that, for the good of the nation and the Party, they would cooperate with Mrs. Wilson and Dr. Grayson and downplay the seriousness of the President's illness.

On October 17, the Radio Corporation of America (RCA) was incorporated, reflecting the rapid expansion of that new form of communication. The creation of the corporation was encouraged and aided by the Federal Government. Under RCA's control would be a host of patents held by such companies as General Electric, AT&T, Westinghouse, and United Fruit, which could be used in complimentary arrangements to standardize and advance the technology of this new form of communications. RCA's immediate aim was to produce versatile and affordable "radio music boxes" for public consumption.

ISSUES IN FRANCE

On October 12, 1919, the wartime state of siege in France was lifted, which took away from Clemenceau much of his authority to rule by decree. This was a signal to the French labor unions that wartime controls over strikes were off and that labor was free to assert itself. In the coming months, labor troubles in France would increase significantly.

On October 14, French President Poincare, as head of the French armed force, ordered a general demobilization of those forces. In Germany, there was joy because, now a large-scale Allied invasion to enforce the Diktat was much less likely.

In Paris, still a focal point for Allied interactions, there was concern about the ineffectiveness of the remnant of the American delegation that remained a part of the Supreme Council. The Americans spent their days without orders from Washington, and because the US had not yet ratified the Versailles Peace Treaty, no Americans were assigned to serve on the various commission and agencies being created. For most of the Europeans, this put an extra burden on them and a general disappointment with American policies in general.

In the French Assembly, criticism of Clemenceau increased and the election was coming. On one occasion, Clemenceau said to the British Ambassador, "What on earth is the Lord Almighty doing that He does not take him (Wilson) to His bosom."

And Clemenceau had other problems. Industrial production was still only 43% of that of 1913, and with winter approaching, coal was still in short supply because repairs on the French coal mines in the north were still incomplete. France was also fifteen billion francs in debt and Clemenceau's opponents were quick to point out that, before the war, France was one of the world's largest creditor nations holding some 40 billion francs in foreign obligations. This brought forward the unhappy prospect of an income tax — something that France had never had.

There was some good news, however, for Clemenceau. Czechoslovakia showed every indication of wanting to become France's ally and France needed allies in the East. Czech Foreign Minister, Eduard Benes, had come to Paris to discuss this issue and the talks were fruitful. In return for an alliance, Clemenceau promised to back Czechoslovakia on the Teschen issue. This, of course, did not sit well in Warsaw.

PADEREWSKI APPEALS TO CHURCHILL

On October 15, Polish Premier Paderewski sent an urgent message to Britain's Secretary for War, Winston Churchill. It began "Sir, I have just received news from our Bolshevik front. The situation there is desperate. The promises of Mr.

Lloyd George made on 27 June to assist our army have not materialized…" Paderewski went on to ask for an extensive list of military supplies including some 300,000 complete uniforms for the Polish Army's new recruits. Furthermore, he asked Churchill's help in recovering "From our supply of railway rolling stock now in France… at least 200 locomotives and 2000 wagons at once." The message concluded, "If such an assistance is not granted immediately, the entire line of our Bolshevist front may break down at any moment and the worst can be expected." The message closed with "Sir, Your obedient, humble servant, I. J. Paderewski."

Churchill's reply came on the 24th and it was negative. Churchill told Paderewski that, with regret, the British Cabinet had refused to accede to the Polish request. He added that the Cabinet had adopted the principle that "…help for the Polish Army rested with the Allies generally and only to a very minor degree with Great Britain." Ironically, Churchill was very much in favor of helping Poland, but his opinion did not prevail at Whitehall.

A NEW DYNAMIC PARTY MEMBER

On the evening of October 16, the DAP held another public meeting at the Hofbraukeller in Munich, and Corporal Hitler, still contemplating party membership, was in attendance. This was something of a milestone for the Party in that they had advertised the meeting, for the first time in a local right-wing newspaper, the *Munchener Beobachter*. Heretofore, the party members had handed out individual invitations, some of them handwritten. The newspaper announcement worked very well. One hundred and eleven people showed up — more than twice the number of their previous public meeting.

The speaker was Dr. Erich Kuhn, the editor and co-publisher of the right-wing magazine *Deutschlands Erneuerung*

(Germany's Renewal), and his subject was "The Jewish Problem — A German Problem."

Hitler, because of his performance at the previous meeting, was asked by Harrer and Drexler to speak after Kuhn concluded his talk and open the meeting for discussions. Hitler was to endorse and emphasize Kuhn's comments and was to speak for only 20 minutes. This was an historic event in that it was Hitler's first scheduled address before a cross-section of the German public — and it was a great success. Hitler spoke for 30 minutes and held the audience's rapt attention all the while. He railed against the Diktat, the Jews, and Germany's former enemies. In a way, he had upstaged Dr. Kuhn because Hitler had a very dramatic way of speaking which, in time, he would develop to perfection. He would begin his speeches in a quiet and subdued manner and then gradually raise his voice to ranting and screaming at the end. He used short, powerful sentences with much gesturing, quoted slogans, and sayings, and he used many absolutes. He spoke in glowing terms of Germany's future and in angry terms of present-day conditions. At the end of a speech, he was usually drenched in perspiration and his hair hung down over his forehead which he would, in one of his often-repeated gestures, brush to the side with his hand.

A reporter from the *Munchener Beobachter* was present and would write in the next day's issue "Herr Hitler... used inflammatory words in urging the necessity for concerted action against the common enemy of all nations, and he particularly stressed support for a true German press, so that the people can learn what is suppressed by the Jewish-controlled newspapers."

As the meeting concluded, donations were requested and some 300 marks were collected, a substantial sum for the little group and about 40 times the Party's current treasury balance. Harrer and Drexler attributed much of this windfall to the Corporal's address.

A short time later, buoyed by his performance at the meeting, Hitler made up his mind — he would join the Party. With the approval of his commanding officer, Captain Mayr, he wrote a letter to the DAP Executive Committee, dated October 19, 1919, asking to join the Party. A second letter followed in which Hitler stated that it was his desire to become a political speaker. The Committee readily accepted Hitler's application and he became party member number 555. Actually, he was the 55th person to join the Party because Harrer and Drexler had started the numbering system at 500 in order to make it appear that the Party was larger than it actually was.

PARTY MEMBER #7

When Hitler came to power, he had the Party's records altered to show that he was Party member #7. There is some justification for this because, at the time, there were six members on the Executive Committee and he was soon given a high post which made him the de facto seventh member of the Committee.

Hitler began attending the weekly Wednesday night meetings of the Executive Committee which were held at a reserved table in the Cafe Gasteig. These were planning sessions, and Hitler was given a voice in the decisions. With the 300 marks, it was decided to advertise the next meeting again in the *Munchener Beobachter* and utilize four speakers, one of which would be Hitler. The Committee also agreed to print and hand out leaflets for the next meeting. All of the committee members expected that these efforts would attract an even larger crowd. In the enthusiasm of the moment, Hitler suggested that an admission charge be instigated of 50 pfennigs. This would be entirely new on the Bavarian political scene since none of the other parties charged admission. Harrer objected, but the other five members, with further persuasion from Hitler, outvoted him and accepted the idea. The next meeting was scheduled for November 13 and the Party leaders would not be disappointed.

Harrer and Drexler were so impressed with Hitler that they created a new post for him — Chairman of the Propaganda Committee, a one-man committee. With this, Hitler was awarded the opportunity to speak to the public on a regular basis, and he would make full use of it. Plus, he was making a little money in the process. Captain Mayr began paying him an extra 20 marks a week from a secret Army fund to cover his expenses.

THE REDS BEGIN TO WIN IN RUSSIA

During October 1919, the news from Russia was all bad. Earlier in the month, Iudenich's Northwest White Army had advanced steadily on Petrograd, and on the 11th, captured Iamburg, 80 miles west of Petrograd. On the 16th they took Gatchina, 25 miles southwest of the city and, by the 20th, had stormed the Polkovo Heights south of Petrograd and were within rifle range of the city's suburbs. At this point, Iudenich proclaimed "Victory is Near." But it was not to be.

THE POLKOVO HEIGHTS

In the Fall of 1941, German forces reached and occupied the Polkovo Heights overlooking the city which, by then, had been renamed Leningrad. Like Iudenich, it would be as far as they would get. They held the Heights for many months but were never able to enter the city.

But Iudenich's successes were not necessarily due to his army's strength but more so to the Bolshevik's weaknesses and commitments elsewhere. Iudenich had some very major problems; he had few tanks and aircraft, the morale of his troops was low, there were desertions, winter was coming, and he was arguing with his second-in-command, Gen. Rodzianko, over command decisions.

On the other hand, both Trotsky and Stalin were working together to rally the troops in the Petrograd area and prepare for a counterattack. On the 17th, Trotsky arrived in the city to personally direct that attack.

On the 21st, the counterattack was launched and the Reds quickly recovered the Polkovo Heights. They moved on to take Tsarkoe Selo and Pavlovsk, some 20 miles to the west, and on the 31st, they took Luga, 85 miles southwest of Petrograd. Iudenich's offensive had been stopped and his hopes of taking Petrograd were now dashed.

In the south of Russia, the situation was similar. During the summer months, Denikin's White Armies had been advancing steadily northward toward Moscow. But Denikin, like Iudenich, had problems with discipline and morale, and his situation was complicated by extended lines of supply and a never-ending broad front that could be penetrated at any of a number of points by a well-organized enemy counterattack.

On the 24th, a major battle between the Red and White horse cavalries took place at Voronezh and the Reds won. Now, there was a large hole in Denikin's front and it would prove to be Denikin's undoing.

From Siberia came reports that Kolchak had lost all control over his forces. The Reds were fast approaching Kolchak's capital, Omsk, and resistance was almost nonexistent. From Omsk, the trains on the Trans-Siberian Railroad were packed with refugees and fleeing soldiers hoping to make Irkusk. Now, only the onset of winter could slow the Red advance.

By the end of October, the view in the West was that Iudenich was in retreat in the northwest, Denikin was in retreat in the south and Kolchak was all but defeated in Siberia. On the Polish front, there was little activity but the Poles appeared to be holding their own.

In Germany, the Weimar government issued a statement on October 30, saying that Germany would continue its policy of non-intervention in Russia. The Germans were playing the situation in Russia both ways. If the Reds were defeated, so be it. If, on the other hand, the Reds won, they would be indebted to the Germans for having secretly transported Lenin to Petrograd in 1917 to start this revolution and for having taken no formal actions to suppress the Bolshevik Revolution. As for the Free Corps activities in the Baltic state against the Bolsheviks, the German government would continue to claim that those actions were independent and not authorized by the German government.

And the Germans and Bolsheviks would also have something else in common — they were both outcasts in the post-war world.

From Paris, the Supreme Council announced on October 10 that the Allied blockade against Russia would not only continue, but would become more restrictive. The neutral nations were warned that their ships, attempting to reach Bolshevik-held ports, would be stopped and turned away, and it was decreed that citizens of the Allied nations would be forbidden to visit Russia and would not be allowed to communicate with individuals in Russia by letter, telegram, or radiogram.

THE VOLSTEAD ACT

The recently-passed 18th Amendment to the US constitution made it legal to outlaw alcoholic beverages in the US, but an act of Congress was needed to implement it and spell out the necessary details. That was the Volstead Act. It was named after Congressman Andrew J. Volstead (R-Minn.) who introduced it into Congress. It forbade the manufacture, sale, or transportation of intoxicating liquors within the US, defined intoxicating beverages as being "one-half of one per centum or more of alcohol by volume," and charged the Commissioner of the Internal Revenue Service within the Department of the Treasury with enforcement. Some years later, enforcement was transferred to the Department of Justice and its recently-formed investigative agency, the Federal Bureau of Investigation (FBI).

The Act was passed by Congress on October 27, 1919, but was vetoed by President Wilson. Congress then overrode his veto, making the Volstead Act the law of the land.

$105 MILLION A YEAR

History duly records that prohibition in the US was a miserable failure. Instead of tax money going into the nation's coffers and legitimate business profits going into the pocket of American businessmen, it went into the pockets of the nation's criminals. In 1927, Al Capone, the prohibition kingpin in Chicago, made $105 million that year — the highest gross income ever received to date by an American citizen. Capone would later go to prison for income tax evasion.

In 1933, during the Roosevelt Administration and in the depth of the Great Depression, prohibition was repealed by another constitutional amendment, the 21st, and the tax dollars began, once again, to flow into the US Treasury.

NO ALCOHOL OR GUNS FOR THE AFRICANS

During the month, the colonial powers held an international conference in which they agreed not to supply alcohol or guns to any of the African peoples under their control.

A TIME TO RATIFY

On October 13, the French government ratified the Versailles Treaty. On the 15th, the British government did likewise and was followed by Italy on the 18th and Japan on the 30th. Peace was breaking out in Europe but the United States was still at war with Germany, Austria, Hungary, and Bulgaria.

AND THE AMERICANS READ IN THEIR NEWSPAPERS...

...that on October 16, President Wilson suffered another malady. He had been suffering from an enlarged prostate for some time and now he could not urinate. Two urologists were called to the White House but their attempts to catheterize the President failed, and the doctors recommended an operation. Mrs. Wilson objected to the operation and said that "nature will take care of things." Nature did.

Journalists on the Washington scene reported that attacks on the President by Senator Lodge and his compatriots had been greatly reduced. It was generally understood that this was being done out of human compassion rather than a change in Lodge's political stance.

On the 24th, it was reported that Wilson had decreed from his sickbed that he, and he alone, would decide Democrat Party's policy toward the Versailles Treaty and the League of Nations.

The next day, the President was heard from again. He was quoted as having said that a strike of coal miners, which had been brewing for several weeks and scheduled for November 1, was unjustifiable and unlawful. It was a clear indication that the Federal Government might get more deeply involved in America's labor problems.

On the 26th, there were news reports that Wilson was on the mend and that Mrs. Wilson had said that his mind was as "clear as ever."

On the 29th, newspapers reported that in Gary, Indiana, where federal troops had taken over, the steel workers' strike had turned bloody. With this, many eyes turned toward Washington.

CHAPTER 17
EUROPE, THE US SENATE AND THE CHAIRMAN OF THE PROPAGANDA COMMITTEE

IN THE US — A COAL STRIKE, A SICK PRESIDENT, AND MORE...

On November 1, 1919, 425,000 coal miners went on strike across the US. The timing of the strike was most unfortunate because millions of Americans heated their homes with coal and winter was coming. But the mine owners, the federal government and the Justice Department were ready. Within hours of the beginning of the strike, a federal judge issued a permanent restraining order to stop the strike and authorized the use of 800 federal troops to back up the order. Wilson had warned the miners of this so it came as no surprise. The miners were also reminded that the wartime Fuel Administration Act was still in force which gave the government extraordinary powers in such matters.

Now faced with a confrontation and a court case which the miners would very likely lose, John L. Lewis, President of the United Mine Workers union (UMW), ordered the miners back to work. Many of the miners did not comply and simply stayed home. This forced both sides to talk to each other because the only other option was to start some sort of punitive action which neither side wanted. The talks dragged on but the mines began producing some coal.

On the 5th, Calvin Coolidge — the man who broke the Boston Police Strike — was reelected governor of Massachusetts.

On the 6th, Senator Lodge introduced fourteen more reservations to the Versailles Peace Treaty into the US Senate and it was becoming clear, by now, that the final vote on the Treaty would be very much along party lines.

The next day, Senator Gilbert Hitchcock, (D Neb.) Democrat minority leader in the Senate, went to see Wilson to discuss Lodge's latest move. Hitchcock later told colleagues that he could see that Wilson's left arm was paralyzed and said, "I beheld an emaciated old man with a thin white beard which had been permitted to grow."

Lenin and Trotsky (saluting) surrounded by other party dignitaries and ordinary citizens in Red Square at the celebrations of the second anniversary of the beginning of the Bolshevik Revolution. Stalin is nowhere to be seen.

This report stimulated rumors, already circulating around Washington, that Vice President Thomas Marshall, who had been denied access to the President, might begin legal proceedings to replace Wilson.

November 7, 1919, was the second anniversary of the beginning of the Bolshevik Revolution in Russia and Attorney General Palmer had a surprise for the Reds in America. His men began rounding up Reds for interrogations and possible deportation. The roundup started in New York City with Greenwich Village being the focal point of his activity. Most of those rounded up were immigrants who were suspected of un-American activities. And this was only the beginning. In the days that followed, more arrests were made in the various parts of the country until some 5000 suspects were in custody. This action was hailed by the press and the public. Palmer, who had presidential aspirations, was elated. He hoped to become to the nation what Coolidge was to Boston.

RUSSIA: REDS WINNING, WHITES LOSING

On November 4, 1919, London informed Denikin that British aid to his forces would end on March 31, 1920. This reversal of policy reflected the influence of Curzon on Lloyd George's government. It was Curzon's belief that it was time to cut and run in Russia. He could also see that the Reds could become a valuable trading partner while the Whites would continue to be a liability.

On the 7th, Bolshevik forces from the east and south linked up at Iamburg west of Petrograd. Now, this combined force would strike at Iudenich's weakened and

THE COMMISSARS VANISH

When Stalin came to power, he had Trotsky airbrushed out of this by-then-famous photograph. Also removed was Artashes Khalatov, with black pointed beard, standing to Lenin's right in the original picture. Khalatov was, in 1919, commissar for all of the Soviet government's published activities. He fell from favor and perished in 1937 during the Stalin purges.

outnumbered forces which were already demoralized and retreating to the west.

Trotsky, who had directed the counteroffensive, rushed to Moscow to personally report the victory to the Central Committee. He also predicted a complete victory in the northwest by the beginning of 1920. It was a moment of glory for Trotsky. He had bought about another major victory; it was the second anniversary of the beginning of the Bolshevik Revolution and it was his 40th birthday. In the halls of the Kremlin, Trotsky was the hero of the hour. Stalin withdrew and sulked.

In southern Russia and the Ukraine, the Reds continued to advance using a new tactic — massed horse-mounted cavalry attacks against the enemy's front. By this time, the Reds had some 16,000 cavalrymen for such attacks and had formed them into an elite unit known as the "1st

Cavalry Army". Heretofore, cavalry units usually worked independently in small groups against the enemy's flanks and supply routes. The massing of cavalry was not new. Genghis Khan and others had used it in centuries past.

To add to the effectiveness of the cavalry charges, the Reds utilized aircraft to support the attack. The combination was deadly because Denikin's infantrymen had no effective air defenses and could not outrun a horse. One of the young officers in the 1st Cavalry Army was Georgi Zhukov.

Denikin had nothing to match the 1st Cavalry Army. He depended mainly on the difficult-to-control Cossacks for his cavalry support, and it would have been virtually impossible to form them into one large cohesive force that could be used as Denikin commanded.

By the end of the month, the 1st Cavalry Army had made it possible for the Red Army to drive a deep wedge between Denikin's center and right. With this, Denikin was in serious trouble and his forces were heading for safety of the Caucasus and the Crimea.

FROM HORSES TO TANKS TO "BLITZKRIEG"

The Germans were quick to learn from such examples as the 1st Cavalry Army and the few times the British had successfully massed tanks for attacks during the Great War. The Germans built on these examples and perfected a form of attack that would become known as the "Blitzkrieg." It would consist of massed tanks, with strong air support and motorized infantry to break through a segment of the enemy's front and charge into his rear areas. It was used with great success in September 1939 against Poland and later in France and Belgium in 1940. By June 1941, when the Axis Powers attacked the Soviet Union, the Blitzkrieg tactic had been perfected, and during the first months of the invasion, devastated the static Soviet defenses. The Soviets, who had numerous and very good quality tanks available, eventually began using the same tactic against the Germans, also with great success, and were eventually able to out-Blitzkrieg the German Blitzkriegers.

In London, Lloyd George announced in a speech that his government was beginning an initiative to reach a trade agreement with the Bolshevik government in Moscow. He said that its main purpose would be to bring the new Russian government into the world community. He had never said anything of this sort about the Russian Whites.

In Siberia, Kolchak's government abandoned Omsk in great disorder on November 12. Kolchak personally had to bribe three railroad officials in order to get his train out of the city. On the 14th, the Reds occupied the city. Kolchak's withdrawal was so chaotic that some 40,000 of his troops surrendered to the Reds without a fight and the Reds captured over 200 locomotives, three armored trains, 3000 freight cars, and a half million rounds of artillery shells. Luckily for Kolchak, he was able to get his government's gold reserves aboard his train. On his way to Irkutsk, his personal bodyguards deserted him. Some members of his entourage suggested that they flee south into Outer Mongolia and/or place themselves under the protection of the Allies. Kolchak, however, was not ready to give up.

POLES AND BOLSHEVIKS NEGOTIATE

Since mid-October, Polish and Bolshevik representatives had been meeting under the guise of the Red Cross at the remote railway stop of Mikaszewice 60 miles east of Pinsk. The purpose of the meeting, which was announced by both sides, was for humanitarian reasons, but it was much more than that. Both sides were feeling out the other for a possible armistice. The Poles had recently improved their bargaining position by adding, in the last two months, over 100,000 new troops as the result of conscription. And the British had recently sent the Poles fifty airplanes. The Reds' bargaining position had not improved. They were still deeply committed in the south, in Siberia, and in the northwest and their Polish front was still weak.

Two humanitarian agreements were quickly reached and publicized; the first was on November 2 in which the Bolsheviks agreed to return to Poland a number of hostages in their possession,

Die Patienten werden gebeten, infolge der Kohlennot zur Heizung des Wartezimmers bei jedem Besuch ein Brikett mitzubringen.
Dr. med. Wagner

This sign in a doctor's office reads, "Due to the coal shortage, patients are requested to bring a coal briquette with them to help heat the waiting room."

and the other agreement was reached on November 9 which arranged for a mutual exchange of prisoners. Agreements beyond this point were much more difficult and the negotiations would continue on until mid-December with time being on the side of the Bolsheviks.

IN GERMANY

In Germany the government shut down the country's rail system for ten days to save coal that was destined to go to France.

In Berlin, the German communists were still trying to make their mark. On the 4th, in a joint meeting, the "Communist Factory Councils" called for yet another strike. Much to their disappointment, many workers resisted the idea. It appeared that the people of Berlin had had enough strife from the politicians. They now wanted law and order and peace.

On the 10th, President Ebert, as commander-in-chief of Germany's armed forces, made a secret agreement with the Army's General Wilhelm Groener which committed both the government and the Army to work together to prevent a revolution from either the left or right. It was a good sign for the stability of the country.

On the 18th, Field Marshal Hindenberg testified before a committee of the German National Assembly and stated that the German Army was close to victory in November 1918 but was "stabbed in the back" by civilian authorities and socialists in the government. Right-wingers applauded the Field Marshal while the left-wingers claimed that Hindenberg was simply trying to conceal his role in the Army's failings and in his agreeing to the armistice. The political moderates were divided and the political atmosphere within Germany was no better off than before.

HITLER — CHAIRMAN OF THE PROPAGANDA COMMITTEE

As head of the newly-formed Propaganda Committee, Hitler had the responsibility for filling the halls for the Party's public meetings. To this end, he made use of the typewriter in his regiment's office and typed out dozens of invitations. He then distributed many of them personally to known supporters and, if he had extras, stuffed them into mailboxes. This was in addition to the Party's advertising efforts in the newspapers. These efforts paid off. At the next meeting, on November 13, there were 126 people in attendance, the largest to date, and they each paid the 50 pfennigs admission fee. In his speech, Hitler, as usual, railed against the Diktat and the Jews, and he referred to "Der Tag," the day when Germany would strike back. This phrase had already become much-used in Germany. Hitler said, "The misery of Germany must be broken by German steel. That time must come."

There were hecklers in the crowd planted by leftist organizations who interrupted Hitler's speech several times.

Hitler realized this might happen and was prepared. He had asked several of his fellow soldiers to attend the meeting to serve as bouncers. They did their job well. Hitler later wrote of the incident, "The disturbers flew down the stairs with gashed heads."

A police officer in the crowd, taking notes, reported that Hitler's speech was "masterful" and that he received "tumultuous applause." There was no mention in the police report of the ejection of the hecklers.

The DAP leaders now knew that Hitler was a great asset to the Party, and on November 16, they admitted him into the Party's most exclusive inner circle, which they called the "Political Workers' Circle." This was the name of the original small group formed by Harrer from which the DAP evolved. The minutes of the meeting read: "Introduction of Herr Hitler into the spirit of the Circle by Herr Harrer."

It was also decided at this meeting that the Party should adopt a formal program to publicize its political position. A five-man committee was formed for this purpose with Hitler being one of the members.

At the next meeting of the Party leaders a week later, Hitler was authorized to begin a program to train other speakers.

Along with these developments, it was generally agreed that publicity would be the key to the Party's future success. Hitler fully agreed, knowing that he would be the kingpin of such efforts. At this point, he began to look around for a mimeograph machine, as the regiment's typewriter was no longer sufficient.

ARMISTICE DAY USA

On November 11, 1919, the first anniversary of the ending of the Great War, there were parades and celebrations all over the US. In Centralia, Washington, however, there was trouble. The IWW Wobblies were still strong in that town and operated out of a union hall in the center of town. On this day of celebration, the newly-formed American Legion held a parade through Centralia which passed by the union hall. For some unknown reason, the Legionnaires doubled back and began attacking the hall and those inside. It turned into a bloody conflict in which three Legionnaires were killed, while one Wobbly, who was thought to have killed one the Legionnaires with a hand gun, was lynched.

News of the "Centralia Massacre," as it became known, spread cross the country accompanied by an outcry of the US citizenry against the Wobblies, Bolsheviks, and other leftist radicals. This sparked some ugly attacks in other cities on known and suspected Reds. Such attacks were especially prevalent on the West Coast.

Back in Centralia, the local coroner recorded the death of the lynched Wobbly as a suicide. Ten Wobblies were taken to court, and seven of them were found guilty of second degree murder and given prison sentences ranging from 25 to 40 years.

In Washington, DC, Attorney General A. Mitchell Palmer took note of the public's heightened attitude against Reds and would use it to his advantage.

The next day, in North Dakota where a miners' strike was threatening, the state's governor declared martial law in the mines which were then taken over by the North Dakota National Guard. This gave Palmer more political ammunition.

ITALY, D'ANNUNZIO, AN ELECTION, THE SOCIALISTS, AND A TRAVELING VIOLIN PLAYER

On November 14, d'Annunzio expanded his domain beyond Fiume. An armed group of his followers landed at the small seaport of Zara (Zadar) on the Dalmatian coast 100 miles south of Fiume. Here was another grab of land to which a large segment of the Italian people believed they were entitled. Italian warships were in the area but did not interfere. There was much joy in Italy, anger in Jugoslavia, and confusion and disapproval in most of the western capitals.

On the Italian mainland, however, the large and powerful Italian Socialists were pursuing an altogether different agenda. Following up on their proclamations of October, and campaigning for the upcoming election, the Socialists called again for the recognition of the Bolshevik regime in Russia, the disbanding of the Italian army, the confiscation of large fortunes and war profits, and other measures which would cast Italy into the camp of the international socialists. The upper and middle classes of Italy were petrified and there was talk, once again, of revolution and civil war.

It was in this atmosphere that, on November 16, an election was held throughout Italy for members of the Chamber of Deputies and for some local offices. In Milan, Mussolini's stronghold, the Fascists fielded a slate of candidates — the only Fascist slate in Italy. Heading the slate was the famous conductor, Arturo Toscanini. He had been nominated by the Fascists without his consent but upon discovering this he, nevertheless, allowed his nomination to stand. The election results for the Fascists were miserable. Out of 270,000 votes cast in Milan, the Fascists got only 4795. Their primary opponent, the Socialists, acquired 176,000 votes. After knowing the results, a mob of Socialists besieged the offices of *Il Popolo* hoping to put a quick end to this troublesome newspaper. But, enough black-shirted Adriti were assembled at the office to prevent that from happening.

Nationwide, the Socialists got 1,840,593 votes out of 6½ million cast and another leftist party, the Italian Popular Party

Mussolini was an accomplished violin player.

(PPI), got 1,175,000. Together, they won control of the Chamber by a very narrow margin. In some cities, however, the leftists took over the local administration. One of the cities was Bologna where the red flag was hoisted over the town hall.

Mussolini was in despair. He talked of giving it all up, of becoming a traveling musician with his violin, or a pilot, or a writer and possibly leaving the country. Clearly, the Fascists had a long way to go.

The next day, the Socialist newspaper *Avanti* headlined, "The Italy of the Revolution is born." In Milan, the victorious Socialists held a parade and a gang of Adriti hurled a bomb into the parading ranks, injuring nine people. The police made some arrests, and in their investigations, searched the offices of *Il Popolo* where they found several revolvers and hand grenades. Mussolini and two others were arrested and held for 48 hours, then released.

Italy was now a polarized nation with a large segment of the citizenry leaning toward the far left as demonstrated by the election, while the Italian military, the political right, and d'Annunzio and his supporters, were tilted toward the far right. In Rome, the Italian government was about to be taken over by the socialists.

Eventually, Mussolini recovered from his bout of depression and decided to keep himself in shape for the battles to come. To do this, he instigated a program of physical exercises. Furthermore, he had always wanted to become an airplane pilot and began taking flying lessons and, as part of his exercise program, bicycled 18 miles, one way, from his residence back and forth to the airfield. On his first solo flight, he crashed the plane upon landing and spent 20 days in the hospital. This did not discourage him, however. He stayed with it, got his pilot's license, and throughout his lifetime, logged some 17,000 hours of flight.

THE BRITISH PULL OUT OF SYRIA

In Syria, the British withdrawal was underway. The British announced that they would withdraw only from Syrian territory north of the disputed area in northern Palestine. Along with the pullout, the British government cut its subsidy to the Damascus government in half. It was understood that Damascus and eastern Syria would be under Faisal's control and that his regime would collect the taxes. Western Syria and The Lebanon would be under French control. In their area, however, the French were noticeably building up their military forces — an ominous sign for Faisal.

Since the border between The Lebanon and Faisal's Syria had not yet been defined, both French and Syrian troops moved into the Biqa Valley on the eastern side of The Lebanon and one of the main areas of dispute. Not surprisingly, there were armed clashes.

Faisal, who was still in Paris, had yet another problem — a family problem. His father, King Husain of Hijaz, turned out to be the Woodrow Wilson of the Middle East. He would not compromise. As for Syria, it would be all or nothing. The King announced from Mecca that he would not support any agreement that his son Faisal might make with the French.

US SENATE REJECTS PEACE TREATY

Debate on the Peace Treaty was winding down in the US Senate and a vote was expected soon. On November 17, the Senate's Democratic leader, Gilbert Hitchcock, went to see Wilson one last time to see if he would accept any reservations. At this point, there were fourteen reservations attached to Senate bill. Wilson told Hitchcock that he wanted all or nothing, and that if the Republicans rejected ratification, they would have to answer to the people. Many now saw in Wilson the stubbornness of his Calvinist upbringing.

On the 19th, the vote was taken. The US Constitution required a two-thirds vote of the Senate for ratification but that figure was not reached. The Peace Treaty was defeated with 55 yeas and 39 nays. It was reintroduced a second time with only five reservations and was defeated again 51 to 41. Then it was entered a third time with no reservations and defeated 53 to 38. Then the Senate adjourned, but it was not the end. All expected the bill to come up for another vote in several months because the feeling in Washington was that the public demanded it. For now, though, ratification had failed and the public reaction was surprising mild.

The Senate's rejection of the Treaty did not sit well with America's European Allies and also signaling that Wilson's Fourteen Points program was a dead issue. This caused considerable concern in the smaller nations, within national minorities, and with the millions of people in the world's colonies.

Over in the House of Representatives, they were making headline too. Its members were debating what to do about the Red scare. On the 22nd, the House Committee on Immigration held a high profile meeting on Ellis Island and one of the announcements forthcoming from the meeting was what everyone already knew, that New York City was the center of Red activity in the US and that the Justice Department should investigate Red activities there with great intensity.

Three days later, New York City police and Attorney General Palmer's agents discovered bomb-making equipment in the headquarters of the "Union of Russian Workers." The authorities had warrants for the arrest of several people associated with the Union, but none of those individuals could be found. This was the sixth raid by authorities on the Union's headquarters in less than a year and signaled the beginning of a large-scale roundup of Reds under Palmer's direction.

OTHER HEADLINES

On November 16, 1919, they held an election in France to select members for the French Chamber. This was the first election in which women voted and there was a dramatic shift to the right of center. Ironically, on this same day, the election in Italy showed a pronounced shift to the left. In France, a coalition of right-wing parties, known as the "Bloc National," had emerged and won 380 of the French Assembly's 616 seats. Another 57 deputies, not associated with the Bloc, could be counted upon to support it. These political factions found a common unity due to the on-going, and seemingly non-ending Red scare permeating Europe and the fact that a huge communist state was about to emerge in the east. Furthermore, and

Admiral Miklos Horthy, as war hero and father-figure for the Hungarian people. He was well-educated, spoke six languages, and had a wife of "majestic beauty."

very much unlike the situation in Italy, the French Socialists had lost favor due to their association with France's troublesome unions and with the international socialists and communists.

Unfortunately for the Bloc National, however, victory brought on greed and the Bloc members began squabbling among themselves. It was not good news for Clemenceau. He now had a new set of problems and his ability to hold on to the Premiership had come into question. And the people would soon speak again in January 1920, when there would be an election for the members of the Senate.

On this same fateful day, November 16, Admiral Horthy and his relatively small force of counter-revolutionaries entered Budapest, Hungary, to the rejoicing of most of the city's population. The Romanians, who had ruled and looted the city, were gone — under strong pressures from both Britain and France. Horthy was seen as a Savior and as a highly admired father-figure in a land where radicals, scoundrels, and Jews had ruled for too long a time. All knew he stood for law and order and was a true Hungarian patriot. One of his first acts was to call an election for a new National Assembly which would determine Hungary's future. On November 23, Count Mahaly Karolyi, a former Head of State, member of the right-wing "Christian National Unity Party," and a highly-respected individual, became the interim Premier under Horthy's authority. Horthy also sought to increase his military resources and called for a sizeable increase in the Hungarian army.

On the darker side, a large segment of Budapest's citizens rose up against the Jews and a low-key pogrom swept the city for several days during which an unknown number of Jews was murdered.

In Paris, the political developments in Budapest were welcomed while the pogrom was all but ignored. Now, the Supreme Council could proceed with the peace treaty for Hungary.

On November 19, Switzerland joined the League of Nations. This paved the way for the League to move from Paris to Geneva, Switzerland.

On November 23, there were reports from the Middle East that the Turks were, once again, attacking the Armenians. In the US, the leaders of the growing isolationist movement reminded the Ameri-can public that if the proposed American mandate over Armenia had come to pass, American boys would be over there now, trying to protect Armenians from Turks.

At the end of the month, world health officials declared that the worldwide flu epidemic had come to an end.

PEACE WITH BULGARIA — THE TREATY OF NEUILLY

In Paris, they signed another peace treaty. This one was signed on November 27 with Bulgaria and the ceremony was held in the Paris suburb of Neuilly. The terms of the treaty were harsh on Bulgaria but not nearly so harsh as those that had been imposed on Germany. Bulgaria's biggest territorial loss was that of western Thrace which went to Greece and cut off Bulgaria's access to the Aegean Sea. Bulgaria also lost southern Dobruja to Romania and four small enclaves to Jugoslavia. The Bulgarian Army was reduced to 33,000 professionals and there were reparations set at $445 million; and Bulgaria was required to recognized the independence of Jugoslavia.

US Under-Secretary of State, Frank L. Polk; the US Ambassador-at-Large, Henry White, and General Tasker Bliss signed the treaty on President Wilson's behalf. However, after a period of time, the US Senate failed to ratify this Paris-generated treaty also. The US then concluded a separate peace treaty with Bulgaria at a later date.

BULGARIA IN WW II

During WW II, Bulgaria, once again, allied itself with Germany and participated in the invasion of Yugoslavia and Greece and the dismantling of Yugoslavia and the partitioning of Greece. Bulgaria regained western Thrace and the areas it had lost to Jugoslavia including a large part of Macedonia, a portion of which was disputed with Italy. On at least one occasion, Bulgarian and Italian troops clashed inside the disputed area.

In 1944, Soviet forces invaded Bulgaria and forced the country out of the war. In the postwar years, Bulgaria again lost western Thrace to Greece and those parts of Jugoslavia it had gained during the war.

CHAPTER 18
36.75%

||||||||||||||||||||||||||||||||||||||||||||||||||||||||||||||||||||||||||||||||||||||||||||||||||||||||||||||||||||||||||||||||||||

ITALY HEADING FOR SOCIALISM

On December 1, 1919, a new Chamber assembled in Rome, the first new Chamber since the armistice. As was the custom, the first session of the new Chamber was to be opened by the King. But a great insult awaited him. As he entered the Chamber hall, 156 Socialist delegates rose en masse and walked out shouting leftist slogans such as "Down with the King," "Hurrah for Socialism," "Up the Socialist Republic," and singing the song, "The Red Flag." The sloganeers, however, had no place to go. As they left the building, they encountered a large crowd that had gathered to witness the King's arrival and were now awaiting his departure. Quite naturally, the crowd was heavily monarchist. The crowd, of course, learned what had happened in the Chamber and when the socialist delegates came out of the building, they were heckled, spit upon, attacked, and chased down the streets. If this was an example of socialist political wisdom, it was a very poor one. The socialists should have seen this coming and prepared for a better getaway.

News of these events in Rome spread rapidly throughout Italy and the country's socialists went into a frenzy and called for a nationwide general strike to go into effect immediately. For the next several days Rome, Milan, Genoa, and Naples were, once again, paralyzed. In Turin, a mob of some 120,000 socialist sympathizers attacked the local Technical Institute and beat up students and faculty members. In other places, socialist mobs vandalized and looted a railroad station, warehouses, and arms factories, and they set fire to a prison. Once again, if this was an example of socialist political wisdom, it was a very poor one.

These actions served only to polarize the nation further and more and more of those who were polarized to the right were finding Mussolini and his Fascist Party which, under the current conditions, appeared to be the voice of moderation and reason.

In Paris, the Supreme Council was, at this time, meeting on the question of Fiume. The general consensus was that Fiume should become a free state similar to that of Danzig. Shortly, however, the US Paris delegation was called home as a result of the Senate's failure to ratify the Peace Treaty and, with this, the Big Three now became the "Big Two" — Britain and France. Discouraged by the departure of the Americans and the turmoil in Italy, the Big Two lost interest in Fiume and the question of Fiume was still without resolution.

IN THE US — COAL, ALCOHOL, THE PRESIDENT, AND OTHER ISSUES

In America, the coal miners were still staying home. Their coal strike had been officially called off, but they simply refused to go back to the mines — and the nation was running out of coal. The only options left were to send soldiers into the mines, or to talk. They decided to talk. It was agreed that the miners were, in fact, due an increase in wages and an increase of 14% was granted (the UMW had demanded a 60% increase) with no increase — at least for the moment — in the price of coal. With this, the miners went back to work and both sides claimed victory. For John L. Lewis, the President of the United Mine Workers, it was a great personal victory. He was now the miner's hero and a hero to the entire American labor movement. And he was acceptable to both the mine owners and to the government because he was strongly anti-socialist and anti-communist.

In the final analysis, it was the mine owners who got squeezed.

In other actions in the US, the use of alcohol in medicines and hair tonic was banned and the sales of hair tonic, which had experienced a recent surge in sales, went back to normal.

On December 3, the *New York Times* reported that the President was better and that his handwriting was "much firmer."

Two days later, two members of Lodge's Senate Foreign Relations Committee visited Wilson on a matter that had arisen with Mexico. This was merely a ploy to gain firsthand information on Wilson's health. The President was propped up in bed, the lights were low, his left side was covered, but he was mentally alert and as defiant as ever. This report, quietly circulated around Congress, went a long way to dispel rumors that Wilson was mentally incapacitated, but it was obvious that, physically, he was not the man he once was. And it was common knowledge by now that Mrs. Wilson was playing a significant role in the President's daily routine. Senator Albert Fall (R-Mass.) summed up the situation by saying, "We have a petticoat government."

BACK IN EUROPE

With a stable government in power in Budapest, various nations of the world began the process of resuming diplomatic relations with Hungary.

On December 1, 1919, the Hungarians were invited to come to Paris to discuss their forthcoming peace treaty with the Allies. The invitation was accepted and the Hungarians made plans to leave for Paris in early January.

That same day, December 1, 1919, the Sultan's government in Constantinople was invited to send representatives to Paris to discuss Turkey's peace treaty. The Turks, too, made plans to leave in early January.

At Paris, the Allies agreed, on December 8, that they would recognize a new border of their own making between Poland and Russia. The border, suggested by British Foreign Secretary Curzon, became known as the "Curzon Line." The

Line favored Poland but took away Vilna to the north and awarded it to Lithuania. This decision was an outgrowth of the new Allied policy of containment toward Russia. Getting the Poles and Bolsheviks to agree to it was now the next step, and the prospects of this was bleak. Pilsudski rejected the Curzon Line out-of-hand because his forces had conquered territory to the east beyond the Line and he was not about to give it up to satisfy the politicians in Paris. Furthermore, Pilsudski was adamant about retaining Vilna, his hometown, which was also occupied by Polish troops.

On December 14, the Polish-Russian talks at the rail junction of Mikaszewicze ended on a civil note, but without accomplishing anything of political significance.

In Warsaw, the pronouncement from Paris, which was made without consultation with the Poles, and the breakdown of the talks at Mikaszewicze, spelled the end of Paderewski's government. He resigned on the 14th and was replaced by Leopold Skulski who, like Paderewski, was subordinate to Pilsudski.

Paderewski returned to Switzerland, resumed his concert career, and never returned to Poland.

At mid-month, there was another triumph in the air. Australian pilots flew from Australia to Britain for the first time in history. Now it was possible that the journey to and from Britain and Australia, the Empire's most distant Dominion on the other side of the globe, could be reduced from weeks to days.

And to the north of Australia, there was another aviation first. The Japanese laid down the keel for their first aircraft carrier to be called the "Hosho" (Flying Phoenix). None of the navies of the Western Powers had yet made such a commitment and were still relying on ships that had been converted into carriers from vessels that had been designed for other uses. The

British, however, were soon to follow and within a year laid down the keel of the "Hermes." The Hosho was commissioned in December 1922 while the "Hermes" was commissioned in early 1924.

THE HOSHO AT MIDWAY

During WW II, the Hosho was used by the Japanese Navy at the Battle of Midway in June 1942. By that time, she was slow and small compared to the more modern carriers of the day, but she was, nevertheless, used to provide air support for the Japanese attack. In 1944, the Hosho was relegated to training duty in Japan's inland sea and in 1947 she was scrapped.

RUSSIA AND CONTAINMENT

In Paris, the Big Two made a major change in their policy toward Russia. Both Britain and France agreed that the policy of intervention had been a failure and that it should be abandoned in favor of one of containment. As Clemenceau put it "... surround them... with barbed wire entanglements and [spend] no money."

This position, however, was soon to be compromised when the British began to pursue trade opportunities in Russia. Yet, something had to be done and containment seemed to be the best answer, at least, for the moment.

From London, Churchill warned that such a policy would throw Germany, Russia, and possibly Japan, into each others' arms. Privately, Lloyd George said to a colleague, "Winston has gone mad," but the Prime Minister let his Secretary of War speak out because the Conservatives in his coalition government liked to hear what he said and Lloyd George needed their support to remain in office.

From Paris, Foch announced that he had an alternate plan for Russia. His plan was to use other nations' soldiers to invade Russia and dispose of the Bolsheviks once and for all. The soldiers to be used would be Finns, Poles, Czechoslovaks, Romanians, Greeks, and Russian prisoners of war still held by the Central Powers. With the Red Army now standing at an estimated strength of between 2.5 and 3 million men, this would be a most formidable task and there would be no way Clemenceau could save money with a venture like this. Plus, after Russia was conquered, someone would have to feed the Russian people and it was very doubtful that Herbert Hoover would return to his post to feed those every-squabbling Europeans. Not surprisingly, Foch's plan found few supporters.

In Russia itself, there were shortages of every kind on both sides of the fronts. There were areas where law and order had broken down, reports of massive executions, reports of peasant risings against the Bolsheviks in the Ukraine, reports of typhus in the north, and reports on a host of other problems. There was still hard fighting in the Ukraine and southern Russia and the reports from there indicated that the Red Army was still advancing. During December, Kiev, the capital of the Ukraine, fell once again to the Reds. To the east, the Reds had completed their conquest of the Donets Basis. That rich industrial area's infrastructure was in shambles, but the iron ore and coal deposits were still there, although most of the miners were not. Most of them had fled with the Whites.

As the Reds advanced, Denikin's forces fell apart. They looted, raped, got drunk, sold protection, and deserted.

In the northwest, Iudenich's army was all but defeated and the Estonians would not let them cross into their territory as armed combatants. The Bolsheviks had warned the Estonians that if they did, the Red Army would follow and invade Estonia. As a result, and for humanitarian reasons, Iudenich's men were allowed to enter Estonia in small groups without their weapons or uniforms. In this manner, some 10,000 of Iudenich's soldiers crossed into Estonia, along with an estimated 20,000 civilian refugees. Many others surrendered to the Reds and a few die-hards made their way to the south to join Denikin.

The Estonians were not prepared to accept such a large number of people, so conditions for the refugees were primitive and the Estonian people suffered as well. Iudenich entered Estonia but soon left for the comforts of Britain. For this, he was vilified by his former soldiers and civilian supporters.

In Siberia — frigid Siberia — the Reds were advancing slowly along the Trans-Siberian Railroad, struggling more against the horrible Siberian winter than Kolchak's meager forces.

In Washington, Secretary of State Lansing now urged that the Americans withdraw from Siberia. He had many supporters.

In Europe, the New York symphonic Orchestra was making a tour of the continent and some of their music selection included American Jazz. This helped to legitimize this new and uniquely American form of music in the lands of Bach, Beethoven, and Brahms. It also indicated that the American wanted to be on good terms with the Europeans.

IN POLAND, PILSUDSKI SAW OPPORTUNITIES

With an impressive string of victories to his credit, Pilsudski believed he could gain still more. His eastern front now stretched from the Latvia to Romania, and at its furthest point, was 350 east of Warsaw. It included the major cities of Lvov, Sarny, Pinsk, Minsk, and Vilna. The Bolsheviks, he reasoned, would be occupied for many months, yet doing away with the last remnants of the Whites in Siberia, the Ukraine, the Crimea, and the Caucasus and would remain weak in the west. After that, they would have to consolidate their gains within the former Russian Empire which, if the reports from the east could be believed, would be a formidable, resource-consuming and long-term tasks. This would give the Poles an opportunity to charge into the territories to the east which, at various times in the past, had been Polish. Those "lost" territories included much of Belorussia and the western Ukraine. Therefore, Pilsudski and his staff began planning a major offensive to regain those territories. The target date for the beginning of the invasion was set for April 1920 — when the warm weather returned.

In Moscow, the thinking was very different. Lenin, Trotsky, Stalin, and others believed that the Whites would soon be suppressed to the point where powerful Red Army units could be shifted to their western front to settle issues with the Poles. As it worked out, the Poles had the advantage with regard to time and circumstances, but the Bolsheviks had the advantage in manpower and resources. Thus, the Poles and Russians were embarking on a collision course without either side knowing it.

The leaders in Moscow also deemed it time to begin implementing "Zakalennya Bolsheviki" (Hardened Bolshevism), the process of putting communist economic and social theory into practice and eventually bring about the workers' paradise that Marxism promised. Little heed was given to Bela Kun's Zakalennya Bolsheviki in Hungary that had failed so miserably.

IN DEFEATED GERMANY

In Germany, militarism was still alive and well — and going underground. Across the political spectrum, various individu-

als and organizations were creating paramilitary organizations such as sports and hiking organizations, social groups, patriotic associations, youth groups, and student groups. These groups had pronounced, but disguised, political and/or military overtones. Such groups had long been common in Germany, but had always been more socially oriented. Now, that was changing.

The right-wing Nationalist Party created the "Bismarck Youth," the Center Party started the "Windthorst League," and there were others, including a group calling itself the "National League of Large Families." Many of the groups had uniforms, rituals, and symbolism; held parades and rallies; printed periodicals; preached against smoking, free love, easy divorces, birth control; and refused to admit Jews. They were seen by many as a form of volkisch defiance against the Diktat and a bulwark against socialism and communism. Some of these groups were well-supported by Germany's upper and middle classes who had nowhere else to turn. Some of them claimed to have memberships in the thousands. Drexler's little group in Munich was still minuscule by comparison.

One organization, known as the "German Racial Defense and Defiance League," operating out of Hamburg, used the swastika as its symbol which, by this time, was becoming a symbol of the political right. It will be remembered that the Thule Society had used the swastika as did several of the Free Corps. And to many, it was still considered a symbol of good fortune at a time when Germany's fortunes were at a very low ebb.

The swastika had come into such wide use by now that some stores were offering swastika jewelry.

On the other side of the political spectrum, the international socialists and communists were creating their organizations too, not necessarily as a form of defiance to the Diktat but as a form of support for their political philosophy and a counter to what was happening on the political right. These groups and organizations were generally supported by the working class, and in some cases, had secret financial support from Russia. Their symbol, which was also growing in use, was the Bolshevik's hammer and sickle.

With time, these phenomena would continue and increase, and the scene of men and women in uniforms and wearing politically-oriented adornments would become commonplace throughout Germany.

Also in defeated Germany, a year after the armistice, there was continuing unemployment, shortages of many things, inflation, and other social ills. Industrial production for 1919 was only 42% of that of 1913 and grain production was down by 50%.

On the positive side, German physicist, Johannes Stark, won the Nobel Prize for 1919 for discovering the "Stark Effect," the splitting of spectral lines of light when an emitting atom is in an electrical field. Because of this and other scientific advancement, the people of Germany and other industrialized nations were learning what an atom was.

The word "atom," a Greek word meaning "not cuttable," was an old word relating to basic matter, but it had recently taken on a new scientific meaning. The modern-day version of the atom, which was first defined by British physicist Ernest Rutherford in 1911 and explained further by Danish physicist, Niels Bohr, in 1913, was that the atom might, actually, be cuttable. By 1919, it was widely accepted in scientific circles that the atom, was a source of immense energy and that by cutting the atom that energy would be released and harnessed. Also during 1919, Ernest Rutherford came forward again to explain that there were protons in the nucleus of atoms, and another Britisher, Francis Aston, concluded that the fusion of hydrogen and helium atoms — the coming together of atoms as opposed to the splitting of atoms — would also release large amounts of energy. It was an exciting time for theoretical physicists.

SPLITTING THE ATOM

In 1938, two German scientists, Otto Hahn and Fritz Strassmann, succeeded in splitting a minuscule amount of uranium atoms. From that humble beginning, the world was eventually blessed with atomic energy.

DREXLER'S LITTLE GROUP IN MUNICH

In Munich, Propaganda Chairman Hitler was proving his worth. He was attracting new followers with his gift of oratory and was filled with ideas for expanding the Party. By the end of the years, Party membership had reached 200, mainly as a result of Hitler's efforts. And Hitler wanted to bring better organization to the Party — the cigar box would no longer suffice. He suggested that the Party acquire an office, a mimeograph machine, a safe, a membership roll, accounting books, and rubber stamps. Harrer thought him extravagant, but Drexler listened. Hitler also proposed that the Executive Committee take onto itself more authority and abandon the democratic ritual of voting.

The latter proposal was too radical for the moment, but the former proposals were doable. Acquiring an office, and paying rent and utilities was not yet within the financial realm of the Party, but Hitler was authorized to begin the search for a possible office site. In Mein Kampf he would later write "... I started out and visited a number of Munich restaurants and taverns with the intention of renting a back room or some other space for the party."

Another project that the Corporal got involved in at this time was the writing of the Party's formal political platform. Heretofore, the DAP had had no such document and the new Propaganda Chairman needed such a document to further his work and define the Party's goals.

Included in this effort was a declaration that the DAP would resist all efforts at being taken over by any "side government" or "circle or lodge." This was Hitler's idea and a direct challenge to First Chairman Harrer whose small group of associates, the Circle, still was a dominant force within the Party.

Drexler understood and worked closely with Hitler on the project. In doing so, he was choosing Hitler over Harrer.

It was approaching Christmas time and these tasks were welcomed by the Corporal. Christmas was not a happy time for Hitler. He had no family, both his mother and father were dead, and his siblings were all adults pursuing their own lives and were not very close as a family. For Hitler, there were no invitations to Christmas dinners or presents under a tree. Therefore, he busied himself with other matters. He had done this during the war by volunteering for extra duty so that his comrades could go home for Christmas. Now, he would devote the Christmas season to the Party.

THAT GROUP OF ISLANDS OFF THE EUROPEAN COAST

That group of islands off the European coast, known as Great Britain, was beginning to distance itself from those nations on the other side of the English Channel. The appointment of Curzon was a most visible indication of this.

The British army was now down to about one-third the strength that it was at the end of the Great War. If military action was required in Europe, that burden would now fall mostly on France.

Furthermore, Britain was no longer the financial capital of the world — the US was — and the British treasury owed great sums of money to the world's new banker.

The British were also watching events in the US very closely for other reasons. With the US Senate having failed to ratify both the Peace Treaty and the proposed defensive pact among the US, Britain, and France, Lloyd George was losing confidence in the wartime alliance. Thus, it was becoming more and more unlikely that there would be a post-war alliance among the Big Three.

Just before Christmas, John Maynard Keynes released his now-famous book *The Economic Consequences of the Peace*. It was an instant best-seller and was soon translated into eleven languages, including German. It was discouraging reading for those who hoped for a permanent peace defined by the Versailles Treaty and administered by the League of Nations.

In Germany, Keynes' book was praised; in France, it was condemned, and in Britain, it an embarrassment for Lloyd George.

Then, for those islands off the European coast, there was the "Empire" with its separate multitude of problems. One of the most pressing was in India where Gandhi and his Indian nationalists were gaining support. Fortunately, the British had faced this type of activity before and one of their most successful countermoves was to grant the colony in question more autonomy but yet keep them within the Empire. In this respect, Parliament, on December 23, 1919, approved a new constitution for India which would go into effect within a year. Supporters believed that is would possibly convert India, one day, into a dominion on the order of Canada, Australia, South Africa, and New Zealand. Gandhi and his followers were not impressed. His "Indian National Congress" rejected the offer. There were, however, less radical elements of his movement that wanted to accept it. This resulted in a schism within Gandhi's movement. Those who would accept the offer from London soon left Gandhi's group and established a rival organization, the "National Liberal Federation." In the final analysis, the British had won a victory in that their actions split and weakened the Indian nationalist movement.

Then, of course, there was Ireland. None of the other major European powers had a problem like Ireland. This was a matter that Britain had to face alone and would drain men, money, resources, and the British public's interests in matters on the Continent.

IN SUNNY ITALY

At least it was sunny and warm in Italy in December 1919, but in Fiume, it was still political stormy. D'Annunzio, now called "The Commander," was forced by political pressures to hold a referendum in which the people of Fiume were given the choice of joining Italy or remaining under his independent rule. The referendum was held on December 18, with the voters opting, by a sizeable majority, for union with Italy. This was not what The Commander expected or wanted. He voided the referendum, destroyed the ballots, and announced that Fiume would become an independent country.

D'Annunzio then went into seclusion to write a new constitution for his domain which he proposed be renamed "The Carnaro," a name that had been used in earlier time to describe this part of Eu-

rope. He also began preparing military operations to take over some of the islands and other areas in the immediate vicinity. The success at Zara was his inspiration. Fiume was not yet an Ireland, but it was moving in that direction.

The political situation in Italy made it unthinkable to launch military operations against Fiume. The nation was so polarized that such actions might possibly touch off a civil war. And there were no signs that things would get better. The Italian right-wing continued to demonstrate in the streets, hold their rallies, publish their newspapers while the workers of the left-wing did likewise, and conducted strikes and work stoppages. During the year of 1919, there had been 1663 strikes and work stoppages in Italy — more than four per day.

Neighboring France fared even worse in the category of strikes. Two thousand twenty-six strikes were recorded there — more than five per day.

AND STILL — THAT MESS IN THE MIDDLE EAST

During the month of December, British troops continued their withdrawal from Syria and began to reduce their military strength in northern Mesopotamia as well. As they did, age-old tribal and religious feuds reignited in both areas. In Syria, bands of nationalists, not necessarily under Faisal's control, came into conflict with the French in The Lebanon. As a result, France's relations with Faisal began to deteriorate rapidly because it was becoming clear that Faisal was not in control of his people.

One of the border areas which, since the end of the war, had been caught up in a four-way dispute among the French, British, Syrians, and Mesopotamians, was the district of Dayr al-Zor between eastern Syria and northwestern Mesopotamia.

Faisal, determined to settle that issue in Syria's favor, issued a jihad and sent his troops into the disputed area, taking several British officials hostage in the process. By doing these things, Faisal was doing a very unwise thing — alienating his chief supporter, Britain. British troops were too few to stop the Syrian advance, but the RAF was called in. It, however, could do little more than harass the advancing Syrians. For the moment, however, Faisal was biting the hand that fed him.

Once Dayr al-Zor was secure, Faisal sent in a large group of anti-British Mesopotamians, who had been living in exile in Syria, into Mesopotamia to establish a pro-Syrian political organization on Mesopotamian territory. They arrived and soon called for the complete withdrawal of the British from all of Mesopotamia and the creation of an independent Arab state that would extend from the Syrian border to the Persian Gulf. The weakened British forces in Mesopotamia could do little to counter this move. Their weakness gave many Arab groups, in and outside of Mesopotamia, hope that much of the Middle East would soon be theirs, even though there was no consensus as to what shape that all-Arab Middle East would take.

And in the northern part of Mesopotamia, around the oil-producing area of Mosul, the Kurds were still causing trouble. They were at odds with everyone — the Syrians, the British, the non-Kurdish Mesopotamians, and even each other. In London and Paris, the leaders of the Big Two were still harboring the dream that they may, somehow, control and share the Mosul oil. But, with the on-going turmoil in the area, this was very unlikely for the foreseeable future.

In Afghanistan, Amanullah, the man who had tried to liberate India from the British, found a new friend — Lenin. Amanullah had sent a representative to

Moscow to meet with Lenin and they were warmly received. As a result, Moscow and Kabul found common ground and exchanged diplomatic representatives. This was a quid pro quo for both parties. With Afghanistan now a friendly nation, a long segment of Lenin's southern border was now secure and Amanullah had a new and powerful friend.

"COLD WAR" — 1919 STYLE

In the US, on December 20, the 249 communists and suspected communists who had been rounded up during November and December by A. Mitchell Palmer's Justice Department were informed that they would be deported the next morning. All were immigrants, most of them lived in the New York City area, and there was a disproportionate number of Jews. This action was made possible by the wartime 1918 Alien Act which was still in effect.

The most prominent person to be deported was Emma Goldman, who had made headlines and served time in jail during the war for her anti-war and supposedly anti-American activities.

At 6:00 AM on December 21, Goldman and the others were put aboard a ship in New York Harbor bound for Russia. As they walked up the gangplank on this cold and snowy day, they sang the *Internationale*, the Comintern's theme song, and shouted communist slogans. Upon departing, Emma Goldman made a statement that was duly reported in the American press, "I shall be back... We shall all be back." The press responded by labeling the ship the "Soviet Ark."

When they reached Russia, the deportees were given a hero's welcome.

EMMA GOLDMAN'S RETURN

Emma Goldman was allowed to return to the US for short visits but not to reside permanently. In 1936, she went to fight for the Loyalists in the Spanish Revolution. Soon afterwards, she was allowed to take up residence in Canada where she died in 1940.

||||||||||||||||||||||||||||||||||||||||||||||||||||||||||||||||||||||||||||||||

In the US, A. Mitchell Palmer was making headlines and he had moved up to the Big Leagues. A popular saying evolved, touting the nations' most recent and best-know Red fighters, "Ole, Cal and Mitch" (Ole Hanson, Calvin Coolidge and A. Mitchell Palmer) — and next year was a presidential election year.

Palmer, however, had a problem at the White House. Wilson had come up with an idea suggesting that the Senators who had voted against ratification of the Peace Treaty stand for a special election to see if their constituents supported them. If they did, Wilson said he would appoint a Republican as Secretary of State and then he and Vice President Marshall would resign, thereby elevating the new Secretary of State to the Presidency. According to the Constitution at that time, the Secretary of State was third in line for the Presidency.

Palmer and others thought the plan was too bizarre, unworkable, and fraught with legal questions. He, and others, were eventually able to talk Wilson out of the idea.

Palmer's anti-Red campaign was now in full motion. A week earlier, he, along with some supporters in Congress, had gained assurances and support from non-governmental entities. For example, the leaders of the movie industry announced that they would cooperate in the fight against Bolshevism and the new veterans' organization, the American Legion, would do likewise. The American Legion, now one million strong, also announced that it approved of the deportations and other measures being taken by Palmer against the Reds in America. The Legion was, by now, known of its very strong anti-Red

stance and at times, Legionnaires had banded together in vigilante groups to right some of the wrongs created by local Reds in their respective communities. This was a very popular grassroots anti-Red movement and the slogan evolved — "Leave the Reds to the Legion."

And then there were the labor unions. Neither Palmer nor the President nor Congress seemed to be able to adequately cope with them because they had a large body of law protecting their rights and millions of voters under their control. Strikes continued to plague the American economy; one of the worst was the ongoing strike in the railroad industry. During 1919 there had been some 3600 strikes and work stoppages in the US — almost ten per day. By this statistic, the unions in Italy and France were in the minor leagues. One in every five American workers had gone on strike at one time or other in 1919. But unlike in Italy and France, most of the strikes were won by management because the American public was not polarized like those in Italy and France, because the great body of American moderates favored moderation and the status quo which tended to support management.

On December 24, Wilson sent a message to Congress stating that he would give Congress until March 1, 1920, to resolve the railway strike. After that, he would rescind the wartime government controls that still existed over the railroads and this action would dump the problems into the laps of the railway owners and the public. This issue smacked of politics with regards to the upcoming election.

Over at the War Department, it was reported that the American Army was down to its peacetime strength. If major military actions were required in Europe, all the Americans could offer on short notice were the troops doing occupation duty in the Rhineland.

From Detroit came a new and controversial pamphlet entitled, "The Eternal Jew." It was written personally by one of the world's most powerful industrialists, Henry Ford, who drew some of the book's material from the *Protocols of the Elders of Zion*. It was a scathing denouncement of the Jews whom, according to Ford, wanted to dominate the US economy.

And Henry Ford had a power base. During 1919, the Ford Motor Company produced over half of the world's automobiles, a high percentage of the world's farm tractors, and was building the world's largest industrial complex in the Detroit suburb of River Rouge. During 1919, American bought over $2 billion in automobiles, and over half of them were Fords.

Ford, who was of Irish decent, was a man of strong convictions, one of which was that Ireland should be free. Another was that the working man should be paid a fair wage, which he demonstrated throughout his company. As a result, there were no unions at Ford's.

Corporal Hitler would soon learn about this man and come to admire him.

By the end of 1919, there were an estimated 30 million aliens living in the US, 18,000 new millionaires — thanks to the war, a distinct rise in anti-Semitism, and more black lynchings than in any previous year. What's more, bootlegging was becoming a new growth industry and women's skirts were rising.

During 1919, the US Navy mothballed many of its destroyers. These ships were of little use in peacetime but were too valuable to scrap out.

DESTROYERS FOR BASES

By September 1940, the British Navy was hard-pressed to combat the German submarine menace. Churchill and Roosevelt came to an agreement, known as the "Destroyers for Bases Deal," in which the World War I destroyers were given to the British in return for temporary control by the Americans of certain British bases in the Western Hemisphere.

Also in America during 1919, the cost of living had risen by 104% since 1914, and because of this, war bonds had lost much of their real value. And there were still a lot of Doughboys still looking for work or out of work because of strikes. Nevertheless, Americans bought $50 million worth of chewing gum, $250 million worth of ice cream, $300 million in furs, $800 million worth of theater and movie tickets, $1 billion in cigars and cigarettes, and an unknown amount in bootleg liquor. The good times in America were beginning to roll.

GOOD TIMES — BOLSHEVIK STYLE

On December 24, 1919, Admiral Kolchak relinquished his command of the White forces in Siberia to a Cossack Chieftain, Nicolai Semenov. This was a transfer in name only because many of the White soldiers would not follow a Cossack leader and the Cossacks were not really capable of leading an army on non-Cossacks.

What Kolchak did not transfer to the Cossacks was his stash of bullion he carried on his train.

In Irkutsk, anarchy reigned with political and military factions fighting each other. And the Reds were approaching.

To the west, the war lord Semen Petlura was driven out of the Ukraine by the advancing Red Army and withdrew into Poland where the Polish government continued to recognize him as head of the Ukrainian People's Republic-in-exile.

In Moscow, Stalin had married his second wife (his first wife had died of natural causes in 1907). The new Mrs. Stalin was

"THE UNFORGETTABLE YEAR 1919"

In 1952, the Soviets made a movie with the above title. It mainly glorified Stalin but emphasized the events in Russia during 1919.

The movie also took considerable license with history. It relates that Lenin brought Stalin to Petrograd to strengthen the Bolshevik Revolution which he, Lenin, had started.

According to the movie, there are British spies in Petrograd being directed by Churchill, and the British Navy attacked the Bolshevik Navy off the island of Kronstadt, and under Stalin's command, the British were defeated. A magnanimous Stalin then invited several of the captured British sailors to dinner where they swapped stories and told jokes.

In the final scene, Stalin gives a rousing patriotic speech with red flags waving, crowds cheering, and cannons booming.

It was later reported that Stalin watched the movie over and over.

Stalin never downplayed Lenin but promoted the concept that he, Stalin, was Lenin's closest confidant. This drawing is typical of such works during the Stalinist era. Note that Lenin has a halo of light around his head — Lenin was regularly displayed in this saintly manner in art and movies in Stalinist Russia. And Stalin was regularly portrayed as Lenin's protege and was usually depicted several inches taller than Lenin.

Nadezhda Allilueva, the daughter of a working-class "Old Bolshevik." Together they would have a daughter, Svetlana.

EXIT WIFE #2

In 1932, Nadezhda committed suicide.

EUROPE AT THE END OF 1919

With the Bolsheviks visibly winning in Russia, fears were high all over Europe that the Reds would soon attack Poland en masse and move on to invade Germany, Hungary, and Austria whose armies had been severely reduced by the various peace treaties and unable to stop the Red onslaught. There were some who predicted that the Allies would soon be fighting the Reds along the Rhine River.

Romania, which bordered the Ukraine and was the largest of the Allied nations in eastern Europe, was, like Poland, thought to be a target of the Bolsheviks. Romania was still relatively unstable having had three governments during 1919. As yet, however, there was no significant Bolshevik threat along their border, nor within the country. But if and when the Bolsheviks captured the western Ukraine, Romania would be on the front line against the Reds. And the Reds had announced that they intended to recover the province of Bessarabia, situated between the Pruth and Dniester Rivers, which the Romanians had invaded and annexed earlier in the year when the Bolsheviks were at a low ebb.

This fear of the Reds once again came down on the heads of the Jews. Many of the refugees who had fled into Romania were Ukrainian and Russian Jews. These people tripled the number of Jews in Romania and were most unwelcome. And many believed that the refugees, especially the Jews, were the secret advanced guards of the Bolsheviks.

For the Western Allies, Romania was seen as a bulwark to Bolshevism second only to Poland. For this reason, the Allies took steps to strengthen the Romanians by overlooking many of the transgressions that they had carried out against the Hungarians, their annexation of Bessarabia, and their territorial acquisitions from Bulgaria.

In 1914, Romania was a country of 80,000 square miles with a population of 7.2 million, and now the country encompassed 176,000 square miles and had 16.6 million people.

In Transylvania, which the Romanians had taken from Hungary, all vestiges of Hungarian rule had, by this time, been removed and income taxes had been adjusted to favor ethnic Romanians at the expense of Hungarians, Jews, Germans, and Ukrainians.

The Allies, however, prevailed upon Romania to comply with the Allied recommendations on the division of The Banat, an area disputed with the Jugoslavs. That area was to be divided between the two countries.

36.75%

Of all the baby boys born in Germany during the year 1919, 36.75% of them would perish in World War II.

1919 has been called the "Year of the Cynic."

THE SECOND YEAR
OF WORLD WAR II
1920

||||||||||||||||||||||||||||||||||||||||||||||||||||||||||||||||||||||||||||||||||||||||||||||||||||||||||||||||||||||||||||||||||||||||||||||||||||||||

CHAPTER 19
ONGOING WOES IN
1920

||||||||||||||||||||||||||||||||||||||||||||||||||||||||||||||||||||||||||||||||||||||||||||||||||||||||||||||||||||||||||

In the US, as the new year began, Attorney General A. Mitchell Palmer, now being called the "Fighting Quaker," made another series of large-scale arrests of Reds. During the first few days of January, his agents arrested and/or detained several thousand Reds and suspected Reds and held them without charge and without access to counsel. His legal authority for this came from the wartime Alien Act of 1918 which was still in effect.

When the dust settled, Palmer announced that his men had rounded up 2720 individuals who would face deportation and that more raids were being planned. In the end, only 591 individuals were deported, and Palmer was criticized for his harsh and arbitrary measures. Some called him the "Fighting Faker."

By January 8, it was reported that the steel industry was back to work. The workers had lost their strike.

On January 15, the US government approved a loan of $150 millions to Poland, Armenia, and Austria to combat the Red menace. The next day, at midnight, the 18th Amendment to the Constitution took effect. When the hour struck, the bars and saloons across America were packed.

IN EUROPE

On January 1, 1920, the Bolsheviks and Estonians signed a truce. Iudenich's White Forces had disintegrated and were no longer a threat to either party.

On January 3, the last American forces left Europe except for those doing occupation duty in the Rhineland.

In ceremonies conducted in Paris on January 10, the League of Nations came into being as required by the articles of the Versailles Treaty.

In Britain, the government began soliciting volunteers to fight the rebels in Ireland.

On January 9, the British government announced that it would build one million new homes of war veterans.

EAST OF THE RHINE

On the evening of January 7, Propaganda Chairman Hitler gave another rousing speech to the members and supporters of the DAP. His topic was "The Jewish Question."

On the 14th, there was another large-scale Red disturbance in Berlin. A groups of radicals, estimated at about 40,000 people, demonstrated and attacked the Reichstag building. The government declared martial law, the police rushed in, there was a pitched battle, and 42 people were killed and 103 injured. This was upheaval #4 for Berlin.

At various places around Germany, the dismantling of war plants, ordered by the Diktat, began under the watchful eyes of the Inter-Allied Control Commission.

FRANCE

Because of the diplomatic intricacies of the Versailles Treaty, a second document, a protocol for peace, was required to be signed by the contracting parties to formally end the Great War. That protocol was signed in the office of the Minister of Foreign Affairs in the Quai d'Orsay at 6:15 PM on January 10. The German had sent two low level diplomats to Paris to sign. The Americans, of course, were not invited.

The next day, January 11, France held the national election for members of the Senate. The result was very much the same as the election for members of the Chamber in November. There was a significant move to the right of center and a dramatic rejection of the left.

On January 14, the new Senate elected Leon Bourgeois as the Senate's President and the date for the election of the President of France was set, by the combined Chamber and Senate, for January 17.

The two most important candidates for President were Clemenceau and Paul Deschanel, a former President of the Senate and a well-respected career politician. Field Marshal Foch's name was also placed on the ballot but he was seen as a distant third.

Clemenceau, seeing that he would not have the votes to win the Presidency, withdrew his name from nomination. When the formal vote was taken on January 17, Deschanel secured 734 of the 888 votes cast.

On January 16, world history was made when the League of Nations Council, the administrative body of the League of Nations, held its first business meeting in Paris. The Council consisted of four permanent members: Britain, France, Italy, and Japan, and four rotating members, the first of whom were Belgium, Spain, Brazil, and Greece.

Issues debated called for the lifting of the blockade of Russia and the encouragement of trade and the extradition of the Kaiser from The Netherlands and his subsequent prosecution for war crimes. The Dutch responded on January 23, stating that they would not allow the Kaiser's extradition.

THE KAISER

The Kaiser remained in The Netherlands until his death in 1941. Hitler paid him respect but would not allow him, or any of his three sons, to participate in German politics.

On January 18, Clemenceau resigned as Premier of France and President Poincare, who would continue to serve as President until mid-February, appointed Alexandre Millerand as the new Premier. Clemenceau, now a very bitter man, soon left France to tour the world and stayed away for nine months.

IN THE US ONCE MORE

On January 19, a vote was held in the US Senate on whether or not the US should join the League of Nations. It was technically possible for the US to join the League even after rejecting the Versailles Treaty. The vote on joining the League was a strong "no."

GERMANY–BELGIUM

On January 20, plebiscites mandated by the Versailles Peace Treaty were held in the three enclaves of Eupen, Malmedy, and Saint Vith, along the German/Belgian border. The Germans had conquered the enclaves during the war and annexed them to Germany. Now, the people would decide — and they voted to join Belgium.

THE MALMEDY MASSACRE OF WW II

During WW II, the Germans once again captured and annexed the three Belgian enclaves. During the Battle of the Bulge, in December 1944, elements of the German First SS Panzer Division captured approximately 100 American soldiers in Malmedy and summarily executed them. This became known as the "Malmedy Massacre."

Allied forces recaptured Malmedy and the two other border enclaves and they were returned to Belgium without plebiscites.

Seventy-three German soldiers were later prosecuted for the massacre, found guilty, but served light sentences.

RUSSIA — SIBERIA — LATVIA

In Siberia, the Bolsheviks now had a relatively free hand.

At this point, French General Maurice Janin, Commander of Allied troops in Siberia, took Kolchak into custody. This order almost certainly came from Paris. Once in custody, Kolchak was handed over to the Bolsheviks in a deal that awarded the French one-third of the gold bullion Kolchak had been carrying on his train.

A few days later, the Reds entered Irkutsk, unopposed, and virtually all resistance to the Reds in Siberia ceased.

Trotsky began at once to withdraw his forces from Siberia into European Russia. They were needed to finish off Denikin and the Poles.

In southern Russia, Denikin's forces were still in retreat. The Red Army captured the city of Rostov, the gateway to the Caucasus, and now were within reach of the Caucasus oil.

IN THE MIDDLE EAST

In Paris, Clemenceau and Faisal finally reached an agreement. Syria would have its independence but with exclusively French advisers. For Faisal, it was the best he could do and it was not much. Faisal then returned to Damascus with little to show for his efforts in Paris. Upon learning of the details of the agreement, there were large-scale popular demonstrations in Damascus against the French and in support of Faisal. Many Syrians, including many women, volunteered to join the Syrian Army and fight for independence. Relations between France and Syria were at a very low ebb.

In central Turkey, Kemal established his capital in the city of Angora (Ankara) in central Anatolia, 225 miles southeast of Allied-occupied Constantinople.

In the Upper Galilee area of Palestine, a political no-man's-land between British and Syrian control, violence broke out between Bedouin tribesmen and Jewish settlers. Out of the need for self-defense, the Jews had organized an armed militia

General Hans von Seeckt, Commander of the down-sized post-Versailles Treaty German Army and called "The Sphinx with a Monocle."

comprised mostly of veterans of the "Jewish Legion" that had served under British General Allenby during the war. The Jews tried to buy arms from the British but were refused. Stepping into the void, however, came American gun runners, and the militia was thusly equipped with mostly American weapons. America's involvement in Palestine in favor of the Jews would grow from this humble beginning.

ITALY

In Italy, there were ongoing and very troublesome strikes. Railroad workers refused to service trains, longshoremen refused to service warships, leftist workers in some areas had taken over factories and estates, there were clashes in the streets, organized prison guards threatened to release prisoners, and in Rome, disgruntled workers at the local electric utility created nightly blackouts to press their demands. Workers all over Italy were talking of forming "soviets" (revolutionary committees) to take control of local public and private assets and services.

In Milan, Mussolini's newspaper, *Il Popolo*, which was now enjoying national distribution, railed at the excesses of the left and the inadequacies of the elected authorities. Because of such printed rhetoric and the unstable conditions in Italy, Mussolini now had a growing voice in Italian politics. He also had a permanent bodyguard of Adriti.

GERMANY

During January, the German mark reached an exchange rate of 65 to the dollar. In 1914 it had been 4.2.

In the realignments that were taking place within the steadily shrinking German Army, General Hans von Seeckt had come to the fore as Germany's top military leader. He was the epitome of a firm, strict, and dedicated Prussian general, and his dour personality and appearance had earned him the title of "The Sphinx with a monocle."

Seeckt, known to be politically rightwing and perhaps a monarchist, was seen by the leaders of the right, such as Drexler and Hitler, as a supporter and potential ally. Due to his position, however, Seeckt had to remain detached from any particular political philosophy and/or organization. Nevertheless, Seeckt's name was often mentioned by right-wingers as a possible authoritarian leader of a post-democratic Germany.

Seeckt was pragmatic, however, in seeing that he had to do everything in his power to prevent a revolution from any quarter, lest it give the Allies cause to invade Germany. This forced him to cooperate with the elected government at Weimar — at least for the foreseeable future.

The "Bund Oberland," one of several right-wing paramilitary groups in Bavaria. Their symbol was a red flag with a black swastika in a white circle. When Hitler designed the flag for the Nazi Party, it was identical to this flag except that he turned the swastika 45 degrees.

Seeckt, approved of underground and private right-wing para-military units and saw them as a possible reserve for his army.

Hitler knew this and realized that the door was open for the DAP to form such an organization, when the time was right.

Seeckt, moreover, saw Germany as a bulwark against Bolshevism and had said in public, "We are ready to stand as a wall against Bolshevism in Germany itself." In private, however, he told his closest aides that Germany would never support Poland even if that country was in danger of being overrun by the communist. Also, he was quoted as saying privately, "A future political and economic agreement with Russia [is] an irreversible purpose of our policy."

Around mid-January, another round of DAP leaflets were seen posted around Munich and being handed out by men on street corners. They were addressed to "The Suffering Public" and announced another DAP meeting scheduled for February 25. The posters stated that Dietrick Eckart, Hitler's close friend and who was fairly well-known as an editor, would speak. Eckart had a reputation for being an excellent speaker and his topic for the evening would be, "Why Did the German Workers' Party Come into Being? What Does it Want?" Hitler was not listed on the posters as a speaker, apparently in an effort to enhance Eckart's position as the meeting's main speaker.

Hitler realized that there might be hecklers and troublemakers at the meeting, so he again enlisted the aid of some of his fellow soldiers and asked them to attend the meeting to keep order. They were also to act as courteous and helpful ushers. Hitler called this little group the *"Ordengruppe"* (Stewards troop) and he instructed them to be very aggressive in dealing with troublemakers. The idea of such an organization was not Hitler's original idea. Some of the other political groups in Munich already had similar groups.

THE SA

Hitler's *Ordengruppe* would grow steadily in the coming years and would be known by various names; "Monitor Service," "Beer Hall Guards," "Civil Guards," "Temporary Volunteer Corps," and was sometimes identified as a gymnastic or sports organization. Eventually, it had acquired the name by which it is best known; "SA" (*Sturmabteilungen* — Storm Troopers) and would be led by an individual who would become one of Hitler's closest associates, Ernst Roehm. In 1933, when Hitler became Chancellor of Germany, the SA had over 1.2 million members and was a private army unto itself.

Behind the scenes, however, there was a crisis in the DAP leadership. Hitler had grandiose plans for expanding the Party and moving swiftly into the local Munich, and perhaps national, political arenas. Drexler favored this as did the other members of the Executive Committee, but Harrer did not. He wanted to keep the organization small, narrowly focused, easy to manage, and inexpensive to operate. The Executive Committee outvoted him and he resigned from the Party. Drexler then became the First (and only) Chairman and Hitler remained head of the one-man propaganda committee.

The DAP's previous meeting in January had brought in a few more members and by the end of the month, the Party counted 190 with the average age of 31. Hitler was 30. One of the new members was Captain Ernst Roehm, a wounded war veteran and a man with some valuable connections within the local Munich military establishment. These connections would prove to be very helpful to the DAP.

IN THE USA

During the month, one of Wilson's doctors revealed publicly that the President had suffered a cerebral thrombosis, a disease that sometime adversely affects the patient's mental capacity. This caused another nationwide surge of negative publicity and even a debate on the Senate floor.

In Massachusetts, Calvin Coolidge began another term as the state's governor. His campaign had been based on a growing issue of the day — taxes — and he had won a solid election victory.

VLADIVOSTOK

On January 30, the Bolsheviks tried to take control of Vladivostok, Russia's only major seaport on the Pacific Ocean and the eastern terminus of the Trans-Siberian Railroad. The seaport had, however, been under Allied control for most of the Bolshevik Revolution so it was Allied forces that the Bolsheviks confronted here and not the remnants of Kolchak's failed regime.

The Japanese contingent was, by now, the largest Allied contingent in the city and it was mainly they who beat back the Bolshevik attempt to take control. Vladivostok remained under Allied — mainly Japanese — control.

CONCERNS ABOUT VLADIVOSTOK IN DECEMBER 1941

In the latter part of 1941, German forces were rapidly approaching Moscow and the Soviets were fighting for their very existence. Most world leaders believed that the city would fall and, if it did, the Japanese might try to take advantage of the situation and seize Vladivostok and other parts of Siberia. Stalin foresaw this and had placed some of best troops — the Siberians — along his eastern border to guard against a Japanese attack. These troops were well-trained and well-equipped to fight in cold weather.

Stalin, however, had a spy in the German embassy in Tokyo, a German communist named Richard Sorge, who reported that the Japanese would soon strike to the south rather than to the north. On this flimsy information, and other bits of information he possessed, Stalin took a major gamble and pulled his Siberian troops out of the Vladivostok area and placed them in front of Moscow. Subsequently, the Siberians were thrown into the battle for Moscow at a critical time and contributed significantly in stopping the German offensive. Moscow was saved and much of the credit was given to the Siberians. But, Vladivostok was virtually undefended.

On December 7, 1941, Sorge's information proved to be accurate. The Japanese attacked and decimated the US Pacific Fleet at Pearl Harbor, Hawaii, and proceeded to advance into Southeast Asia just as he had predicted.

HANG 'EM

On February 3, 1920, the Allies sent a note to the German Foreign Minister with 890 German names on it. These were individuals whom the Allied wanted handed over to them to be tried for war crimes, as called for by Articles 227-230 of the Diktat. The "Black List," as it was called, included Hindenburg, Ludendorff, and others perceived by the Germans to be war heroes, not criminals. A few days later, General von Seeckt said publicly that the German Army would fight before it would hand over such people to the Allies. Meanwhile, his planners went to work on another defensive plan to fight the Allies if they invaded.

The Bauer government bitterly complained about the Allies' demand; and an agreement was subsequently reached and on February 16, whereby the Germans agreed that 113 individuals would be tried, not by the Allies, but by German courts in Leipzig. This was a significant about-face for the Allies and seen as a victory for von Seeckt which, in turn, helped to strengthen von Seeckt's position as Germany's top military leader.

RUSSIA AND EASTERN EUROPE

On February 1, Latvia and Soviet Russia signed an armistice that ended the armed conflict between those two countries.

On the 2nd, Estonia and Soviet Russia signed a peace agreement, the "Treaty of Tartu," in which the Russians recognized Estonia's independence. In the Treaty, the Russians agreed to renounce "in perpetuity" all right to the territory of Estonia. The little state of Estonia seemed secure and the Russians had another segment of their border pacified — for 20 years.

In Siberia, Admiral Kolchak was in the hands of the Reds. His trial began in Irkutsk and on February 6, he was found guilty the next day and was executed within hours. His body was then dumped into the Angara River through a hole in the ice.

THE LEAGUE OF NATIONS CHARGES INTO ACTION

On February 11, 1920, the League of Nations Council held its second meeting, this time in London. A decision was reached with regard to the large and coal-rich island of Spitzbergen north of the Arctic Circle whose ownership had been in dispute. It would go to Norway.

Then too, the Council accepted the results of the two plebiscites recently carried out: that of the three border enclave between Belgium and Germany, and a recently held plebiscite in Schleswig-Holstein. Furthermore, two new commissions were formed, one to manage the Saar during its fifteen years of French control, and the other to manage the Free City of Danzig.

A French jurist, Leon Bourgeois, was charged with creating an international court system as called for in the League Covenant.

On February 10, Jugoslavia, still known formally as The Kingdom of Serbs, Croats, and Slovenes, was admitted to membership in the League.

On the 11th, the League commission took over the administration of the Free City of Danzig.

On the 13th, the League recognized the perpetual neutrality of Switzerland in preparation for the establishment of its permanent headquarters in the Swiss city of Geneva.

On the 16th, the nation of Columbia, in South American, was admitted to membership in the League.

On the 19th, The Netherlands, another traditionally neutral county in Europe, joined the League.

On the 26th, the League took over formal administration of the Saar.

IN EUROPE AGAIN

During the first weeks in February, the Bulgarian Government ratified its peace treaty.

In France, as was customary, Premier Millerand faced a vote of confidence in the French Assembly. He was supported by a vote of 513 to 68.

On February 12, the day after the League Council began its meeting in London, interested parties met at the Prime Minister's residence at 10 Downing Street to discuss the forthcoming treaty with Turkey. One decision, already taken, was confirmed that the all-important Turkish Straits were to be internationalized. Other matters would not be so easy to conclude.

On the 15th, Article 99 of the Versailles Treaty went into effect which gave the East Prussian seaport of Memel to Lithuania. To ensure a smooth transition, Allied troops moved into the port to maintain order. As the Allies moved in, the last of the German troops moved out.

In France, the railroad unions went on strike again.

On the 18th, Raymond Poincare stepped down as President of France and Paul Deschanel assumed that office. Clemenceau did not attend the ceremony. Poincare returned to his seat in the Senate and was soon elected chairman of a committee to oversee reparations.

In Czechoslovakia, a new constitution was adopted. It was both democratic and liberal and was held up by democrats around the globe as an example that democracy could succeed in some of the more troubled areas of the world. In the White House, President Wilson was cheered by the news.

In Austria, the Austrian National Socialist Party (DNSAP) began using a party flag which consisted of a black swastika in a white circle on a red field.

In Italy, Mussolini learned of d'Annunzio's plan to make Fiume into an independent nation. For Mussolini this was totally unacceptable. To him, Fiume was a part of Italy. Thus, Mussolini and d'Annunzio parted ways and the Fascist Party and *Il Popolo* began attacking d'Annunzio.

In Upper Selesia which was scheduled for a plebiscite, there was violence between the Poles and the Germans. On the German side, the local Free Corps was the main combatant while the Poles had organized a counter-militia known as the "Polish Volunteers." Because of this strife, the Inter-Allied Commission of Control deemed it necessary to send Allied troops to the area to keep the peace until such time that the plebiscite could be taken. During the latter part of February these troops arrived — mostly French troops — and began to restore order. Nonetheless, unstable conditions would exist in Upper Selesia for over a year until the plebiscite was finally taken in March 1921.

In Berlin, General Ludendorff had returned from his self-imposed exile in Sweden. He was as bitter as ever against the politicians whom, he still maintained, had stabbed Germany in the back in November 1918. He spoke, not too privately, of hanging Ebert and Scheidemann. Upon his return to Berlin, he was looked upon, now more than ever, as the most prominent leader of the political right.

Ludendorff had retired from the army and now lived in an apartment in Berlin, which soon became a gathering place for right-wing political and military figures. Two such individuals who were frequent guests were Wolfgang von Kapp, a member of the Reichstag and an outspoken proponent of the political right, and General Walther von Luttwitz, Reichswehr commander of the Berlin district and the man who had led the loyalist forces against the Spartacists in Berlin in January 1919.

There was also disturbing news coming from the town of Doberitz, a small community on the western edge of Berlin. The now-famous Ehrhardt Free Corps Brigade had taken up residence there, and,

if conditions warranted, was in position to march into the heart of Berlin within hours. Given Berlin's recent history of turmoil, this was a comfort to some, but a threat to others.

On the 22nd, anti-Jewish violence broke out in Berlin. The police stepped in, restored order, and arrested 21 people.

DOWN IN MUNICH

Drexler and Hitler were getting ready to announce to the world their new Party platform. It consisted of 25 points and would be announced at a public meeting on February 25. On the 20th, however, the DAP leaders approved a name change for the Party from "The German Workers' Party " (DAP) to *"Nationalsozialistische Deutsche Arbeiterpartei"* (The National Socialist German Workers' Party" — NS-DAP). From the word, *Nationalsozialist-ische*, came the word "Nazi."

Since the Party was actively promoting a neo-socialist program which would be created specifically for the German people, the addition of the phrase, "National Socialist," was appropriate. This too, would be announced at the meeting. In the discussions that brought about the name change, Hitler was not happy with the word "Socialist," but Drexler convinced him that it would attract the working class and draw them away from the leftists. Therefore, Hitler acquiesced.

On the day of the meeting at the Hof-brauhaus, there was, once again, a large crowd, estimated to be 2000, each paying 50 pfennigs admission. This event brought in more than 50 times the number of people who had attended the meeting in September at which V-man Hitler made his first appearance.

It was feared, once again, that many hecklers might be in the audience, and one report received stated that the speakers might be shot. So the men of the Ordentruppe were on the alert. Several people spoke, but Hitler had the honor of reading the new Party platform. Several of the speakers praised Hindenburg and Ludendorff, but there was no praise for the Kaiser.

Just before Hitler was to speak, Dr. Johannes Dingfelder, founder of the "German Socialist Party," another right-wing party with a left-wing sounding name, and an ally of Drexler's group, gave his speech. Dingfelder's speech was entitled "What We Want." In it, he likened the mission of his and Drexler's Parties to that of Christianity. As he finished and Hitler was seen approaching the rostrum, Dingfelder concluded his speech by saying, "For us too, a savior is approaching." As Hitler mounted the rostrum, he was given tremendous applause.

When the applause died down, Hitler began to speak in his usual mellow tones and began reading the 25 Points. As he enumerated the various Points, he was interrupted several times with applause, and at times, with chants. Also the hecklers added their caustic shouts but there were no confrontations or rowdiness. With the Ordentruppe nearby, the hecklers almost certainly concluded that it was better to remain and heckle rather that start a confrontation and be thrown out.

A police reporter in the audience, furiously taking notes, wrote that he expected violence to erupt at any minute.

The 25 Points were:

1. We demand the unification of all Germans in the Greater Germany on the basis of the right of self-determination of peoples.

2. We demand equality of rights for the German people in respect to the other nations; abrogation of the peace treaties of Versailles and St. Germain.

3. We demand land and territory for the sustenance of our people, and colonization for our surplus population.

4. Only a member of the race can be a citizen. A member of the race can only be one who is of German blood, without consideration of creed. Consequently no Jew can be a member of the race.

5. Whoever has no citizenship is to be able to live in Germany only as a guest, and must be under the authority of legislation for foreigners.

6. The right to determine matters concerning administration and law belongs only to the citizen. Therefore we demand that every public office, of any sort whatsoever, whether in the Reich, the county or municipality, be filled only by citizens. We combat the corrupting parliamentary economy, office-holding only according to party inclinations without consideration of character or ability.

7. We demand that the state be charged first with providing the opportunity for a livelihood and way of life for the citizens. If it is impossible to sustain the total population of the State, then members of foreign nations (non-citizens) are to be expelled from the Reich.

8. Any further immigration to Germany of non-citizens is to be prevented. We demand that all non-Germans, who have immigrated to Germany since August 2, 1914, be forced immediately to leave the Reich. (Hitler, an Austrian citizen, immigrated to Germany before that date.)

9. All citizens must have equal rights and obligations.

10. The first obligation of every citizen must be to work both spiritually and physically. The activity of individuals is not to counteract the interests of the universality, but must have its results within the framework of the whole for the benefit of all. Consequently we demand:

11. Abolition of unearned incomes, breaking of rent-slavery. (Some of the Party's largest contributors were wealthy people living off of investments such as rental properties).

12. In consideration of the monstrous sacrifice to property and blood that each war demands of the people, personal enrichment through the war must be designated as a crime against the people. Therefore we demand the total confiscation of all war profits.

13. We demand the nationalization of all associated industries (trusts).

14. We demand a division of profits of all heavy industries.

15. We demand an expansion of a large scale or old age welfare.

16. We demand the creation of a healthy middle class and its conservation, immediate communalization of the great warehouses and their being leased at low cost to small firms, the utmost consideration of all small firms in contracts with the State, county or municipality.

17. We demand land reform suitable to our needs, provision of a law for the free expropriation of land for the purposes of pubic utility, abolition of taxes on land and prevention of all speculation in land.

18. We demand struggle without consideration against those whose activity is injurious to the general interest. Common national criminals, usurers, Scheibers (small fish) and so forth are to be punished with death without consideration of confession or race.

19. We demand substitution of a German common law in place of the Roman Law serving a materialistic world-order.

20. The State is to be responsible for a fundamental reconstruction of our whole national education program, to enable every capable and industrious German to obtain higher education and subsequently introduction into leading positions. (As a young man in Vienna, Hitler was rejected from both an art school and an architectural school because of his weak credentials.)

21. The State is to care for the elevating national health by protecting the mother and child, by outlawing child-labor, by the encouragement of physical fitness, by means of the legal establishment of a gymnastic and sport obligation, by the utmost support of all organization concerned with the physical instruction of the young.

22. We demand abolition of the mercenary troops and formation of a national army.

23. We demand opposition to known lies and their promulgation through the press. In order to enable the provision of a German press, we demand that... all writers and employees of the newspapers appearing in the German language be members of the race... non-German newspapers be required to have the express permission of the State to be published... non-Germans are forbidden by law any financial interest in German publications... publication which are counter to the general good are to be forbidden.

24. We demand freedom of religion for all religious denominations within the State so long as they do not endanger its existence or oppose the moral senses of the Germanic race. The Party, as such, advocates the standpoint of a positive Christianity without binding itself confessionally to any one denomination. It combats the Jewish-materialistic spirit within and around us...

25. For the execution of all of this we demand that formation of a strong central power in the Reich. Unlimited

authority of the central parliament over the whole Reich and its organization in general. The forming of State and professional chambers (guilds) for the execution of the laws made by the Reich within the various states of the confederation. The leaders of the Party promise, if necessary by sacrificing their own lives, to support by the execution of the points set forth above without consideration.

After reading the Points, Hitler opened the meeting for discussion which had been, since its inception as a discussion group, the norm. Most speakers ardently supported the new platform. One member suggested that the meeting go on record as opposing the distribution to the Jews of Munich a relief shipment of flour recently received. At this point, the hecklers stood up on chairs and tables and shouted their opposition, but the bulk of the audience responded and shouted them down with chants of "Get out!" A hand vote was taken, and the members of the audience supported the proposal overwhelmingly. One of the hecklers stood up and suggested that communist dictatorship would be the solution to Germany's problems. Like the others, he was shouted down.

Hitler did not let this go on for too long and eventually adjourned the meeting. It would not be good press if a riot was started after the announcement of the 25 Points.

But the leftists had a plan. As the members of the audience filed out of the Hofbrauhaus, about 100 leftists formed up in the street and began to march toward city hall. They shouted communist slogans, demanded that an Eisner-type of government be re-instated in Munich, praised the Comintern, and chanted "Down with Hindenburg, down with Ludendorff and down with the German

nationalists." The leftist demonstration eventually petered out without violence.

Overall, Hitler was pleased. He later wrote in Mein Kampf "...there stood before me a hall full of people united by a new conviction, a new faith, a new will."

IN 1933

In 1933, when the Nazis came to power, some of the 25 Points were implemented, some were compromised, and some were ignored.

In the next few days following the meeting, the Party accepted 47 new members. One of them was Hans Frank, a 20-year-old veteran of the Free Corps and a law student.

HANS FRANK

Hans Frank would serve in the SA, rise rapidly in the Party structure, become the Party's primary legal advisor, a Bavarian state minister of justice, the Reich's Commissioner of Justice in Hitler's cabinet, President of the Law Academy and, ultimately, Governor General of the "General Government," the area around Warsaw that was to be the reservation-like homeland for the Polish people. He would be instrumental in cleansing the General Government of its Jews and subjugating the Poles. For these things, he was tried as a war criminal and hanged in 1946.

With crowds ever growing, the Party leaders decided to have weekly meetings. This would only increase Hitler's importance within the Party. The meetings were, by now, held almost exclusively at the Hofbrauhaus and, with time, the

Hofbrauhaus would become a Party shrine. Hitler wrote in *Mein Kampf* "... the Munich Hofbrauhaus assumed an almost sacred significance for us National Socialists."

RUSSIA, ODESSA, VICTORY

In southern Russia, the Red Army captured Odessa, one of the nation's most important ports on the Black Sea.

In the Caucasus, Denikin's forces had been pushed back to the Kuban River, 150 miles south of Rostov. With this, a large percentage of the Caucasus oil was in Bolshevik hands.

In the north, the Allies were abandoning Archangel and Murmansk. The White commander there, General Eugeni Miller, on February 14, 1920, formed his own government which was called the "Government of Salvation." Miller had little chance, however, of fending off a Bolshevik attack when it came. Miller's government became known to those who would soon face the Bolsheviks as the "Government of Evacuation," and/or the "Government of Stupidity." By the 20th, Bolshevik forces had occupied both Archangel and Murmansk and Miller fled to Finland.

In Siberia, there was anarchy. Semenov's Cossacks and other remnants of Kalmykov's had descended into banditry. Also, the Trans-Siberian Railroad and many of the towns along its route, were very much in disrepair as a result of the years of fighting. White Forces, being supplied by the Japanese, still held out at Khabarovsk on the Amur River, a natural defensive line, 400 miles inland from Vladivostok. This line would prove to be difficult for the Reds to crack and the Whites would hold out there, with Japanese help, until February 1922.

By now, there were only some 5000 American troops in the Vladivostok area and they were due to depart soon.

Also at this time, Lenin told his military leaders to withdraw whatever forces possible from Siberia and send them to the West for the forthcoming attack on Poland. He also authorized the release of a new slogan for the people: "Make Ready for War with Poland." In the Far East, the conquest of Vladivostok could wait.

FAR EASTERN CONCERNS IN THE US

With Japan in near-total control of the Russian Pacific Maritime provinces, and with strong influence elsewhere in the Far East, there was concern in Washington that the Japanese would never leave and continue building their empire. US Secretary of the Navy, Josephus Daniels, Franklin Roosevelt's boss, told his associates that war with Japan was inevitable unless the great powers worked together now to force them to leave both Russia and China. With the US heading into isolation, Daniels' warning fell on deaf ears and US participation in such a venture was most unlikely.

On the US West Coast, where there was ongoing opposition to the influx of Japanese immigrants and the Hearst Newspapers, based in San Francisco, took up the issue and spread it throughout the nation via its nationwide chain of papers. Rumors circulated, mainly in the West, that Japanese spies were at work in the Western States, in Mexico, and in Panama and that their loyalty to America was questionable.

THE JAPANESE RELOCATION OF 1942

Long before the Japanese attack on Pearl Harbor, there was fear and animosity toward the ethnic Japanese in the US. Rumors circulated frequently that the Japanese residents were disloyal to America and in the service of the Japanese government. After Pearl Harbor, such rumors exploded. Some of the most audacious were these: the Japs (now seldom referred to as Japanese) were building secret airfields in the desert and in Mexico; Jap fishermen were bringing spies and saboteurs ashore from submarines and taking out supplies and secret information; and there were Japanese terrorist cells ready to assassinate people, blow up bridges and tunnels and poison water supplies. Rumors also had it that the Japanese truck farmers were poisoning their vegetable, before bringing them to market.

It was rumors such as these and the long-standing distrust of the ethnic Japanese that so frightened the American public that the US government was forced to act. It acted by forcefully evacuating most of the Japanese living on the West Coast into relocation camps in the Interior.

In both Canada and Mexico there were similar fears, and both countries also forced many of their ethnic Japanese into relocation camps.

OTHER CONCERNS IN THE US

During early February, President Wilson discovered that his cabinet had met 25 times since October and that he had not been informed. The meetings had been called by Secretary of State Lansing. To Wilson, this was treasonable behavior and he demanded Lansing's resignation.

On February 12, 1920, Lansing resigned and on February 25, Wilson appointed Bainbridge Colby, a New York lawyer, to take his place. Colby had no diplomatic experience but was a strong supporter of Wilson and his policies. Colby's appointment was greeted with some praise and much silence.

Lansing, in his anger, wrote a scathing letter to Wilson, accusing him of not listening to the advice of others and treating his subordinates in a most haughty manner. Lansing wrote that he left his post "with profound relief." He then sent the letter to the media and more bad press for the Wilson administration followed.

Lansing was not the only cabinet member to resign because of this flap, William G. McAdoo, Secretary of the Treasury, and Franklin K. Lane, Secretary of the Interior, also resigned.

Quite understandably, the public wondered what was going on in the White House and the answer came through loud and clear — Edith. The public knew Edith quite well by now and knew that there were people around the President that she liked and people she disliked. Lansing had been at the top of her black list. Few people knew it, but also on her black list was Assistant Secretary of the Navy Franklin D. Roosevelt, but he was not asked to resign. The Republicans and newspapers had a field day with these developments and rumors.

In Central America there was another revolt. In Honduras, former President Alberto Membreno led a second unsuccessful revolt against the government. He had led an unsuccessful revolt in October 1919. US Marines had been put on alert ready, once again, to go into Honduras to maintain law and order. This time, however, they were not needed.

POLAND MAKES READY

In Poland, Pilsudski was proceeding with his plans to conquer parts of Russia, Belorussia, and the Ukraine.

In London, War Minister Winston Churchill authorized the sale of surplus German rifles to the Poles. Curzon protested, but Lloyd George allowed it to happen.

In Paris, the French extended a credit of 375 millions francs to the Poles for military purposes. With this money, the Poles purchased arms from various sources.

The US government extended the Poles a credit of $65 million to purchase some of the US war materials that were still in France. Clearly, a new war was coming between Poland and Soviet Russia.

HUNGARY GETS A REGENT

On February 25, the last Romanian troops left Hungary and in Budapest, Horthy was still forming the new Hungarian government.

Hungary was still technically a monarchy, but the throne was vacant and no suitable candidate for the throne was in sight. Furthermore, neither the Allies nor Hungary's neighbors would tolerate the return of any of the Hapsburgs. Therefore, a regent was called for. On February 29 (leap year) Admiral Horthy appointed himself to that post and the decision was confirmed by the Assembly.

HUNGARY AFTER WW II

In October 1944, with the Red Army fast approaching Budapest, Horthy, still in power and still regent, resigned his posts under pressure from the Germans. Ferenc Szalaski, a former President and puppet of the Germans, became Head of State in a Fascist-like government. Szalaski's government lasted until April 1945, when the Soviets occupied Budapest. Szalaski was captured by the Soviets and later executed. Following that, the Soviets converted Hungary into a communist state.

Horthy fled to Austria where he was captured by the Americans. After the end of hostilities, Yugoslavia, which had become a communist state, wanted to try Horthy for war crimes but the US refused to allow him to be extradited. He went into retirement in Portugal and died there in 1957.

IN TURKEY, KEMAL TAKES ON THE FRENCH

In Turkey, fighting between the Kemalists and the French had begun in Cilicia, an area in Turkey south of Angora bordering northwestern Syria. The area had been claimed by France as part of Syria, but Kemal wanted to recover it for Turkey, along with the Turkish people there who were in the majority in the area. Surprisingly, the Kemalists began inflicting one defeat after the other on the French. In Paris, Millerand caught between the popular demand to scale now the French Army, yet maintain French interest in Syria, offered to negotiate. Kemal, however, seeing that he had the upper hand, rejected the offer — and the fighting continued.

GO BACK TO DOBERNITZ AND BE QUIET

The German government was under strong pressures from the Allies to comply with their order to disband the Free Corps, and on February 29 they announced that two of the three most famous of the Free Corps would be disbanded. One of those units was the swastika-bearing Ehrhardt Brigade, commanded by Navy Lt. Commander Hermann Ehrhardt and stationed at Dobernitz on the outskirts of Berlin.

The Brigade was in fine fighting order and had recently received new members from the disbanded Latvian Baltikum Army. When Ehrhardt learned of the order, he went to see General von Luttwitz, the top German Army commander in the Berlin area, to protest the order. Luttwitz was very sympathetic with Ehrhardt and knew that something big was about to happen in Berlin but could not reveal it to Ehrhardt. Luttwitz simply told Ehrhardt to go back to Dobernitz and be quiet.

ANOTHER STRIKE IN FRANCE

On the 29th, French rail unions called a general strike, once again, over a dispute involving the Paris-Lyon-Mediterranean Railroad. The union call was only partially heeded by the workers and in this atmosphere of weakness, the union was forced to accept a settlement within 24 hours. Labor problems on the French railroads would continue to simmer, however, just under the surface.

CHAPTER 20
HITLER LEAVES THE ARMY

||||||||||||||||||||||||||||||||||||||||||||||||||||||||||||||||||||||||||||||||||||||||||||||||||||||||||||||||||||||

EUROPE

On March 2, 1920, another war in Eastern Europe came to an end when the Bolsheviks and Romanians signed an armistice. The disputed territory of Bessarabia went to Romania and the Bolsheviks were assured that Romania would not support Poland in the coming conflict. This agreement completed the pacification of another segment of the Bolshevik's western border. Only the borders with Poland and Polish-occupied Lithuania remained unsettled.

On the 5th, Germany and Latvia signed a treaty of friendship and cooperation. Both countries were in need of friends and potential trading partners.

During these first two weeks of March, the League of Nations gained more new members: Venezuela, Denmark, Cuba, The Netherlands, Norway, Sweden, Switzerland, and El Salvador. Greece joined on the 30th.

On the 13th, Nitti, now being criticized by both the right and the left, and having virtually lost political control of the country, offered to resign. The King, however, asked him to stay on and form a new cabinet, which he did. But, Nitti and his new cabinet were on very shaky ground from day one.

MEXICO

On March 9, three Mexican generals, Adolfo de la Huerta, Alvaro Obregon, and Plutarco Calles, formed a military junta, took over the Mexican state of Sonora, and proclaimed it the "Republic of Sonora." This, of course, was a direct challenge to the government of Carranza Venustiano in Mexico City and sparked a renewal of the ten-year-old Mexican civil war. Most disconcerting for the Americans was the fact that the new Republic of Sonora bordered the state of Arizona.

The three generals commanded a substantial army and soon launched a march on Mexico City. In the US, the newspapers kept the American public well-informed.

IN THE MIDDLE EAST

On March 3, 1920, the Sultan's Cabinet in Constantinople resigned upon receiving word that, in the forthcoming peace treaty, the Allies intended to reduce Turkish territory to that of the province of Anatolia and take away Turkish control of the Straits. Because of this reduction in territory, Turkey would lose some 24 million inhabitants.

In Syria, on March 8, an all-Syrian Congress proclaimed Faisal King of Syria. His official title became Faisal I ibn Husain ibn Ali. The congress also defined Syrian territory as stretching from the Euphrates River in Mesopotamia to the Sinai desert in Egypt and the Taurus mountains in Turkey. This included all of The Lebanon, much of Palestine, and much of southern Turkey. Throughout the country, there was great rejoicing and claims that the Greater Arabia that the Husain family had long planned for was coming into being.

By issuing this proclamation, however, the Syrians angered many people: the French, the British, the Lebanese, the Zionists, the Mesopotamians, and the Turks. And it would prove to be another nail in Faisal's political coffin.

But it was not the end, King Faisal wanted more. The pro-Syrian Mesopotamian political organization that Faisal had sent into Mesopotamia in December now proclaimed the creation of a Mesopotamian government headed by Abdullah Husain, Faisal's older brother. They then proclaimed Abdullah as Amir of Mesopotamia in absentia, a preliminary step to his being proclaimed King at some future date.

In the camps of the opposition, this group was seen as a puppet organization beholding only to Faisal with no real authority or support in Mesopotamia.

Over in The Lebanon, the Lebanese Christians, on the 20th, announced their position. They proclaimed their loyalty to France (a relationship going back to the Crusades) and called for an independent Lebanon. The Lebanese Christians also defined their territory as that previously outlined by the French, which included the Biqa Valley to the east, the seaport of Tyre in the south, and that of Tripoli in the north. By claiming these areas, millions of Muslims would be incorporated into a Christian Lebanon. In Paris, the Lebanese proclamation met with approval from the Millerand government.

In Egypt, on March 10, the Egyptian legislative assembly passed a resolution demanding independence from Britain.

INDEPENDENT EGYPT

Independence for Egypt would come in 1922 but with the stipulation that British military forces would remain in the country to protect it and the Suez Canal. In 1936, a new agreement provided for the withdrawal of British forces from all of Egypt except for the Suez area.

In the Fall of 1940, when Italian forces invaded Egypt from Italian-controlled Libya, it was the British Army that met them at the border, not the Egyptian Army. The Egyptian Army had withdrawn to the safety of Cairo. In the battles to come, it was the British that defended the country while the Egyptian Army remained on the sidelines. All the while, the Egyptian government remained neutral. At the very end of the war, however, when it became apparent that the Axis Powers would be defeated, Egypt declared war on Germany in order to gain charter membership in the forthcoming United Nations Organization and a seat at the peace table. After the war, the British, still observing the 1936 agreement, withdrew back into the Suez area.

IN GERMANY — DER TAG AND COLLECTION CAMPS

In Munich, Thomas Mann, who would become one of Germany's best- known authors, wrote in his diary, "Anger at the French is very strong among the populace. The people are saying `In the next war we won't take any prisoners.'" This was another reference to Der Tag and it defined the attitude of the people who lived in Munich and were hearing more and more about Adolf Hitler.

On March 10, in Munich, the headlines of the *Munchener Beobachter* read "Clean out the Jews once and for all." The paper went on to call for the deportation of all Jews who had entered Germany after August 1914. As for the others, the paper demanded that all Jews in governmental positions, the entertainment business, the news media, and other important segments of the economy be replaced. It went on to recommend that these things should be carried out by the "most ruthless means," including the creation of "collection camps" to hold the displaced Jews.

THE BOLSHEVIKS START TROUBLE WITH POLAND AND FINLAND

On the 7th, Bolshevik forces launched measured attacks against the Poles on Poland's eastern frontier. This was seen as probing attacks in preparation of larger ones to come.

A week later, the Bolsheviks increased the stakes by launching similar attacks against Finland.

IRELAND

In London, Parliament offered a solution to the Irish question. On March 10, they passed a law called the "Home Rule Bill" which would divide Ireland into two components, northern Ireland, known as "Ulster" which was predominantly a Protestant area, and southern Ireland, which was predominantly Roman Catholic. In both segments, the Irish would have a generous measure of home rule but remain within the British Empire.

In the north, the "Ulster Unionist Council," which spoke for the Protestant majority, promptly accepted the plan. The Irish rebels, however, in both the North and South, totally rejected the Home Rule concept and announced that the rebellion would continue.

Coincident with the Home Rule plan, the first contingents of the Royal Irish Constabulary (RIC) arrived in Ireland. They had had three months of training and were paid ten shillings a day, a high wage for military service at the time. The RIC would soon acquire another name, the "Black and Tan," because of the uniform they wore which was a mix of police and military garments.

THE IRISH FREE STATE

In 1923, the leading Irish factions signed a peace treaty with Britain which was based on the Home Rule Bill of 1920. It established two political entities: southern Ireland became an independent nation known as the Irish Free State, and Ulster remained a part of the British Empire.

However, the Catholic factions in Ulster refused to accept these peace terms and began an insurgency that would last for generations.

When WW II erupted, London asked the Republic of Ireland, as it was known by then, to join in the war against Germany. The Irish agreed to do so, but for a price — the return of Ulster. London rejected the proposal and Ireland remained neutral throughout the war.

The Ehrhardt Free Corps entering Berlin during the Kapp Putsch.

IN GERMANY, THE KAPP PUTSCH

Late on the evening of March 12, the 8000-man Ehrhardt Free Corps left its barracks at Doberitz, marching in the direction of Berlin.

In the early morning hours of the 13th, Chancellor Bauer and his cabinet met to confront the issue. They could not reach agreement on what to do but ordered the Germany Army troops in the Berlin area remain in their barracks until the situation was clarified. Then, Bauer and the cabinet left Berlin at once for the safety of Dresden.

While the government had no plan of action, General Luttwitz, who had organized the march, and the Ehrhardt Free Corps had one worked out in detail. The Free Corps would occupy the government offices in Berlin, peacefully it was hoped, and install a new government. With that, they would proclaim Wolfgang Kapp Chancellor with Luttwitz as Defense Minister. Ludendorff, if he announced his support for the takeover, would be offered a high governmental post.

The rebels believed that once Kapp had been proclaimed Chancellor, Seeckt would abandon his support of the troubled Bauer government, which was now on the run, and declare for this new right-wing government in Berlin.

Meanwhile, when the Inter-Allied Control Commission in Berlin learned of the situation, they warned all right-wing elements within the Berlin area not to support Kapp and threatened that the Kapp Putsch could trigger an Allies invasion of Germany.

General Seeckt, however, chose not to cooperate with Kapp and Luttwitz, but neither did he make statements of support for the Bauer government. He declared that the Army would remain neutral and not support either the Bauer government or the rebels. Then, Seeckt issued himself leave and simply went home to await developments.

Meanwhile, the Freecorpsmen were entering Berlin from the West marching in formation and accompanied by a band playing martial music. At the Brandenburg Gate, General Ludendorff, dressed in full uniform, joined Luttwitz, who was also in full uniform and Kapp, who was in formal attire, and together they marched into the center of the city at the head of the column. There, the Freecorpsmen soon took possession of the governmental offices as planned and Kapp moved into the Chancellory. A short while later, an announcement came forth stating that Kapp had assumed the office of Chancellor and was forming a cabinet in which Luttwitz would be Defense Minister. Ludendorff who, as yet, had not been offered a political post and, it appeared, was having second thoughts, simply emulated Seeckt's actions and, he too, went home.

In the Defense Ministry, however, Luttwitz was having unexpected problems. The personnel there were not supportive of the takeover and delayed and/or impeded all of Luttwitz's outgoing orders as best they could.

News, of course, of the takeover spread fast and virtually all of the Free Corps announced support for Kapp. Throughout Germany, however, there was no such leap into the Kapp camp by other right-wing organizations and other political entities. The other top military leaders throughout Germany remained ominously silent, waiting to see where Seeckt stood.

In an effort to discredit the rebel regime in Berlin, the Bauer government, traveling on the road to Dresden, called for a general strike to paralyze the rebel regime. This was quickly supported by the leftists and began to take hold in various places in Germany and in Berlin. It was a bad sign for Kapp.

On the morning of Sunday, March 14, Berlin was paralyzed. There was no

electricity, gas or running water, and the streets were empty and shops closed.

Meanwhile, Bauer and the others reached Dresden only to discover that the military governor there, General Ludwig von Maercker, was sympathetic to the Putsch. Bauer and his associates then decided to go on to Stuttgart. So, off they went again on the road.

Back in Berlin on Sunday, there was chaos as the various forces interacted with threats of violence, and at the same time, offers of compromise. It had, by now, become clear who in Germany supported the Putsch and who did not. The only major part of the civilian population that announced a unified support for Kapp was the Junker (land owner) community in East Prussia which was traditionally on the political far right and monarchist.

In Bavaria, support for Kapp was modestly strong, but not organized. Throughout the rest of Germany it was a mixed bag — and, to add to the confusion, the men of the Ehrhardt Brigade were demanding their pay which consisted of generous bonuses for having participated in the Putsch.

By Monday evening, it was clear to Kapp that his Putsch was in serious trouble. As for the various Free Corps, they were all unable or unwilling to come to Kapp's support.

By Wednesday, March 17, Kapp had more troubles. The Security Police who, four days earlier, had announced their support for the Putsch, now renounced that support and were demanding Kapp's resignation. At about the same time, the men of an Army unit, the Guards Engineer Battalion of the Army's Berlin Garrison, mutinied, seized their officers, and declared for Bauer.

On Wednesday, Kapp realized that all was lost and resigned in favor of General Luttwitz. That afternoon, Kapp took a taxi

Dr. Wolfgang Kapp at Templehof Airfield on his way to exile in Sweden.

to Templehof Airfield, boarded a waiting airplane, and flew to exile in Sweden.

Luttwitz briefly toyed with the idea of conducting a vengeful blood bath but was talked out of it and fled to safety in the Hungarian Embassy.

Ludendorff also fled the scene by train on Wednesday evening for Bavaria where he was worshipped as a war hero and knew he could find safety. To insure his safety, however, he assumed the name "Herr Lange," wore civilian clothes, a false beard, and blue-tinted glasses — the same disguise he had worn on his flight to Sweden in November 1918. Ludendorff reached the Inn River Valley where friends hid him in an old hilltop castle.

In Munich, there was another abrupt change of government sparked, in part, by the events in Berlin. Gustav von Kahr, an ardent right-winger, come to power in a local right-wing putsch, and took over the state government. This was another factor in Ludendorff's choice to go to Bavaria.

Now, with Kapp out of the picture, and Berlin, once again reverting to the control

of the Social Democrats and their allies, Munich would soon become a gathering place for the political right and many of its prominent individuals. There Ludendorff would learn of, and meet, Hitler.

In Berlin, Ehrhardt, now without a political leader, demanded that his Brigade be allowed to leave the city and return honorably to Doberitz. Still powerful, and having no opponents able to stop them, they did just that. They departed Berlin as they had arrived, marching in military order, with bands playing and with the old Imperial flags waving.

A few days later, the Bauer government returned to Berlin from Stuttgart. But, because of the Putsch, Bauer's government was weakened and his days were numbered. On March 26, he resigned and Hermann Muller, another Social Democrat, took office. Muller's government was, like Bauer's, a coalition of several parties.

In the overall picture of German politics, the moderates had survived the Putsch, but they were still very weak. And Berlin had experienced its fifth political upheaval in Berlin since January 1919.

HITLER TRIED TO JOIN IN

When Hitler learned of the Putsch, he decided after some contemplation to go to Berlin and offer what support he could to Kapp. In the company of his close advisor, Dietrich Eckart who had connection in Berlin, and in a borrowed open-cockpit airplane, and wearing disguises — Hitler wore a false goatee — they arrived at Templehof Airfield on Wednesday afternoon. His pilot was Robert Ritter von Greim, a war ace with 28 kills and holder of the "Pour le Merite."

ROBERT RITTER VON GREIM

By WW II, Greim had become a senior general in the Luftwaffe and was one of Hitler's favorites. When, in late April

1945, Hitler, holed up in the Berlin Bunker with the Russians closing in, perceived that Goering was trying to take over command of the Reich, Hitler fired him from all of his positions and ordered his arrest and execution. To replace Goering as head of the Luftwaffe, Hitler chose von Greim. As Germany collapsed, von Greim committed suicide a few days later.

Hitler was not feeling well when they landed; he had gotten airsick and vomited. They soon learned that the Putsch had failed but decided to drive into the city to get more details. It is very possible that Hitler and Kapp passed each other either on the road or at the airfield.

Upon reaching the center of the city, Hitler and Eckart saw that the atmosphere was quite hostile toward right-wingers and scurried back to the airfield and on to the safety of Munich.

In a backlash of the Putsch, the leftists, on March 19, seized control of the cities of Essen and Dresden (Saxony). In Dresden, they demanded that the city and state revert to the former communist-style government that existed there in early 1919. And in Berlin, by March 24, the Reds gained control of about half of the city and it was feared that they might attempt to pull off a leftist coup.

On the 27, the new Muller government struck back at the leftists, ordering that all people with Russian connections be arrested. This was eagerly carried out by the Berlin police and the army garrison, thus greatly easing the situation. A sixth upheaval in Berlin had been suppressed before it could get underway.

BRITISH TAKE CONTROL IN CONSTANTINOPLE

On March 16, 1920, British troops, acting under direct orders from Lloyd George,

suddenly and without warning, took control of all governmental positions in Constantinople. To justify this, they claimed that law and order had broken down in the city which, to a large degree, was true.

The British promptly declared martial law, disbanded the city's police force, and arrested some 150 military and political officials. They then instructed the Sultan to form a new government headed by one Damad Ferid whom they, the British, felt would cooperate fully with the Allies in the forthcoming peace treaty negotiations.

It was soon discovered, however, that the high-handed British action had the opposite effect in that the Turkish people now began to look, more than ever, toward Kemal as their national leader. One-by-one, influential individuals in Constantinople fled the city for Angora to offer their services to Kemal. In Angora, Kemal retaliated against the occupation of Constantinople by arresting every Allied officials within his reach, most of whom were middle and low level personnel.

THE US SENATE REJECTS THE VERSAILLES TREATY AGAIN

In Washington, on March 19, the US Senate refused, once again, to ratify the Versailles Treaty. The vote was 57 yeas to 39 nays, not enough to meet the two-thirds majority (64), required by the US Constitution.

In the White House, Wilson commented to Dr. Grayson, "Doctor, the devil is a busy man."

With the rejection of the Versailles Treaty, the US was still, technically, at war with Germany.

POLAND AND RUSSIA MOVING TO THE BRINK

In eastern Europe, the Poles and Bolsheviks resumed peace negotiations, but at the same time, both sides continued building up their armed forces as rapidly as possible.

Pilsudski was planning a preemptive strike and was rapidly training and equipping some 75,000 new conscripts. On the 19th, in preparation for the pending attack, Pilsudski promoted himself to Field Marshal.

During the month, Petlura and his Ukrainians came to life again. Petlura, still recognized by Warsaw as the head of the Ukrainian People's Republic, and still with about 20,000 men under his command, signed a military alliance with the Poles to fight Bolshevik aggression. It was agreed that the Zbruch River would become the new boundary between Poland and Petlura's Republic. It was also agreed that the eastern boundary of the Ukrainian People's Republic would extend as far eastward into the Ukraine as could be accomplished, hopefully even beyond Kiev, the Ukrainian capital.

Back at the peace talks, negotiations were heading downhill, but they continued because both sides still needed time.

DENIKIN OUT, WRANGEL IN

On March 31, 1920, British aid to Denikin was terminated in compliance to the British announcement of November 4, 1919, to that effect.

During the latter days of March, the Red Army in southern Russia overran Denikin's last defenses in the Ukraine at the town of Perekop on the narrow isthmus that connects the Crimea to the southern Ukraine. With this, the Ukraine was lost to the Whites and the Crimea would be the Red's next objective. It also spelled Denikin's end as commander in the south. He resigned his command and passed it on to Baron Pyotr N. Wrangel who had commanded White forces in the Volga region of southern Russia and the Caucasus. Wrangel's great accomplishment had been that he had led the

successful advance in 1919 that resulted in the capture of Tsaritsyn and the thrust toward Moscow.

Wrangel, like Denikin, had been forced to retreat in recent months and had been operating in the northern Caucasus. In taking over Denikin's command, he also retained his command in the Caucasus as well. Wrangel renamed his new army the "Armed Forces of South Russia" but it was weak, and most believed, doomed.

IN THE US — REDS AND THE ELECTION

Attorney General Palmer made headlines again by claiming that there were some 60,000 Reds in the US, enough he said, if organized, to bring down the government.

And it was coming — the election. All eyes were turning toward the forthcoming Republican national convention because there were many contenders for the nomination with a wide range of political views. Leading contenders were General John J. Pershing and General Leonard Wood, war heroes; Senator Hiram Johnson of California, arch isolationist; Frank Louden, Governor of Illinois; and Herbert Hoover, humanitarian. Further down in the pack were Senator Warren Harding of Ohio, a moderate, and A. Mitchell Palmer, the Red chaser.

HITLER LEAVES THE ARMY

It had been a beneficial seven months for both the German Army and for Corporal Hitler. The Army had paid his room and board and he had helped to bring forth a political organization in Munich that supported many of the Army's views.

But the time had come to part. Hitler was now drawing a small salary from the Party, thanks to admission fees and contributions from supporters, and he could now afford to live on his own, albeit very frugally.

Furthermore, Corporal Hitler needed to get out from any obligation the Army might impose upon him in the event of a national emergency. So on the 31st, he submitted his resignation. Hitler's income at this time is a bit clouded. There were indications that he was still being subsidized by the Army.

Hitler's love for the Army, the real Army and not the Reichswehr of the Diktat, would never wane, and the Army would ultimately give Hitler its full support even unto its death in 1945.

As mustering out pay, the Corporal received 50 marks, and a set of civilian clothes consisting of a hat, coat, jacket, pants, underwear, shirt, socks, and shoes.

Hitler rented a one-room apartment on the third floor of 41 Thierchstrasse in a middle class district near the Isar River.

His landlord was a Frau Reichert who would later describe her tenant as "... such a nice man, but he has the most extraordinary moods. Sometimes weeks go by when he seems to be sulking and does not say a word to us... He always pays his rent punctually in advance, but he is a real bohemian type."

A visitor to Hitler's apartment wrote of Hitler's living conditions: "He lived there like a down-at-the-heels clerk... His room itself was tiny. I doubt if it was nine feet wide. The bed was too wide for its corner and the head projected over the single narrow window. The floor was covered with cheap, worn linoleum and a couple of threadbare rugs, and on the wall opposite the bed there was a makeshift bookshelf, apart from a chair and a rough table, the only piece(s) of furniture in the room." All in all, however, for the ex-Corporal these humble quarters were a step up from a bed and a trunk in an army barracks.

In the small front yard of his building was a statue of the Virgin Mary.

CHAPTER 21
TROUBLES IN THE RUHR AND MANDATES BEGIN

|||||||||||||||||||||||||||||||||||||||||||||||||||||||||||||||||||||||||||||||||||||||||||||||||||

IN THE RUHR

One of the most glaring mistakes made by the peacemakers in Paris was the belief that the German police, alone, could maintain order in the Ruhr, the country's most industrialized and most unionized area. The Versailles Peace Treaty was very clear in that it forbade the Germany government from placing elements of the German Army there because, as the Diktat demanded, it was to become a demilitarized zone. The leftists in the Ruhr saw this weakness and exploited it. By April 1920, the area was peppered with workers' councils, semi-armed and armed militias and leftist organizations of various kinds. The failure of the Kapp Putsch, along with the discrediting of the German Army, the Free Corps, and Germany's political right, gave the Ruhr leftist incentives to act. Soon, an army of some 50,000 workers — so they claimed — emerged calling itself the "Red Army of the Ruhr." With this army to back them up, the leftists took over factories, newspapers, and other enterprises and there were pronouncements from various red leaders that they would endeavor to take over all of Germany and turn it into a communist state.

Obviously, this was unacceptable to the German government and to the Western Allies. But, most of the major Allies had, by now, distanced themselves from continental Europe, which meant that France and her ally, Belgium, were the only nations prepared or even willing to address such a problem.

In Berlin, the Muller government knew that it had to act but was faced with several major problems. The Army was still not all that reliable following the Kapp Putsch and, per the Diktat, the army was forbidden to enter the Ruhr. This left the Free Corps. But they had been ordered by the Allies to disband and had lost a great amount of credibility among the German people because of their freebooting ways.

Finally, the Muller government hit on a plan. They would delay the disbanding of the Free Corps as long as possible and, taking a page from Kapp's brief tenure, would offer Freecorpsmen financial bonuses to serve in a newly-organized and government-controlled Free Corps in the Ruhr to oust the Reds. By offering bonuses, the government could pick and choose, to some degree, who would serve and who would not. And it was Berlin's interpretation of the Diktat that, while the German Reichswehr were forbidden in the Ruhr, the Free Corps were not.

Seeckt approved this plan and offered Muller the Army's full cooperation.

Things then happened with great speed. By the beginning of April, men from twenty-one Free Corps had been organized into the new fighting force and on April 3, they entered the Ruhr. Encounters were immediate, but as had happened before, one-sided. The rag-tag, worker-led Red Army was no match for the military capabilities and skills of the Free Corps commanders and their experienced veterans.

The Allies — the French and Belgians — were also forced to act. In Paris and Brussels, there was no thought of sending French and Belgian troops to do battle with the Free Corps or the Red Army in the Ruhr, but they took another course. French troops moved out of the occupied Rhineland, and on April 6, with the support of the Belgian Army, occupied the major city of Frankfurt and the smaller nearby towns of Darmstat and Hanau. This area was some twenty miles inside Germany from the occupied Rhineland. There was, thusly, an unofficial understanding among Berlin, Paris, and Brussels that Frankfurt and the other two cities would be held hostage until the issues in the Ruhr were favorably resolved and the Free Corps would withdraw.

Inside the Ruhr, the Free Corps made short work of the workers' Red Army. By April 8, the last organized resistance ended and on Easter Sunday, a band of diehard Reds made a last ditch stand in a water tower in Essen as the townsfolk watched.

With the pacification of the Ruhr, the Ruhr police were strengthened and allowed to take control once again, and on April 17, the Free Corps withdrew from the Ruhr. A few days later, the Allies withdrew from the Frankfurt area. Conditions in the Ruhr once again conformed to the Diktat but tensions were high.

TROUBLES IN JERUSALEM

Easter Sunday was approaching in Palestine and the Muslim leaders in Jerusalem, apparently looking for an opportunity to press their demands, planned a "Nebi Musa," a march to Moses's tomb, for the same day. This set the stage for trouble.

On that fateful Sunday, the Nebi Musa began and quickly degenerated into Muslim attacks on both the Jews and the British. The Jews had seen it coming and called in the Haganah. For the next 4 days, there were riots and clashes throughout the city. In the end, five Jews were killed, four Muslims killed, some 200 people injured, and many arrested.

The British authorities eventually restored order, but tensions in Palestine showed no signs of lessening.

THE MUFTI

One of the instigators of the Jerusalem revolt was the local "Grand Mufti" (expounder of Muslim law) and aptly demonstrated that, with the Arabs, religion and politics were one and the same.

In 1921, the Grand Mufti was succeeded by his brother, Haj Amin al-Husayne, who became the new Grand Mufti. Haj Amin, like his brother, soon became one of the most prominent Palestinian leaders in opposition to the Zionists and the British occupiers.

During WW II, Haj Amin went to Germany, met Hitler and offered his services to the Axis cause. Hitler was impressed with the Mufti because he was well-educated, hated the British, was articulate, had red hair and blue eyes which, to Hitler, indicated Aryan blood. Hitler, subsequently, gave the Mufti the task of forming an all-Arab legion for the German Army. He did this by recruiting Arabs living in Europe and Arabs who were prisoners of war that had served in the British and French armed forces.

Later on, he aided in the formation of a Muslim unit for the Waffen SS which operated against the Partisans in the Balkans.

The Mufti survived the war, returned to Palestine, and in the post-war years, cooperated with Yasser Arafat and the PLO.

IN HITLER'S WORLD

Thanks to the recent expansion of the Nazi Party, Hitler now had at his command several gifted speakers that he, himself, had selected and trained. Two of his best speakers were Dietrich Eckart and Alfred Rosenberg.

With these new human resources, Hitler expanded the Party's operations outside of the city of Munich. During April, a new branch of the Party was established in the town of Rosenheim, 30 miles southeast of Munich. The procedure for establishing this branch, and later others, was to advertise the arrival of the Nazi Party in the local media, invite interested parties to the initial meeting at which Hitler would speak, and then press them for Party membership and charter membership in the branch. Thereafter, it was hoped that local leaders could be found, and Hitler's corps of trained speakers would become the primary speakers at the branch's public meetings on a rotating basis. Hitler, of course, would speak from time-to-time at the local branches.

Local branch leaders, when selected, would be required to attend a coordinating meeting in Munich once a month that Hitler would organize and chair.

Hitler, always with an eye on finances, ordered that 20% of all dues money collected by the branches, and 50% of all volunteer contributions, be sent to the main branch in Munich.

To coordinate all of these growing Party activities, the Party hired a paid employee to manage the newly-acquired office and do the necessary paperwork.

Hitler later wrote of the office in *Mein Kampf*; "In the former Sterneckerbrau in the Tal, there was a small vault-like room... It was dark and gloomy... The alley on which its single window opened was so narrow that even on the brightest summer day the room remained gloomy and dark. This became our first business office...the monthly rent was only fifty marks... the room really gave more the impression of a funeral vault than an office."

IN OTHER PARTS OF EUROPE

In Italy, strikes were rampant. In Rome, student volunteers were cleaning the streets because the street cleaners were on strike and middle class and right-wing vigilante groups were forming.

On April 6, 1920, *Il Popolo* predicted anarchy throughout Italy and emphasized that the Fascist Party was the only party in Italy that could unite the Italian people. Privately, Mussolini said that this unity could only come an armed conflict. He told his associates, "The Italian Proletariat needs a bloodbath for its force to be renewed."

A FEW THOUSAND DEAD

When Italy entered WW II, Mussolini was quoted as saying that he needed "a few thousand dead" in order to have a seat at the peace table.

On April 8, 1920, Portugal joined the League of Nations.

On April 9, in Paris, the League of Nations Council held its fourth meeting and between April 13 and 17, the League hosted an international health conference in London to help improve and standardize international health-related activities and issues.

In Ireland, the rebels began confiscating British tax records and publicly burning them. Such records were a much-hated symbol of British rule.

On April 20, the 7th Olympic Games opened in Antwerp.

IN WILSON'S WORLD

In Washington, Wilson attended his first cabinet meeting since he was stricken in October 1919. It became immediately apparent to all that his mental capabilities were impaired and the meeting was quickly halted by Dr. Grayson and Mrs. Wilson. In private, and to some of his closest aides, Wilson was still talking of running for a third term.

On April 7, some 50,000 railroad workers went on strike, affecting 25 railroad companies.

On the 9th, the US Senate voted to do away with military conscription and depend on an all-volunteer army.

On the 14th, C. Mitchell Palmer declared that the discredited IWW union (Wobblies) was behind the rail strike and that it was part of a worldwide communist conspiracy. He told the rail workers that they had been duped by the communists and urged them to go back to work.

In South Bainbridge, Massachusetts, a paymaster and guard at a local shoe factory were killed and $16,000 stolen. Two Italian immigrants, Nicola Sacco and Bartolomea Vanzetti, were arrested and charged with the crime. It was revealed that the two men had anarchist sympathies, and given the temper of the times and the nationwide anti-immigrant attitude of the public, many believed, without question, that they were guilty.

Their ordeal would dragged on through the courts until August 1927 when they were both executed.

On April 21, there was a confrontation between IWW workers and police in Butte, Montana, and 14 Wobblies were shot. A. Mitchell Palmer reminded the nation of his recent words.

POLAND STRIKES BACK

By the third week in April, Pilsudski had his forces mobilized and positioned and was ready to launch his preemptive attack against the Russians.

On the 22nd, Pilsudski moved to his advanced field headquarters at Polish-occupied Rovno in the Ukraine some 250 miles southeast of Warsaw.

On April 24, the Poles, along with Petlura's forces, launched their attack. They struck out from the Rovno area in the direction of Kiev, a city that had once been ruled by the Poles in the 1600s. Success was immediate as the Red Army forces in their path displayed weakness and confusion. The fighting, at times, was heavy and bloody and in most cases, prisoners were shot by both sides.

Behind the Bolshevik lines, however, a new unity quickly emerged as the various political and military factions of the new Soviet state united to face the common enemy. Seeing that Kiev was the Pole's objective, the Soviet leaders began accumulating forces in that area. This was one of the oldest Russian tactics on record: draw them in, force them to extend their lines of supply and then strike. It had been used with great success against Napoleon and would be used again in WW II.

Within a few days, the Poles had captured the city of Zhitomir, 110 miles east of Rovno and only 80 miles from Kiev.

The new war in Eastern Europe had widespread repercussions. All of Europe was now on edge and the details of the war were amply reported throughout the continent. Also, the various communist and leftist organizations in Europe found a new unity and were openly supportive of the Reds.

Most European leaders knew that a Bolshevik counterstroke was inevitable, and given Russia's superior numbers, that that counterstroke would, very likely, be the deciding factor in the war. Lloyd George was one of those who was worried. He said to a colleague, "The Poles are inclined to be arrogant and they will have to take care that they don't get their heads punched." From the British government, however, came only neutralist statements. Even Winston Churchill, who usually was outspoken on everything, remained silent.

In Russia, two of Lenin's most pressing issues were put on hold- the advance into the Caucasus and the Zakalennya Bolsheviki (the hardening to the Russian economy along orthodox communist lines).

And in the Far East, Lenin made a major concession to keep that area pacified while he dealt with Poland. He authorized the creation of an independent nation, to be known as the "Far Eastern Republic," that would serve as a buffer state between his Bolshevik regime in Siberia and the Allied-occupied areas of eastern Siberia. The capital of the new Republic was Chita, on the Trans-Siberian Railroad 400 miles east of Irkutsk.

Two years later, on November 15, 1922, after the last of the Allied forces had withdrawn, the Far Eastern Republic was absorbed by Soviet Russia.

THE SAN REMO CONFERENCE — APRIL 9-27, 1920

On April 27, the Allied powers — less the US — concluded a meeting at San Remo on the Italian Riviera which formalized,

and distributed, the colonial mandates that were created out of both the German Empire and the defunct Ottoman Empire. With regard to the Ottoman Empire, Article 22 of the Versailles Treaty directed their hands reading in part, "Certain communities formerly belonging to the Turkish Empire had reached a stage of development where their existence as independent nations can be provisionally recognized by a Mandatory until which time as they are able to stand alone." It was also acknowledged by all mandatory powers that the League of Nations would have oversight authority.

Ironically, Italy, the host for the San Remo Conference, was not given any mandates, although some of her earlier colonial acquisitions were confirmed.

To many in Italy, this was seen as yet another betrayal by Italy's wartime allies, and Mussolini would refer to the disgrace of San Remo often in his rise to power.

With regard to Fiume, the Conference decided to leave that issue to the parties involved, Italy and Jugoslavia. With this, the Italians were given a free hand to hopefully resolve the Fiume issue on their terms. In other areas, the issues were resolved thusly...

PALESTINE: The British and French agreed that Britain would take Palestine and that the Balfour Declaration could go forward, which meant that the immigration of Jews into Palestine could resume.

At French insistence, the British agreed to protect Palestinian Christians.

As for the Palestinian Arabs, they were not represented at San Remo and it was understood that they would become wards of the British.

It was also agreed that the land east of the Jordan River, known as Trans-Jordan, was acknowledged to be a part of the British Palestine mandate, but it would not be a part of the Jewish homeland.

These actions caused a new governmental post to be created in London, the "High Commissioner for Palestine." It was given to Herbert Samuel, a member of the Liberal Party, a cabinet minister, and one of Britain's most prominent Jews.

SYRIA and THE LEBANON: France was authorized to have a mandate over The Lebanon, and if it became necessary, over Syria. The Lebanese willingly accepted the mandate, but the mandate over Syria would have to be worked out with King Faisal's regime in Damascus.

MESOPOTAMIA: The mandate over all of Mesopotamia was given to Britain. Behind the scenes, and in secret, the British and French reached an agreement on the control of Mesopotamia's oil assets. France would recognize the British mandate and, in return, would have liberal access to the oil and a promise from London to support France with regard to future issues with Germany. This arrangement shut out all others in Mesopotamia, including the US, who had hoped to attain a part of the country's oil resources. The US government soon learned of the secret agreement and vigorously protested the decision, albeit secretly.

Also shut out of the arrangement with regard to Mesopotamia was Turkey. The Turks wanted control over the Mosul area, claiming that this heavily Kurdish area could be administered along with the adjacent Kurdish areas in Turkey. Everyone knew, however, that the major interest for Turkey was not the Kurds, but the oil.

The British countered this move by declaring that the mountains between northern Mesopotamia and Turkey provided a natural border that could be well-defined and adhered to. The British also argued that the Assyrian Christians in the Mosul area would be more secure under a British mandate and, eventually,

under a British-structured independent Mesopotamia. Another British argument was that the Mosul area contained many Sunni Muslims and they were needed in Mesopotamia to balance out the distribution of Sunnis in the north with the large number of Shiite Muslims in the south.

The participants at San Remo sided with Britain and the Mosul area was incorporated into Mesopotamia.

KEMAL OBJECTED

In Turkey, Kemal would not acknowledge the San Remo decision with regard to Mosul until 1925. By then, he had come to power in Turkey and accepted the decision after the issue had been submitted to the Court of International Justice in the Hague, which decided in favor of Britain.

TURKEY: The decisions regarding Turkey, which had been made in February with regard to the partitioning of that country and the placing of international controls over the Straits, were confirmed and submitted to the Sultan's government in Constantinople. The Sultan's government was told that these conditions would be embodied in the coming peace treaty. To be assured that ratification of the peace treaty would not be a problem, the British ordered the Sultan, on April 11, to dismiss his parliament which was, by now, very nationalistic and pro-Kemal.

Other decisions agreed to at San Remo were that the Turks would retain Constantinople but that Greece would acquire Western Thrace, and that the Greeks in Smyrna would have a sphere in influence which extended into western Anatolia. With regard to Smyrna, it was agreed that a plebiscite would be taken there within the next five years for the people to decide upon union with either Greece or Turkey.

It was further agreed that France would also have a sphere of influence in southern Anatolia.

Armenia's independence was confirmed and an autonomous area would be created in eastern Turkey for the Turkish Kurds. In Paris, the Allies had searched for a nation that was willing to accept a mandate over Kurdistan, but found no takers. Therefore, the Turks would keep their Kurds. As for the Kurds in Mesopotamia, they would come under the British mandate and those in Persia would, as had been the case before the war, remain under Persian control. Consequently, the Kurds would be divided into three political entities with little chance of forming a united Kurdistan.

It was also agreed at San Remo that the foreign concessions (Capitulations) in Turkey, granted to foreigners over the years, would continue to be recognized and that Turkey's governmental finances, which were notoriously corrupt, were to be placed under joint British, French, and Italian controls.

Not surprisingly, Kemal and his Grand National Council refused to accept any of these conditions. On April 23, at a meeting of the Council in Angora, they issued a forceful denunciation of the Sultan's government and issued a draft for a new Turkish constitution. With this action, Kemal and his supporters created a de facto provisional government that would be a rival to the Sultan's government in Constantinople and would, of course, not comply with any peace treaty signed by the Sultan.

In the Caucasus, an issue between the Turks and the Bolsheviks was resolved but outside the realm of the San Remo Conference. On the 28th, while the San Remo Conference was in progress, the Bolshevik took control of oil-rich Azerbaijan and the Turks acknowledged that takeover. This left Armenia and Georgia to be contested between the two neighboring powers and the remnants of the Russian Whites.

Once the Bolsheviks became established in Azerbaijan, a mostly Muslim nation, Zinoviev, head of the Comintern, convened a congress there of representatives from other Muslim countries outside Soviet Russia. Zinoviev urged the world's Muslims to declare a holy war against the British, French, and Greek occupiers of their lands. There was no significant response to this call, however. It was very naive of the communists to expect that these very religious peoples would, in any way, cooperate with the godless communist.

ARABIA: It was agreed that the great desert land of Arabia would remain "independent." This was a euphemism which meant that the Arab tribes and clans there could continue their age-old rivalries and warfare. Arabia was seen by the Western Powers as a burden rather than an asset. That would change in a few years when oil was discovered there.

EGYPT: Britain's dominant position in Egypt was accepted by all parties. In London, Winston Churchill received much of the credit for the British successes at San Remo.

As for the German Empire, Article 119 of the Versailles Peace Treaty read: "Germany renounces in favor of the Principal Allied and Associated Powers, all her rights and titles over her overseas possessions."

Article 22 of the Treaty further defined the responsibilities of the Mandatory powers in Africa where the majority of German colonies were located. It read in part: "Other peoples, especially those of Central Africa, are at such a stage that the Mandatory must be responsible for the administration of the territory under consideration which will guarantee freedom of conscience and religion, subject only to the maintenance of public order and morals, the prohibition of abuses such as the slave trade, the arms traffic, and the liquor traffic...." It was also agreed that the former German colonies would be demilitarized zones, supervised by mandatory powers and open to international trade and commerce.

To oversee the management of the mandated territories, the League had created the "Permanent Mandatory Commission."

Subsequently, the German colonies were divided thusly...

EAST AFRICA: Germany's largest East African colony, Tanganyika, was mandated to Britain which subsequently administered it, along with its two existing colonies to the north, Kenya and Uganda.

A small portion of southern Tanganyika, known as the Kiongo Triangle, was mandated to Portugal and would be administered along with the Portuguese colony of Mozambique to the south.

The two smaller German colonies of Rwanda and Urundi, adjacent to the Belgian Congo, were mandated to Belgium.

WEST AFRICA: In West Africa, the small colony of Togo was divided into two parts with the western part given a British mandate and the eastern part a French Mandate. Six hundred miles to the east, in the elbow of the West African coast, the colony of Kameroons was divided with the western, and smaller part, mandated to the British, and the larger part to the French. British Kameroons was administered along with the British colony of Nigeria, and French Kameroons was administered along with the federation of French colonies known as French Equatorial Africa.

At the southern tip of West Africa, the colony of South-West Africa was mandated to the Union of South Africa.

PACIFIC — NORTH OF THE EQUATOR: In the Pacific, north of the Equator, the German island groups of the Marianas, the Carolines, and the Marshalls were mandated to Japan. Japan, of course, had already been given control over Germany's large concession in northeastern China, Shantung.

The mandating of these islands to Japan was of considerable concern to the US because Guam, America's Western Pacific outpost, was now surrounded by Japanese-controlled islands and the Philippines were seen as being more militarily vulnerable. Furthermore, America's direct sea route between Hawaii and the Philippines now passed through about 1000 miles of Japanese-controlled water and her trade routes to China passed through some 2000 miles of Japanese-controlled water.

In Washington, the War Department had began updating war plans that had existed since the 1890s in the event of a future war with Japan. These plans would eventually call for a series of amphibious invasions of various islands that would culminate with the invasion and capture of the island of Okinawa, in the Ryuku Island group south of Japan. Such conquests would facilitate a further invasion of Japan. During WW II, this would become known as "Island Hopping."

"PLAN ORANGE"

By the late 1930s, American military strategy in the Pacific had been consolidated into an operation named "Plan Orange" which eventually became the blueprint for the American war in the Pacific.

PACIFIC — SOUTH OF THE EQUA-TOR: South of the Equator, the German colony on the northern shore of the island of New Guinea, known as "Kaiser Wilhelm Land," and the guano-rich (fertilizer) island of Nauru were mandated to Australia. Three thousand miles to the east, German Samoa was mandated to New Zealand.

In all, 1,043,910 square miles of German territory was given away, along with some 13.6 million colonial subjects.

THE MANDATES AT THE BEGINNING OF WWII

By the advent of WW II, all of the countries in the Middle-East, as well as Egypt, had gained their independence and most of them had joined the League of Nations.

In Africa and the Pacific, all of the former German possessions were still under their respective League of Nations Manditories.

After WW II, the United Nations inherited the League's responsibilities to oversee what was left of the mandated territories, but this obligation was terminated in 1947 when other arrangements were made.

SHUT UP AND GO BACK TO WORK

In Italy, the ongoing labor troubles reached a new zenith. In mid-April, some four million workers went out on another strike, crippling the Italian economy. One of the main issues was the use of official time, which the factory owners preferred, versus solar time which the workers preferred.

As before, the strike turned into demonstrations, riots, and plant takeovers and the Army had to be called out, one more time, to restore order. By now, the general public had become disgusted with the labor movement and the strikers had little sympathy. Finally, after ten days of disorder, the union leaders concluded that striking over such petty issues was counterproductive, and on April 24, they ordered the workers back to work. With this, the strike ended peacefully. But this became a turning point in the Italian labor movement in that it began to lose public support.

During the strike, Mussolini supported the use of solar time, because there were more votes to be had that way than with official time.

CHAPTER 22
MORE
TREATIES

‖‖‖

KIEV

In Russia, during these first days of May, the Poles were advancing on Kiev. Trotsky had appointed a new commander in the area, General M. C. Tukhachevsky, who had proven to be one the Red Army's best commanders and was now given the task of saving Kiev and dealing with the Poles.

On May 7, the Poles and their Ukrainian allies occupied the city and moved on to take Brovari, 30 miles northeast of the Kiev. As events would show, this would be the high-water mark of their advance.

Pilsudski announced that the Poles would remain in the city until a functional and independent Ukrainian government was in place, and Petlura was charged with creating that government as well as a Ukrainian national army.

The response from the citizens of Kiev was lackluster at best. There was no great love for Petlura and the city had changed hands so many times in the recent past that the political rhetoric of this new conqueror was not much different from the last.

On May 15, Tukhachevsky struck. His Red Army launched a massive and well-coordinated counterattack on the Poles and Ukrainians in the Kiev area on several fronts. A hard battle ensued for several days, but the Reds won the contest and the Poles and Ukrainians were forced to withdraw from the city. Their conquest of Kiev had been brief.

MESMERIZED

On May 10, 1920, Hitler spoke again in a Munich beer hall on the subject "The Workers and the Jews." In the audience was an angry young man, a wounded veteran of the Great War, and an ex-freecorpsman, Rudolph Hess. Hess was mesmerized by Hitler's words, and by the end of the evening, knew he had found his leader.

Hess joined the Party, caught Hitler's eye, and began a rapid rise within the Party's leadership. Hitler needed men like Hess — Especially now. Hitler had secretly decided to maneuver around the Party's existing leadership that had rejected his proposals and form a group of loyalists he could depend upon to support his position. It was the beginning of a coup within the NSDAP.

IN THE REST OF EUROPE

A new book appeared in Germany that was to have earth-shattering consequence. It was written by Professors Karl Binding, a jurist and Alfred Hoche, a psychiatrist, titled *Die Freigable der Vernichtung Lebensunwerten Lebens* ("The Sanctioning of the Destruction of Lives unworthy of Being Lived"). This was euthanasia, a policy that the Nazis would aggressively pursue in the 1930s.

On May 14, the League of Nations Council held another meeting, this time in Rome.

On the 21st, Premier Nitti of Italy formed his third cabinet but his government was still very much in trouble.

"NORMALCY"

On May 14, Senator Warren Harding of Ohio made a speech before the Market Club of Boston and said, "America's present need is not heroics but healing, not nostrums but normalcy, not revolution, but restoration..." The newspapers picked up on Harding's use of the unusual word "normalcy" and with time and repetition, it became associated with him and a word that supported isolationism. Harding took advantage of this and made use of it in his campaign for the presidency.

MESOPOTAMIA AND TURKEY

In Mesopotamia, the call for Mesopotamian independence by Syria's King Faisal found some followers. In northwestern Mesopotamia, near the border with Syria, local Mesopotamians took up arms and clashed with the British occupiers. The British appealed to Faisal to call an end to the violence, but he disclaimed any responsibility. The British, then, moved out of the area. This action was seen as a British abandonment of a significant part of Mesopotamia and as a victory for the insurgents. It only encouraged the dissidents even more and the clashes continued and spread.

On May 24, the Sultan's government formally denounced the peace terms presented to it at San Remo, but in the final analysis, the Sultan would have no options but to sign and everyone knew it.

THE CRIMEA AND KIEV

At this time, there were two major military campaigns underway in Russia: one in the Crimea and one west at Kiev.

In the Crimea, Wrangel's hard-pressed White Army was struggling in an effort to keep from falling apart. Wrangle offered political and social reforms, spoke of "Holy Russia," and renamed his army. But it was too little and too late.

Foreign support for his cause had all but dried up and many of the World's leaders were positioning themselves for the coming, and inevitable, Red victory.

West of Kiev, it was a different story — there was still hope. The French called for Allied unity to aid Poland and protect Europe from the Bolsheviks. The British had other thoughts on the matter. They looked toward trade as the new way to deal with the Red, and as a sidebar to the French proposal, called for a humanitarian effort to save Wrangel. From Whitehall came a lone voice calling for military support for Wrangel. It was Winston again.

From Washington, there was indifference and silence.

In the Kiev area, Pilsudski's Poles and Petlura's Ukrainians were in orderly, but steady, retreat. Tukhachevsky's forces were simply too strong, and now, with captured British tanks, too mobile.

Tukhachevsky also had two very capable and experienced officers under his command, Generals Kliment Voroshilov and Semen Budennyi.

IN FRANCE AND BRITAIN

In France, as in Italy, the populace had had its fill with labor. The latest general strike in France, thought to be communist-inspired, was petering out and more and more of the union members refused to follow their command. Also, union membership began to drop. On May 21, the labor leaders sheepishly declared an end to the latest strike.

On the 31st, a Russian trade mission arrived in London with great publicity. Lloyd George was enthusiastic; Churchill was skeptical.

COUNTERCLOCKWISE

In Munich, the Nazis, in imitation of the Austrian Nazis, introduced a new flag for their party. It was red, with a counter-clockwise black swastika in the center of a white circle.

THE TREATY OF TRIANON

On June 4, 1920, representatives of the Horthy government in Hungary signed a peace treaty with the Allies at the Trianon Palace near Paris. The ceremony was brief and unceremonious.

The treaty confirmed the breakup of the old Austria-Hungarian Empire and the loss of land by Hungary that had already been divided among Hungary's neighbors. This meant that Hungry lost two-thirds of its pre-war territory and her population was reduced from 22 million to 8 million. Hungary's former partner in

empire, Austria, had been reduced to a population of 6.2 million and her age-old adversary, Romania, now had 15.6 million. Hungary's new neighbors, Czechoslovakia and Jugoslavia, had 13.6 and 11.9 million respectively. In contrast, Germany had 62 million.

The treaty stipulated that the Hungarian Army would have no more than 35,000 members, no tanks, no heavy artillery, and no air force. Furthermore, Hungary was to pay reparations.

The French, unlike the hard line they had taken toward Germany in the Treaty of Versailles, now took a softer line toward Hungary, indicating that they might be interested in a future positive relationship with Hungary. French Premier Millerand generated a letter in which he stated that the Trianon Treaty carried with it many injustices toward the Hungarian people and that the Treaty should be reviewed and possibly revised.

All over Hungry, however, flags flew at half-mast and the word "Trianon," like the word Diktat in Germany, became a dirty word.

HUNGARY'S SHORT-LIVED REVENGE

During the late 1930 and early 1940s, Hungary, with the help of Nazi Germany, regained sizable amounts of land and population from Czechoslovakia, Romania, and Yugoslavia.

When the Germans invaded the Soviet Union in June 1941, Hungary declared war on the communist giant and sent troops to help with its conquest. As a reward, Hungary was to receive land in westernmost Russia up to the Dniester River.

On December 12, 1941, five days after the attack on Pearl Harbor, Hungary declared war on the US.

In late 1944, the Red Army overran Hungary, ousted Horthy, and installed

Warren Harding

300,000 – REALLY?

In the years to come, the US Army never really reached the 300,000 figure until 1940. The actual size of the Army throughout the 1920s and 1930s was about half the allotted amount, kept low primarily because Congress refused to grant enough funds for it to reach it full strength.

The Navy did somewhat better and acquired a number of new and modern warships because it took years to design and build such warships. Those ships were of great value in the early days of WW II.

a new pro-Soviet government which declared war on Germany on December 28, 1944.

After WW II, the borders of Hungary were restored to those defined by the Treaty of Trianon.

IN THE US

On June 4, 1920, the Republican-controlled Congress passed the "National Defense Act of 1920" which, among other things, reduced the US Army to an all-volunteer force of 300,000 members.

All of this was good politics. The election was coming, the American people were sick of war and its costs in lives and money, and the politicians knew it.

President Wilson signed the Act for the same reasons.

On June 8, the Republican National Convention began in Chicago at the Blackstone Hotel. Senator Lodge gave the keynote address and served as the convention's chairman. This convention would be like previous conventions: gaudy, loud, long, and hot. And while the delegates made their speeches on the convention floor, the party leaders made the important decisions behind closed doors. And herein lay a problem. The party leaders could not agree on any of the major candidate and had to settle for a compromise candidate. On June 12, a decision was reached- on the tenth ballot. The nominations would go to Senator Warren Harding of Ohio and, for Vice President, Boston mayor Calvin Coolidge.

Since this would be the first presidential election in which the ladies would participate, it was felt that the candidate had to be attractive to women. Harding, a very handsome man, met that qualification.

One observer wrote of Harding's family-oriented domestic image " ... Harding exuded the atmosphere of a sleepy Ohio town, the shady streets, the weekly lodge meeting, the smoking-room stories, golf on Sunday morning followed by a fried chicken dinner and an afternoon nap."

GERMANY

On June 6, 1920, there was an election in Germany for representatives to the Reichstag. It was a typical multi-party European election in which no party gained a majority. The Social Democrats led the pack with 102 seats followed by their break-away former members, the Independent Social Democrats with 84 seats. The Nazis did not participate in the national election, and, therefore, had no representation in the government.

At this time, there was an interesting change in the German Communist Party. Under the leadership of Paul Levi, a Jew, the Party began the policy of trying to gain respectability. Strikes and other punitive actions were downplayed and Rosa Lux-embourg's newspaper, *Rote Fahne*, which had had a measure of notoriety during the latter part of the war, was resurrected. This was to be the new way of spreading the message of communism. The editor of *Rote Fahne* was Josep Borenstein, also a Jew. As future elections would show, progress in this endeavor would progress, but slowly.

On June 8, the Muller government resigned — after serving for only three months — and, in the negotiating that traditionally took place after European elections, Konstantin Fehrenbach of the Catholic Center Party became Germany's new Chancellor. Fehrenbach's government was a broad-based coalition tilting to the political right. By any standard, it was a weak government in which political compromises were the order of the day.

WHO'S IN CHARGE THIS MONTH?

On June 9, the day after the Muller government in Germany resigned, the Nitti government in Italy resigned. The last straw came for Nitti when, on June 4, he decreed an increase in the price of bread.

Giovanni Giolitti, who had served three times previously as Premier, assumed that post once again. Giolitti was well-respected and known to be supportive of some of the Fascist Party's views.

In Austria, Chancellor Karl Renner's government fell on June 10 and was replaced by a government formed by Michael Mayr. Renner had signed the Treaty of St. Germain, which cost him considerable public support.

In Britain, Lloyd George was still very much in control, but he had his ongoing problems, one of which was Palestine. On the 13th Cabinet Minister Churchill sent him a depressing note on British prospects there. It read, in part, "Palestine is costing us six millions a year to hold... The Palestine venture... will never yield any profit of a material kind."

IN WESTERN EUROPE

On June 14, the League of Nations Council met in London, and on June 16, the "Permanent Court of Justice," an offshoot of the League of Nations, began to function.

THE WAR IN EASTERN EUROPE

On Poland's eastern front, the Reds were advancing slowly, and by the end of the month, was approaching the important Polish city of Lvov.

But the Poles had their strengths, one of which was that they had broken the Bolsheviks secret codes and were reading messages from Trotsky on down.

ULTRA-ENIGMA

The Poles became very adapt at ciphering and deciphering coded radio messages which led to the development of an advanced and high-quality ciphering/deciphering machine that, in the

1930s, became know as "Enigma." The first versions of this machine appeared in the 1920s. During WW II, the Enigma machine became the basis for one of the Allies most successful intelligence operations known as "Ultra."

IIIIIIIIIIIIIIIIIIIIIIIIIIIIIIIIIIIIIIIIIIIIIIIIIIIIIIIIIIIIIIIIIIIIIIIIIIII

MIDDLE EAST – OIL – PALESTINE – A HAREM OF YOUNG BOYS

More troubles were brewing in Mesopotamia. Various tribes were now fighting each other, the Americans were pressing for a share of the oil, and the Kurds were still very unhappy.

Politically, Mesopotamia was a mess. Plus, the massive irrigation system, so important to the economy of the area, needed major repairs, as did the rail system. To accomplish these things, the British tried to enforce payment of the land taxes and tenure laws which were still on the books from the days of the Turkish administration. This met with little success. Large-scale anti-British demonstrations erupted in Najaf and Karbala and the British, not having enough resources to deal with the problems, simply withdrew from those cities.

Another factor that galled the local people was that most of the British troops were East Indians.

Demonstrations turned into hit-and-run attacks and a general insurgency threatened. As the revolt spread, the British abandoned more garrisons and outposts and concentrated their forces around Baghdad, in the middle area of the Euphrates River valley and Basra in the south. With time, the insurrection stopped spreading, but uncoordinated hit-and-run attacks continued, and anarchy was the order of the day in most of Mesopotamia.

In an effort to placate the Mesopotamians, the British announced, on June 23, 1920, that they were removing the chief

British administrator in the area, A. T. Wilson, who was known to favor Mesopotamia being made into a British colony. Wilson's replacement was Sir Percy Cox who had served in Mesopotamia with distinction and had a large measure of respect from the local people. It was also announced that a Mesopotamian council of state would be formed to prepare the country for elections and, eventually, a national assembly — vital steps toward independence. These advancements, however, would not come easily. Mesopotamia not only needed a new political structure, but a modern judicial system, an educational system, public health services, and many more things before it could function as an independent country.

To finance all of this, the British looked to the revenues that would be available from the sale of the oil in the Mosul area — once that oil began to flow to the world markets.

MESOPOTAMIAN/IRAQI OIL

IIIIIIIIIIIIIIIIIIIIIIIIIIIIIIIIIIIIIIIIIIIIIIIIIIIIIIIIIIIIIIIIIIIIIIIIIIIIIII
Negotiations among US oil companies, the British, and the government of Iraq (Mesopotamia), dragged on until the summer of 1928. At that point, the US received a share of the oil in what was called the "Red Line" Agreement.
IIIIIIIIIIIIIIIIIIIIIIIIIIIIIIIIIIIIIIIIIIIIIIIIIIIIIIIIIIIIIIIIIIIIIIIIIIIIIII

In western Turkey, the conflict between the Greeks at Smyrna and Kemal's forces in Anatolia erupted again and it was clear that neither side had the advantage. In London, there were those who believed that Lloyd George was backing a losing horse and that the Greeks had little chance of defeating Kemal's fast-growing, and very nationalistic, army. Time would tell.

If this were not enough, clashes in northeastern Turkey between Turks and Armenians were also escalating.

And the peace treaty with Turkey was only weeks away.

In Palestine, the British finally made the decision to replace the military government in Jerusalem with a civil government. In keeping with the spirit of the Balfour Declaration, the British chose Sir Herbert Samuel to be the new High Commissioner for Palestine. This had the full support of Balfour as well as the Jewish leaders, Weizmann and Theodor Herzl, and was in keeping with the probability that Palestine was to become a British-mandated territory. Soon, the news media was calling Samuel, Balfour, Weizmann, and Herzl the "Big Four" of Palestine. Throughout the Muslim world, the British action was seen as an "Anglo-Zionist conspiracy."

Samuel arrived at Jaffa in late June. There was a brief ceremony at dockside and then he was whisked away in an armored car to a camouflaged train which took him to Jerusalem. On his person, Samuel carried a loaded pistol. In Jerusalem, Samuel's reception was subdued and cool.

Once established in Jerusalem, however, Samuel set up a Jewish advisory board and allowed local Zionists to establish a "Constituent Assembly" as a step towards Jewish self-rule. The local Arabs soon created on their own a rival organization called the "Arab Executive." Out of fairness, Samuel recognized both organizations as representatives of their respective constituents but it was no secret where his sentiments lay.

In Turkestan, that vast desert area east of the Caspian Sea and north of the Persian and Afghanistan borders, the Reds moved in to claim this former Tsarist territory. One of the local potentates they dislodged was a perverted Muslim Emir that had two harems, one of women and the other of young boys.

The Reds made no effort to advance into Persia or Afghanistan and announced, much to the relief of the West, that they would respect the old Tsarist boundaries. Turkestan was renamed the "Bukhara People's Republic."

CHINA

In Shanghai, library assistant Mao Tse-tung made a life-altering decision. He later wrote of this time, "In theory, and to some extent in action, (I) became a Marxist." Mao plunged into party activity and soon became recognized by his fellow comrades as a man with potential leadership abilities.

THE US – TRADE AND POLITICS

From the White House came a statement that the President had declared that the US had every right to instigate trade relations with the Bolsheviks, as was now being done by the British in London. There were a lot of people in the US who thought that that was a bad idea, and the Democrat National Convention was about to begin where this decision would be anything but a uniting force.

On June 28, 1920, that convention opened in San Francisco. The behind-the-scenes wrangling was not nearly as intense as it had been with the Republicans in Chicago, although it took 44 ballots to get the job done. Emerging from the convention were James M. Cox of Ohio as presidential candidate, and young and handsome Franklin D. Roosevelt as vice presidential candidate. Roosevelt was extremely popular with his party and was nominated by acclamation.

President Wilson did not attend the convention but sent telegrams of congratulations to both men. Rumors in Washington circulated, however, that Wilson was not happy with Cox and was not very fond of Roosevelt.

The Party's political platform was broad and pledged unequivocal ratification of the Versailles Treaty. Cox announced

Democrat presidential candidates for 1920, James Cox (right) and Franklin D. Roosevelt (left).

that, as soon as he took office, he would apply for US membership in the League of Nations.

It was a grand time for the Buckeyes. Both Cox and Harding were from Ohio.

TWO MORE MEMBERS

On June 30, 1920, the League of Nations gained two more members, Haiti and Liberia.

CHAPTER 23
MIRACLE ON THE VISTULA

‖‖‖

"TO THE WEST..."

On July 2, Soviet General Tukhachevsky issued the order to begin the summer offensive against Poland. Zero hour was to be dawn on July 4. Tukhachevsky's order read in part, "To the West... on to Vilna, Minsk and Warsaw...."

In the early morning hours of the 4th, the attack began on the northern part of the front. The Red infantry was supported by captured French-made Renault tanks and Cossack calvarymen on their flanks. For the first time in their revolution, the Reds were able to put together a large and modern force similar to those that had been used by both sides during the Great War.

In Warsaw, the Premier's office was empty. Premier Wladyslaw Grabsky was in Belgium at the Spa Conference where he had hoped to gain some meaningful support from the Allies. Back in Poland, Pilsudski was in full command.

At the front, the Poles were outnumbered, had little defense against tanks and were soon overwhelmed. Pilsudski ordered a retreat.

By the 6th, the Reds were within 45 miles of Vilna and two days ahead of schedule. They then crossed the Berezina River and turned south toward Minsk.

On the other side of Lithuania, a small Lithuanian force entered the conflict and began to advance on Vilna from the west, and at this time, Lenin's government announced that it would recognize Lithuania as an independent state.

By the 10th, the Poles had been pushed back to their April starting point. On the 11th, the Reds took Minsk.

At Vilna, however, the Poles put up strong resistance and hard fighting raged for several days. The Reds, however, were able to surround Vilna and the Poles were cut off from their supplies. The Poles broke out of the city at considerable expense in men and material and the city then fell to the Reds and Lithuanians on the 14th. The announcement soon came from Moscow that Vilna would be given to the Lithuanians.

Now, the Poles were retreating toward Warsaw.

THE SPA CONFERENCE

On July 4, the premiers of the leading Allied governments met with German representatives at Spa, Belgium, to discuss various matters, including the crisis in Poland.

Spa was chosen because it had been the Kaiser's headquarters for a greater part of the Great War and was, therefore, a place of honor to the Germans. By meeting with the Germans in Spa, and, as anticipated, insisting that they live up to the dictates in the Versailles Peace Treaty, the Allies hoped to destroy the favorable image the Germans had of Spa.

NUREMBERG

After WW II, the Allies held the well-publicized Nazi war crimes trials in Nuremberg to diminish the favorable image the Germans had of that city, which had been the site of many Nazi Party rallies. Furthermore, the Nazis had often touted Nuremberg as a "Nazi city."

Lloyd George, Millerand, and Foch had met beforehand, and, in a rare show of unity, agreed upon an agenda for the Spa meeting. This was that the Poles should give up Vilna and the territory they had conquered in Belorussia and the Ukraine, that neither France nor Britain would send much in the way of military aid to Poland, and that the Poles should seek peace with the Bolsheviks.

This was not what Polish Premier Grabsky had hoped to hear but he had no other options.

British Foreign Secretary Curzon suggested a new boundary between Poland and Russia which, in his opinion, was fair and reasonable. It provided for an en-larged and independent Lithuania which included Vilna, along with a generous span of Polish territory east of Warsaw. On the 17th, the Spa proposals were rejected outright by Lenin who suggested direct negotiations with the Poles without the mediation of a third party. Here was a hint that the Soviets did not intend to conquer all of Poland and charge on into Germany. It was a positive sign for the West.

On the 21st, the Western Allies announced that they would send an Inter-Allied Control Commission to Poland to put pressure on Poland to seek peace.

The Polish-Soviet conflict was not the only issue on the agenda at Spa. German reparations were discussed, and still, no total could be agreed upon, but it was agreed that, whatever that total would be, France would get 52%, Britain 22%, Italy 10%, Belgium 8%, and the remainder divided among the lesser powers. Eventually an amount was agreed to: 132 billion gold marks of which France would get 83.8 billion. These were enormous sums of money in 1920.

Another topic discussed at Spa was the delivery of coal that was to be sent to France by Germany under the provisions of the peace treaty. Those deliveries were well behind schedule. The Germans made excuses but the French threatened to march deeper into Germany if the Germans would not agree to increase coal deliveries. In the end, the Germans promised to deliver two million tons of coal per month to France. This figure proved to be unattainable. The best the Germans could do was 1.2 million tons per month.

General Seeckt was at Spa and emphasized that Germany would very likely become the bulwark against the Bolsheviks, depending on what happened In Poland. In this respect, he demanded that the strength of the German army be increased from the mandated 100,000 to 200,000 members. The Allies rejected this demand outright and insisted that the deadline for the German Army to be at the 100,000 level on January 1, 1921 be observed.

The Germans left the conference with nothing but more and renewed demands that they live up the peace treaty. Throughout Germany, the Spa Conference was branded as another great insult to the German people and an example of the ongoing oppression being conducted against Germany by the Allies.

On July 15, as the Spa Conference was coming to an end, Hitler spoke to an audience of 1200 people at the Hofbrauhaus in Munich. He railed against the injustices heaped upon the Germans at Spa, saying "...the hour of vengeance tolls." It was another reference to *Der Tag*.

A USELESS PLEBISCITE

On July 11, a plebiscite was taken in the Allenstein and Marienwerder areas in the southwestern part of East Prussia. The issue was that of joining Poland or remaining with Germany. The area in question composed about 30% of East Prussian territory and was the homeland of a great part of Germany's elite Junker community, which considered itself the most German of the Germans. The vote was overwhelming: 97.9% in favor of remaining with Germany. Anyone could see this coming.

THE "KAGA"

In Japan, they laid the keel for another aircraft carrier, the "Kaga" (a province of Japan). Construction was delayed and the ship was not commissioned until March 1928.

THE KAGA IN ACTION

The Kaga was first used in combat during the Japanese invasion of China in the summer of 1937. Later, it participated in the attack on Pearl Harbor in December 1941, operated in the Indian Ocean against the British during the first half of 1942, and was sunk by the Americans at Midway in June 1942.

IN THE US, THE ELECTION CAMPAIGN

In the US, Harding, Coolidge, Cox, Roosevelt, and many others were on the campaign trail and the Democrats had a new campaign song "The League of Nations Song."

On July 18, candidates Cox and Roosevelt paid the obligatory visit to the White House. There, they witnessed firsthand, and for the first time, the decrepit condition of the President. Wilson conducted the session from a wheelchair.

The meeting was cold and formal. Cox and Roosevelt knew that Wilson would not do much to advance their campaign.

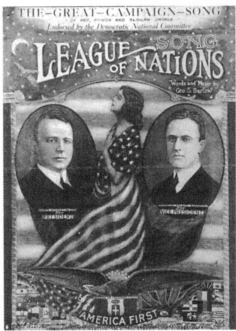

The sheet music of the Democrat's new campaign song.

The Democrats had another liability, the 18th Amendment — it had happened on their watch and the public was beginning to become disenchanted with the whole concept of prohibition. And it was known that both Cox and Roosevelt enjoyed a libation now and then.

THE CHILDREN'S HOUR

When Franklin Roosevelt became President, he developed a daily routine which included cocktails — martinis mostly — at five PM. He called it "the children's hour."

About this time, another Presidential candidate entered the race. He was prisoner #9653 at the Federal penitentiary in Atlanta — Eugene Debs. He was running on the Socialist Party ticket.

BACK TO THE POLISH-BOLSHEVIK WAR

On July 15, the German dock workers in Danzig went on strike, thus closing one of the supply routes into Poland.

On July 22, the Reds captured the city of Grodno. Warsaw was only 150 miles away. The next day, Tukhachevsky issued orders for the attack on Warsaw. And he set a deadline for the city's capture — August 12.

On July 23, the Poles asked the Soviets for a peace conference, but Moscow was not ready yet. The military operations were greatly in their favor. That same day, the Grabsky government fell and was replaced by one headed by Wincenty Witos, another close associate of Pilsudski.

At Warsaw, the Poles were digging in and putting up stiff rear guard actions to slow the Reds' advance.

On the 25th, the Inter-Allied Commission reached Warsaw. There was little it could do.

On the 26th, the German announced their neutrality in the Polish-Soviet conflict, but this was just a cover. Behind the scenes, the Germans, with Seeckt's full approval, began to feel out the Soviets for future German-Soviet military cooperation.

On the 28th, the Czechs took advantage of Poland's weaknesses and sent their troops into the disputed territory of Teschen. The French and Italian troops occupying the area did not interfere. But, on one hand, the Czechs taketh and with the other hand, they giveth. At the same time they entered Teschen, the Czechs sent a large part of their army into Slovakia, the eastern part of their country, to guard against a possible Soviet invasion across their northern border. They also allowed some arms to flow to the Poles through Slovakia, aided Polish refugees, and arrested some leftist agitators.

If the Reds tried to cross into Czechoslovakia, the Czechs would fight.

On the 29th, in Poland, there was a major clash between Polish and Red forces at the village of Lohza northeast of Warsaw. At this point, the Reds halted their advance. They needed to resupply and regroup for the final advance on Warsaw.

On July 31, the Reds responded to the Polish peace offer of the 23rd. They did not reject it; they demanded a postponement. In the West, there was hope that this was another indication that the Reds would not go beyond Warsaw.

A DARK TIME FOR THE MUSLIMS

In Paris, the French concluded that they had to take action against the troublesome and incompetent Faisal regime and activate the mandate over Syria given to them at the San Remo Conference. That agreement authorized the French to use force if necessary. Since Faisal was creating troubles for the British in Mesopotamia, London gave its tacit approval for the French to act in Syria.

The French then issued King Faisal an ultimatum to accept the French mandate or face the consequences. The King rejected the ultimatum, and the French advance on Damascus began during the third week in July from their stronghold in The Lebanon.

Faisal's small and poorly-equipped army met the French on the road to Damascus, a clash ensued at Khan Maysalun, twenty miles west of Damascus, and the Syrians were forced into retreat. On the 24th, the French occupied Damascus. Faisal, his family, and some of his closest aides fled into Palestine and eventually made their way to Egypt and then to Italy. All of this was done with the aid and protection of the British. In the process, Faisal, once again, became a British pawn.

The French force that occupied Damascus was comprised mostly of Moroccans, Algerians, and black Africans and many in the Middle East saw this as an affront to Islam by using Muslims against Muslims. In the weeks that followed, the French occupied the rest of Syria and began restructuring the area as they saw fit. They divided the area into two mandates, one for The Lebanon and the other for Syria. They also drew the new boundaries of Lebanon which gave that country a generous amount of territory which included the disputed Biqa Valley to the east, the ports of Tyre, Sidon, and Tripoli, and the territory in the south all the way to the yet-to-be-defined border with Palestine. With these actions, the French created a new state that was dominated by Christians but contained hundreds of thousands of Muslims.

In Turkey, the war with Greece was not going well. The Greeks seized the city of Brusa on July 9 and the city of Adrainople, in Thrace, on the 25th.

Throughout the Muslim community in the Middle East, it was a dark time. The French had placed The Lebanon under the Christians, the British were placing Palestine under the Jews, Faisal's regime in Damascus had been wiped out, the British had occupied Constantinople, the Sultan was about to be presented with a humiliating and oppressive peace treaty, and there was a growing insurrection in Mesopotamia. To add to their hatred for the West, the word mandate in Arabic translated into "domination."

THE TREATY OF SEVRES

On August 10, 1920, the Turkish Sultan's representatives signed the peace treaty with the Allies under very degrading circumstances. The ceremony was low key and took place in the showroom of a porcelain factory in the Paris suburb of Sevres. The Turkish delegation, which was treated very rudely, was headed by the Sultan's premier, Damad Ferid. The "Treaty of Sevres," as it became known, was very lopsided and was, in reality, a treaty between the great powers of Europe and a man under house arrest in his royal palace in Constantinople. The real ruler of what remained of Turkey, Mustafa Kemal, was not represented at Sevres. Kemal's response to the Treaty of Sevres was that it was a sham and totally invalid because he claimed that the Sultan was a prisoner of the Allies and was unable to act freely.

Nevertheless, the Allies forged ahead using the Treaty to justify their actions. The Treaty gave both France and Italy spheres of influence within Turkey, confirmed the centuries-old system of foreign concessions in Turkey known as the Capitulations, internationalized the Straits, and gave Greece western Thrace and the Smyrna area and most of the formerly-owned Turkish islands in the Aegean Sea. The Treaty stipulated that within five years, plebiscites were to be conducted in western Thrace and Smyrna.

The French sphere of influence was to extend northward from Syria some 200 miles and to within 50 miles of the Black Sea. The Italians' sphere included the entire southern coast of Turkey and extend inland 150 miles northward into central Anatolia and then 200 miles inland in western Anatolia to border with the international zone in the Straits area.

Turkey was to retain eastern Thrace, its capital city of Constantinople, and what remained of Anatolia.

The Treaty required Turkey to recognize Armenia as an independent state and that the border between Turkey and Armenia was to be established at a later date.

And the Kurds of eastern Turkey were to be given a large measure of autonomy.

Section IX of the Treaty confirmed the distribution of most of the former Turkish empire in the Middle-East which had already been decided upon and distributed.

The Turks were also required to recognize the French mandates over Syria and Lebanon, the Britain mandates over Palestine and Mesopotamia, and to affirm that the Kingdom of Hijaz was to be granted independence. Turkey was also required to renounce all territorial claims in Egypt, Sudan, Cyprus, Libya, Tunisia, and Morocco. Some of these claims went back hundreds of years.

With regard to the vital Turkish Straits, they were to remain under Turkish sovereignty, but in addition to being internationalized, were to be demilitarized and opened to all the world's seaborne traffic, including warships in both peace and war. A League of Nations Commission, consisting of representatives from ten nations, was to be established to oversee the management of the Straits.

The Turkish military was drastically reduced to the point where it became a self-defense force and a force capable of only maintaining internal order.

Just as had happened in Germany, Bulgaria, and Hungary, the Sultan's government decreed several days of national mourning after the Treaty was signed.

In the secret Allied negotiations that were conducted before the Treaty was finalized, the Allies' military leaders warned the political leaders that the Treaty was unenforceable. In one estimate, the military leaders estimated that it would take 27 army divisions to enforce the Treaty — a force that the Allies no longer commanded.

THE BOLSHEVIKS ADVANCE DEEP INTO POLAND

In Poland, the Reds were steadily advancing toward Warsaw, but the Poles were putting up a very determined resistance. Days earlier, the Reds crossed the Bug River, but were thrown back by a strong Polish counterattack. They crossed the river again but their advance was stopped at Sokolow only 50 miles northeast of Warsaw. Red military successes were, for the most part, accomplished by overwhelming numbers and not by military skills. By now, the Red army consisted of many conscripts and a large number of non-commissioned officers (NCOs) who had served in the Tsar's army and been forced to serve in the Red Army because of a chronic shortage of NCOs.

Following the Red Army was a "Provisional Polish Revolutionary Committee" (Polrevkom) ready to take political control in Warsaw when the city was captured. Under the auspices of Polrevkom, the nucleus of a future communist Polish army had been formed out of Polish units serving in the Red Army and Polish prisoners of war willing to serve Polrevkom. That army-to-be waited in Minsk.

Also following the Red Army was the "Galician Revolutionary Committee" (Galrevkom) which hoped to establish a new soviet republic in the western part of the Ukraine — Petlura's domain. The new republic was to be known as the "Galician Soviet Socialist Republic."

THE LUBLIN GOVERNMENT

When the Red Army took Warsaw in 1944, they had a ready-made Polish communist government that took control in the Polish capital. It was known as the "Lublin Government" because it had been formed originally in the city of Lublin. That government formally took control in Warsaw on January 5, 1945, and the Soviet Union recognized it as the legitimate government of Poland. The Western Allies had, all along, recognized the Polish-Government-in-Exile in London. Therefore, this became one of the issues that would help bring about the Cold War.

In Moscow, the astute political and military leaders around Lenin could see that the Red army was stressed to its limit, and considering the strength of the Polish opposition and the growing problems at home, the Red Army might not be able to take Warsaw.

Lenin believed what he was told, and within a short while, called for a renewal of the peace talks with Poland. Their chief negotiator this time would be a high-level official, Georgi Chicherin, the Commissar for Foreign Affairs. On August 9, Chicherin sent word to the Poles through neutral sources that Moscow wanted to talk and that terms for a proposed armistice would be forthcoming. The Poles soon received those terms, and a series of back-and-forth negotiations developed between Warsaw and Moscow. Meanwhile, the Red advance crept forward, and on August 10th, reached the

environs of Warsaw. The Reds had three armies, while the Poles had only one, but the Poles were hastily reconstituting their Second Army, which had been disbanded after the battle for Kiev. To build the Second Army the Polish government called for volunteers age 17 through 42 with officers being accepted up to 50. Also formed was a "Citizens Watch" organization to serve behind the lines. Furthermore, Polish boat owners along the Vistula were organized to perform military chores if asked to do so.

These efforts soon produced enough volunteers so that the Polish force reached an estimated 737,000 men. And, supplies, though small, were still arriving steadily from the West.

Upon reaching the outskirts of Warsaw, the Reds halted to prepare for the final assault on the city. On the maps it looked as though Poland was doomed.

And in Europe's capitals, it was never forgotten that from Warsaw, it was only a ten-days march to Berlin.

Unbeknownst to most in Europe, however, the Red armies were, by this time, nearly spent. There were shortages of many military supplies, desertions were increasing, and there were internal conflicts between commanders.

On August 13, the foreign diplomatic corps began to leave Warsaw for Poznan where the Polish government was expected to take refuge if ousted from Warsaw.

Elsewhere in Poland, however, the Reds were still advancing. On the 15th, they laid siege to Lvov, 200 miles southeast of Warsaw and only 75 miles from the Czech border. Two days later, in the north, the Reds cut the main railroad line between Warsaw and Danzig.

As for armistice negotiation, both sides promptly agreed to talk and a meeting was set for the 17th in Minsk.

In Poland the weather was misty and overcast, which limited the use of reconnaissance aircraft for both sides. Therefore, neither side had reliable intelligence about the other. Clashes on the ground were more by chance than by design.

August 14 was a day of bitter fighting around Warsaw, often hand-to-hand but the Poles held their own. Pilsudski was encouraged.

On the 15th, he launched a counterattack which pushed the Reds back toward the suburb of Radzymin. The next day, the Poles attacked again and pushed the Reds back again. This advance cut the Bolshevik's line of supply, and, at the same time, the Poles captured a large number of the Reds' artillery pieces. The tide of battle was turning.

The Poles attacked again on the 17th and the Reds showed more signs of weakening.

That same day, the 17th, the Polish armistice commission arrived at Minsk but it was promptly locked in a room by its ungracious host until the results of the battle at Warsaw were known.

On the 18th, the issue was decided. The Poles launched yet another attack and the Reds fell back again and began to show signs of disintegrating. Seeing what was happening, Tukhachevski ordered a general retreat in order to save what was left of his armies. Warsaw was saved and this epoch battle would go into the history books as the "Miracle on the Vistula."

The Poles followed up their victory quickly, and with skill and vigor. On the 19th, they reached Ciechanow and on the 20th they took Ostroleka and Bielsk. The advance continued, and on the 22nd and 23rd the Poles succeeded in nearly encircling the Red's IV Army which was cut to pieces when it tried to withdraw.

To the north and south of Warsaw, the Reds also retreated. In some places the retreat turned into a route. In the north

many Red soldiers fled into East Prussia and were interned by the Germans.

Of the five Red Armies that began the campaign in early July, one had been destroyed, two decimated, and two badly mutilated.

The Poles gathered in 66,000 POWs and the Red suffered an estimated 40,000 dead and wounded.

In Moscow and the various field headquarters, the Red leaders began to blame each other. Trotsky blamed Stalin, Stalin blamed Trotsky, Tukhachevski blamed Budennyi, and Voroshilov who, together, blamed Tukhachevski. Everyone blamed Kamenev. Lenin had not only lost his western army but its command structure as well. In the capitals of Western Europe, there was elation but also indecision. What to do next? Some western leaders wanted, now, to actively support the Poles. Some die-hard militarists wanted to declare war on Soviet Russia, march on Moscow, and destroy the communist menace once and for all. Still others advised doing nothing. In the long run, it was the latter view that prevailed.

In Poland, there were hard feelings against the western allies, especially the French. And many in the West responded in kind. Pilsudski was not hailed as a great hero but rather as a greedy and inept leader who had sparked a war that he could not win.

But there was euphoria in Poland, and at various places around the country, there were sightings of the Virgin Mary which confirmed that the victory at Warsaw had been the will of God.

At Minsk, the Polish peace delegation was released from confinement and peace negotiations got underway. They would be arduous and slow and a final peace treaty would not be signed until March 1921. In the meantime, sporadic fighting between the Poles and Reds continued.

On hand in Warsaw to witness the Miracle on the Vistula were two members of the French military mission who would play significant roles in the next war: General Maxime Weygand and Major Charles de Gaulle. The Poles were very impressed with de Gaulle and offered him a high rank in their army, but he declined.

THE RED SCARE SUBSIDED

For all of Europe, the Polish Miracle on the Vistula greatly reduced the Red Scare for the foreseeable future. That being the case, the Europeans could now direct their attentions to other matters. In Germany, that meant that much more attention could be given to *Der Tag*.

CHAPTER 24
ON TO
DER TAG

||||||||||||||||||||||||||||||||||||||||||||||||||||||||||||||||||||||||||||||||||||||||||||||||||||||||||||||||||||

SEPTEMBER 5, 1920: In a speech, Hitler declared, "We are tied and gagged. But even though we are defenseless, we do not fear a war with France!"

MID-SEPTEMBER 1920: A series of powerful and prolonged strikes begin again in Italy.

SEPTEMBER 16, 1920: A bomb exploded on Wall Street in New York City. Thirty people were killed and 300 injured. Mario Buda, an Italian immigrant, was charged with the crime.

MID-SEPTEMBER 1920: In Turkey, Kemal's forces launched a major attack on the Armenians in the northeastern part of the country. The Armenian Army was no match for the Turks and began a series of retreats that would not end until November.

SEPTEMBER 21, 1920: Polish-Soviet talks resumed, this time in Riga, Latvia. An armistice was the first order of the day.

LATE SEPTEMBER/OCTOBER, 1920: Poles continued their advance into Russia and won major victors at the Nieman River and Wlodzimierz.

EARLY OCTOBER 1920: Hitler began a two-weeks speaking tour in Austria, the land of his birth, on behalf of the Austrian Nazis who were campaigning for a coming election. That election, held on October 17, brought forth a strong right-wing government and it was generally agreed that Hitler's efforts had helped. All of this helped Hitler acquire more speaking engagements which, in turn, increased his notoriety.

In eastern Europe, the Poles continued their eastward advance and soon crossed the line which had been proposed by the British as the future boundary between Poland and Soviet Russia.

OCTOBER 6, 1920: On this day, the Polish and Soviet representatives meeting at Riga, Latvia, agreed to an armistice. By this time, Tukhachevsky's retreat had deteriorated into a route.

OCTOBER 9, 1920: A Polish force under General Lucien Zeligowski, seized Vilna and much of Lithuania from the disintegrating Soviet forces. This was a direct violation of the soon-to-be-signed armistice but Warsaw labeled Zeligowski's force as a renegade organization over which they had no control. This was an out-and-out lie and everyone knew it, but the Poles stuck with their story and the Reds were too weak to do nothing about it.

In the West, this action was all but ignored. Throughout Europe, there was universal joy in that the Bolsheviks had finally been defeated. The threat of communist hoards charging into Europe was now eliminated for the foreseeable future.

OCTOBER 12, 1920: Poland and Soviet Russia signed an armistice at Riga. The cease fire line was drawn along the line of the Poles current military position with a 15 Km neutral zone between the opposing forces.

MIDNIGHT, OCTOBER 18, 1920: The Poles and Reds began to honor a ceasefire agreed to by both sides. Talks soon began at Riga on a formal peace agreement.

LATE OCTOBER-EARLY NOVEMBER, 1920: The Red Army was still strong in the Crimea and continued to push back Wrangel's forces.

In the US, election campaigning was at its peak and the polls showed that the Democrats were trailing badly. Ethnicity had become a big factor. The Wilson administration had simply alienated too many ethnic groups: the Irish, Germans, Italians, Poles, Chinese, and Armenians. Plus, there was creeping inflation and the Administration was seen as weak in dealing with labor.

Cox and Roosevelt tried to offset these losses by attacking the "old guard" of the Republican-controlled Senate for rejecting the Versailles Treaty and the League of Nations.

Roosevelt, in touting his experience in foreign affairs, made an offhand remark that he had written Haiti's new constitution. This was not true and the Republicans pounced on this and made it a major campaign. Roosevelt also made uncomplimentary remarks against some of the hyphenated Americans and at one point called Italian-Americans "50-50 citizens." This young and handsome man with a famous name had a few things to learn yet about politics.

The Republicans, sensing victory, straddled many issues, including the Versailles Treaty and the League of Nations. As would be expected, they attacked Wilson for all of his shortcomings and failures. Harding did little traveling and remained at home in Marion, Ohio. Delegation after delegation came to see him. All of this was reported in the media and he, and others, made the point that the US should return to its historic mind-your-own-business roots, and in touting that thought, made generous use of the word normalcy.

By the end of the month, odds-makers were giving ten-to-one in favor of a Republican victory.

The odds-makers were right. On election day, November 2, it was a landslide, with the Republicans winning 37 of the 48 states. Roosevelt lost his home state of New York and New York City.

Along with their victory, the Republicans won larger majorities in both the House of Representatives and the Senate. Political liberalism in the US was all but dead — America had moved to the right.

For the brooding and wheelchair-bound President, there was some good news. He was informed that he had won the Nobel Peace Prize for 1919. The prize was formally presented to him on December 9, 1920.

NOVEMBER 3, 1920: There was much celebrating in Germany at Wilson's defeat.

NOVEMBER 11, 1920, was the second anniversary of the end of the Great War. In France, an elaborate ceremony at the Arc de Triomphe to bury France's unknown soldier was held. All of the major French dignitaries were in attendance except for Clemenceau.

That same day, President-elect Harding made a speech in Brownsville, Texas, saying that the US would back away from Wilsonianism. He said the US had fought the Great War to protect American rights but not to make the world safe for democracy.

NOVEMBER 12, 1920: The major powers met at Rapallo, Italy, to settle some outstanding problems. Among other things, the border between Italy and Jugoslavia was fixed and it was agreed that the city of Fiume would become a free city but under the supervision of Italy; the surrounding territory would go to Jugoslavia. *Il Popolo* supported the Rapallo decisions. In Fiume, D'Annunzio, who had not been invited to Rapallo, rejected the settlement.

NOVEMBER 15, 1920: The League of Nations held its first meeting in its new home of Geneva, Switzerland. Membership, at this time, consisted of 41 nations.

MID-NOVEMBER 1920: During the second week in November, a massive evacuation began in the Crimea, as tens of thousands of Russian Whites and their families evacuated by sea. This was, for the most part, an orderly multi-national effort that included over 200 ships. Before it ended, 145,000 people had been evacuated. The Reds followed up their conquest with a horrible bloodbath against those who were not fortunate enough to escape. This marked the end of the Russian Revolution. The Bolsheviks were in control of all of Russia and most of the former Tsarist empire. The Revolution had lasted three years and nine days.

On November 25, Lenin announced the reduction of the Red Army by two and one-half million men. It was now time to start building the communist utopia.

NOVEMBER 1920: In the Middle East, the brief but bloody war between the Turks and Armenians ended. On November 17, an armistice was signed, leaving Armenia a small but independent nation. The Turks had conquered the territories that they had claimed were theirs.

In December, the Bolsheviks took over Armenia and made it a part of the Soviet Union, renaming it the "Soviet Republic of Armenia."

DECEMBER 1, 1920, D'Annunzio declared war on Italy over the Rapallo decision. Italian forces gathered at the border with Fiume and on the 24th, the Italians shelled the city. This was enough to end the war, and on the 31st, Italian troops occupied Fiume. D'Annunzio surrendered but was still hailed throughout Italy as a hero. The edicts of Rapallo were then put into place and Fiume became a free city under Italian supervision.

LATE DECEMBER 1920: In the US, Attorney General Palmer resumed his "Red raids," arresting scores of aliens suspected of having communist sympathies, and on December 28, deportations began anew.

Also in the US, the American public was better informed than it had ever been before, because now, many families had an RCA radio music box. They cost about $10.

DECEMBER 1920: In Munich, the Nazis bought the local newspaper, *Munchener Beobachter*, with the intention of making it a nationwide publication and the voice of the Party. This was made possible with secret funds funneled to the Party from the German Army. The paper which, at this time, had 11,000 subscribers, was renamed *Volkischer Beobachter* and Hitler's close associate, Dietrich Eckart, became its editor. Now, both Hitler and Mussolini had national newspapers.

At Christmas time, the Nazis held a party. It would become an annual affair and Hitler would no longer spend Christmases alone. The Nazi Party now had over 3000 members. In Italy, the Fascist Party had over 20,000 members.

END 1920: By this time, thousands of Ford Model T automobiles were on the streets of Germany. The Ford Motor Co. of Detroit, Michigan, was now producing and selling half of the world's automobiles. Hitler and many others were annoyed by this — seeing their people drive about in foreign-made vehicles. They rightfully believed that German industry was capable of producing a reliable, low-priced automobile for the German volk and that that should become a national goal for Germany.

Of all the baby boys born in Germany during the year 1920, 36.64% of them would perish in World War II.

JANUARY 3, 1921: The first issue of the new Nazi Party newspaper, the *Volkischer Beobachter*, appeared. In it was a poem written by Adolf Hitler which ended, "You must make a supreme effort, and bury the Jews!" The newspaper also carried the announcement of Hitler's next speech.

The next issue of the *Volkischer Beobachter* appeared on January 7 with a large-type article on the front page entitled, "Take the Jews into protective custody, then there will be peace in our country."

JANUARY 7, 1921: The Polish Army was ordered to stand down to a peacetime

basis for the first in its history. Soon afterwards, Pilsudksi went to Paris to negotiate a new treaty of friendship with France.

JANUARY 22, 1921: The Allies announced that Germany's reparation bill would be 216 billion gold marks with payments scheduled up to 1963.

FEBRUARY 17, 1921: In the Caucasus, the Red Army invaded independent Georgia and occupied its capital, Tiflis, on the 25th. Months earlier, Lenin's government had recognized Georgia's independence. Now the world was learning the true value of treaties with the Soviets.

By the end of the month, all of the Caucasus, and its rich oil resources, were under Red control.

To allay fears of further Soviet expansionism in the region, Moscow initiated talks with Persia, Turkey, Afghanistan, and Outer Mongolia for treaties of friendship. Those countries had few options but to agree to the talks.

In Persia, Colonel Reza Shah Pahlavi, commander of the elite Persian Cossack Brigade, overthrew the existing government. In this effort, he had British support. Pahlavi would still be in control of Iran (Persia) when WW II started, but by then, he had changed his loyalty from Britain to Germany.

FEBRUARY 19, 1921: France and Poland signed a secret military convention. The convention would still be in force in September 1939 when Germany invaded Poland.

FEBRUARY 23, 1921: In Munich, the Nazis held their largest public meeting to date. They rented a hall that held 6000 people and 6500 showed up and paid one mark each admission. Hitler spoke for two-and-a-half hours, railing against the reparations figure recently announced, the French in the Rhineland, the British in Ireland and India and, of course, the Jews. Hitler later wrote, "After the first hour, the applause began to interrupt me in greater and greater spontaneous outbursts...." Hitler was carving a larger niche for himself in German politics.

Hitler scheduled two more meetings in the same hall and each was a resounding success.

FEBRUARY 1921: During February 1921, Mussolini's Fascist Party began moving noticeably to the political right by openly courting the Italian upper and middle classes and issues of interest to them.

As for labor, the Party created its own labor organization that would toe the Party line and, hopefully, weaken the appeal of the old line unions.

Also during the month, Lloyd George transferred Churchill from Minister of War and Air to the post of Colonial Secretary.

MARCH 4, 1921: In the US, Warren Harding was inaugurated as the President of the United States. Herbert Hoover became his Secretary of Commerce. Franklin Roosevelt lost his position as Assistant Secretary of the Navy and went into the private business sector as vice-president of the Fidelity and Deposit Company of Maryland, heading up their New York office. He was still highly respected in the Democrat Party and still seen as a leader of its progressive wing.

Former President Wilson remained in Washington and moved into a small bungalow on S Street. He was a bitter and broken man. He brooded over his defeat, was bitter toward the American public for not supporting him, still saw himself as the leader of the Democrat Party, had recurring mood swings, never admitted his mistakes, refused interviews, and still harbored hopes for a comeback in 1924.

MARCH 16, 1921: Britain and Soviet Russia signed their long-considered trade

agreement. There were benefits for both parties. Britain had a new, and gigantic customer, as well as a source for raw materials, while the Soviets had access to western technology and manufactured goods, and a significant measure of political recognition by one of the world's major powers. For Lenin, the timing was most beneficial because the Soviet economy was not responding well to his communist economic theories.

MARCH 18, 1921: On this date, Poland and Soviet Russia signed a peace agreement at Riga, Latvia. That agreement became known as the "Treaty of Riga." It ended the Polish-Soviet war and settled the boundary between the two nations in Poland's favor.

MARCH 21, 1921: In troubled Upper Selesia, the League of Nations-dictated plebiscite was taken and the results were predictable. The German majorities in their home districts voted for union with Germany while the Poles in their home districts voted to join Poland. Essentially, the plebiscite settled nothing and the issue was now thrown back to the League of Nations.

MARCH 22, 1921: Germany defaulted on a one billion mark reparations payment.

MARCH 23, 1921: In Italy, things were going so well for Mussolini that he wrote in *Il Popolo*, "In a few months the whole of Italy will be in our hands." And this prediction would come to pass.

APRIL 1921: By now, it had become obvious to Lenin and the other Bolshevik leaders that orthodox communist economic theories were unworkable. The workers could not run their factories, the bureaucracy was mushrooming and become unwieldy, discipline in the armed forces was melting away, the peasants were not producing and delivering food, there was banditry in the countryside, unemployment and famine were widespread, and an economy without money and taxes simply did not work.

It was a very bitter pill for the communist leaders to accept, but they had to act. The result was the "New Economic Plan" (NEP), a drastic overhaul of the communist system under the guise of progressive reform. In reality, it was simply a return, in a very large measure, to the capitalist system that had prevailed before the communists came to power.

Money was printed, factory managers were returned to their posts, officers regained authority within the armed forces, a large measure of private enterprise was permitted, relief was accepted from the West, amnesty was granted to rebels if they promised to return to the farms and produce food, and taxes were re-introduced.

Lenin, reluctant to place blame on communism's cockamamie economic theories, blamed the war. He told the 10th Party Congress "The transition from war to peace confronted us with a whole number of difficulties and problems, and we had neither the experience, the training, nor the requisite material to overcome them."

The implementation of the NEP would take years and have to be directed from above which, with time, gave the rulers in the Kremlin strong dictatorial powers — powers that Stalin would inherit.

APRIL 1921: The League of Nations and Britain agreed that Palestine would be divided into two parts. The land west of the Jordan River would be known as Palestine, subject to the edicts of the Balfour Declaration and other agreements reached regarding the Jews. East of the Jordan River, a future Arab Emirate would be created, known as "Trans-Jordan." It would be an all-Arab state and would come into effect in September 1923 with Prince Abdullah, the second son of the King of Hijaz and Faisal's older brother becoming King. The chief British negotiator for this arrangement was Lloyd George's new Colonial Secretary, Winston Churchill.

MAY 4, 1921: French troops occupied the German Ruhr in response to Germany's default on the recent reparations payment. They remained in the area until the end of September 1921 after Germany had promised — once again — to make reparations payments.

MAY 1921: In Italy, Mussolini's new policy of supporting the upper and middle classes, the industrialists, and the landowners, had paid off. During the month, a national election was held and Mussolini and 34 other members of the Fascist Party were elected to the Chamber of Deputies.

Also during May, an election was held in Ulster, now being called "Northern Ireland," and Ulster Unionists won a large majority in the new Parliament. Belfast was chosen as the new capital. This arrangement was ratified by a treaty in December 1921 in which Northern Ireland remained a part of Great Britain and southern Ireland, known as the Irish Free State, became a dominion within the British Empire. In the Free State, however, the political leaders were at odds with each other and an internal crisis, sometimes bloody, continued for over a year.

JUNE 1921: In Turkey, Kemal reached an agreement with the Italians to withdraw from southern Turkey. In return, the Italians got several more islands in the Aegean Sea.

JULY 2, 1921: In the US, President Harding signed a separate peace treaty with Germany. On August 25, the Germans ratified the treaty and the Great War between the US and Germany ended.

JULY 29, 1921: After an internal power struggle, Hitler took control of the Nazi Party. The vote of the assembled party members at this crucial meeting was 553 to 1. Drexler was relegated to a secondary position and Hitler soon eliminated the democratic structure within the Party and made it a totalitarian organization under his absolute command. In 1933, Hitler would do the same with Germany — he would be democratically elected to power and then destroy the democratic system.

JULY 30, 1921: The day after Hitler took control of the Nazi Party, he wrote a memo to one of his associates and signed it, for the first time, "der Fuehrer der NSDAP." Within a short time, party members began greeting their new Fuehrer with the word "heil," adopted from the Austrian Nazi Party which had been using the greeting for some time. And from that day forward, the Nazi Party's executive committee never met again.

MID-AUGUST 1921: Franklin Roosevelt, while at his summer home at Campobello, New Brunswick, contracted polio. It left him crippled for life and barely able to walk. He was 39.

AUGUST 23, 1921: In Mesopotamia, the British occupiers and the local political leaders reached an agreement. Faisal, the deposed King of Syria and a direct descendent of the Prophet Muhammad, became King of Mesopotamia and the country became a British protectorate.

AUGUST 29, 1921: The US signed separate peace treaties with Austria and Hungary, thus ending the Great War with those two nations.

OCTOBER 20, 1921: On this date, France and Turkey signed the "Treaty of Angora" which concluded peace with Kemal's regime. It also established the border between Turkey and Syria to Turkey's benefit.

NOVEMBER 7, 1921: In Italy, Mussolini took unto himself a new title, "Duce" (leader — of the Fascist Party) because the titles President and Chairman had no place in Fascist ideology. They were words used by democracies.

NOVEMBER 1921: Early in the month, Hitler restructured the paramilitary wing of the Nazi Party and renamed it the *"Sturmabteilungen"* (Storm Troopers or SA).

In Turkey, Kemal's Grand National Assembly voted to eliminate the Sultanate. The road was then open for Turkey to become a republic.

DECEMBER 13, 1921: In the US, the Washington Naval Conference ended, which set limits on naval strengths in the Pacific for Japan, Britain, the US, and France.

DECEMBER 1921: In Russia, a terrible famine was developing in which many would die. The League on Nations refused to send aid, blaming the famine on the failure of the communist economic system. A famine was also well under way in China.

During the month of December, the US established a consulate in Munich. Now, reliable information with regard to the Nazi Party would reach Washington.

By the end of the year, membership in Mussolini's Fascist Party reached 248,000, up from 20,000 at the end of 1920. The Fascist Party was now a major force in Italian politics.

Also, by the end of the year, the Berlin government reached a secret understanding with the Bolsheviks that German troops would be able to train secretly in Soviet Russia in exchange for German technical assistance.

Of all the baby boys born in Germany during 1921, 38.95% would perish in World War II.

FEBRUARY 4, 1922: A Sino-Japanese accord restored Shantung Province to China.

FEBRUARY 6, 1922: In Washington, an international agreement was reached to forbid submarines from sinking merchant ships in wartime, to outlaw the use of poison gas, and for the next fourteen years, to ban fortification in the Aleutian Islands.

FEBRUARY 26, 1922: Britain and France agree to extend their military alliance for 20 years — until 1942.

MARCH 20 — JUNE 4, 1922: US-German negotiations reduced American strength in the Rhineland to 1000 troops. American troops began leaving in January 1923 to bring their strength down to that number.

APRIL 16, 1922: German and Soviets representatives signed their own Treaty of Rapallo, which had nothing to do with the Allied Treaty of Rapallo of November 1920. Under this agreement, the Germans and Soviets agreed to extend diplomatic recognition to each other, renounce mutual debts, and grant Germany favorable trade concessions within Soviet Russia. Thus, Germany became the first major western nation to formally recognize Soviet Russia.

MAY 26, 1922: Lenin suffered a stroke that paralyzed his right arm and leg and slurred his speech. But he remained at the helm of the Soviet empire.

AUGUST 1, 1922: In Italy, Mussolini's Black Shirts were now so powerful that they were able to crush a massive Socialist-led general strike in Milan, Genoa, and Livonia.

AUGUST-SEPTEMBER 1922: In Turkey, Kemal's forces drove the last elements of the Greek invaders out of western Turkey. Kemal was now the master of the Turkish heartland and on October 11, 1922, an armistice was signed between the two parties. By now, Kemal was the uncontested ruler of Turkey. By using both negotiations and military might, Kemal had cleansed Turkey of the Greeks, the Italians, the French, and the Armenians.

SEPTEMBER 1922: In the US, aviator Jimmy Doolittle set a flight record by flying from San Diego, CA, to Jacksonville, FL, in 22.5 hours. This was the first in a series of air records that Doolittle would set, and in the process, he would become one of America's foremost aviation pioneers.

OCTOBER 23, 1922: In London, Lloyd George's rule had come to an end. In an orderly transition of power, he resigned office and was replaced by Arthur Bonar Law.

OCTOBER 25, 1922: In a speech in Naples, Mussolini demanded that all governmental powers be given to his Fascist Party peacefully or he would seize them by force. It was widely believed that he had King Victor's approval to make such demands. This belief was substantiated when the King ordered Premier Luigi Facta and the army not to interfere with a takeover of the government by the Fascists. The King then sent a special train to Naples and invited Mussolini to come to Rome and form a government. All of this was highly irregular and almost certainly unconstitutional, but the forces of the political right were united and they had found their man.

OCTOBER 30, 1922: With the way cleared to Rome, Mussolini and his followers boarded their train and "marched" on Rome. In all, some 40,000 Black Shirts converged on Rome. There was some opposition, but it was easily overcome by the Black Shirts' superior numbers. Upon arriving in Rome, Mussolini was met with wild frenzy by the citizens of the city. He went directly to see the King, who as promised, asked him to form a non-elected, authoritarian government. Mussolini did as the King instructed and formed a government composed mostly of Fascists, but in a show of solidarity with the Italian people, also included non-Fascists in the new government. Even a few individuals who had openly opposed him were given posts. In any case, democracy was dead in Italy and this, the "March on Rome," was Mussolini's finest hour. It was also an inspiration to right-wing political groups everywhere. In Munich, the Fuehrer was one who was very much impressed with the success of the Duce.

NOVEMBER 4, 1922: In Turkey, Kemal's Grand National Assembly voted the Ottoman Empire out of existence and declared that Turkey was, henceforth, a republic.

NOVEMBER 21, 1922: Clemenceau gave a speech in New York City in which he warned of the rebirth of German militarism under that radical upstart in Munich, Adolf Hitler.

NOVEMBER 25 1922: In Italy, the Fascist-dominated Italian Assembly granted Mussolini dictatorial powers until the end of 1923.

DECEMBER 13, 1922: Lenin suffered two more strokes this day, both minor, but three days later, he suffered a more serious one. After this, it became obvious that he could no longer rule as before and a power struggle began quietly behind the scenes and out of view of the Soviet people. Lenin's voice, however, was still heard when he wanted it to be heard. In memos,

letters, and newspaper articles, he tried to clear the way for Trotsky to become his successor and was very critical of Stalin whom he saw as evil and scheming.

DECEMBER 30, 1922: From his sick bed, Lenin decreed that the nation be renamed the "Union of Soviet Socialist Republics" (USSR).

END DECEMBER 1922: Germany was in the beginning stages for run-away inflation. At this time, the mark was rated as 12,000 to the dollar and strikes, once again, were paralyzing the economy. Also, the government's ability to make the next reparations payments was becoming doubtful.

JANUARY 11, 1923: Once again, French and Belgian troops entered and occupied the German Ruhr to enforce the Diktat and force Berlin to make the scheduled reparations payments and coal deliveries. This had an ugly ripple effect. Immediately in the Ruhr, there were strikes, work stoppages, sabotage, and passive resistance. Longer term, there was thievery, an increase of people on welfare, another surge in inflation, and another noticeable movement of the German public to the political right.

On the night the French and Belgian troops arrived, Hitler spoke to a crowd of 9000 in Munich and said, "France thinks less of Germany than it does a nigger state." Privately, Hitler was talking to associates about the possibility of guerilla warfare against the invaders. And, in the days that followed, there was another surge in Nazi Party membership.

The French and Belgians responded by advancing into Germany out of the French bridgehead on the east bank of the Rhine and occupying the towns of Offenburg, Appenweier, and Buhl. There, they began to confiscate automobiles, coal, private salaries, and other things of value.

On the 27th, the Nazis held their first public "congress" with thousands of SA members, Party members, and supporters marching through the streets of Munich, protesting the occupation of the Ruhr and the action being taken by the French and Belgians in the Offenburg area.

MARCH 9, 1923: Lenin suffered another major stroke and was unable to speak. In the halls of the Kremlin, the power struggle intensified.

MARCH 12, 1923: Hitler met with General Seeckt, Commander of the Reichswehr, and offered him the services of his SA to oust the French and Belgians from the Ruhr. He also hinted that he would support an attempt by Seeckt to take over the government and that the SA would support him in that effort. Actually, Hitler was "feeling out" Seeckt to see if he would stand by inactively, as he did during the Kapp Putsch, if the Nazis tried a Putsch. Seeckt was non-committal and Hitler took this as a positive sign.

MAY 11, 1923: In late 1922, war hero Hermann Goering had walked into the Nazi office in Munich and joined the Nazi Party. Hitler quickly brought him into his inner circle, and on this date, appointed him head of the SA. This was another signal from Hitler to Seeckt.

MAY 20, 1923: In Britain, Bonar Law resigned as Prime Minister due to health reasons and was replaced by Stanley Baldwin. Baldwin would serve three times as Prime Minister until May 1937.

During the month, the King and Queen of England made a highly-publicized trip to Italy. They met with Mussolini, praised him for stabilizing Italy, and the British King awarded Mussolini the Order of the Bath.

JUNE 20, 1923: France announced that it would take over all Ruhr industry as credit against reparations.

JULY 10, 1923: Mussolini dissolved all political parties in Italy except for the Fascists.

JULY 24, 1923: "Treaty of Lausanne (Switzerland)" was signed between Western Allies and Kemal's regime in Turkey. This Treaty nullified the Treaty of Sevres with the Sultan and recognized Turkey as an independent republic under Kemal's regime. The treaty also settled questions regarding the Turkish Straits, borders, trade and economic matters, population transfers, refugee matters, and other related issues.

Kemal would go on to strengthen the Republic, promote democracy, separate religion from politics, and build a Muslim state oriented to the West. With regard to Islam, Kemal once said that it was "... a poisonous dagger which is directed at the heart of the people." This would be the Turkey that existed when WW II began.

AUGUST 1923: In Germany, inflation was soaring. On August first, the mark was pegged at one million to the dollar and by mid-month it was six million. Revolution and secession threatened and there was talk of a march on Berlin — Mussolini's March on Rome was fresh in everyone's mind. On August 13, Chancellor Wilhelm Cuno resigned and was replaced by Gustav Stresemann — Germany's seventh Chancellor in five years.

And Hitler referred again to *Der Tag* saying, "The day must come when a German government will have the courage to proclaim to the Foreign Powers `The Treaty of Versailles is founded on a monstrous lie and we hereby dissolve it!...If you want war, you can have it!'"

AUGUST 2, 1923: From the US — shocking news — President Harding was dead. He died suddenly in San Francisco after a brief illness. Within hours, Calvin Coolidge became the new President of the United States.

OCTOBER 13, 1923: In Germany, with a national crisis emerging, the Reichstag passed an "enabling act" which authorized Chancellor Stresemann to rule temporarily by decree. At this point, Germany became a dictatorship.

OCTOBER 20, 1923: The nation of Germany began to disintegrate. On this date, the state government of Bavaria broke relations with the German Federal Government in Berlin. Secession for the German Federation would be the next step. The next day French-supported separatists in the Rhineland seceded from the German Federation and proclaimed the Rhineland an independent republic. On the 21st, the exchange rate for the mark was twelve billion to the dollar. The next day, it soared to forty billion to the dollar. On the 24th, there was a communist uprising in Hamburg and there were rumors that the states of Saxony and Thuringia might go communist.

NOVEMBER 8, 1923: PUTSCH! Hitler and the Nazis pulled off an attempted coup in Munich with the intent of marching on Berlin to take over the government. It failed, and Hitler and others were arrested and charged with treason.

NOVEMBER 23, 1923: In Berlin, the Stresemann government resigned and was replaced by one headed by Wilhelm Marx. By the end of the month, the mark was rated at 4.2 trillion to the dollar. Money was useless.

DECEMBER 1923: With the German economy in collapse, Berlin took some strong economic measures, including the issuing of new currency known as the Rentenmark. With time, effort and the cooperation of the public who had been shocked and frightened by the run-away inflation, these measures were successful. Within a few months, the German economy became relatively stable.

JANUARY 1924: Mussolini annexed Fiume to Italy and was cheered throughout Italy and in Fiume.

JANUARY 21, 1924: Lenin died at age 53. The power struggle in the USSR became even more deadly. Six days later, Petrograd was renamed Leningrad.

JANUARY 25, 1924: France and Czechoslovakia signed a treaty of military alliance. This treaty would be in effect in 1938 when Hitler threatened to take, by force if necessary, the westernmost portion of Czechoslovakia known as the Sudetenland. If he did, France would be obligated to come to Czechoslovakia's aid and war between Germany and France would, very likely, have resumed.

FEBRUARY 1, 1924: Britain extended full diplomatic recognition to the USSR. Other nations soon followed, but not the US.

FEBRUARY 3, 1924: President Wilson died at his home in Washington, DC, at age 68. He was a shattered man and his wife, Edith, asked that Senator Lodge and Col. House not attend the funeral. In Washington, DC, the German embassy refused to lower its flag to half-staff.

APRIL 1, 1924: Adolf Hitler and others were convicted of treason by a Munich court. Hitler was sentenced to five years imprisonment with the possibility of parole in six months. Also, the SA was ordered disbanded. Hitler appointed Alfred Rosenberg, one of the few Nazi leaders not in jail or in hiding, to head the Nazi Party in his absence. Hitler was sent to Landsberg Prison in Berlin where he began to write a book on his life, his plans for the future and his political philosophy. That book would be called "*Mein Kampf*" (My Struggle).

APRIL 7, 1924: In Italy, another national election was held and the Fascists received 64% of the popular vote, a clear mandate to rule as they saw fit. Hitler watched these developments from his jail cell.

MAY 26, 1924: In the US, the House of Representatives passed the Johnson anti-Japanese immigration bill which virtually ended Japanese immigration into the US. The Japanese government strongly protested but to no avail. This action would stabilize the ethnic Japanese community in the US into three distinct age groups. When the US entered WW II in December 1941, the original Japanese immigrants, who had flocked to the US before, during, and after the Great War, were in their fifties. Their children were in their teens and early twenties (military age) and their grandchildren were babes and toddlers.

In July, the newly-enacted "Quota Act" was authorized by Congress which put strict limits on immigrations from all areas outside of the Western Hemisphere. It strongly favored Europeans and strongly discouraged Orientals, Africans, and others. US immigration policy within the Western Hemisphere was to be determined on a country-by-country basis.

LATE AUGUST 1924: In Europe, Germany, France, and Belgium reached an agreement on the Allied occupation of the Ruhr. Germany agreed to begin reparations payments as spelled out in the "Dawes Plan," a plan devised by the Americans that substantially reduced such payments. In return, French and Belgian troops withdrew from the Ruhr.

OCTOBER 28, 1924: France and the USSR established diplomatic relations.

NOVEMBER 4, 1924: In the US, President Coolidge was re-elected to office.

DECEMBER 20, 1924: Hitler was released on parole from prison after serving

eight months. To many, he was a hero and a martyr. The Party was in shambles and he began, at once, to rebuild it. Per his parole, however, he was not allowed to speak in public until 1927 and he was to stay out of the state of Prussia.

LATE 1924: Enter Joseph Goebbels! While Hitler was in prison, Joseph Goebbels joined the Nazi Party. He soon came to Hitler's attention as a well-educated and loyal follower. When the Nazis came to power in 1933, Hitler made Goebbels the Gauleiter (political leader) of Berlin and Propaganda Minister in his cabinet. And for a few hours on April 30, 1945, following Hitler's suicide, Goebbels served as Chancellor of Germany.

EARLY JANUARY 1925: In Italy, Mussolini began to restructure the Italian government. One of his first acts was to create a "Fascist Grand Council" which would, within a short time later, replace the Italian Assembly. It would be the Fascist Grand Council that would oust Mussolini from power in 1943.

MARCH 1925: In China, the nation was still in great turmoil. Dr. Sun Yat-sen, founder and President of the Republic of China, had died and one of his closest aides, General Chiang Kai-shek, became his successor. Chiang was the commander of Sun's 40,000-man army. Chiang's assumption of power in south China worsened the relations with his rivals in the north, and within a short while, another civil war erupted, this time, in the Hankow region.

May 12, 1925: In February, German President Friedrich Ebert died in office. An election was held, and on this date war hero, Field Marshal Paul von Hindenberg, became the President of Germany. This was a good omen for the political right because Hindenberg was known to support right-wing causes. Hindenberg would still be President when Hitler came to power in January 1933.

JULY, 1925: *Mein Kampf* was published and initial sales were brisk.

AUGUST 1925: Heinrich Himmler joined the Nazi Party. Hitler soon recognized him as a very loyal and absolutely ruthless individual. Hitler needed a man like Himmler.

AUGUST 6, 1925: Former Italian premier Orlando, his political fortunes in ruins, left public life and went into voluntary exile. The Big Four was no more.

OCTOBER 16, 1925: The "Treaty of Locarno (Switzerland)" was signed this date by the major non-communist powers of Europe. They pledged never to fight one another again but rather to settle their differences through negotiations.

DECEMBER 18, 1925: In the USSR, at the 14th Soviet Communist Party Congress, Joseph Stalin won a major political victory when Congress voted to adopt his policy of "socialism in one country" as opposed to continuing to call for world revolution. Leon Trotsky, now Stalin's arch enemy, was the leading proponent advocating the continuation of the spread of communism and revolution and force.

LATE 1925: During November, 1925, Hitler formed a personal bodyguard which he named the *"Schutzstaffel"* (Protection Detachment — SS).

By the end of the year, proceeds from the sale of his book were providing Hitler with a respectable income. On his tax report for 1925, he claimed an income of 19,843 marks.

FEBRUARY 23, 1926: In the US, President Coolidge announced his opposition to the US having a large air force, claiming it was a threat to world peace. A smaller air force, however, would be considered. Three days later, he signed a $388 million tax cut.

MARCH 16, 1926: In Auburn, Massachusetts, Professor Robert H. Goddard launched the world's first liquid-fuel rocket.

APRIL 7, 1926: Mussolini was wounded in the nose in an assassination attempt.
APRIL 24, 1926: The "Treaty of Berlin," a treaty of friendship and neutrality, was signed by Germany and the USSR.

MAY 19, 1926: In Rome, Mussolini announced that democracy in Italy was dead and had been replaced by Fascism.

JULY 4, 1926: The US Army Air Corps was created by act of Congress.
JULY 23, 1926: In Rome, Mussolini announced a new expansionist policy for Italy, saying the Italy must expand or explode. All knew that Mussolini's focus would be on Africa.

SEPTEMBER 8, 1926: Germany was admitted to the League of Nations.
SEPTEMBER 11, 1926: In Italy, there was another failed assassination attempt on Mussolini. On October 7, 1926, Mussolini decreed that the Fascist Party was now an agency of the national government.

MID-OCTOBER 1926: In the USSR, the post-Lenin power struggle concluded with Stalin's faction gaining control of the government and Trotsky's faction forced to admit defeat. The world waited and watched to see if this transfer of power, the first in the USSR since Lenin, would be peaceful or otherwise.

OCTOBER 31, 1926: In Italy, there was yet another failed assassination attempt on Mussolini. Pope Pius XI stated that it is a clear sign "... that Mussolini had God's protection."

DECEMBER 3, 1926: A British report stated that German troops were being secretly trained in the USSR.

MARCH 10, 1927: In Germany, the court-imposed ban on speaking was lifted on Hitler.

MARCH 24, 1927: In China, there was another revolution, this time at Nanking. The Chinese communists, heretofore cooperating with Chiang Kai-shek's Nationalist regime, split with Chiang over ideology and took control of the city. Chiang was forced to move his headquarters to Shanghai. Chiang, however, still in command of a substantial army, began making plans to recoup his losses.

APRIL 19, 1927: In China, civil war broke out between the Chinese communists and Chiang Kai-shek's Nationalists.

MAY 20/21, 1927: US aviator, Charles Lindbergh, age 25, flew a single-engine airplane nonstop from New York City to Paris. In the process, he become an instant and world-wide celebrity.

MAY/JUNE 1927: The civil war in China became more intense when the northern Chinese warlords banded together to fight the Chinese communists. It was now a three-sided civil war. In Shantung Province, the Japanese intervened to block Chiang Kai-shek's attempt to invade that province and march on Peking. At this point, it was a four-sided civil war.

JULY 15, 1927: Austrian Communists instigated an uprising in Vienna and burned the government's Palace of Justice.

AUGUST 2, 1927: President Coolidge announced that he would not seek another term as President.

OCTOBER 23, 1927: Joseph Stalin, having gained control of the Russian Communist Party, expelled Trotsky, Zinoviev, and some 30 others, from the Party. Most were sent off to gulags in the East. Trotsky was later expelled from the Soviet Union, and after years of searching, finally found safe exile in Mexico. In 1940, he would be murdered there by a Stalinist agent. Stalin would go on as undisputed dictator of Soviet Union until his death in 1953.

DECEMBER 14, 1927: Britain recognized Iraq's independence.

END 1927: Membership in the Nazi Party had risen to 40,000.

MAY 1, 1928: A communist May Day celebration in Berlin ended in a bloody riot.

SECOND WEEK IN MAY 1928: After three days of hard fighting, Chinese Nationalist troops under Chiang Kai-shek were defeated by Japanese forces in Shantung and lost control of that province. Chiang, however, continued his advance on Peking, and in June occupied the city, driving out his northern Chinese rivals. By October, Chiang was the dominant leader in China. Chiang established his capital at Nanking, in the south of China, a city that was friendly to his regime, and not Peking, the traditional capital of the country, which was not friendly toward him.

MAY 28, 1928: In Germany, the Nazis fielded a slate of candidates for the national election and won 840,000 votes which gave them 12 seats, out of 491, in the Reichstag. Two of the 12 winners were Hermann Goering and Joseph Goebbels.

OCTOBER 1, 1928: In the Soviet Union, Stalin announced a five-year economic plan to expand industrial production, take farm land out of private hands, create schools to train government workers, and implement other progressive measures. These policies soon replaced Lenin's New Economic Policy.

NOVEMBER 7, 1928: Herbert Hoover was elected President of the United States and Franklin Roosevelt was elected governor of New York.

NOVEMBER 10, 1928: In Japan, Hirohito, age 27, was proclaimed Emperor after having succeeded to the throne following the death of his father. Hirohito pledged to work for world peace and improve the lot of his subjects. He was also considered by the Japanese people to be divine, having inherited that state from his father.

JANUARY 6, 1929: In Germany, Hitler appointed Heinrich Himmler to head his bodyguard unit, the SS.

FEBRUARY 13, 1929: The US Congress authorized the construction of, and provided funds for, 16 naval cruisers and one aircraft carrier.

MAY 1, 1929: In Berlin, the annual leftist-sponsored May Day celebration, once again, turned into a bloody riot. Eight people were killed and 140 injured.

MAY 20, 1929: Under international pressures, Japan began evacuating Shantung.

May 29, 1929: The German government agreed to accept the scaled-down reparations figure of $27 billion as proposed by the American Young Plan. Payments would run to 1988. Hitler became one of the most outspoken opponents to this plan.

OCTOBER 24, 1929: In New York City, the US stock market crashed with an unprecedented wave of selling. It was called "Black Thursday" and portended great economic problems ahead for the US and most of the industrialized world. A wave of bankruptcies, foreclosures, and suicides soon followed.

NOVEMBER 24, 1929: Former French Primer Clemenceau died of uremia at the age of 88.

NOVEMBER 30, 1929: A large contingent of Allied troops evacuated the Rhineland but some French troops remained.

JANUARY 5, 1930: In the Soviet Union, Stalin decreed that collective farms and agricultural cooperatives would be instigated throughout the country. This meant the end of private ownership of land and the age-old tradition of peasant farming.

END JANUARY 1930: In the US, prohibition was ten years old and proving to be a failure. Alcoholism persisted, enforcement was becoming impossible, bootlegging was flourishing, gangsters were getting rich, and calls for repeal were mounting.

MARCH 7, 1930: In the US, facing an ever-increasing economic downturn, President Hoover tried to bolster public confidence by claiming that "Prosperity is just around the corner."

APRIL 22, 1930: The London Naval Treaty was signed by Britain, France, Italy,

Japan, and the US, putting tonnage limits on various types of warships and reducing the overall number of battleships in the world. Under the treaty, the US was required to scrap 49 warships and reduce the US Navy by 4800 men.

JUNE 30, 1930: French troops withdrew from the Rhineland five years ahead of the date set by the Versailles Treaty. The Rhineland, however, was to remain demilitarized.

AUGUST 5, 1930: General Douglas MacArthur was named US Army Chief-of-Staff.

LATE SUMMER 1930: By this time, the economic downturn sparked by the stock market crash of October 1929 was having negative repercussions around the world. Unemployment was on the increase in many countries, people were losing faith in the democratic economic and political processes, and were turning to political extremes. The communists were quick to take advantage of this, recommending that it was time now for the people of the world to turn to communism. This, in turn, stimulated fellow travelers in various countries to resort to action in the form of strikes, protests, marches, and riots.

The economic downturn now had a name, "The Depression," and later "The Great Depression." One of the nations hardest hit by the Depression was Germany.

SEPTEMBER 14, 1930: In Germany, another national election was held and the Nazi Party made a spectacular gain by winning 107 in the Reichstag, up from 12 seats in 1928. The Nazis were now the second largest party in the Reichstag and the communists became the third largest with 77 seats. The moderate Social Demo-

crats, however, remained the largest with 143 seats. The Nazi delegates soon began emphasizing their newfound notoriety by attending Reichstag sessions in uniform. Hitler was now in the big leagues of German politics.

DECEMBER 11, 1930: In the US, one of the nation's largest banks, the Bank of the United States, closed its doors.

END OF YEAR: Adolph Hitler filed his income tax return for 1930, claiming an income of 48,472 marks. Much of his income now came from the sale of his book, *Mein Kampf.*

JANUARY 20, 1931: In Europe, it was announced that unemployment had set new all-time records.

MAY 19, 1931: In the Soviet Union, Stalin's government announced the beginning of the second Five-Year Plan, claiming that the first had been a great success. On June 1, the hard-pressed American steel producers announced an agreement with the Soviets to build 90 steel plants in the Soviet Union. There was no depression in the Soviet Union.

JULY 13, 1931: In Germany, one of the nation's largest banks, the Danatbank, declared bankruptcy. This caused a general banking crisis within Germany and capital began to flee the country. To halt this situation, German government closed all of the banks for three weeks.

AUGUST 28, 1931: From Albany, NY, Governor Roosevelt proposed a 50% increase in income tax to help the nation's unemployed. This, and other comments made by the governor, propelled him into the limelight for the upcoming 1932 presidential elections.

SEPTEMBER 1931: In the Far East, the war between China and Japan flared anew when Japanese forces, moving north out of Japanese-controlled Korea, invaded Manchuria. Chinese defenses were very weak and the Japanese moved deeply into Manchuria and seized the capital, Harbin. The League of Nations protested but was powerless to act.

SEPTEMBER 30, 1931: There was an unemployment riot in London.

OCTOBER 11, 1931: The US Navy mothballed 17 more warships because of budget cuts.

DECEMBER 7, 1931: In Washington, DC, hundreds of communist-led hunger marchers attempted to converge on the White House but were stopped by police.

JANUARY 1932: In China, the Japanese were advancing toward Shanghai. The Japanese clearly had the military advantage, but the sympathies of the West were with China. Therefore, the Americans, British, French, and Italians sent troops and warships to Shanghai to protect their interests in that important international city. In March, the warring parties reached an agreement regarding Shanghai and a truce was agreed to. The Japanese abandoned their hope of conquering Shanghai.

In Manchuria, however, the Japanese had prevailed. On January 2, 1932, they established a puppet regime in Harbin, the capital, and proclaimed Manchuria an independent nation which was to be called Manchukuo. Manchukuo would become a member of the Axis alliance, and in December 1941, soon after the Pearl Harbor attack, would declare war on the US and Britain.

FEBRUARY 25, 1932: On this date, Hitler was granted German citizenship.

Heretofore, he had been an Austrian citizen which prevented him from holding public office in Germany. And Hitler intended to run for public office — not just any office, but for the Presidency itself. His major opponent would be the venerable Field Marshal von Hindenburg, the current President of Germany.

MARCH 12, 1932: In the German presidential elections, Hindenburg won re-election but the contender, Adolf Hitler, gained a very respectable number of votes and came in a strong second. The political atmosphere in Germany had moved substantially to the right.

MAY 1, 1932: Two British scientists announced that they had split the hydrogen atom and produced 60% more energy than used in the process.

JUNE 1932: Reparations again! Finally, and primarily as a result of the Depression, the Western Powers realized that Germany could no longer pay her reparations debt. Therefore, the major parties met at Lausanne, Switzerland, and agreed that German reparations payments would be postponed until better economic times returned.

JULY 2, 1932: In the US, at the Democrat Convention in Chicago, Governor Franklin Roosevelt was nominated for President by the Democrats. He announced that he would have a "New Deal" for the American people.

MID-JULY 1932: In China, yet another war started as Chiang Kai-shek's Nationalists launched a major campaign against the Chinese Communists.

JULY 31, 1932: In Germany, another national election was held and the Nazis more than doubled their number of seats

On To Der Tag

in the Reichstag, winning 230 seats, up from 107 in the previous election. The Nazi Party was now the largest party in the Reichstag. In this election, however, the communists also gained ground, winning 89 seats, up from 77 before. But then, the Nazis made a surprising announcement by declining to form a government because it would require the inclusion of coalition members. Hitler announced that it would be all or nothing for the Nazis. As a result, the government of Franz von Papen, a Social Democrat, remained in office and the Nazis were not included.

AUGUST 4, 1932: There was another bloody confrontation in Berlin between Nazis and communists. Berlin had not really been a safe city since 1919.

AUGUST 22, 1832: Unemployment in US reached 11 million. Many people were living in shanty towns called "Hoovervilles."

AUGUST 30, 1932: Hermann Goering was elected President of the Reichstag.

SEPTEMBER 1, 1932: Jimmy Doolittle became the first person to fly faster than 300 mph.

NOVEMBER 6, 1932: In Germany there was yet another national election. It appeared that the German people were having second thoughts about the Nazis because they lost ground, winning only 196 seats, down from 230. But the communists gained ground, winning 100 seats up from 89. Papen, however, was unable to form another government and in the negotiations that went on, Hindenburg asked Hitler to form a government, but under certain restrictions. Hitler refused and on December 2, a new, and very weak, government was formed by General Kurt von Schleicher.

NOVEMBER 8, 1932: In the US, Franklin Roosevelt won the presidential election by a landslide. His platform was based on the need to eliminate the Depression and provide a New Deal for Americans. The era of Republican conservatism was over and the era of Democrat liberalism was dawning. The US had turned to the left and the Germans had turned to the right.

EARLY JANUARY 1933: In China, Japanese troops, operating out of Manchukuo, marched further into northern China, capturing Shuangyashan.

JANUARY 30, 1933: In Germany, von Schleicher's government had failed and Hindenberg, once again, asked Hitler to form a government. This time he agreed, and on January 30, 1933, he took the oath of office and became Germany's 16th Chancellor since 1919. Because the reins of government were now in the hands of the far right, there were mounting fears throughout the country that the communists would never accept these conditions and the possibility of a revolution was just over the horizon. Hitler was obliged to form a coalition government with the Nationalists who had won enough seats in the Reichstag to give the coalition a majority. Hitler's new government had Hindenburg's full approval. All knew that the Nazis would do everything in their power to destroy democracy, but then democracy had not worked well in Germany over the past fourteen and a half years; many voters concluded that a firm hand was needed at the helm. Many believed that Hitler's government would provide strong and authoritarian leadership such as that which the Kaiser had provided before and during the Great War.

Two of the eight cabinet posts were given to Nazis: Wilhelm Frick became Minister of the Interior, which controlled the police, and Goering was given the post of Minister Without Portfolio, with the understanding that when Germany became able to create a new air force, he would become the Minister of Air. Goering's duty would be to work toward that goal. A new cabinet post was created, that of Minister of Propaganda and Public Enlightenment, which was given to Goebbels. Hitler, having been very successful as Propaganda Chairman for the Party in its early years, was a strong believer in the power of the written and spoken word.

FEBRUARY 2, 1933: On this date, Hitler dissolved the Reichstag and called for a new election. This was an old tactic used in European politics, whereby the party in power hoped to gain more power in a repeat election. In this case, it was Hitler's goal to rid himself of his coalition partner, the Nationalists. On this same day, Chancellor Hitler placed all the curbs that his office allowed on his leftist opponents and on the 6th, he imposed media censorship.

FEBRUARY 15, 1933: In Miami, there was an assassination attempt on President-elect Roosevelt. The assassin's bullet missed Roosevelt but fatally wounded Anton Cermak, the Mayor of Chicago.

FEBRUARY 24–25, 1933: On the 24th, the Assembly of the League of Nations voted unanimously to censure Japan for her actions in China. The next, day, Japan announced that she would withdraw from the League in 1935. And in China, the Japanese continued their advance. On March 3, they took the city of Chengteh, capitol of Jehol Province, and showed no signs of halting. It appeared to many that Japan was intent on setting up another puppet regime in northern China similar to that of Manchukuo.

FEBRUARY 27–28, 1933: In Berlin, the centerpiece of the German government, the Reichstag building, was destroyed by fire. A young Dutchman, Marinus Van der Lubbe, was caught inside the building, stripped to the waist and shouting communist slogans. He was arrested, and

interrogated, and it was determined that he had come to Berlin from Holland to be a part of the forthcoming communist revolution. When it did not happen, Van der Lubbe believed he could make it happen by touching the Reichstag building.

This action served only to enhance the general belief that a communist revolution was imminent which, in turn, played extremely well into the hands of the Nazis. Within hours, Hindenburg signed an emergency decree authorizing Chancellor Hitler to take extraordinary measures to preserve law and order. Hitler then ordered the German police, assisted by his SA, to round up and incarcerate all known communists. This was a day Hitler had longed for. He had his first taste of dictatorial power and was now legally empowered to strike a major blow at the communists.

MARCH 4, 1933: While the crisis in Germany was at its worst, the US got a new President. On this date Franklin Roosevelt took the oath of office in Washington, DC. And, as in Germany, there was a crisis brewing — not over a possible revolution, but over a possible collapse in the nation's financial infrastructure. In his inaugural address, Roosevelt made a statement for which he would long be famous, "The only thing we have to fear is fear itself."

On the 5th, Roosevelt took action and ordered all of the nation's banks closed for four days. And on the 12th, he went on radio to explain his actions to the American people and to try to calm their fears of an economic disaster. This would set a pattern for the rest of his career as President. Throughout his tenure, he would, from time-to-time, make radio addresses to the American public, calling them "Fireside Chats."

MARCH 5, 1933: In Germany, they held the special election ordered by Chancellor

Hitler. With the burning of the Reichstag building and the threat of a communist revolution, the Nazis played the crisis to the hilt, hoping that the German people would give them an undeniable mandate to save the nation. They were disappointed. The Nazis won more seats in the Reichstag — which was now meeting in a theater — but not enough to form a government without the Nationalists.

But the Nazis were not deterred and had powerful support. Hindenburg, the Army, the police, the industrialists, and the upper and middle classes realized that drastic measures had to be taken, and these segments of the German state were united enough to let Hitler have his way.

MARCH 20–22, 1933: In the US, Roosevelt, now being referred to nation-wide as "FDR," signed the "Economic Act," which had been hastily passed by the new Democrat-controlled Congress. The act called for a number of emergency economic measures, including the reduction of salaries of federal workers and the reductions in veterans' benefits. At this time, he also signed a bill legalizing beer and wine. To legalize hard liquor, it would take a constitutional amendment.

MARCH 23, 1933: In Germany, the Reichstag delegates were cajoled and, at times, threatened by the Nazis, to pass an emergency bill known as the "Enabling Act." This was an action, permitted by the German constitution, which granted the Chancellor the authority to rule tempo-rarily by decree. This was a measure that had been utilized in Germany on several occasions during the 1920s when other crises loomed and it had worked well. The clause in the Enabling Act that made this possible for Hitler was buried deep in the bill and simply stated that the Chancellor could "deviate from the Constitution." The duration of this power was to be until April 1, 1937, an extraordinary length of time.

Hindenburg signed the Enabling Act and at this point, Hitler became the dicta-tor of Germany. But he was not yet an ab-solute dictator. He could still be removed by Hindenburg or whomever was Presi-dent. For the foreseeable future, however, there was little chance of this.

Meanwhile, the roundup of commu-nists, and especially Jewish- communists, continued at a rapid pace.

MARCH 31, 1933: In the US, Congress passed, and FDR signed the "Reforesta-tion and Relief Act," which provided for government funding to hire many of the unemployed and put them to work on public projects. The primary organiza-tion created to do this was the "Civilian Conservation Corps" (CCC). During its lifetime, the CCC saved many American families from abject poverty.

The US Congress and the President would go on to enact many more such measures in the next three months which would become known as FDR's first "hun-dred days" in office.

MARCH 1933: In Germany, the jails were filling to capacity and a program was begun to build new prison camps in various parts of the country. One of the first camps was built near the village of Dachau in Bavaria near Munich. At this time, SS leader Heinrich Himmler was given the post of chief of police of Munich to oversee its construction. This camp, and subsequent camps, became the nucleus for the infamous Nazi Con-centration Camp system. It also marked the beginning of the takeover of German police organizations by Himmler.

In 1934, the SS would take control of the Prussian State Police which had in its organization a unit called the "*Geheime Staatspolizei*" (Secret State Police — GESTAPO). Under Goering's and Himmler's control, the GESTAPO would become a very aggressive and evil organizations and a hallmark of the excesses of Hitler's Nazi regime.

MAY 2, 1933: On this date, the Nazis disbanded all labor unions in Germany, confiscated their property and assets, and replaced the unions with a Nazi Party-controlled labor organization known as the "Deutsche Arbeitsfront" (German Labor Front).

MAY 31, 1933: In northern China, under strong international pressures, a truce was signed between the Japanese and Chinese. It would last for about four years.

MAY 1933: On the Arabian Peninsula, the warlord Ibn Saud had defeated all of his rivals and created the Kingdom of Saudi Arabia with himself as King. Soon afterwards, oil was discovered in the northeastern part of the country and during May 1933, King Saud signed an agreement with US oil companies to exploit that new and very valuable resource. Progress would be slow, however, and the first well would not be brought in until 1938.

Oil was also known to exist in neighboring Kuwait, a British protectorate, to the north of Saudi Arabia. In 1934, the Kuwaiti government signed an agreement with a joint British-American consortium to develop their oil. Thus was born the Kuwait Oil Co.

JULY 14, 1933: In Germany, Hitler abolished all political parties except his own. On the 26th, he issued a decree permitting the sterilization of German citizens who, according to Nazi racial and medical guidelines, should not reproduce.

AUGUST 3, 1933: In the US, Congress authorized the US Navy to acquire 37 new warships.

AUGUST 29, 1933: In Germany, it was now time for the Hitler government to address the "Jewish question." Confirmed reports came out of Germany that the Nazis were rounding up Jews, mostly on trumped-up charges, and sending them to the concentration camps. Underground anti-Nazi sources in Germany reported that there were now 65 concentration camps with Dachau the largest.

SEPTEMBER 8, 1933: In Iraq, King Faisal died suddenly of a heart attack and was replaced by his son, Crown Prince Ghazi.

OCTOBER 23, 1933: Germany withdrew from the League of Nations. Hitler justified this action by claiming that the conditions in the Versailles Treaty were grossly unfair, had been forced on Germany, and that Germany had been poorly treated by the Allied nations ever since the end of the Great War.

NOVEMBER 12, 1933: In Germany, another national election was held and the Nazis, the only party of the ballot, won all of the seats in the Reichstag. This would be the last major election in Germany and the farce of maintaining democracy in Germany would come to an end.

NOVEMBER 17, 1933: The Roosevelt Administration extended diplomatic recognition to the USSR. William D. Bullitt was named US Ambassador to Moscow.

DECEMBER 5, 1933: In the US, the 21st Amendment to the Constitution was ratified and prohibition came to an end.

END DECEMBER 1933: By the end of the year, Hitler was a wealthy man primarily from the brisk, and in many cases obligatory, sale of his book *Mein Kampf*. He also had income from his public offices and other unnamed sources.

DURING 1934: The US Army began to rise in numbers following a long period of decline since 1919.

JANUARY 26, 1934: Germany and Poland signed a ten-year non-aggression pact in which both promised not to attack the other. It would last for five years and eight months.

MARCH 21, 1934: In Germany, Hitler announced a new program to build superhighways all across Germany to be called "Autobahns."

MARCH 26, 1934: In the US, Congress passed a law stating that the Philippines would be granted independence by 1946.

MAY 5, 1934: Poland and the USSR extended their non-aggression until 1945.

MAY 19, 1934: In a Bulgarian coup, a fascist-like government came into being supported by the King, Boris III.

JUNE 14, 1934: Hitler decreed that Germany would stop paying all foreign debts, including reparations.

JUNE 16, 1934: Hitler and Mussolini meet for the first time in Venice. The meeting was proper but not warm.

JUNE 30, 1934: In a bloody coup, Hitler, in collaboration with Heinrich Himmler and his SS organization, eliminated the leadership of the SA whom, Hitler suspected, was planning to oust him as Chancellor and take control in Germany. This coup became known as "The Night of the Long Knives." The SA was then relegated to a secondary role and Himmler and his SS (Hitler's bodyguards) became the nucleus for a newly-structured Nazi Party paramilitary organization.

JULY 3, 1934: In Germany, Franz von Papen, the Vice Chancellor and the leading member in the Nationalist's coalition component in Hitler's government, resigned under Nazi pressure. This gave Hitler complete control of the government. Subsequently, the post of Vice Chancellor was eliminated and Hitler had no constitutionally-designated successor. In this regard, Hitler would deviate from the constitution and name his own successor.

JULY 27, 1934: In a national election in France, a far leftist coalition of French socialist and communists, calling themselves the "Popular Front," won control of the government. This was another example of how European politics was polarizing to the right and left. The effects of the Great Depression, the renewed threat from Germany, and the apparent successes of the communist regime in the USSR created an atmosphere which all but destroyed confidence in European democracy. Democracy in Europe was dying a slow and painful death in many places.

AUGUST 2, 1934: In Germany, President von Hindenburg died while still in office. The Germany constitution stated that an election for a new president was to be held, but Chancellor Hitler, with the powers given him by the Enabling Act, deviated from the constitution and ordered the Reichstag to appoint him President, which they did. At this point, Hitler became the absolute dictator of Germany and there was no legal authority in the country that could remove him from office.

SEPTEMBER 5, 1934: In a speech, Hitler predicted that his new Reich would last for 1000 years.

SEPTEMBER 18, 1934: The USSR became a member of the League of Nations.

OCTOBER 16, 1934: In China, following the truce between Chiang Kai-shek's Chinese Nationalists and the Japanese, the Nationalists used this opportunity to begin hostilities against the Chinese Communists, now controlled by the former library assistant, Mao Tse-tung. After a series of pitched battles, Chiang's forces defeated the Communists and they began a lengthy retreat into a remote area of northern China. This trek would become known as the "Long March." The Chinese Communists would remain is this area throughout most of WW II and would emerge at its end and with support from the USSR, renew their challenge with the Nationalists for the control of China.

NOVEMBER 13, 1934: Ever since Hitler came to power in Germany, there were rumors that Germany was rearming. On this date, Germany's Commissioner of Disarmament, Joachim von Ribbentrop, admitted that this was so. Protests were forthcoming from many sources, but no actions were taken against Germany. Hitler had become confident that that would be the case.

END DECEMBER 1934: In the wake of a political murder, Stalin became convinced that a conspiracy of high-level political figures and military men were conspiring against him. Thus, he began arresting those he suspected of plotting his downfall and the beginning of the infamous "Stalin Purges" began. They would last into the late 1930s and decimate much of the Soviet government's political and military leadership.

JANUARY 13, 1935: In the Saar, the plebiscite decreed by the Versailles Treaty was held and the people of the area voted 90.8% to join Germany. In Germany, this was seen as a great victory for Hitler.

MARCH 11, 1935: From Berlin came the announcement that Germany would begin building an air force to be known as the "Luftwaffe." In response, Britain announced that it would triple the strength of its air force by 1938.

MARCH 16, 1935: Hitler decrees the renewal of military conscription.

JULY 8, 1935: From Berlin came the announcement that Germany was building two battleships and 28 submarines. Also from Germany came reports that the Nazis were significantly increasing their persecution of the Jews.

AUGUST 31, 1935: In the US, Roosevelt signed the "American Neutrality Act of 1935." This law prohibited the sale of American-made arms to any nation at war, as well as forbidding American citizens to serve in the armed forces of any such nation. In the late 1930s, this law would become a major obstacle in America's efforts to aid her former European Allies and would gradually be amended into impotency.

SEPTEMBER 15, 1935: In Germany, the swastika flag of the Nazi Party was adopted as the national flag of Germany.

OCTOBER 2, 1935: In East Africa, a large Italian army, striking out from the Italian colonies of Eritrea and Italian Somaliland, invaded the neighboring, and independent, nation of Ethiopia. Italy had long coveted this land because its acquisition would create a very large Italian colonial empire in the region.

To most of the world, his was seen as out-and-out aggression by Fascist Italy and was denounced in many quarters. The League of Nations took action and imposed economic sanctions on Italy but they were widely violated and had little effect on events in East Africa. The Ethiopians, surprisingly enough, put up a determined defense and it would take the Italians almost a year to conquer the country.

This action showed the world that the Italian Fascists would not hesitate using military force when it suited their needs. And this image of this aggressiveness spilled over onto the Fascists' political soulmates, the Nazis, as well as other far right political organizations around the world.

MARCH 7, 1936: On this day, German troops marched into the demilitarized Rhineland and Hitler proclaimed that that area was now under his full control. The Western Powers complained bitterly but, once again, took no action. With this, Hitler had won another great victory in the eyes of the German people and his power and authority within Germany had reached a zenith.

MARCH 30, 1936: The British government announced that it would construct 38 new warships.

MAY 3, 1936: A national election in France retained the leftist Popular Front in power.

MAY 22, 1936: On this date, Germany and Italy signed a political and economic protocol that eventually grew into a military alliance known as the "Pact of Steel." Mussolini, in explaining the pact to the Italian people, stated that an "axis" had been drawn on the map between Berlin and Rome around which the rest of Europe would now rotate. The word, axis, caught the attention of the media and others, and the relationship between Germany and Italy became known as the "Axis" (capital "A"). This word would be used throughout WW II to describe the enemies of the Allied nations.

JUNE 17, 1936: In Germany, Heinrich Himmler was named chief of Reich police. Every policeman in Germany was now a member of the SS.

JULY 19-20. 1936: In Spanish Morocco, a rebellious faction of the Spanish Army took control of that protectorate and the rebellion quickly moved into parts of southern and northern Spain.

Spain was one of the European nations where the government had polarized to the far left, imposed communist-like controls on the economy, and the church, and imposed many other radical programs on Spanish society. Public reactions to these measures had been violent and frequent, and had by now, reached a point where law and order was breaking down throughout the country. As a result, a clique of Spanish Army officers decided to take military action to oust the neo-communist regime in Madrid. Thus began the long and bloody "Spanish Civil War." This conflict soon took on the aspect of a contest between far left and the far right political organizations and factions throughout the Western world. The rebels formed a provisional government which soon came under the control of General Francisco Franco. Both Germany and Italy soon recognized that government and sent arms and military personnel to support it. Meanwhile, the Soviets sent "volunteers" to fight for the loyalists. In hindsight, the Spanish Civil War was seen as a preliminary conflict to the coming of WW II.

SEPTEMBER 18, 1936: Lloyd George, now retired from political office, visited Hitler in the latter's mountain retreat at Berchtesgaden, Germany. In his conversation with Hitler, Lloyd George admitted that the Versailles Treaty had been a failure and that Germany had been ill-treated by the Allies. He blamed these actions on Wilson and Clemenceau.

LATE SEPTEMBER 1936: The German Army held large maneuvers, the largest since 1914.

NOVEMBER 3, 1936: In the US, Franklin Roosevelt won a second term as President in another landslide vote.

NOVEMBER 26, 1936: In Berlin, the German and Japanese government signed a new political agreement designed to oppose the actions of the Soviet Union's worldwide Comintern organization. That pact, known as the "Anti-Comintern Pact," stated that international communism was the greatest threat to world peace and it was hoped that other nations would join the Pact to create a worldwide anti-communist bloc.

JANUARY 30, 1937: In the face of growing war fears in Europe, Hitler guaranteed the neutrality of Holland and Belgium.

MAY 28, 1937: In Britain, Neville Chamberlain became Prime Minister and promised peace in Europe.

JULY 7, 1937: On this date — 7/7/37 — Japanese forces near Peking sparked an armed clash with Chinese forces at the Marco Polo Bridge just outside of Peking. The Chinese were quickly routed and the Japanese blamed Chiang Kai-shek's government for the incident and used it to begin a full-scale invasion of China. By mid-August, the Japanese had captured Peking and other parts of northern China and set up a Japanese military government in the Chinese capital. On August 25, the Japanese set up a naval blockade along the entire coast of China. With this, western supplies were all but cut off from Chiang's government in Nanking.

OCTOBER 1937: By this time, Japanese forces had captured all of Shantung Province in northern China and were marching on Nanking.

OCTOBER 6, 1937: The Roosevelt Administration denounced Japan as an aggressor nation and declared its full support for Chiang Kai-shek's Chinese Nationalist government.

NOVEMBER 6, 1937: Italy joined the German-Japanese Anti-Comintern Pact.

MID-NOVEMBER 1937: Japanese forces occupied Shanghai.

DECEMBER 11, 1937: Italy withdrew from the League of Nations.

DECEMBER 13, 1937: Japanese forces occupied Nanking and began a reign of terror unparalleled in the Twentieth Century. Tens of thousands of Chinese were slaughtered in what became known as the "Rape of Nanking." In the weeks that followed, the Japanese government was universally condemned for these horrendous actions.

Chiang Kai-shek's government fled to the west and eventually established a new capital in Chungking but was weak and desperate for military aid. To remedy the latter, the Chinese and British began building a road across the Himalaya Mountains from the British colony of Burma to the Chinese city of Kunming, 350 miles southwest of Chungking. This undertaking would be a grueling and lengthy task and would not be completed until late 1939. Once completed, however, the highway through the mountains became known as the "Burma Road."

JANUARY 28, 1938: President Roosevelt asked Congress for a significant increase in military spending.

FEBRUARY 4, 1938: In Berlin, Hitler abolished his cabinet's War Ministry and created a new organization called *"Oberkommando der Wehrmacht"* (OKW). This organization would take direct command of Germany's armed forces with Hitler, himself, at its head.

FEBRUARY 20, 1938: Hitler sparked a new controversy in Europe by demanding self-determination for the German population in the westernmost part of

Czechoslovakia, Sudetenland. This was a land with a mixed German and Czech population that had been a part of Austria-Hungary, but it was awarded to Czechoslovakia by the Allies in 1919.

MARCH 12, 1938: On this date, Germany and Austria became one. After a dangerous conflict between Hitler and the rulers of Austria, German troops marched in that country unopposed and Hitler then proclaimed its union with Germany. This action was called the "Anschluss" and was the culmination of a long-standing desire by many to unite Germany and Austria into one nation. This action had been forbidden by the Versailles Treaty, but the Allies took no actions to prevent it. And in Germany, Hitler was being hailed as the greatest German leader since Bismarck.

APRIL 10, 1938: In France, the leftist Popular Front was defeated in a national election and Edouard Daladier, a moderate, became the new Premier. This was the twenty-first change in the French premiership since the end of the Great War, and it clearly indicated that democracy in France was not working well.

MAY 17, 1938: In the US, the Congress voted funds to create a two-ocean navy.

JUNE 9, 1938: Britain ordered 400 war planes from the US.

SUMMER 1938: During the summer of 1938, the world witnessed a new and very disturbing aspect of modern warfare, the aerial bombing of civilians. Several instances of this had occurred in both China and Spain. Heretofore, civilians had been relatively safe in wartime, but this was now changing and in future wars, it was very likely that civilian populations would be targeted.

In Europe, Germany continued to press its demands regarding the Sudetenland, and the French and British advised the Czechs to comply. This policy soon had a name — "appeasement." Tensions reached a new height when, on August 12, Hitler called up one million reservists in the face of the Sudeten crisis and on the 15th, the German armed forces began a series of war maneuvers. On August 27, the Chamberlain government warned Hitler that an attack on Czechoslovakia would mean war.

In Italy, Mussolini decreed an end to Italy's democratically-elected parliament and replaced it with a Party organization known as the "Fascist Grand Council."

SEPTEMBER 15-30, 1938: In a series of meetings, Chamberlain and Daladier met with Hitler in an effort to save the peace in Europe. This culminated in an agreement signed September 30 in Munich in which the British and French agreed not to come to Czechoslovakia's support if the Germans took the Sudetenland. In return, Hitler promised that this would be his last territorial demand in Europe. This arrangement became known as the "Munich Agreement," an agreement to which the Czechs had not been a party.

OCTOBER 3, 1938: German troops marched into the Sudetenland unopposed and the area was soon annexed to Germany. In the days and weeks that followed, Czechoslovakia, now defenseless, was besieged on all sides by its neighbors who had lost territory to the new republic in 1919. The Czech government in Prague became fully discredited and powerless. Accordingly, the Poles seized the Teschen area, the Hungarians seized land in the southern part of the country, and Slovakia seceded from its union with the Czechs and proclaimed itself independent. Ultimately, the Germans entered the Czech provinces of Bohemia and Moravia to maintain law and order and proclaimed the area a German protectorate called the "Protectorate of Bohemia-Moravia." Czechoslovakia that, in 1919, had been the great hope for the spreading of democracy in Eastern Europe, was no more.

NOVEMBER 7-9, 1938: In Paris, a young Jewish man charged into the German embassy and shot and killed the first German official he encountered. He did this in retaliation for the severe treatment that his mother and father had just experienced in Germany. The Nazis pounced on this opportunity to come down even harder on the German Jews. The SS took to the streets, killed and beat Jews, burned synagogues, and smashed Jewish businesses. So much glass littered the streets after this rampage that the event was given the neo-comical name of "Crystal Night."

DECEMBER 6, 1938: In Paris, Germany and France signed a treaty of friendship, and on January 11, 1939, Chamberlain traveled to Rome to meet with Mussolini. Many saw these actions as continuation of appeasement.

JANUARY 28, 1939: On this date, the noted Italian physicist Enrico Fermi announced that two of his German colleagues, Otto Hahn and Fritz Strassmann, had split uranium atoms by bombarding them with neutrons and thereby released a very large amount of atomic energy.

FEBRUARY 10, 1939: Japanese forces occupied the large Chinese-controlled island of Hainan off the south China coast. Japanese military presence in this region posed a new military threat to all of Southeast Asia, especially the US-controlled Philippines and French Indochina.

FEBRUARY 14, 1939: Germany launched the battleship "Bismarck," one of the most powerful ships in its fleet.

FEBRUARY 24, 1939: Hungary signed on to the Axis-sponsored Anti-Comintern Pact.

MARCH 22, 1939: German troops marched, unopposed, into the Lithuanian port of Memel that had been a part of Imperial Germany, but given to Lithuania in 1919. With this action, Hitler's promise made at Munich not to seek any more territorial acquisitions in Europe was seen to be meaningless. Appeasement was not working.

MARCH 28, 1939: In Spain, rebel forces under Generalissimo Franco occupied Madrid and the Spanish Civil War came to an end. Franco promptly set up a fascist-like government on the order of those in Germany and Italy. And, as Hitler was called Fuehrer and Mussolini Duce, he took unto himself the title "Caudillo," (Leader) of Spain.

MARCH 31, 1939: On this date, Japanese forces moved deeper into Southeast Asia by occupying the Spratly Islands, a cluster of seven islands 700 miles south of recently-occupied Hainan and whose ownership was disputed between France and China. This was seen as yet another Japanese threat to US, British, French, and Dutch interests in the region.

APRIL 1, 1939: Britain and Poland signed a treaty of military alliance.

APRIL 8, 1939: Italian forces invaded and occupied Albania.

APRIL 11, 1939: Hungary left the League of Nations.

APRIL 13, 1939: In Rome, air raid drills were conducted.

APRIL 23, 1939: Britain began peacetime conscription.

APRIL 26, 1939: Roosevelt signed an order to build 571 military aircraft.

MAY 7, 1939: Spain left the League of Nations.

JUNE 15, 1939: The French submarine "Phoenix" sank mysteriously off the coast of French Indochina with all hands aboard. The Japanese were suspected.

AUGUST 2, 1939: Albert Einstein, one of the world's most renounced scientist, wrote a personal letter to President Roosevelt, informing him of the recent developments with regard to atomic energy and informed the President that an extremely powerful bomb could be made using atomic energy.

AUGUST 8, 1939: In Germany, all individuals between the ages of five and seventy were required to register for possible wartime assignments.

AUGUST 11, 1939: The US government announced that it had placed an order for $85 million for military aircraft with America's aviation industry — the largest such order ever.

AUGUST 19, 1939: Hitler approved an order to send 14 U-boats into the North Atlantic.

AUGUST 20, 1939: Poland rushed troops to the German border.

AUGUST 22, 1939: France and Britain reaffirmed their pledge to aid Poland if she were attacked.

AUGUST 23, 1939: From Berlin and Moscow came the startling news that Germany and the USSR had signed a non-aggression pact. In a secret protocol within this agreement, Germany would have a free hand to take military actions without Soviet interference, and in return, the USSR could take steps to regain territory lost in eastern Europe during and after the Great War without German interference.

AUGUST 23, 1939: The French Army began mobilization.

LATE AUGUST 1939: In both Paris and London, children were being evacuated to the countryside.

SEPTEMBER 1, 1939: Powerful German forces invaded Poland and Danzig to reclaim territory lost in 1919. This was *DER TAG* — SEPTEMBER 1, 1939.

REMINDER:
"This is not peace; it is an armistice for 20 years."
— Field Marshal Ferdinand Foch, 1919

BIBLIOGRAPHY

ALBJERG, VICTOR L. & MARGARITE H. *Europe from 1914 to the Present,* NYC: McGraw Hill 1951

ALLEN, LOUIS. *Japan: The Years of Triumph: From Feudalism to Pacific Empire.* NYC: American Heritage Press, 1971.

ASINOR, ELIOT. *1919: America's Loss of Innocence,* NYC: Donald L. Fine, Inc. NY, 1990.

BARRACOUGH, GEOFFREY. *The Soviet Achievement.* NYC: Harcourt Brace & World, Inc., 1967.

BLEUEL, PETER. *Sex & Society in Nazi Germany.* London: Bantam Books, 1973.

BUKEY, EVAN BURR. *Hitler's Hometown: Linz, Austria.* Bloomington, IN: University Press, 1986.

BUTLER, RUPERT. *SS & SA: The Black Angels: A History of the Waffen SS.* NYC: St. Martin Press, Inc., 1979.

BUTTERFIELD, ROGER. *The American Past: A History of the U.S. from Concord to the Great Society.* NYC: Simon & Shuster, 1966.

COLLIER, RICHARD. *Duce: The Life & Death of a Dictator.* NYC: Viking Press, 1971.

CREEL, GEORGE. *The War, the World and Wilson.* NYC/London: Harper & Bros., 1920.

DEGRAZIA, VICTORIA. *How Fascism Ruled Women: Italy 1921–1946.* Berkeley: University of California Press, 1992.

DELMER, SEFTON. *Weimar Germany.* London: Library of the 20th Century, 1972.

DEZELL, CHARLES F. *Mediterranean Fascism 1919–1945.* NY: Walker & Co., 1970.

FISHER, JOHN. *Curzon & British Imperialism in the Middle-East, 1916–1919.* UK: Frank Cass Publications, 1999.

FLEMING, THOMAS. *The Illusion of Victory: America in World War I.* NY: Basic Books, Inc., 2003,

FROMKIN, DAVID. *A Peace to End All Peace: The Fall of the Ottoman Empire & the Creation of the Modern Middle-East.* NYC: Henry Holt & Co., 1989.

GALLO, MAX. *Mussolini's Italy: Twenty Years of the Fascist Era.* NY: Macmillan Publications, 1973.

GENTILE, EMILIO. *The Origins of Fascist Ideology.* NY: Enigma Books, 2005.

GREEN, JONATHAN. *The Book of Political Quotes.* NYC: McGraw Hill, 1982.

GRENVILLE, J.A.S. *The Major International Treaties 1914–1973: A History Guide with Texts.* NY: Stein & Day Publications, 1975.

HAYWOOD, JOHN. *Historical Atlas of the 20th Century.* NY: Barnes & Noble Books, 2000.

HIRO, DILIP. *Dictionary of the Middle-East.* NY: St. Martin Press, 1996.

HITLER, ADOLPH. *Mein Kampf.* Houghton Miffin Co., 1971.

JONES, NIGEL. *The Birth of the Nazis: How the Freikorps Blazed a Trail for Hitler.* NY: Carroll & Graf Publications, 1987.

KIRBY, D. G. *Finland in the Twentieth Century*. London: C. Hurst & Co., 1979.

LEGRAND, JACQUES. *Chronicle of the 20th Century*. Liberty, MO: J & L International Publications, 1991.

LEWIS, JON E. *The Mammoth Book of Eyewitness World War II*. NY: Carrol & Gray Publications, 2002.

LENTZ, HARRIS M., III. *Encyclopedia of Heads of States and Governments 1900 through 1945*. Jefferson, NC and London, 1994.

LINCOLN, W. BRUCE. *Red Victory: A History of the Russian Civil War*. NY, DaCapo Press, 1919.

MACMILLAN, MARGARET. *Paris 1919*. NYC: Random House, 2003.

MARTIN, BENJAMIN F. *France and the Apres Guerre 1918–1924*. Baton Rouge, Louisiana State University Press, 1999.

MASON, HERBERT M., JR. *The Rise of the Luftwaffe: Forging the Secret German Air Weapon 1918–1940*. NY: Dial Press, 1973.

MOOREHEAD, CAROLINE. *Dunant's Dream: War, Switzerland and the History of the Red Cross*. NY: Carroll & Graf Publications, 1998.

ORLOW, DIETRICH. *The History of the Nazi Party: 1919–1933*. Pittsburgh: University of Pittsburgh Press, 1969.

OSBORNE, RICHARD E. *If Hitler Had Won*. Indianapolis, Riebel-Roque Publications, 2005.

OSBORNE, RICHARD E. *World War II in Colonial Africa*. Indianapolis, Riebel-Roque Publications, 2003.

OVERY, RICHARD. *The Penguin Historical Atlas of the Third Reich*. NY: Penguin Books USA, 1996.

PELISSIER, ROGER. *The Awakening of China*. NY: G. P. Putnam's Sons, 1967.

PINE, LISA. *Nazi Family Policy 1933–1945*. Oxford & NY, Berg, 1997.

REDLICH, FRITZ. *Hitler: Diagnosis of a Destructive Prophet*. Oxford, Oxford University Press, 1999.

ROGERS, AGNES & FREDERICK L. ALLEN. *I Remember Distinctly, A Family Album of the American People 1918–1944*. NYC: Harper & Bros. Publications, 1947.

ROOSEVELT, JAMES AND BILLY LIBBY. *My Parents: A Differing View*. Chicago: Playboy Press, 1976.

ROSSER, RICHARD F. *An Introduction to Soviet Foreign Policy*. Englewood Cliffs, NJ: Prentice-Hall, Inc., 1969.

SACHAR, HOWARD M. *Dreamland: European Jews in the Aftermath of the Great War*. NYC: Alfred Knopf, 2002.

SCHLESINGER, ARTHUR M. JR. *The Crisis of the Old Order, 1919–1933: The Age of Roosevelt*. Boston: Houghton Miffin Co., 1957.

SETON-WATSON, HUGH. *The East European Revolution*. NY: Frederick A. Praeger, Inc., 1983.

SHANNON, DAVID A. *Between the Wars: 1919–1941*. Boston: Houghton Miffin Co., 1965.

SIMKINS, PETER. *Imperial War Museum: Cabinet War Rooms.* London: Imperial War Museum, 1983.

SMITH, DENIS MACK. *Mussolini's Roman Empire.* NYC: Penguin Books, 1977.

STURMER, MICHAEL. *The German Empire 1871–1919.* London: Weidenfeld & Nicolson, 2000.

TURNER, HENRY ASHBY, JR. *German Big Business & the Rise of Hitler.* Oxford: Oxford University Press, 1985.

WAITE, ROBERT G. L. *The Psychopathic God: Adolf Hitler.* NY: DaCapo Press, 1993.

WARNER, PHILIP. *World War One: A Chronological Narrative.* London: Brockhampton Press, 1995.

YU TE-JEN. *The Japanese Struggle for World Empire.* NY: Vantage Press, 1967.

BOOKS WRITTEN BY GREAT WAR PERSONALITIES

BARUCH, BERNARD, *My Own Story.*

CHURCHILL, WINSTON, *The World Crisis, 1911–1918.*

DANIELS, JOSEPHUS, *Our Navy at War.*

DEGAULLE, CHARLES, *The Enemy's House Divided.*

GRAYSON, DR. CARY T., *Woodrow Wilson: An Intimate Memoir.*

HINDENBURG, FIELD MARSHAL PAUL VON, *The Great War.*

HINDENBURG, FIELD MARSHAL PAUL VON, *Out of My Life.*

HOOVER, HERBERT, *American Individualism.*

KEYNES, JOHN MAYNARD, *The Economic Consequences of the Peace.*

LAWRENCE, T. E., (LAWRENCE OF ARABIA) *Seven Pillars of Wisdom.*

LLOYD GEORGE, DAVID, *Memoirs.*

LLOYD GEORGE, DAVID, *The Truth About the Peace Treaties.*

LLOYD GEORGE, FRANCES, *Lloyd George: A Diary.*

LUDENDORFF, ERICH, *Warfare & Politics.*

MAO TSE-TUNG, *Communism and Dictatorship.*

PILSUDSKI, ALEKSANDRA, *Pilsudski: A Biography by His Wife.*

PILSUDSKI, JOSEPH, *ROK 1920.*

REED, JOHN, *Ten Days that Shook the World.*

TROTSKY, LEON, *My Life.*

TUKHACHEVSKY, MIKHAIL, *New Problems of War.*

WILHELM, CROWN PRINCE, *Memoirs of the Crown Prince of Germany.*

WILHELM II, *The Kaiser's Memoirs.*

WILSON, EDITH, *My Memoir.*

WRANGEL, PYOTR N., *Memoirs.*

INDEX